Augustan England

AUGUSTAN ENGLAND

Professions, State and Society, 1680–1730

GEOFFREY HOLMES

Professor of History, University of Lancaster

London
GEORGE ALLEN & UNWIN
Boston   Sydney

**George Allen & Unwin (Publishers) Ltd,
40 Museum Street, London WC1A 1LU, UK**

George Allen & Unwin (Publishers) Ltd,
Park Lane, Hemel Hempstead, Herts HP2 4TE, UK

Allen & Unwin Inc.,
9 Winchester Terrace, Winchester, Mass 01890, USA

George Allen & Unwin Australia Pty Ltd,
8 Napier Street, North Sydney, NSW 2060, Australia

First published in 1982

British Library Cataloguing in Publication Data

Holmes, Geoffrey
    Augustan England.
1. Great Britain – History – 1660–1714
2. Great Britain – History – 1714–1837
I. Title
942.07   DA470
ISBN 0–04–942178–6

Library of Congress Cataloging in Publication Data

Holmes, Geoffrey S., 1928–
    Augustan England: professions, state and society, 1680–1730.
Includes bibliographical references and index.
1. Professions – England – History – 17th century.
2. Professions – England – History – 18th century.
3. England – Social life and customs – 17th century.
4. England – Social life and customs – 18th century.   I. Title.
HT687.H6   1982   305.5′53′0942   82–11485
ISBN 0–04–942178–6

Set in 10 on 11 point Times by Grove Graphics, Tring
and printed in Great Britain by Mackays of Chatham

Contents

To the memory of my father

Preface

Literary scholars have long made use of the word 'Augustan' or the phrase 'Augustan England' to identify that brilliant age of English letters which had its heart in the reign of Anne, but which stretched back as far as the heyday of Dryden and forward to the high noon of Pope. They are labels which historians, too, can most usefully appropriate; for one of the most invigorating currents in seventeenth- and eighteenth-century English historiography during the past ten years or so has been the one which has carried the study of themes once regarded as peculiar to either one century or the other over the sacred dynastic watershed which for so long divided them. It is creating, in effect, a new 'period'.

For something like three generations students of history have been reared, at school and at university, on textbooks whose authors knew with invincible certainty when the seventeenth century in England ended and when the eighteenth century began. The eighteenth century began, self-evidently, in 1714; and a myriad research hours, my own included, have been conditioned by this fundamental presupposition. Not all the great Victorians, it is interesting to recall, Whiggish in their history though they may have been, shared these certainties. Lecky, for one, did not. And perhaps, if the study of the social history of the whole period from 1660 to 1780 had not been so astonishingly neglected for over three decades after 1930, that growing awareness of the essential continuity between the development of late Stuart and early Georgian England, now overtaking us, would have dawned much earlier. Be that as it may, whether we study the social evolution or economic progress of our ancestors, or whether our concern is more with their political institutions, ideologies or religion, it is beginning to be accepted that there is more historical cohesion, in many ways, about the five decades from the 1680s to the 1720s than one can hope to find under 'the later Stuarts' from 1660 to 1714 or within that time-honoured half-slab of Hanoverian history which ends with the accession of George III. We need a word, therefore, to classify this bridging period historically, and what better word than *Augustan*? For it was not in its literature alone that it was marked by outstanding achievement and by progress that was at once self-consciously exciting and quietly fruitful.

In a period which saw a striking growth in England's influence, self-confidence and material well-being there was one group of Englishmen, the members of the professions, whose range of activities permeated almost all walks of life – public, private and corporate – and touched at some point almost every branch of the economy. In the public field alone, professional men were largely responsible between the 1680s and the 1720s for engineering the most important overhaul and extension of their machinery of government and revenue raising which Englishmen had known; for creating the instruments of maritime and naval supremacy and for giving the country its first sustained and effective military presence on the Continent since the fifteenth century. In their private capacity, to take only three examples, they were closely involved in the progress of estate management and agrarian 'improvements', in aesthetic, cultural and scientific advances, and in the growth of towns and enrichment of urban life – all features of this period which put a distinctive stamp upon it. The professions, in short, were an integral part of the fabric and the very texture of Augustan England. Its achievements, and some of its travails too, are illuminated by their history. And yet far too little is known about their members, either as individuals, as occupational groups or as social entities.

The significance of the years from 1580 to 1640 in the progress of the older English professions has been brought to our attention by, among others, Professors Lawrence Stone and G. E. Aylmer, Dr Prest, Dr O'Day and Dr Raach. Unpublished work, too, such as that of Dr C. W. Brooks on the Elizabethan and early Stuart attorneys supports the view that those years did see a notable advance of the common lawyers, significant changes in the practice of medicine and a growth of 'professional' consciousness among Anglican clergy and royal officials. This apart, however, historians have given extraordinarily little attention before the nineteenth century to a process which was fundamental to the evolution of modern English society. Students can be forgiven for assuming, on the strength of what is available in print, that only a heavily urbanised and industrialised society can support a vigorous growth and diversification of professional services and produce a significant professional element in the social structure. In 1951 Edward Hughes wrote a brief pioneering paper on the eighteenth-century professions calculated to dispel this fallacy. Unfortunately he interred it in the pages of the *Durham University Journal*. Where work has been undertaken since then on individual professions or subprofessions in the pre-industrial century, and has found its way into print, it has tended to concentrate on their 'professional' rather than their social faces; so it is with W. A. L. Vincent's investigation of the grammar-school masters of 1660–1714, with D. A. Baugh's admirable essay on the naval officers in the age of Walpole or the important research of R. S. Roberts into seventeenth-century medicine. In the 1950s Robert Robson and Bernice Hamilton, with their studies of the eighteenth-century attorneys and medical professions, seemed to be blazing a trail; but few followed it, the undergrowth swallowed much of it up, and in any case the trail started in both cases at a relatively late point in the process of change.

It will be argued in this book that there was in fact a period of at least fifty years, beginning in the latter part of Charles II's reign and with the reigns of William III and Anne at its core, when much of that sector of English society which would now unquestionably be called 'professional' was in flux: undergoing changes more remarkable in themselves and far-reaching in their implications, both for the state and for society, than anything which had taken place in comparable areas before the Civil Wars or the Restoration. They constituted neither an exclusive 'seventeenth-century' phenomenon nor an 'eighteenth-century' one. They were quintessentially 'Augustan'. In examining them my chief concern has been to produce a work of social history. Of course I have not ignored the functional and institutional aspects of professional development: to do so would have been artificial and distorting. But above all I have conceived this as a book about people – about individuals and groups who shared some measure of common identity – and about the social changes which their experiences and professional evolution involved.

It is not a book of extravagant pretensions. It is written principally for the student and the general reader interested in the history of both seventeenth- and eighteenth-century England, and puzzled by some of its lacunae. I naturally hope that scholars of these periods, too, even specialists in some of the fields into which I have ventured, will find something here to satisfy them, and perhaps even to stimulate them (if only into disagreement!). But I have to caution them from the start that the original scholarship underpinning the essays which follow makes no claim to profundity. The primary material I have used has left some mark on every chapter, and in a number of essays – especially those on the clergy and on the legal and medical professions – it has played a very important part in shaping several of my hypotheses and conclusions. But what I have written is not the fruit of long years of archive-delving, and my indebtedness to other historians' work, in many areas, has been immense.

My original intentions were twofold. I could see a need to lay a broader and more solid foundation than exists at present for future work both on the seventeenth- and eighteenth-century professions and on a sadly neglected aspect of English social history. At the same time it seemed I might assemble between one pair of covers something that would at least meet the interim needs of students and non-specialists. Both ends, I cheerfully imagined, could be largely served by bringing together what was already known but widely scattered and often not easily accessible (material located, for example, in periodicals which few undergraduates ever encounter); but occasionally I would add from my own researches a certain amount that was not known or had so far been only vaguely comprehended. Not surprisingly the personal as opposed to the synthesising role bulked larger as the work proceeded: partly because the groundwork previously done proved so much thinner in some places than in others, and partly because my natural curiosity proved, predictably, as difficult to contain as a frisky puppy. Such unevenness of treatment, however, as may strike the reader (the fact, for example, that lawyers get a good deal more space than naval officers or even clergy, and doctors more than either) has been deliberate. I set out to write a series of semi-autonomous essays, loosely connected. In the end they have cohered. But I have held to my early assumption that more was necessary on some groups than on others. On the one hand, I have had to allow for such vagaries as that there already exists a valuable book on Georgian attorneys but nothing remotely comparable on, say, Augustan civil servants. On the other hand, I have had to accept that in dealing with some professions, certainly schoolmasters and to some extent the clergy, I had to contend not so much with a vacuum as with the wrong kind of substance: vague but stubborn images which owe little to what serious work has been done on these groups as professionals but a great deal to common misconceptions about both education and religion in the century following the Restoration.

While the book has been in the making, a much longer process than anticipated, there have been heartening signs that basic research on the Augustan professions is getting under way again. Richard Pearce, formerly of St John's College, Cambridge, has begun work on social aspects of the Common Law élite, David Harley (St John's College, Oxford) on the social history of medicine in late Stuart England, and Michael Miles (Birmingham University) on taking much further Dr Robson's investigations of the eighteenth-century attorneys. Mrs J. G. L. Burnby has completed a London doctoral dissertation on the provincial apothecaries. Dr Howard Tomlinson's book on the Ordnance Office has illuminated an obscure corner of the bureaucracy in the years 1660–1714. D. L. Hirschberg and J. H. Pruett have investigated the Anglican clergy and Dr Bruce has published a revised version of his thesis on the purchase system in the British army from the seventeenth to the nineteenth centuries. If what is offered here, whatever its shortcomings, encourages the taking up of other torches of this kind, a great deal of labour will have been worthwhile.

In part because of the character of the book, in part because I have had in mind the expense, in these inflationary days, of complex typesetting, I have taken a decision which will be unpopular with some fellow scholars, though if experience is any guide on this score it will leave most of my readers undismayed. In the final version footnote references have been left out, and explanatory notes reduced to the merest handful. Even cross-references have been included in brackets in the text – an inelegant but serviceable device. I have, however, listed all the sources I have used, chapter by chapter, in the course of a very extensive bibliographical commentary at the end of the book, acknowledging my most important debts to existing work, and providing pointers, quite often explicitly, to the derivation of much of the matter that has gone before, especially to the sources of quotations and to the authority behind passages based on primary material. To those who wish for chapter and verse either for quotations whose origins cannot be deduced or for statements they may find particularly startling, I can only promise to be patient in answering queries.

Acknowledgments

My thanks to the authors of various unpublished dissertations on which I have drawn and to the Curators of the Osborn Collection at Yale University Library are expressed in the notes at the end of the book. I have, however, incurred many particular debts which no bibliography can adequately acknowledge.

Professor Henry Horwitz and Drs Wilfred Prest, David Hayton and Peter Borsay brought to my attention material on lawyers and doctors which I might otherwise have missed. Two past members of my Special Subject class at Lancaster, Peter Le Fevre and Ruth Roughton, likewise passed on to me information on naval officers and schoolmasters which they had unearthed. Charles Parker, Christopher Clay and Robert Beddard answered my queries about, respectively, Lord Macclesfield, Lord Cowper and Edward Greene, the surgeon, and the two former were very generous with the fruits of their own researches. So, too, were Professor David Hirschberg and Mr Michael Miles in communicating to me unpublished papers on the episcopate and state patronage over the Church (referred to in the bibliographical notes on the clergy) and on attorneys. In helping to clarify some of my ideas on the lawyers and on university dons two discussions I had in Oxford in 1978, with Dr Prest and with the late Dame Lucy Sutherland, were most valuable.

The Council of the British Academy, having invited me to deliver the 1979 Raleigh Lecture on 'The Professions and Social Change in England, 1680–1730', was subsequently kind enough to allow me to reproduce several paragraphs of that lecture, parts of them verbatim, in Section II of the introductory chapter that follows. Clyve Jones, of the Institute of Historical Research, has helped me in more ways than I can possibly detail here; not the least of his kindnesses was to make sure that I always had somewhere congenial to lay my head whenever I was pursuing my researches in London. I am deeply grateful, too, for the sympathetic encouragement and wise counsel of John Bright-Holmes. I was fortunate in having the help of Lesley Ferrari as well as of my wife in preparing the final typescript. My wife's invaluable support must have shortened the completion time of the book by at least twelve months; since as well as typing earlier drafts she also took scores of *précis* and transcripts for me during the precious year when I was able to work at the book full-time.

Lastly, I must mention my debts to the institutions and persons who made that year, from April 1977 to March 1978, possible: to the University of Lancaster for first granting me two terms of study leave and then, on a special plea, extending that leave by a further term; to my colleagues in the History Department, in particular Mike Mullett and Eric Evans, for shouldering a good deal of the teaching work I would otherwise have been doing; above all, to the Warden and Fellows of All Souls College, Oxford, first for electing me to a Visiting Fellowship in Michaelmas Term 1977 and then for allowing me to hold it for a further term. There I enjoyed idyllic conditions for committing a first draft to paper. I had the Codrington Library available at any hour at the turn of a key, guidance whenever I needed it from John Simmons, the Librarian, and his staff, and the contents of one of the finest wine cellars in England at hand to restore the tissues. What more could any scholar desire? If this book falls short of the expectations of all whose assistance has helped it along the way, the fault is entirely my own.

GEOFFREY HOLMES
Burton-in-Lonsdale
January 1981

PART ONE

The Augustan Professions and English Society

1

Introduction

I The Professions in Transition, 1680–1730

Both those who study and those who inhabit a twentieth-century society have their notions of what constitutes a profession. These notions may not at all points coincide, especially when they involve adjudging the claims of particular occupations to 'professional status'. But there would be a large measure of agreement that a profession is a calling or vocation, exclusive (as one dictionary puts it) of occupations 'purely commercial, mechanical, agricultural or the like'; and that what gives it its distinctive social stamp is the fact that, through education and a career-oriented training, a particular body of specialised knowledge is acquired and is then applied to the service (or it may be, the instruction or command) of others. The notion of service – of skilled service to the community in ways more highly esteemed socially than the skills of trades and crafts – is inseparable from a modern image of a profession. The assumption that this is usually expressed within some kind of institutional frame-work, and often under the auspices of some professional organisation or association with a supervising and regulating function, must be almost as widespread. Such concepts as these were not alien to the seventeenth- or early-eighteenth-century Englishman; neither was the term 'profession' itself, used in roughly these senses, a stranger to his vocabulary. It was a word, however, which could also mean both less and more to him than it does to us.

As early as 1605 Francis Bacon had found it strange that the great colleges of Europe were 'all dedicated to professions, and none left free to Arts and Sciences at large'. Implicit in his remark are two ideas, both of which were firmly implanted in the seventeenth-century mind, although they were never entirely consistent with each other. One was that the profession presupposed a lengthy training, basically intellectual in nature, and a recognised qualification; the other, that the training was vocational and the profession itself a means of livelihood. The idea died hard that the only true professions were 'learned' professions and that the learning they demanded was primarily of an academic kind, to be acquired at a university or – stretching a point – through an alternative medium of higher educa-tion. During the first half of the seventeenth century a training at one of the inns of court was conceded (in some quarters, only grudgingly conceded) comparable status to the vocational degree courses of the universities; although there were still civil lawyers even in the second half of the century who were perfectly serious in regarding their calling as superior to the profession of the Common Law because it was grounded in an academic discipline. By this criterion 'the profession of Divinity', as Dryden termed it in 1682, was then securely based; for by the 1680s ordination into priests' orders in the Anglican Church was almost invariably confined to men with an Oxford or Cambridge degree; and most Augustan clergy were Masters of Arts who had pursued their theological studies after taking their bachelors' degrees, even if only a very small minority in due course acquired BDs or DDs. By the same token the credentials of physicians who were qualified with a university doctorate of medicine were unimpeachable, and those of 'doctors' who practised under licence with a plain MB were wholly respectable; whereas Francis Brown, putting *The Case of the College of Physicians* at the beginning of Queen Anne's reign, argued against allowing apothecaries freely to 'practise physic' on the grounds that it would not only 'deprive the gentry of one of the professions by which their younger sons might honourably subsist' but would 'be a great detriment to the Universities'.

On the other hand, the fact that references to 'the profession of arms' can be traced back as far as the Elizabethan period suggests that the English vocabulary was even then beginning to find a useful way of classifying means of employment which were not 'trades', in the usual sense, but whose specialised training was akin to an apprenticeship and certainly owed nothing to the syllabuses of any university. A century and a half later the word was in widespread use to cover such cases. Two writers of the 1740s, for example, had no hesitation in describing architecture as a 'profession', though one of them, himself a professional artist, preferred to term it 'the profession of building' in conscious contradistinction to the 'trade of building'. The idea that a profession was, by definition, a means of livelihood was also bound in the end to be destructive of purely academic criteria. And, conversely, it meant that when the new breed of 'men of science' became an important and permanent feature of the intellectual scene in England under the later Stuarts, they were not thought of as together constituting a 'profession' since they had no common *occupational* identity. Most of the leading astronomers, mathematicians or natural philosophers in Restoration and post-Revolution England earned their bread as teachers in the universities or, in a few cases, at Gresham College; a few did so as beneficed clergymen; one or two – Newton after 1696 being the most famous case in point – as civil servants.

The predictable result of the steady undermining of traditional assumptions about 'professions' was to introduce for a long period in Augustan England, and after, a greater ambivalence into contemporary usage than had existed in 1600 or for that matter in 1680. As late at 1755 Lord Chesterfield, in discussing the 'breeding up' of sons 'to some profession or other', considered the claims of 'trade' in almost the same breath as those of the army, the navy or the

Church. If this confusion seems strange, we need only recall that although there were by George II's reign many forms of service to the community that had established a claim, and often a strong claim, to be considered 'professional' since the time of Charles II, it was still difficult to differentiate in a technical sense between certain professions and the superior trades. Just as youths of good or respectable family were apprenticed to mercers and drapers, merchants and goldsmiths, so a formal apprenticeship was the only way in the seventeenth and eighteenth centuries of entering and training for some occupations which we should unhesitatingly consider professional. It was the automatic route for apothecaries, solicitors, attorneys and surgeons. It was also practised elsewhere, to an extent that was growing rather than declining – in fitting boys for careers of authority in the merchant navy, for example, and in the training of such specialists as music masters, writing masters, surveyors and those architects with a technical rather than a theoretical grounding. Even in the government service a clerkship was frequently the recognised equivalent of an informal apprenticeship, since for some it offered the definite prospect of a rise to higher things ultimately: indeed in certain departments, for instance the Exchequer, the Customs and the Excise, the bonds taken on entry from clerks or trainee revenue men in one respect paralleled the premiums required of tradesmen's apprentices, although their prime purpose – security against fraud – was not, of course, strictly the same.

Grey areas, therefore, there undoubtedly were between professions, on the one hand, and commerce or crafts, on the other. Writing masters played a role of increasing importance in education; yet a man such as John Baskerville was not merely a craftsman (calligrapher and japanner) but a manufacturer (typefounder, ink- and paper-maker). Scriveners remained technically adjuncts of the legal profession in the early eighteenth century; but in London, at least, they had long since become an integral part of the world of business and finance. Discussing their functions in a popular handbook of 1747 to the 'Trades, Professions, Arts, both liberal and mechanic' currently practised in London, R. Campbell sat firmly and without obvious discomfort astride the fence:

[Conveyancing] is the most profitable branch of the Law; for to that of drawing deeds, they commonly add the *trade* of a money-scrivener; that is, they are employed to find out estates to purchase, or have money to lay out for some, and borrow for others, and receive fees from borrower and lender; and of course are employed to draw the securities . . . This business is engrossed in the hands of a few, who suddenly make estates . . . Fancy and whim governs the public in this, as in *other professions.* (My italics).

Apothecaries, too, were in an ambivalent position. They made up and sold medicines in their shops; yet they also rendered consultancy services to the sick which were eminently professional, and – what was perhaps the most important criterion of all, and the decisive one – they were by the end of the seventeenth century clearly *perceiving* their own function as more of a professional than a commercial one. When seeking statutory sanction in the winter of 1694–5 for their exemption from certain onerous local offices, it was not with shop-keepers and tradesmen but with lawyers and doctors that the apothe-caries sought parity on the grounds of the indispensability of their contribution to the common weal – 'knowing that the profession of the common and civil law (in all their branches) were excused from such services, and that the physicians and chirurgeons were by parti-cular acts of Parliament discharged from the like'.

Another contrast with the professions of the late nineteenth and twentieth centuries is that in Augustan England there existed more overlap between certain groups. Thus over the whole period from 1680 to 1730 it remained the case that nearly all university dons, a majority of grammar-school headmasters, a substantial number of assistant masters in such schools, and a fair proportion of private tutors were clergymen; and more than is often realised were beneficed priests. But lay teachers, too, not infrequently wore two vocational hats. Mathematics masters with the right training and experience happily freelanced as surveyors and map-makers. On the other hand, Edward Faulkner of Limehouse described himself early in George I's reign as 'Schoolmaster and Notary Public' and took duly bound apprentices – though it is not clear whether he undertook to give them likewise two strings to their bows. While clergymen were less likely than heretofore to venture beyond spheres pastoral or peda-gogic (the old tradition of parish priests practising medicine as a serious by-occupation was fast dying out by 1700), lawyers by contrast were finding increasing scope for versatility. The proportion of lawyers to non-lawyers in Crown employments was very much higher than it is today. Or to take an instance from a more fledgling profes-sion: many estate stewards were attorneys-at--law by training, and some of them still combined private legal practice with land manage-ment.

However, the swift expansion of the market for their services, which was a boon to lawyers in many ways, proved in one respect a serious plague to them, just as a similar expansion brought embarrass-ment to qualified medical practitioners. A great jackal pack of illicit, unqualified operators snarled round the fringes of both professions by 1730, posing problems undreamed of by their modern counter-parts. Running with them in their hundreds were unqualified lawyer's clerks; self-styled 'solicitors' who would not have known the Court of Chancery from the local alehouse in which they did much of their business; a miscellaneous horde of medical quacks or 'empirics', thriving in a land where sickness was endemic and peddling their wares not only in the traditional ways, at markets and fairs, but through the new media provided by a flourishing young newspaper press. Such men fought mostly for the leavings of the true professionals, but in some cases carried off very plump prey indeed. Among many quack doctors who made fortunes in early-eighteenth-century England, two (Sir William Read and Roger Grant) actually became Queen Anne's oculists-in-ordinary. Even successful provincials were sometimes able to live with amazing pomp on the strength of their profits, lording it from one county town to the next in their coaches and six with liveried servants and outriders. One exotic, glimpsed by John Macky in the courtyard of the George in Winchester in 1722, was even accompanied by his own tame apothecary, by his private jester and by the rough equivalent of a modern publicity agent: 'it's a prodigy', Macky reflected, 'how so wise a people as the English can be gulled by such pickpockets'.

Most of the anomalies, or apparent anomalies, we have just noticed – as between professions and trades, between one profession and another, or between *bona fide* professionals and pseudo-professionals – already existed in some degree in England in the 1680s. But they were unquestionably more obtrusive by the end of our period than they had been at its beginning; and this in itself has much to tell the historian. The fact that in 1680 it was a feasible if not a simple task to distinguish those callings which adequately satisfied the contemporary criteria of a profession, whereas by 1720 or 1730 it had become in many respects more difficult, is one measure of the transition taking place in the interim across a whole sector of England's social structure. And the very fact that this was a sector which in numbers, wealth and relative weight was expanding more rapidly than any other in the late seventeenth century and the first half of the eighteenth makes this transition all the more important. But also, of course, the anomalies bear witness to a fact already noticed, namely, that some of the 'professional' criteria themselves were becoming less rigid.

What were these contemporary criteria and characteristics? In three basic respects, and in one that was something less than basic, they differed very little from our own. In the first place, a profession was seen as a vocation for the whole of a man's working life and one which usually, but not invariably, had its own recognised hierarchy of promotion. Not only the ministry of the Anglican Church and the 'higher degrees' of the law but commissioned service in the army and the navy and also the non-political civil service had such hierarchies; and by the early eighteenth century the last three fields of employment had begun to share with the two former that degree of continuity and permanence, essential to the consolidation of professional status, which they had not possessed in Charles II's reign. In the second place, entry to a profession normally presupposed a long and at times carefully regulated vocational training. Such courses of training would not necessarily end in qualifying examinations, but examinations in one form or another were the norm in the Royal Navy after 1679, in the Church, in preceding a call to the bar (in form, at least), in every branch of London medicine and universally among university-trained physicians; and by Anne's reign they had made their first appearance in the bureaucracy – in the Customs department. Gradually, though only gradually, it was conceded that training for a profession need not be strictly 'learned' in the traditional sense, so long as it had a 'bookish' element in it; but this remained for a long time an area of dispute between arch-conservatives and those bent on establishing their claims to professionalism. The nature of their training was naturally closely linked to a third factor, the nature of the services which professional men rendered to the community. They were services in which the hands normally played a subordinate part to the brain. The tradition established by the old 'learned' professions, that these services were not primarily economic, continued to provide a valuable touchstone (although to contemporaries not an infallible one) whereby those who saw themselves as pursuing a 'profession' were distinguishable from those who followed other highly skilled service occupations (for instance, London's private bankers, who still had their goldsmiths' background).

At various times between the Middle Ages and the early seventeenth century regulating societies or other forms of organisation had developed to determine and enforce standards in a number of occupations that were either already professional or destined to become so: the Royal College of Physicians, the London Company of Barber Surgeons and Society of Apothecaries, and the benchers of the inns of court. Among the Anglican clergy the responsibility for maintaining 'discipline' was shared between the archdeacons, the bishops in their periodic visitations, and in dire cases the consistory courts. By the end of the seventeenth century the Admiralty and Navy Commissioners between them had made the naval officers perhaps the most closely regulated of all bodies of professional men; the Treasury Lords had begun to assume a far greater responsibility than hitherto for the efficiency and conditions of work and pay of public office-holders; while individual departments of state, notably the Excise (outside the dockyards the biggest civil employer under the Crown), had started to formulate their own corpora of rules. Apart from being subject to judges' rules, attorneys and solicitors continued to stand aside from this current, but in the 1730s a combination of legislative pressure and their own sense of self-preservation in the face of the piratical activities of unlicensed practisers drove many of them into their first professional association, the forerunner of the Law Society.

Even among the older professions of the early eighteenth century there were few which in their entirety satisfied all these criteria and two – the army and schoolmastering – which displayed particularly idiosyncratic features. But not surprisingly it was the newer, smaller groups emerging from the chrysalis in the half-century after 1680 which were emphatically less successful in fitting into any stereotype mould. The architects of Augustan England, for example, had no standard method of training, and the same was true (despite their much longer pedigree) of officers in the merchant navy, where a formal apprenticeship system made only limited progress. Estate stewards, unless they were lawyers, had no formal training at all.

Musicians and other artists usually served apprenticeships, much as tradesmen did, and there was a great deal more practice than theory to their training. None of these groups had anything approaching an organisational structure, neither did they have watchdogs to supervise entry and performance. With a society that was developing organically as swiftly as that of the Augustans was, it was natural that over half a century the frontiers of the professions should not merely have been pushed further out but should have become, in places, more blurred at the extremities. The more sophisticated a society becomes, the greater the scope within it for the extension of professional services (see below, pp. 11–14); but this is a process that, in the early stages at least, will generally be accompanied by a good deal of improvisation. In the end, therefore, the two most decisive questions in a period of such rapid transition were not so much, how did a particular occupational group measure up to this standard or that? They were rather, how did it see itself, collectively, in social terms? And how did others see its members, individually, in terms of their social status?

A hallmark of the professional man in eighteenth-century England was that he was entitled to nothing less than the prefix 'Mr', that he quite frequently earned the label of 'gentleman', and that in certain circumstances (if, for instance, he became a barrister or a captain in the army) either the nature of his profession or his place in its hierarchy carried with it the rank of 'esquire' or rough social parity with esquires. The gamut of social distinctions thus covered was not wholly unspannable; but it was wide enough to suggest to us that even the major and indisputable professional groups of Augustan England must have had difficulty in experiencing anything resembling a common 'professional' solidarity. There is very little evidence that they did experience this; and indeed it would have been extraordinary had the professions at large approached the self-awareness of the 'landed interest' at this period or even of that much newer phenomenon, the City. If we picture tens of thousands of families by the early eighteenth century inhabiting an imposing apartment block, and mentally label that block 'the professions', we must also envisage within it not merely a great many separate rooms, but a series of floors (on each of which there are representatives of all the larger professions) ranging from a luxuriously furnished upper storey to the most austere of basements. Connecting staircases there were; but there was also a built-in tendency in the structure towards social segregation.

What this did not do was eliminate all development of group identity – of common aspiration and, where appropriate, of a certain *esprit de corps* within individual professions or branches of professions. An outward manifestation of corporate self-awareness, not without significance, was the distinctive dress that was to be found in all major Augustan professions except the bureaucracy. The law furnished an especially rich variety of habiliments: the judges' scarlet and great wigs, the coifs of the serjeants-at-law, the 'long robes' of the King's Counsel, the gowns worn in court by barristers, attorneys and solicitors. But there were also the black coats and Geneva bands of the lower clergy and the lawn sleeves of the bishops; the mortar-boards and gowns of the grammar-school masters and university teachers; and, more colourfully, the uniforms of the army and navy officers. The tradition that doctors of physic should appear in public in a red cloak and full-bottomed wig, wearing a sword and carrying a long cane (preferably silver- or gold-headed) was only spasmodically kept up by the early decades of the eighteenth century. But it did persist here and there down to the 1730s, even in the provinces. William Logan, MD, who practised in Bristol from 1711 to 1747, was said never to stir abroad – or even allow himself to be seen at home – without his full regalia. And the cane and heavy wig, at least, remained in favour with many of the older generation well into George II's reign. William Wadd, an early-nineteenth-century collector of bio-graphical titbits on the medical profession, related how 'even in the middle of the last century . . . Dr Brocklesby's barber's boy was accustomed to carry a band-box through high 'change, exclaiming, "Make way for Dr Brocklesby's wig! " '

There were too many rivalries between the long-established and the newer branches of the medical profession to permit an easy progress towards a common outlook and ethos among all who doctored the sick of Augustan England; though as we shall see (below, Chapter 6) important strides had been made in this direction by 1730. However, sectional loyalties within the profession were very strong indeed, and never stronger than when any section felt its own special interests to be under attack. Oxford- and Cambridge-trained physicians and London apothecaries each exhibited considerable cohesiveness in such circumstances, but the camaraderie of the surgeons was an altogether more spontaneous, widespread and notable growth rooted in a particularly deep sense of professional pride that was fostered by both the technical and social advance of surgery in this period. The barriers within the legal profession were not so high as those within medicine, and the day when consciousness of being part of 'one body' with common interests and aspirations would seem natural to many lawyers was not far off by the end of George I's reign. Even so, what is most remarkable in Augustan England is how tightly the 'lesser degrees' of the profession, the attorneys and solicitors, con-solidated whenever they faced strong pressure or criticism, as they did in 1701, 1706 and 1729. A sense of danger, heightened by the attacks of its political enemies (for example, in the years 1702–6, 1710 and 1730–6), served also to highlight – perhaps in exaggerated colours – the fierce tribal feeling of the clergy, above all of the parish clergy. In theory the Anglican clergy provided the most notable exception to the rule that divergencies of wealth and rank within professions militated strongly against a true sense of homogeneity; but in practice even among divines it was sometimes very difficult, at the extreme poles of bishop's palace and curate's lodging, to en-visage a brotherhood which encompassed such gross inequalities.

In the civil service it was possible to find within certain departments of government by the early eighteenth century, such as the Post Office, the Excise and possibly the Salt Office, a professional *esprit de corps* that was capable of bridging wide differences of income and status. But it would have been quite unrealistic to look for anything comparable throughout the whole bureaucracy, where the gap between key executives earning anything from £500 to £2,000 a year and a lower-clerical and revenue-collecting proletariat earning from £30 to £50 was formidably wide. In fact, from the 1690s onwards it was probably in the armed forces, and more especially in the navy, that the line between success and anonymity, between fame and fortune and threadbare obscurity, was least destructive of an overriding professional consciousness.

Although it is hard to discern much sense of mutual identity suffusing professional men at large during the half-century after 1680, there was one area, at least, in which its slow growth was being encouraged. All through this period the urbanisation of England's pre-industrial society was going steadily but significantly forward. It offered greater opportunities for more regular social intercourse among lawyers, physicians and urban clergy, for their intermarriage and for their common association with the 'town gentry' in those provincial urban centres which acted as natural foci for professional services, and particularly in those towns involved in what Peter Borsay has called 'the English urban renaissance' of the late seventeenth century and the first half of the eighteenth. Into this circle a prosperous schoolmaster, surgeon or apothecary could hope to break, while after the wars of 1689–1713 the retired or half-pay officer of the army or navy enlarged it further. Awareness of a separate social phenomenon, with characteristics marking out its members in certain respects from those whose status rested on land acreage and rent rolls, and even from those whose worldly success was quantifiable in the business ledger, was in this way undramatically enhanced.

II Professional Men and Social Change

At a later stage (pp. 239–42 below) our attention will fasten on those political necessities of the Augustan state which helped to propel the English professions in the late seventeenth century into the most active phase of transition they had yet known. The professions as a whole, however, as opposed to a distinct and relatively novel compartment of them, would never have experienced such remarkable flux and growth between 1680 and 1730 if the social and economic climate of England had not been changing at least as emphatically as the responsibilities and requirements of her government. One powerful agent of this change was the period of fruitful urban development just mentioned: a period which outside London began roughly in the last two decades of the seventeenth century and went on until it was subsumed in the onset of industrialisation. And it had this in common with other relevant factors of a social and economic nature, that as well as being a stimulant to the expansion and diversification of the professions it was also, in its turn, a principal beneficiary of the self-same process. One has only to glance at some of the fine town houses and mansions still surviving today which were built by flourishing lawyers, doctors or clergy of King William's reign and Queen Anne's, monuments to the years of their pomp, to appreciate this. Such buildings as the Cupola House of Macro the apothecary in Bury St Edmunds, Landor House, built for Dr Johnson of Warwick, Dr John Castle's 'Great House' in Burford, Chancellor Tullie's house in Carlisle and the Augustan jewels of many a cathedral close reveal something of the social and cultural enrichment which small communities of professional men could bring to the English urban scene.

In addition to urban development three other aspects of a changing social backcloth to the period had a critical bearing on the fortunes of professional groups and individuals. For one thing standards of material prosperity and comfort rose in England in the fifty years after 1680 to a degree that was wholly without precedent. At the same time, and not of course coincidentally, the economy was growing in complexity and in the process requiring new services from contemporary society to match its developing needs: lawyers who could, for example, facilitate international business transactions or pilot controversial river navigation schemes through the shoals of local opposition and ultimately through Parliament; full-time estate stewards who could apply scientific methods to the maximisation of rents and estate yields; customs officers who could master a tariff which by Anne's reign was bewildering in its ramifications; new Exchequer officials who could administer public loans funded on the basis of the most involved actuarial calculations; or schoolmasters who could instruct youths in mathematics, book-keeping and accountancy, calligraphy and surveying. Meanwhile, in a quite different sphere, the role of private patronage in literature and the arts, whether through individuals or through group initiatives such as music societies, was becoming more ambitious year by year; and this enabled more men to make a living, and occasionally a more than comfortable one, by the pen, or through their talents in music or in one of the other arts, than had been dreamed of in Elizabeth I's reign or even in the years immediately after the Restoration. If to these four broad considerations we add a fifth, the central political fact of the age, that for a total of eighteen years out of twenty-three between 1689 and 1712 England was actively involved in warfare of unprecedented magnitude, we have the main keys to understanding the rapidity with which the Augustan professions evolved and expanded.

At many points in this book we shall find ourselves touching on the links between both urbanisation and economic conditions and the progress of the English professions; and Part Three will take as its dominant theme the role of war. But little of this would be fully comprehensible without recognising the one constant ingredient in the situation, fundamental in so many ways to all else. The growth of prosperity in late Stuart and early Georgian England provides this basic and pervading element, and with it the improvement in the quality of life experienced not simply by a tiny élite but by several hundred thousand English families over two generations. Thanks partly to what historians have termed the commercial and financial 'revolutions' of the later seventeenth century, and partly to a great augmentation of the fiscal resources of the state between 1683 and 1712, Englishmen's private spending power was transformed while public spending power was multiplied at least three times over. The result of this, and also of half a century of uneven but unquestionable agrarian progress, was a society which over five to six decades from the mid-1670s strikingly improved its material well-being; and a society which, for this reason and others, became more sophisticated, probably more status-conscious, certainly more comfort- and amenity-conscious, and furthermore more cultivated, than any previous English generation. In the light of all this it can be no coincidence that it was between the late 1670s and the mid-1680s that the momentum of rapid change in the professions built up: years when, among other things, the formal examination for a naval commission was introduced, London apothecaries took a conscious and overt step towards the assumption of professional status and the country's first really large professional government department, the Excise, was created; that this momentum increased after 1689; and that it scarcely slackened from then on until after the foundation of the great Edinburgh medical school (an event of no less significance for England than for Scotland) and the passing of the Lawyers' Bill in the years 1726–9.

As we have noted, professional men have their *raison d'être* in providing certain specialised services for their fellow citizens and for the state. In England between *circa* 1680 and 1730 there existed a society which increasingly required new services, or a greater volume and variety of existing services, on a scale never before approached. What was equally vital, both private citizens and the king's government had the capacity as never before to pay for these new assets. The former, for instance, were able to foot the bills for a widening range of legal services as well as financing the mounting volume of litigation in the courts, and at the same time they managed to absorb the higher fees which many lawyers were now demanding. Less willing to tolerate discomfort and therefore pain than their more stoical forebears (and also less adequately armoured by religious faith against the malignancy of fate), they looked for relief, with an optimism that in retrospect seems little short of awesome, to those who practised medicine and surgery; and in return for the treatments they received they disgorged sums of money which would have made their mid-seventeenth-century predecessors blench. They not merely craved new houses, or whole streets, terraces and squares *á la mode*, but insisted on the services of experts, professional planners who would express the Augustan aesthetic on their behalf, instead of leaving the business of building, as their fathers and grandfathers had done, to the master masons and master joiners, craftsmen who frequently worked by the thumb. And they were also prepared to invest quite heavily in the kind of education that promised, far more than did a traditional grammar-school training, to fit their sons for employment in a more urbanised, professionalised and economically advanced society. What is more, in defiance of all seventeenth-century precedent, they proved to be as willing, through their taxes and loans, to pay for public benefits as they were to satisfy private needs and aspirations. The large army, navy and bureaucracy of the French Wars, which established the careers of thousands of officers and officials, would as recently as the 1660s have seemed in the realms of fantasy to a penurious monarchy and a cheese-paring ruling class.

These and all other manifestations of society's greater wealth and sophistication, and of its rising and widening expectations, were open invitations to the professions. In such circumstances it was natural that they should expand and that they should prosper; that some of them should adapt their methods of training, or of organisation, to meet the requirements of the changing world about them; and that as time went by they should acquire new offshoots, tiny to start with but destined in time to become large branches. As well as responding to the demands of society and the state, however, professional men played a notable part in keeping the wheel turning full circle. As their own numbers and rewards rose, they themselves helped to generate more and more of the new spending power in a consumer society. They bought land, stocks and securities; they built houses for themselves, sometimes in the country but mainly in the towns; they patronised not only an army of tradesmen, craftsmen and shop-keepers but, increasingly, their fellow professionals. Not least, they developed the keenest interest in improving the amenities of the places they lived in. They involved themselves in such activities as town planning, the improvement of water supplies and of communi-cations, and the founding of charity schools. The lawyers frequently exercised great local influence as Town Clerks, and the civic im-portance of both them and medical men was reflected here and there in their election as mayors. If, in all these respects, their efforts were matched (to say the least) by those of local business communities, their cultural and recreational contribution was more distinctive – frequently outstripping that of the neighbouring country gentry as well as that of the merchants and tradesmen. They were great patrons of local music societies and assemblies. They are also to be found by their own private leisure interests making their neighbourhood a place to be sought out by visiting antiquarians, virtuosi, bibliophiles and collectors. And they were particularly active in supporting (as well as delivering) those infinitely various courses of public lectures to which the educated Englishman of the early eighteenth century was growing so addicted.

Among the many ways in which the development of the professions lent encouragement to the forces working for social change in

Augustan England, one will stand out far beyond the rest in the chapters that follow. Their contribution towards the maintenance of a relatively mobile, yet firmly integrated, social order in the century before the Industrial Revolution is seen as nothing less than crucial: and the more so since this was a time when there might well have been a tendency for other factors (for example, population stability, the state of the land market, and the declining appeal of the universities of Oxford and Cambridge) to work in very much the opposite direction. To argue along these lines may appear to smack of unorthodoxy. After all, that most influential of modern interpreters of pre-industrial society, Lawrence Stone, has made familiar a striking contrast between the century from 1540 to 1640 and what followed the Restoration. In the course of the former, the social fabric of England 'experienced a seismic upheaval of unprecedented magnitude'; whereas 'the increasingly immobile society' which, in Professor Stone's view, evolved between 1660 and 1700 established a pattern of development which lasted from then until the coming of industrialisation. For the years after 1688, especially, he has depicted with a plausibility that students have found hard to resist an oligarchic rather than an open society, one into which the avenues of entry were severely limited and controlled and which held few of those dramatic opportunities for individual advancement which had existed before the Civil Wars: a society in which young men from families engaged in the crafts and small trades, and above all from the great classes of yeoman freeholders and substantial tenantry, who had had so many chances to rise before 1640, now had precious few.

If 'society' is equated narrowly with *landed* society, and the only avenues of mobility to be taken into account are those which allowed families to rise (and fall) solely within the context of landownership and tenancy, there is no difficulty in accepting that the England of 1680–1780 enjoyed far greater social stability than that of 1540–1640, and perhaps suffered some periods of relative stasis. Even so, the upward flow from the ranks of the yeomanry did not dry up, while the cross flow, both into landed society from outside and out of it again, became stronger than it had ever been. Richard Grassby has recently reminded us how popular apprenticeships to merchants still were with the families of the gentry, and in particular of the lesser gentry, by the close of the seventeenth century. As for the role of the professions, both in recruiting from landowning and farming families and in subsequently providing the source of fresh and regular transfusions into landed society, this had not been negligible before the Great Rebellion; yet it expanded beyond comparison after 1680. In any case, English society in the late seventeenth and early eighteenth centuries was becoming less and not more land rooted. Although land remained by far the most important source of political influence throughout the eighteenth century, it was certainly not by the Augustan period the sole prop of social status. And it is only in the context of a society becoming decade by decade more broadly based, in both economic and social structural terms, that we can fully appreciate the extent of the mobility which remained possible within it and the vital importance of the professions as vehicles of this mobility.

One key to their importance, of which we shall be much aware throughout this book, lies in the far-reaching status changes which took place within and among the professions themselves in the late seventeenth and early eighteenth centuries. It was in two of the learned professions, medicine and the law, in schoolmastering, and in the three newer professions which grew and matured in the service of the late Stuart state that they were most profound. Down to the Restoration, and for some time after, the standing of attorneys and solicitors and also of surgeons and apothecaries had been – with the exception of an élite group of London attorneys – very much a subordinate one, that of auxiliaries rather than true professionals in their own right. By 1730, for a variety of reasons which should become clear later, their standing was transformed; and thereby both the law and medicine greatly enlarged their appeal to the sons of the gentry while in no way damaging their ability to attract young men from a far broader social background. Largely through a dramatic increase in the practice of taking in boarders and fee-paying day boys, together with a major expansion in the private and technically specialised sectors of education, the secondary schoolmaster and academy teacher of George I's reign was in many places almost unrecognisable as the successor of the miserably paid drudge so familiar in the mid-seventeenth century. Over a similar period the three youthful professions of Augustan England, the army, the navy and the civil service, hitherto precarious vocations with a very limited capacity, and in the case of the navy a marked absence of social cachet, developed into permanent reservoirs of employment which were acceptable to the members of the existing professional and landed classes and desirable in the eyes of other groups as yet outside their ranks.

A second key to the outstanding importance of the professions as vehicles of social mobility during the years 1680–1730 lies in the great increase they achieved in sheer carrying capacity. A rough estimate – and in the nature of our information it can only be extremely rough – would put the number of *permanent* jobs in the professions by 1730 at between 55,000 and 60,000. Although this is a figure which excludes all apprentices, probationers and part-timers, officers in the merchant navy, on whom it is difficult to come by even approximate information, officials of the Royal Household, and the permanent staff, including craftsmen, of the naval dockyards, my guess is that this still represented an increase since 1680 of very little short of 70 per cent. An expansion of respectable employment opportunities of this order would have been notable in any circumstances. But when supply is considered in relation to demand; when we take account of the minimal increase of population between the 1650s and the late 1720s; when it is borne in mind that with smaller families than before 1640 there were fewer sons and, most significantly, fewer younger sons of well-born families, to be provided for;

and also that the business world had increased its attractions and that there was therefore far less need than before for the landed gentry to seek a lion's share of professional jobs; then it manifestly becomes a factor of prime social significance.

But what made it possible for social classes and groups other than the gentry, including groups far below the ranks of the governing élite, to take up the large surplus thus created and to profit to a degree that would otherwise have been impracticable from the advance of the professions? The answer (and the third and master key to the relationship between the professions and social mobility) lies in the ways in which men trained for the Augustan professions and in the cost of that training. We shall find that many of the more thrusting professional bodies of the years 1680–1730 had one thing in common: they required of their recruits an apprenticeship. Mostly this was a formal, indentured apprenticeship, but in some cases a more informal one. By the beginning of the eighteenth century, as we earlier observed, the whole traditional concept of the English professions as 'learned' occupations, for which young men prepared themselves by attendance not just at a grammar school but at a university or at one of the inns of court, was being fundamentally modified. Dr Charles Goodall had recognised the writing on the wall in his own field in 1684, when in the preface to his treatise on *The Royal College of Physicians* he wrote distastefully (in this context of the apothecaries), 'we have to deal with a sort of men not of academical but mechanic education'. It is unlikely that more than a third of the qualified men in professional occupations by 1730 had been trained in the time-honoured way.

The social repercussions of this process were immense. For although apprenticeship could justifiably be regarded as the equivalent of the vocational training of the ancient professions – and in fact was often more rigorous – it was on the whole, as later studies will emphasise, *much less expensive* than these traditional routes. At a time when entrance to the long-established hierarchies of the Church, the law and 'physic' was becoming costlier (the one major exception being the routes via the Continental medical schools, to which there was increasing recourse), the rest of the expanding professional sector was able to keep its doors remarkably wide open. Even the army before the 1720s was some way short of the bastion of social privilege normally associated, in peacetime at least, with Hanoverian England. Elsewhere men of 'mean originals', or of at best modest family backgrounds, established a firm foothold on the ladder of professional advancement. And not infrequently – as with so many of the successful admirals, apothecaries and surgeons of the period – they succeeded in climbing high.

Relatively low costs of entry had a further implication of great importance for eighteenth-century society, when combined with the rising status of the professions that benefited thereby. Because the Augustan professions, despite some internal tensions, tended by their very nature, their common concerns and mutual respect, to foster identity of interest, so as they expanded and diversified they became increasingly valuable as instruments of social fusion. Professional status in itself became a bond that helped more closely to integrate numerous units of local society as Englishmen in general left behind their Stuart traumas and moved into calmer waters. In this way, by a curious paradox that same transformation of the professions which was so vital a force for social change in England became, almost by the same token, a powerful tranquillising and stabilising agent as well.

2

Nascent Professions and the 'Liberal Arts and Sciences'

When Gregory King, Lancaster Herald, constructed his 'Scheme of the Income and Expense of the several Families of England . . . for the year 1688' he produced six species of 'degrees' or 'qualifications' which we would recognise as professional in character. King himself was at pains to distinguish them both from the 'ranks' of the leisured classes at the top of his table and from those who earned a living on the land and those involved in trade, retailing, craftsmanship and manufacture. He described them as follows: the holders of 'offices and places'; 'persons in the law'; clergymen; 'persons in sciences and liberal arts'; naval officers and military officers (see Table 2.1).

Table 2.1   *The Professions in Gregory King's 'Scheme' for 1688*

Number of Families	Ranks, Degrees, Titles and Qualifications	Heads per Family	Number of Persons	Yearly Income per Family £
5,000	Persons in greater offices and places	8	40,000	240
5,000	Persons in lesser offices and places	6	30,000	120
10,000	Persons in the law	7	70,000	154
2,000	Eminent clergymen	6	12,000	72
8,000	Lesser clergymen	5	40,000	50
15,000	Persons in sciences and liberal arts	5	75,000	60
5,000	Naval officers	4	20,000	80
4,000	Military officers	4	16,000	60

Note: Both the designations and the figures reproduced above are those contained in the revised version of his table, which King communicated to Charles Davenant in 1698. See G. Holmes, 'Gregory King and the social structure of pre-industrial England', *Transactions of the Royal Historical Society*, 5th ser., vol. 27 (1977), pp. 58–9, 63, app. following p. 65.

King never intended his 'Scheme' as a bequest to future historians of the English social structure: hence many of the finer delineations and groupings which appear in his notebooks disappear in the final tabulation into a limited number of broad categories which were chosen with one overriding consideration in mind – quite simply, they served the principal end of the author's work, which was to influence the fiscal policies of King William's government. In any case, King did not have at his disposal the official data on numbers and incomes within particular groups which the modern student can derive from census returns; and the ring of true conviction which the statistics of the 'Scheme' would have derived from such sources is therefore missing. We know, too, that despite the fact that he wrote initially in the mid-1690s, Gregory King was very much concerned to present to his readers what he believed to be a peacetime norm; so that although he must have been well aware of the great expansion which three at least of the professions had experienced since 1689, he takes no cognisance of these wartime changes. The army, the navy and the bureaucracy he submits to statistical analysis are those of James II, not William III.

There are other reasons, too, why this best known of all contemporary classifications of the professions of pre-industrial England is of only limited value. Quite apart from the minor ambiguities it contains – the fact, for example, that the bishops, with their exceedingly wide range of incomes, are listed separately from the higher clergy and that dissenting ministers are not listed at all – there are also major confusions built into this part of the 'Scheme'. For one thing, it is clear both from the numbers and the incomes he attached to them that King's military and naval officers must have included NCOs in the army and petty officers in the Royal Navy as well as commissioned ranks of both services. The office-holders, too, were by no means an exclusively 'professional' body but a motley agglomeration. As King's insertion, on second thoughts, of the word 'places' suggests (it had not been in his original table of 1696), these hybrids included political appointees to both government and Court posts, most of them necessarily impermanent. They also embraced a large number of public employees who were part of the Royal Household rather than the 'civil service' and many others whose duties were too manual or in other respects too lowly for them to be considered, in any realistic sense, professional men: artisans and labourers in the dockyards; doorkeepers, messengers and porters in the central offices of government; gardeners, grooms, yeomen of the guard, cellarers, butterymen, pastry cooks and a score of other types of employee of the Household.

The most blandly unhelpful feature of Gregory King's table is his use of the portmanteau phrase 'persons in sciences and liberal arts', since such a broad variety of professions was obviously comprehended within it. Not that there is anything singular or perverse about King's usage. His two principal heirs as social statisticians, Joseph Massie in 1759 and Patrick Colquhoun as late as 1806, both followed his lead and used the same formula. The only difference was that Colquhoun did see fit to remove from its orbit the biggest single group which King and Massie had silently inserted there, the schoolteachers. All the same, their usage is a frustrating one for historians as the term 'sciences and liberal arts' can only cloud what are two particularly important distinctions for anyone studying the professions in the seventeenth or eighteenth centuries. By subsuming all branches of medicine in the arts or sciences (Augustans themselves were by no means sure which it was), it obscures the distinction between the three 'great professions' of medieval ancestry – one of which was 'physic' – and the rest. Equally confusing is the lumping together of those in well-stocked and long-standing occupations (doctors, surgeons, apothecaries, schoolmasters and university teachers) with a much more miscellaneous company whose vocations were by comparison esoteric and the pursuits of small minorities. Most of the latter were only just beginning in the half-century after 1680 to take on a group identity and one that is recognisably professional in character.

It was those changes in the social and economic climate of Augustan England, of which we are already aware, which encouraged the slow crystallisation of a number of new vocational groups. Most of these were still quite tiny in size even by 1730, but at some stage between the reigns of Charles II and George II each began to take on an embryonic professional identity. They emerged essentially because a maturing society of growing complexity generated certain demands which the existing professions could not meet. By virtue of the new specialised services they managed to provide for the Augustan Englishman, fulfilling his rising and widening expectations, men in these new occupations had earned by the 1730s a certain corporate recognition as something more than the collection of isolated individuals their predecessors had been just after the Restoration. Not all the occupations could have been adequately described as arts, 'liberal' or otherwise, or as sciences. We may call them the nascent or fledgling professions.

Three groups among them, architects, ornamental or landscape gardeners, and surveyors, had some obvious traits in common. Although only architecture was conceded the status of an 'art' (being put in a similar category to other arts of design, like sculpture and painting) all three were products of the great age of baroque and early palladian country-house building in England, together with the accompanying park-and-garden craze which gripped the Augustan upper class like an epidemic after 1690. At the beginning of the nineteenth century, with the Industrial Revolution well launched, Colquhoun was to link surveyors with engineers: he thought that by then there were 5,000 of them in England earning on average £200 a year. But a century earlier the training of surveyors, which for youths who already had a sound mathematical grounding might well cost little more than £30–£40 for a formal seven-year apprenticeship, was encouraged, in the main, by the grandiose approach of Augustan landowners to the planning and mapping of their grounds. Likewise it was their building ambitions which was the prime factor in the emergence of a new breed of specialist architects; although the fact

that the profession burgeoned at this particular time was also connected with urban developments in the late seventeenth and early
eighteenth centuries. It was a period which saw not merely new
building in London at an unprecedented rate but much provincial
activity also, including the rebuilding of Warwick and Northampton
after fire, the creation of handsome suburbs or 'new towns' in such
places as Manchester, Liverpool, Bristol and Birmingham, with the
emphasis on careful, symmetrical planning and homogeneous design,
and not least an appreciable amount of large town-house building. In
this the gentry played a significant part; and such elegant town
mansions as those created for the Plumptres in Nottingham, the
Seymour Portmans in Sherborne or the Sheldons in Winchester often
enlisted the services of specialist architects – even of national figures,
like Archer or Campbell – as well as masons and craftsmen. And as
we have observed (above, p. 12), not only urban and neighbouring
gentry but professional men themselves helped significantly to swell
this demand.

When Defoe described the road from Richmond to London in the
1720s, 'the river sides ... full of villages, and those villages so full of
beautiful buildings, charming gardens and rich gentlemen of quality
that nothing in the world can imitate it', he excused himself from the
prodigious task of cataloguing the fine houses which lined the route.
But he did take pains to inform his readers 'concerning the original
of the strange passion for fine gardens which has so commendably
possessed the English gentleman of late years, for 'tis evident it is but
of late years'. Defoe's explanation – that it was William III who first
made garden-making a fashionable pursuit – was a partial one:
experiences of the Grand Tour were also persuasive, as was the
prolific literature on the subject which became available from the
beginning of the eighteenth century onwards. But it is true that the
king's garden works at Hampton Court and Kensington, like his
well-known passion for evergreens, were widely influential; and it
was certainly from the 1690s onwards that with gathering momentum
'the gentlemen followed everywhere, with such a gust[o] that the
alteration is indeed wonderful throughout the kingdom'.

The rigidly formal, regimented bedding and hedging in the French
mode which typified the seventeenth-century garden called for little
beyond the services of a good head gardener and a nurseryman. But
the far more ambitious garden architecture which held sway under the
last two Stuarts and under George I put a premium on professional
advice of a more elevated kind; and even more was this so of the
indigenous practice of landscaping which, far from being suddenly
invented by William Kent in the 1730s as is sometimes thought, had
been gradually establishing itself through a series of compromises
with established conventions for at least three decades before this.
John Macky, for example, viewing Postmaster-General Frankland's
house at Sutton Court, Middlesex, around 1714, noted that while 'the
gardens are irregular, ... that, I think, adds to their beauty; for every
walk affords variety; the hedges, grottos, statues, mounts, canals are

so many surprising beauties'. Batty Langley, inveighing in 1728 in his *New Principles of Gardening* against 'that abominable mathematical regularity and stiffness' which had marred so many noblemen's and gentlemen's seats in the past, roundly blamed those 'unpleasant, forbidding sort of gardens' on

> the insipid taste or interest of some of our theoretical engineers who, in their aspiring garrets, cultivate all the several species of plants as well as frame designs for situations they never saw: or [on] some nursery-man, who, for his own interest, advises the gentleman to such forms and trees as will make the greatest draught out of his nursery, without regard to anything more: or oftentimes [on] a coxcomb, who takes upon himself to be an excellent draughtsman as well as an incomparable gardener, of which there has been, and still are, too many in England...

The solution, so the new school argued, lay in the hands of experts who would set out, after the most careful assessment of the situation of both the house and estate, to marry art and nature; and in recognising in the case of new building (as Langley's contemporary Stephen Switzer had put it ten years earlier) that 'the gardener and builder ought to go hand in hand, and to consult together'.

As with building design there was, of course, plenty of scope in garden planning for the leisured amateur. Just as Sir Stephen Fox, the Paymaster-General, and Sir William Temple earned a reputation as celebrated gardeners at the end of the seventeenth century, so in the early eighteenth such enthusiasts as James Johnstone, formerly William III's Secretary of State in Scotland, entirely planned their own creations. Johnstone's house at Twickenham 'may [thought Macky] be more properly called a plantation... and Doctor Bradley of the Royal Society, who hath wrote so much upon gardening, ranks him among the first-rate gardeners in England'. Yet the majority of landowners – and this was above all true of the scores of active professional and businessmen who acquired small estates in the Home Counties between the 1690s and the 1720s and were bitten by the garden bug – had neither the time nor the talent to realise their aspirations at first hand. What they could do was to create the demand and furnish the wealth to sustain and reward those who came along to supply the need. There was certainly a select group of specialists at work in England between 1700 and 1740 who can only be called professional landscape gardeners: men such as George London and Henry Wise, Swinburne, Langley, Switzer and Charles Bridgeman. Although employed by many of the best private families in both England and Scotland, and in some cases by royalty, few made their whole living as consultants. London, Wise, Swinburne and Switzer (who at the start of his career worked for London and Wise and learned much of his art from them) were all practical gardeners in their early years and operated big nursery businesses. Langley was fascinated by problems of design and turned his talents eventually to architecture, as did Bridgeman; and indeed some of the finest landscape gardens of the 1720s, 1730s and 1740s were devised by men who were primarily architects, men of the calibre of Vanbrugh, Gibbs and Kent. Also, nearly all the early landscape gardeners supplemented their incomes by copious writing on the subject, much of it embellished by fine draughtsmanship – Batty Langley, for one, to the tune of no fewer than twenty-one books and treatises. And yet it was from this already established professional seedbed that Brown and Repton and their many acolytes and imitators sprang up later to make *le jardin anglais* one of the most admired sights of the civilised world in the second half of the eighteenth century.

With the experts involved in the work of planning and building another fledgling brood, the land agents and specialist estate stewards, had little, if any, affinity. Yet they, too, by 1730 had staked their own claim to professional standing. During the first half of the eighteenth century landlords whose estates were too large or scattered for personal supervision, or were potentially too rich (whether through their fertility or their mineral resources) to entrust to the mercies of the old-style farm bailiffs, accepted the need to employ a full-time agent to tend them. In return for salaries that did not often exceed £40, £50 or £60 a year but occasionally rose as high as £200, and with a house and perhaps a farm thrown in, these agents provided the needful element of continuity, expertise and experienced application in the management of estates. By the beginning of George II's reign they had become an accepted part of the landed community in every part of England; and, as Edward Hughes observed, like the growing class of career bureaucrats in the state's service, 'they not infrequently died in harness, and in the hope that the mantle would eventually fall on their sons and relatives'. It had a habit of doing so.

It is hardly surprising that the nascent professions of our period should all have been, to a greater or lesser degree, loosely textured, uncertain of their pedigree and subject to little, if any, of the internal regulation that characterised most established professions. Nothing conveys this more clearly than the example of the architects, while at the same time revealing the subtle changes in the social structure of Augustan England which such new arrivals were slowly effecting. The backgrounds of the numerous successful architects of the Augustan and early Georgian age were extraordinarily diverse. But broadly four main types can be distinguished: the gifted artisan, who took his chances and, literally, built on them; the dilettante amateur; the gentleman-architect, who learned in any or all of a variety of ways – association, observation, overseas travel, empirical experimentation – but for whom design and building became in the end an absorbing and profitable passion; and the quintessential professional who acquired his skills in the service of, or as assistant to, an already established master.

Of the first type, the traditional one, the years from 1680 to 1730 still saw many interesting and prominent representatives. The man who began the work on Kimbolton Castle before Vanbrugh took over was a joiner by trade, William Coleman. William Thornton, who restored Beverley Minster (according to John Loveday in 1732 'Hawksmoor ... and he had concerted of the affair between 'em'), and who also built Beningbrough Hall and did much work elsewhere in early eighteenth-century Yorkshire, was a York joiner and carpenter. Another carpenter conceived and produced Cottesbrooke Hall and other valuable work in Northamptonshire: his name was Henry Jones. Sir William Wilson, who undertook a good deal of design and building supervision in Warwickshire between the 1680s and the opening years of the eighteenth century, was something of a hybrid: originally a statuary mason from Leicester whose marriage to a wealthy widow enabled him to embark on a new career as gentleman-architect. Both in his own locality and out of it, however, Wilson was outshone by the bricklayer's son, Francis Smith (1672–1738), who as a master mason of Warwick became one of the outstanding builder-architects of the eighteenth century. Among much else Smith was responsible for Lord Leigh's mansion of Stoneleigh Abbey and for Umberslade Hall, home of the wealthy Warwickshire squire and Member of Parliament, Andrew Archer. He also co-operated with Thomas Archer in building Heythorp for Charles Talbot, Duke of Shrewsbury, after the latter returned from Italy in 1706, and in the end he was able to pass his immensely flourishing business on to his son. The whole family presents a fascinating example of social mobility through sheer talent, for Francis Smith's brother, William, became the leading church designer and builder in the West Midlands between 1700 and 1730.

The best-known of the dilettantes was Richard Boyle, Earl of Burlington. Under the influence of Colen Campbell, the young Burlington became in the 1720s a leading propagandist, and a far from negligible exponent of the palladian style of architecture which he had studied intensively in Italy in 1719. The amateur interest in architecture was exceedingly strong in the forty years after the Revolution, and not least among dons. Dean Henry Aldrich of Christ Church designed the great new Peckwater quadrangle at that college, as well as All Saints Church in Oxford, while George Clarke, Fellow of All Souls and Admiralty Commissioner, was largely responsible for the design of Worcester College. In the late seventeenth century it was still customary for all but the most affluent squires, when contemplating the building of a new wing or even a new house, to consult a master mason or a master carpenter, just as their fathers and grandfathers had done. But one who planned his own country residence at this time was Robert Benson of Bramham Park, Yorkshire, a future Chancellor of the Exchequer whom Queen Anne was to raise to the peerage. And Benson was not the only one to follow the precept that was later forthrightly laid down for his fellow landowners by the retired lawyer, Roger North, to 'be your own architect, or sit still': 'for [North claimed] a *profest architect* is proud, opiniative and troublesome, seldom at hand, and a head workman pretending to the designing part is full of paltry contrivances'. (my italics).

More relevant than these amateurs to the concerns of this study were the 'profest' gentlemen-architects. After Wren and Hooke, five men stand out as the most successful members of an increasingly numerous group down to the late 1720s: William Talman, Thomas Archer, James Gibbs, Colen Campbell and Sir John Vanbrugh. Talman and Archer were both younger sons of squires, the first from Wiltshire, the second from Warwickshire. Gibbs was a Scots Catholic of gentle birth who, like Archer before him, learned much of his art from travel and study in Italy. Campbell, who had connections with the Argyll clan, came south to make his fortune after building Shawfield House in Glasgow for his kinsman, Daniel, and further boosted his reputation by the first two volumes (1715 and 1717) of his *Vitruvius Britannicus*. As for Vanbrugh, he was a virtuoso in a class of his own. Erstwhile soldier (like another prominent gentle-man – architect of much the same generation, William Winde) he was also herald and playwright. But it was architecture that immortalised him. Through a combination of flair, publicity and connections he made himself the most spectacular, gold-spangled star in the entire baroque firmament, counting Blenheim, Castle Howard, Kimbolton and Seaton Delaval among his astonishing achievements.

Despite the remarkable creations of Vanbrugh and his like (Colen Campbell, for instance, conceived the splendours of Wanstead for Sir Richard Child and of Houghton for Sir Robert Walpole), the real future lay with the fourth group of architects, the trained profes-sionals, even though, as yet, they were only a small minority of all those who practised. Writing in 1747 in *The London Tradesman*, R. Campbell esquire declared, 'I scarce know of any [architects] in England who have had an education regularly designed for the profession'. But Campbell was a little behind the game. It is true that the English architects of his own and the previous generation pre-sented a picture without uniformity; that most of them still involved themselves directly in the management or financing of building work in a way that would be foreign to most of their modern counterparts; that they had no forum of their own to compare with, say, the French Academy of Architecture, founded in 1671. More to the point, the system whereby practising architects took apprentices or 'pupils' in a formal sense was not inaugurated until after 1750 and not firmly established as the normal basis of a professional training until the last two decades of the eighteenth century. Nevertheless in the seventy years before Campbell wrote, a slowly broadening stream of recruits who had, in effect, been professionally trained had been flowing into English architecture. Of the principal architects of the mid-seven-teenth century, only John Webb (d. 1672), the pupil of his uncle, Inigo Jones, had received a systematic architectural education. After 1680, however, there was a distinct change. Here, as with the involve-ment of the gentry, the growing popularity of good 'mathematical instruction' in school syllabuses was initially important; for, as one contemporary remarked, it was vital that a successful architect should have a 'head mathematically and geometrically turned'. But it was two particular routes thereafter which enabled talented young 'figures men', with a gift for design but without the money to travel, to establish themselves as architects: acting as a private assistant to an established master and securing a public employment in that chief fount of patronage for young architects, the Office of Works.

The trend was set by Nicholas Hawksmoor, Wren's most brilliant pupil, who entered the great man's office in 1680. (Wren was Surveyor-General of the King's Works from 1669 to 1718 and was still actively creating new masterpieces in the early years of Anne.) Later Hawksmoor became clerk of works at a number of the royal palaces. William Dickinson the younger worked on St Paul's and various City churches as Wren's assistant and in due course became a surveyor to the Fifty New Churches Commission (1711). John James, the architect of St George's, Hanover Square who also played a major part in the designing of Cannons for the first Duke of Chandos, was a vicar's son who spent thirty-seven years as assistant clerk and then clerk of works at Greenwich Hospital: in particular, as he told the Bishop of London in 1711, he had 'ten years of instruction in all the practical parts of building by Mr Banks [Master Carpenter to the Crown, 1683–1701], who was well known in their Majesties' Works'. On the other hand, John Talman was brought up to the profession at the feet of his father, William, and was sent by him to study for many years in Italy; while Henry Joynes, another architect who later became very successful in the private sector, had a double training, both as clerk of works to Vanbrugh at Blenheim and, thanks to Vanbrugh's influence, subsequently in the Office of Works.

Whatever the route to a high reputation in the profession, its rewards in Augustan England were plain to see. George Vertue, the celebrated engraver, wrote in 1749:

I must own [that] the branch of the art of building in architecture is much improved and many men of that profession [have] made greater fortunes...than any other branch of art whatever. Their manner of undertakings is so profitable, by their agreements at so much per cent for drawings and direction of works of building.

'This profession of building', he concluded, 'has many profitable advantages which make it worth while to study, travel and labour.' The writer of the chapter on architects in *The London Tradesman* only two years earlier had made the very same point, if more cryptically. 'Few men who have gained any reputation [in the profession]', he wrote, 'but have made good estates.'

'Architecture', the same author pronounced, '... is reckoned of the liberal arts.' Although Gregory King took no explicit notice of such novel and still diminutive phenomena as architects, agents and surveyors, he did estimate optimistically that at the time of the Revolution close on a third of the professional men in England who were heads of families practised what he called the 'liberal arts and sciences'. Architecture was unquestionably regarded as a visual art by the Augustans, but like sculpture and painting (the last an increasingly profitable occupation for the fashionable artist in an age when not only portrait painters but experts in murals and painted ceilings were in great demand), it was disputable whether it truly was a *liberal* art in the strict academic sense; and the distinction between the 'artist' and the 'craftsman' was a hazy one. Among the groups, however, which even social precisians like King would certainly have included with the professors of the liberal arts were mathematicians and musicians. Arithmetic and geometry were two of the seven traditional 'arts' subjects on the syllabus of the medieval university. But mathematics was also one of the boom subjects of the late-seventeenth- and early-eighteenth-century curriculum (see below, pp. 45, 49–50). And it is worth remembering that many qualified mathematical practitioners in Augustan England, Gregory King's own father among them, also practised as surveyors and mappers and quite frequently combined this with teaching. Music was another liberal art of honourable pedigree, and musicians by the 1730s were among the most quickly expanding of the small fledgling professions which had been nurtured by the social climate of the previous half-century.

The consolidation of musicians as a minor profession of fair prospects was one of the most interesting of the occupational effects of a society more leisured and, in general, more cultivated than that of early- and mid-seventeenth-century England. It became a profession reputable enough to be considered suitable, in some quarters at least, for the scions of good families; although there were those who professed unease at this development on social grounds:

> If a parent cannot make his son a gentleman, and finds that he has got an itch of music [wrote Campbell in his guide to trades and professions in George II's reign], it is much the best way to allot him entirely to that study. The present general taste of music in the gentry may find him better bread than what perhaps this art deserves. The Gardens in the summer time employ a great number of hands; where they are allowed a guinea a week and upwards, according to their merit. The Opera, the play-houses, masquerades, ridottoes, and the several music-clubs employ them in the winter. But I cannot help thinking that any other mechanic trade is much more useful to the society than the whole tribe of singers and scrapers: and should think it much more reputable to bring my son up a blacksmith (who was said to be the father of music) than bind him apprentice to the best master of music in England.

The writer was prepared to concede, however, that 'this ... must be reckoned an unfashionable declaration in this musical age'.

It was a 'musical age' in a very particular sense, and a very different sense from that of Pepys's England in the 1660s. Between

1680 and 1740 spontaneous music-making, and indeed amateur music-making at large, was in retreat, in London at least, in face of sharply rising demand for publicly performed music and for the higher standards of performance which visiting artists from the Continent taught Londoners to expect. Professional musicianship gained ground decisively at its expense. Writing far into his retirement, probably in the 1720s, Roger North expressed sadness at the way music had been driven out of the home during his lifetime; and he was in no doubt that the great scourge of domestic music had been the public concert, given by professional musicians of high technical accomplishment. Among the many symptoms of the arrival of a new musical public in the late seventeenth and early eighteenth centuries, including the springing up of music clubs both in London and the provinces and the ambitious publishing ventures of John Playford between 1685 and 1692, the most unequivocal was certainly the opening in London from 1673 onwards of a string of music rooms or concert rooms. The five most frequented before 1690 were Banister's at Whitefriars (opened in 1673), Britton's in Clerkenwell – the unprepossessing but well-patronised premises of 'the musical coal-man', the Villiers Street rooms (1680), Robert King's concert room (1689) and York Buildings, which contained the first purpose-built concert hall in London. Of the post-Revolution reinforcements, Hickford's (1697) was to occupy a unique place in London music for decades and the Hanover Square rooms, opened soon after 1715, became a popular venue for subscription concerts.

There were three other prominent characteristics of the musical life of the period which could only encourage the trend towards professionalism. One was the craze for Italian opera which hit London in Queen Anne's reign and was still not fully appeased thirty years later. A second was the convention, well established by 1700, of having music played before or during virtually every play performed on the London stage. This meant much grist to the musicians' mill: Purcell, for instance, provided music for forty-four different plays and most of it required the recruitment of an orchestra. Opportunities for regular employment were further increased, as Campbell acknowledged, by the practice of employing orchestras to entertain the public at the various wells and pleasure gardens opened in London between 1660 and 1740, particularly from the 1690s onwards. A 'consort' of thirty performers played every Wednesday in the summer of 1697 in the Great Room at Lambeth Wells 'after the manner of the music meeting in York Buildings', and Sadler's Wells capped this in 1698 by laying on an orchestra twice a week in 'Miles's Music House'. Similar fare was provided either regularly or periodically in the Vauxhall Gardens, much later in the Marylebone Gardens (where the entrepreneur-impresario Daniel Gough organised daily concerts in an impressive new hall from 1738), and at Hampstead and Pancras Wells and Islington Spa. The numbers involved in the early-eighteenth-century orchestra were, of course, relatively modest. The thirty employed at York Buildings and Lambeth was about average: it was the size of the celebrated private orchestra of the Duke of Chandos, maintained at Cannons from 1718 until well after 1730 under an eminent foreign director, Johann Pepusch (who was paid a salary of £100 a year). But larger forces were sometimes used – an orchestra of eighty-five played in Dorset Gardens in 1701 – and smaller groups sufficed for such select convivial purposes as to entertain the gentlemen of Lincoln's Inn every Saturday during Michaelmas Term, 1706.

The bulk of the professional musicians in late Stuart and early Georgian England were instrumentalists. There were some native-born singers who were able to make a good living with their voices in the secular field: a few of them, like Robert Leveridge, the bass who made 'The Roast Beef of Old England' a popular hit, became celebrated. But in London the scope for English professional vocalists was limited by the clamour for the fashionable Italians, and the extravagant fees which some of the foreign stars, such as Cuzzoni, Senesino, Fasinelli and Faustina, could command by the late 1720s, rising in some cases to around £1,500 a season, were far above their touch. Native instrumentalists, especially woodwind and string players, were under less pressure from Continental masters; all the same the organiser of a season of garden concerts in Clerkenwell in 1743 made a publicity point of his resolve to engage none but British players, asserting that 'the manly vigour' of their style was 'more suitable to the ear and heart of a Briton than the effeminate softness of the Italian'. Sacred music was a different matter. Not only Westminster Abbey, St Paul's and the Chapel Royal but several of the bigger London churches and all the provincial cathedrals and collegiate churches had their paid 'singing-men'. Those at the Chapel Royal were on salaries of £70 a year, though that was not to say they received them with regularity. Church music also sustained a healthy demand for good organists; and this benefited the profession in more ways than one. Concert-hall proprietors like Gough were encouraged to install first-class organs and employ organists. Composers, however, were the chief beneficiaries of the popularity of church organs. Apart from Henry Purcell and G. F. Handel, no Augustan composer could have earned a decent livelihood without at least one paid appointment. The great majority were organists, among them Purcell himself, John Blow, Michael Wise, Thomas Tudway (later professor at Cambridge), Jeremiah Clarke, Maurice Greene, John Welden, and later, William Boyce. Turner and Kent were professional choristers and several (John Eccles, for instance) had the additional security of the Mastership of the King's Musick or Band. Charles Lulman, composer of vocal and violin music, was a music teacher in Norwich for more than thirty years. At the top of the profession pluralities were commonplace. Thomas Purcell, Henry's uncle, held six appointments in 1679, several of them conveniently overlapping, from which he accumulated £242 1s 8d. Handel, master teacher and great impresario as well as prolific composer, enjoyed a yearly pension of £200 from the Crown from the last year of Anne's reign. He could have survived without it, so shrewdly did he cash in on his prodigious musical output. Twenty pounds was the least he received from his publisher for any of his thirty-six Italian operas and for *Alexander's Feast* Walsh paid him £105.

Small local orchestras on a permanent or semi-permanent footing began to appear here and there from late in Queen Anne's reign, reinforcing the efforts of the traditional 'town waits'. Norwich assemblies were regularly entertained both by 'the City Musick and another set of Musick' from 1718 onwards. Yet with these exceptions, together with the cathedral musicians and the teachers of music (the latter's numbers running into hundreds by the end of George I's reign), the Augustan musical profession was still heavily metropolitan. Even so there existed no single organisation which could give it coherence or maintain standards. The Westminster Corporation of Musick became defunct around 1680. The writ of the Musicians' Company of London ran ineffectually, for the most part, by the early eighteenth century, although the company still had enough influence as late as 1700 to procure from the Corporation a new Act prohibiting any musician who was not a freeman from performing in the City itself. The Royal Academy of Music had only a brief, faction-torn life from 1719 to the late 1720s and was not, in any case, anything like the body recommended by Defoe in 1729 which would, he hoped, produce 'sixty English musicians regularly educated, and enabled to live by their science' and would 'prevent the expensive importation of foreign musicians'. The situation was not, however, anarchic. Some of the cathedrals provided excellent training grounds, as at Norwich under the organist Maurice Greene. The Cannons musical establishment was not just a costly aristocratic indulgence but a first-class private music school, where at one stage Handel, Pepusch and Francesco Scarlatti all taught simultaneously. More influential still was the Academy of Ancient Music, founded in London in 1710, to which the great majority of leading English musicians belonged and which developed into an excellent singing school as well as offering instrumental training. And the foundation of the Royal Society of Musicians in 1738 was a step of some significance along the road to a formal corporate identity.

Just as distinguishable as the musicians among the budding professions of the age were the men who lived – or tried to live – by the pen: its men of letters, who were unarguably professors of a liberal art, and its professional journalists whose claims were sometimes more open to question. Not that the line between man of letters and journalist, or for that matter between high-class journalist and Grub Street mercenary was ever a clearcut one. The examples of some of the literary giants on the Augustan scene attest clearly enough to this; but so does the history of many a lesser figure, too. Thomas Brown is a case in point, a professional writer extremely difficult to pigeon-hole with confidence: part hack, part serious writer following his own bent and fancy; an ex-schoolteacher, a good Latinist and skilled in modern languages; one minute engaged in reputable translation work or contributing sophisticated pieces to the *Gentleman's Journal*, the next bending his pen to the production of a salacious book on *Marriage Ceremonies*, which advertised itself as 'very diverting, especially to the ladies'.

Whatever path they chose to follow all who wrote for profit from the end of the seventeenth century onwards, and those who published their writings as well, benefited from three particular features of the age in which they lived. One was the lapsing of the licensing laws in 1695 which led, not precisely to a 'free' press – no profession which had to endure the political harassment of the years 1702–17 enjoyed complete freedom – but at least a substantial relaxation of censorship. Another was the high literacy rate that characterised most pre-industrial towns after the mid-seventeenth century (the reasons for this will become apparent in the next chapter), and equally, the Augustan Englishman's leisure for reading. The public's determination to use this leisure was only matched by that of printers, booksellers, and even innkeepers and coffee-house proprietors to exploit it for profit. Thirdly, the force of public demand, reflected in a trebling of London's printing presses between 1662 and 1695, was exerted without usurping the traditional role of private patronage. Although this was probably less crucial to the profession as a whole than it had been before 1680, it rose at times to new heights of generosity (as with the £2,000 received by Edward Young from the Duke of Wharton for his *Universal Passion*) and it remained an essential factor in the continued encouragement of serious literature.

Very few poets, dramatists or writers of serious pretension could hope to live prosperously by their literary work alone, even in one of the golden ages of English letters. Publishers, like journalists, were more likely to do so. Henry Clements, who published Doctor Sacheverell's sermons and many other Tory effusions, died a very well-to-do man; William Taylor made a profit of more than £1,000 from the first part alone of *Robinson Crusoe*; and Jacob Tonson left at least £40,000 when he died in 1736, lands in Herefordshire, Gloucestershire and Berkshire and at least two country seats. But *bona fide* men of letters usually had to find other ways to support themselves in comfort: by journalism, as we shall see; by becoming private secretaries to the great, like Mainwaring and, for a while, Addison; by places at Court or in the administration, such as Steele, Congreve and Prior enjoyed, and later Addison; or by practising another profession, like the vicar of Laracor. Nevertheless as the commercial exploitation of literature grew more resourceful and successful the rewards of the leading *littérateurs* did rise appreciably. By Anne's reign a play of average popularity produced in London would usually make between £50 and £150 for its author. Lewis Theobald, though dogged by poverty for much of his adult life, did receive £652 from his publisher for his 1734 edition of Shakespeare. At the top of the tree the full possibilities of the new age were glimpsed when Dryden harvested £1,400 in fees for his translation of Virgil in 1694. Under the early Hanoverians Pope was to be paid

£8,500 by Lintot and Tonson for ten years of work translating the *Iliad* and the *Odyssey*, while John Gay, dramatist and poet, was another whose pen eventually made him a comfortable fortune, though he was much indebted to noble patronage during at least one period of crisis in his career.

While there remained a brisk market for good literature, what most obviously distinguished the Augustan reading public from its predecessors was its hunger for news and commentary on news, for polemic and for popular satire. This is why a large majority of the 'penmen' of the age were engaged for much of their time, if not all of it, on the production of appetising ephemera. The Glorious Revolution, and still more the end of licensing in 1695, transformed journalism within a few years into a crowded occupation. It was a precarious occupation, it is true, and the standing of journalists was generally low. Even Defoe, whom we can now recognise as a master craftsman by the standards of any age, was execrated as a 'mercenary scribbler' by his political opponents and consigned to the same literary dunghill as the most uninspired Grub Street hack. Few members of the established professions would have dreamed of conceding to newspaper editors (of whom there were a score in London by 1710), to newsletter writers or to journeymen pamphleteers who wrote for their bread a status remotely comparable with their own. And yet one of those who was most scathing in denouncing journalists, the clergyman Jonathan Swift, also adorned their fraternity; as, of course, did Steele, the army officer, and Addison, the ex-don. William Arnall, the editor of the *British Journal* in Walpole's heyday, was a trained attorney, though it is doubtful whether he ever practised. Clearly, a profession that created its own subculture and one that by Anne's day could attract such gifted, cultivated pens as those of Swift, Steele and Addison, was not to be over-crudely categorised; for even their talents, and those of Arthur Mainwaring and Daniel Defoe, were not solely deployed at the sophisticated level of weekly journals such as the *Tatler*, the *Medley*, the *Examiner* or the *Freeholder*.

No profession, save the armed forces, had more occupational hazards. Debts; harassment by Whitehall and by the courts, including the ultimate degradation of the pillory and the ear-lopper's knife; enforced Continental exile: these came the way of journalists as prominent as Defoe, Tutchin, Ridpath and Pittis. Yet many made a competent living; and a select few 'scribbled' their way to prosperity. Alan Downie has recently written that 'no-one made a fortune by publishing political literature'. Four years of mercenary service to Robert Walpole, however, earned Arnall well over £10,000, and at the end of it a pension of £400 per annum. John de Fonvive, for many years the painstaking editor of the moderate Whig newspaper *The Postman*, reckoned his average income from that venture alone (consistently the bestselling of all the newspapers of Anne's reign) as 'above £600 a year' by 1705. Lauded by John Dunton, a fellow professional, de Fonvive turned down the editorship of the *Gazette*, which Steele later accepted, as beneath his dignity and commented scathingly on the allowance of £50 annually for the editor's clerk: 'I have given a great deal more in my own business.' The most widely read of the post-Revolution newsletter writers, John Dyer, employed a platoon of clerks, could command a £4 annual subscription from his British readers and £5 from those overseas, and ended his days in affluence; while the talented Huguenot immigrant, Abel Boyer, historian as well as journalist, did more than anyone to lend his embryonic profession what it most obviously lacked, solid respectability.

In addition to the various professions we have briefly surveyed, growing rapidly in their importance to a changing society but physically still relatively small in scale, the 'liberal arts and sciences' were assumed in Gregory King's day, and for that matter right through the eighteenth century, to embrace two occupations which involved not hundreds but many thousands of men: the practice of medicine and the teaching of youth. They were occupations, too, whose functions touched the social order at many points, and well down the scale, as opposed to serving the needs essentially of a small and largely leisured minority. To traditionalists of King's stamp the apothecary was still primarily a shopkeeper in 1680, perhaps even in 1700. In reality the good apothecary had so adequate a training in botany and chemistry and was adding so much more, year by year, to his bedside observation of disease that by the beginning of the eighteenth century he had already established a good claim to be considered a 'man of science'. That the physician had such a status was beyond question. And as for the 'art' of the surgeon, although not acquired through university study, it had become since the sixteenth century increasingly grounded in a careful study of the science of anatomy. Medical men were much more numerous in the 1730s than they had been in Charles II's reign. But as a body they were still heavily outnumbered by what was probably the largest professional amalgam that existed in late-seventeenth and early-eighteenth-century England, the teachers. All those men who in Augustan England were involved in education, whole-time or part-time, and from every level downwards from university professors to purveyors of basic instruction in reading, writing and arithmetic, made up a sprawling, amorphous body and one that defies simple classification. But the sciences and liberal arts could justly claim the vast majority of those employed as far down as what we should now call secondary schools, public or private; almost all private tutors; and a proportion – though how large a proportion is not fully clear – of elementary-school masters.

Of doctors and schoolmasters much more will be said in subsequent chapters of this book. In the present chapter it remains only to look at those who traditionally represented the cream of those Englishmen who practised the liberal arts and sciences between 1680 and 1730. They were to be found in the two ancient universities and among those who taught in them: the Fellows of the nineteen Oxford colleges and six halls established by 1714; the Fellows of the sixteen Cambridge colleges and halls; the heads of all these houses; and the forty-odd professors, readers and lecturers who held university appointments by the mid-1720s. Not counting the Oxford halls, there were endowments for roughly 900 Fellows in the two universities by 1727 – representing a slight increase over the previous half-century. If we include the small group of leading university officers (Librarians, Archivists, Public Orators, Registrars) and throw in, for good measure, the seven professors of Gresham College, who were still going through the motions in 1730 in their now dilapidated premises in Bishopsgate Street, London, we have what seems, on the face of things, to be an 'academic profession' by the early Hanoverian period that numbered just over a thousand.

But was it an academic 'profession' in anything like our sense of the term? Or even in contemporary terms, were its members any more or any less 'professional' as a body than the schoolmasters of the day, whose credentials were by no means secure at all points? So far as the great bulk of the ordinary college Fellows were concerned two very large queries, placed against their character and performance, have an obvious bearing on how we answer these questions. How far, in the first place, did the overwhelmingly clerical status of Augustan academics, and the normal conditions under which fellowships were awarded, retained and resigned, affect their sense of vocation as teachers and scholars? It was only in a very few colleges – Merton being the outstanding example in Oxford – that Fellows were not required by statute to take holy orders as an absolute condition of retaining their places on the foundation (that is, supposing they were not already in orders when elected); and even in those colleges the number of die-hard laymen was small. There was a strong movement among the rampant Whigs in the Parliament of 1709, spearheaded by the anti-clericals in the party's leadership such as the Earls of Sunderland and Wharton, to 'reform' the universities by statute and, in particular, to remove the obligation on college Fellows to take orders. The effects of such a step, had it been taken, on everyone involved in higher education would have been traumatic. However, in the great agitation in the winter of 1709–10 over the case of Dr Sacheverell (himself an absentee Fellow of Magdalen College, Oxford, when he preached the notorious sermon for which he was impeached) this Whig objective was lost sight of, and with the party's fall from power in the autumn of 1710 it was removed from the realms of practical politics for the rest of Queen Anne's reign. Further 'regulating' Bills were considered in 1716 and 1719, after the Whigs were back in the saddle. In the end, despite all alarms, the old order survived intact, eroded only by a certain relaxation of rules concerning the holding of fellowships *in absentia.*

Thus a normal career pattern in the eighteenth century, as in the seventeenth, was roughly along the following lines. A man would be elected by a college to one of its fellowships, usually soon after he had taken his BA degree. Over the next few years he would pursue theological studies and take first deacon's orders and then priest's orders, although meanwhile he might already have begun college teaching or the assumption of other academic responsibilities. He would hold his fellowship, on average, for about ten years, but in the case of a not insubstantial minority tenure might be for as long as fifteen years, even for twenty years or longer. Twenty years certainly became very exceptional later in the eighteenth century, except for a college head; but that it was less so earlier in the century is shown by the fact that a *limitation* on a Fellow's tenure to such a period was a part of the Whig reform package of 1717. Generally speaking, however, some time in his late twenties or early thirties the Oxford and Cambridge don, having as like as not already supplemented his college income with the stipend of a curacy, or the profits of some indifferent Church living too meagre to disqualify him from the foundation, would achieve one of two ambitions. Either he would reach the head of the queue for a college living that would guarantee him 'an independency', or he would attract the favour of a beneficent lay patron. He would then resign his fellowship and leave the university, generally for good, for a clerical career. For this average Fellow, therefore, neither university teaching nor scholarship were ends in themselves; nor was there any prospect of finding a life's vocation in his college or in his university. The fellowship was a stage – a comfortable and coveted stage, for the most part – in the climb up the slopes of Mount Preferment.

Exceptions to the pattern did exist, of course. Fellows who held professorships or readerships were in a separate category. So, too, were those lay Fellows who remained in their colleges for a number of years equipping themselves academically for careers as civil lawyers or physicians. There were also clerical Fellows, and some laymen too, who were content to remain celibate and managed to make a good or, at worst, a reasonable living out of a combination of tutoring and the hogging of college jobs. Such men, if they were clergy, might well hold a modest living close to Oxford or Cambridge which could be tended, after a fashion, while still allowing them to remain resident in college and treat their pastoral function as a purely auxiliary one. If they were Fellows of Christ Church, they might be fortunate enough to become canons residentiary of the cathedral, which was physically an adjunct of the House. This third group of Fellows, along with the holders of university posts, did constitute a stratum of 'career academics'. But it was a thin stratum and it is worth remembering that even heads of colleges were sometimes strangely divided in their professional allegiances. How, for example, can one categorise William Lancaster who, while Provost of Queen's College, Oxford, and for a while even Vice-Chancellor of the University (1706–10), was also archdeacon of Middlesex and rector of St Martin's-in-the-Fields? Such conundrums highlight one of the two major obstacles in the way of envisaging a genuine academic profession in Augustan England.

The second query lies against the way those dons who did have eight, ten or twelve years to give to their colleges and universities spent their time; or even against the seriousness with which the 'full-time' Fellows and professors took their academic duties. The argument so often advanced is that during the later sixteenth and the first half of the seventeenth centuries the universities had enjoyed a golden period, crowded with students and requiring a good deal of commitment to teaching from both short-term and long-term Fellows. Around 1670, however, what Lawrence Stone has called 'the great depression' set in at Oxford and Cambridge, marked by a decisive decline in undergraduate admissions which, with few intermissions, grew progressively worse and was not reversed until the end of the eighteenth century. With the urge to learn (so the argument concludes) ebbing fast, except among clergymen's and some gentlemen's sons bent on a Church career, dedication to teaching, and even to research and publication, among the vast bulk of Oxbridge Fellows correspondingly dwindled away; and the growing wealth of many of the colleges, bolstered by new or appreciating endowments and by the fees of an increasingly upper-class student body, was largely devoted to making life as comfortable and civilised as possible for their senior members. According to this interpretation, then, the years from 1680 to 1730 saw the beginning of a long and demoralising period of stagnation for the universities and of declining, instead of increasing, professionalism among the teaching body in the two main institutions of higher education in the land. Thomas Hearne's strictures, delivered in 1705 against those Oxford professors and readers who were now too idle or apathetic to deliver their lectures, are often quoted as evidence that the process of decay was already well advanced as early as Queen Anne's reign. Although he singled out Sykes of Trinity as being a disastrous successor to Bishop Hall and Dr Maurice in the Chair of Divinity – 'stuffing his lectures with nothing but long quotations out of Fathers, that after a few lectures he could get no hearers, and so makes the place in a manner a sine cure' – he claimed that the neglect of 'public reading' was fairly general, 'much to the disgrace of the University' and to the dismay of foreign visitors. Almost as familiar is the choice witticism of Addison, who claimed that his chief recollection of Oxford when he was an iconoclastic young Fellow of Magdalen in the late 1690s was of senior common rooms full of men who were really dead, though they occasionally made a token show of life.

Leaving aside the literary and the subjective, there is ample evidence of the most concrete kind to support certain parts of the 'depression' thesis. The college admission registers proclaim loud and clear the diminishing attractions to undergraduates of university study after 1670. Professor Stone's revised calculations for Oxford estimate an annual intake that declined from an average of 458 in the 1660s to 321 in the 1680s and then, after three fairly level decades, to 303 in the 1720s and 271 in the 1730s. Although there was still a long way to go before the dismal nadir of the decade 1750–9, with its average of only 182 admissions a year, the figures for the years 1680–1730 indicate a situation that was some way short of being healthy, if a good deal less than disastrous. Side by side with this documentary and statistical evidence we can set the many physical signs, most of them still extant, of the striking advance in standards of comfort and gentlemanly living which the dons of Augustan England enjoyed in these same undemanding fifty years. This has to be seen in the wider context of the value, social and financial as well as professional, of holding an Oxford or Cambridge fellowship.

It is impossible to estimate the average benefit accruing financially from such fellowships at any time in our period. There were so many variables. There had always been vast differences in the wealth of colleges, and in many cases the gaps were widening. The great endowments of Christ Church, Magdalen or New College in Oxford stood in glaring contrast to the poverty of Jesus College and the modest income of unpretentious foundations such as Pembroke. Equally important, the path to prosperity rarely ran via the fellowship alone. It depended partly on how large an ecclesiastical income a Fellow could enjoy, consistent with his tenure, and still more on the academic appendices to a fellowship that could be acquired by the able, the ambitious or the scheming. College jobs – bursarships, lectureships, deanships, and so on – were time-consuming but could be lucrative. In Christ Church there were the cathedral canonries to be coveted and fought for as well. Not least important were tutorships, especially in those colleges such as King's, Cambridge, which by the late seventeenth century were already attracting a particularly high proportion of well-to-do gentlemen commoners. Just how essential tutorships could be is illustrated by the disparities not just between but within colleges. Even in as rich an institution as New College, Oxford, those who held fellowships in civil law, and were therefore more hard-pressed to get students than theologians or 'artists', sometimes preferred to scramble instead for the £30 or £40 a year that could be obtained from the Mastership of Bedford School, which was in the college's gift. By contrast, when Celia Fiennes visited the college around 1694 she

> was very handsomely entertained by Mr [Richard] Cross which was one of my nephew Saye and Sele's tutors when at Oxford. These fellowships in New College are about [£]100, say, and a very pretty apartment of dining room, bedchamber and study and a room for a servant, though the servitors of the college gives attendance; and here they may live very neatly and well, if sober . . .

Fellows who acquired university teaching posts, whether chairs, readerships or special endowed lectureships, might be counted very fortunate. And there were indeed some in enviable circumstances, such as the great scholar and Boyle Lecturer Richard Bentley, who combined the Mastership of Trinity, Cambridge, with the Lady

Margaret Chair of Divinity. Yet the salaries attached to such university appointments were in no case princely and the variations between them were extraordinary. Some chairs were so poorly endowed as to bring in no more than £50 a year (which was the same stipend that the professors of Gresham College still enjoyed under the founder's will of 1597, along with free rooms, for delivering their two lectures a week – both on the same day – for four terms a year). The Cambridge Chair of Greek was by no means in this humble class; yet one late-seventeenth-century incumbent, Thomas Gale, preferred to resign it in order to accept the High Mastership of St Paul's School. Less subject to such temptations were the first incumbents of the two Regius Professorships of Modern History and Languages, established in 1724; for these chairs, thanks to the determination of their instigator, Bishop Gibson, were worth £400 per annum to each of their fortunate holders, less £50 for the employment of assistants. The Lady Margaret Professor of Divinity at Oxford and the Regius Professors of Hebrew and Divinity were still better off, for despite nominal salaries they all held prebendal stalls at Christ Church *ex officio*.

The biggest imponderable, then as today, was the concealed benefits which went with fellowships. In the poorer colleges and halls many dons still lived with something of the austerity of former days. But in general there was a remarkable rise in the material advantages of college living during the Augustan period. St John's, Oxford, in 1676 set a new fashion in providing a handsome common room in which Fellows could converse and imbibe in secluded comfort. But in all respects the years from the 1670s to the 1730s were a spectacular period of new building and rebuilding in both universities: an era in which medieval dilapidation and inconvenience gave way to baroque or classical spaciousness and elegance, making it possible for many Fellows in the fortunate colleges to live henceforward in suites of highly desirable rooms.

The building of Dean Aldrich's vast Peckwater quadrangle in Christ Church (1705), 'equal to anything [one contemporary guidebook writer confidently asserted] one can see abroad of that kind', put an end, for some Fellows of the House at least, to the hazard which George Smalridge had been exposed to as late as 1689, when he had been driven from his living quarters in Canterbury quadrangle by rats. Elsewhere in Oxford, Queen's was totally and magnificently rebuilt in the late seventeenth and early eighteenth centuries, and its Fellows could henceforward luxuriate in Hawksmoor's great south quadrangle and work in his grandiose library. Soon afterwards the same genius undertook the transformation of All Souls, whose Warden was already lodged in George Clarke's fine Queen Anne lodgings on the High. The Fellows of Trinity, Corpus Christi, New College and, from the 1730s, Magdalen, all shared in varying degrees in the benefits of Oxford's great building boom. Fiennes was deeply impressed with the gracious living in the garden quadrangle of New College, with 'several new lodgings added and beautified here, the gardens also with gravel and grass walks, some shady, and a great mount in the middle which is ascended by degrees in a round of green paths defended by greens cut low; and on the top is a summer house, [and] beyond these gardens is a bowling-green...' In Cambridge the monuments to the new era were rather less numerous but, in some cases, hardly less splendid. They were epitomised by the Fellows' building of King's, the work of James Gibbs, which was opened in 1723. And there were telling signs of affluence elsewhere: as in the rebuilding of St Catharine's (1673–1704), where a visitor in 1697 found 'the apartments [provided] for the Fellows and Gentlemen Commoners are very fine, a large dining-room, a good chamber and good study, and this for £8 a year', with only commoners presumably required to pay.

But does all this necessarily mean that the thousand 'persons in liberal arts and sciences' inhabiting the universities had been transformed since the later years of Charles II into a gang of sybarites and soaks, and that all sense of professional obligation had departed? There is a great danger of reading back into the Augustan universities too many of the stereotype conditions associated, not without some justice, with mid- and late-Georgian Oxford and Cambridge. Beyond doubt there was uneasiness, even alarm, in some right-thinking quarters about several of the symptoms that were appearing by the reigns of William III, Anne and George I. It can be seen in some of the provisions which Dean Prideaux of Norwich persuaded Lord Townshend to write into the abortive Universities Bill of 1717, among them the intriguing recommendation that (in W. R. Ward's words) 'fellows who failed to pass a merit bar twenty years after matriculation were to be pensioned off in an institution called Drone Hall'. It is evident, again, in the storm raised about the same time by the bizarre case of the absentee Oxford Professor of Physic, Dr Thomas Hoy, a storm ridden out by Hoy himself from the unacademic waters of Jamaica. Those who had argued that he should never have been elected to the chair in 1698, since his chief claim to scholarly distinction rested on his essays on Ovid and Musaeus, may have had a point. And yet to assume that intellectual stagnation, the pursuit of worldly pleasures and the decay of academic commitment all followed inexorably within two or three decades from the first major sag in undergraduate admissions would be almost as unrealistic as to imagine that they occurred virtually overnight in the 1670s. In reality, their onset was slow and extremely uneven, and even by 1730 the worst was yet to come.

There were striking variations in academic effectiveness between college and college. There were some marked differences, too, between Oxford and Cambridge. The spirit of Newton's genius was still alive in Cambridge in 1700 (he remained Lucasian Professor of Mathematics there until 1703, albeit a largely absentee one in his later years). No university which had a Whiston to succeed Newton in that chair, a Richard Bentley at Trinity, or a Daniel Waterland as Master of Magdalene in the first few decades of the eighteenth century could be bereft of intellectual stimuli. The inauguration of the mathematical tripos at Cambridge was only one indication of how far from exhaustion these stimuli still were. The establishment of new chairs of Chemistry and of Astronomy and Experimental Philosophy early in Anne's reign (1702–3) provided other proofs of continuing Cambridge vitality. It is clear, too, that not a few colleges still provided conscientious, and occasionally inspired, tutoring: and this was especially true of some of the smaller colleges, for example Lincoln, the young Wesley's college, at Oxford and Corpus Christi (earlier Bennet) and Magdalene at Cambridge. As for lectures: no doubt the students of the first post-Revolution generation who were anxious for knowledge were subjected to many a lecture of paralysing boredom or apparent pointlessness (what generation of students has not complained of that?); and perhaps they escaped others only because lecturers were not present to deliver them. Yet here also it would be unwise to generalise. An enthusiastic letter from William Stukeley to a former schoolfriend, Ambrose Pimlow, about his undergraduate experience at Bennet College in 1705 makes plain that in Cambridge, in some subjects at least, college and university lecturing was far from being a ritualistic routine at that time, let alone a dead letter.

... for all the riches of the Indies I would not have changed my college. That regular (though something strict) government of our college so suitable to my genius, the small number of lads to what other colleges have, but above all the continual lectures which we have in classics, ethics, mathematics and philosophy ... makes me esteem (after a diligent enquiry) our college to be the best of all ... We at present with Mr Denny go to lectures in philosophy; we read all Newton's and Boyle's works, those most famous miracles of mankind.

For that matter, it was not as difficult as the acidulous Hearne would have us think to find lectures, nor indeed lecturers, still being taken seriously in Oxford in the 1690s and the early 1700s. There is mention of Atterbury, the brilliant young Fellow of Christ Church, hurrying up from London in 1691 in time to fulfil his lecturing obligations. We know that Henry Sacheverell was a star turn on the rostrum as well as in the pulpit while he was a Fellow and lecturer of Magdalen from 1702 to 1709. Oxford followed Cambridge's lead by offering courses on Newtonian natural philosophy in the early eighteenth century. Courses on chemistry, in which a chair had been founded in 1683, were already well established. More consumed by political agitation and factional in-fighting than Cambridge under the later Stuarts, the university may appear, in some respects, to be on a downward slope of academic achievement after the Revolution. Yet old *alumni* such as John Wallis, Savilian Professor of Geometry, were still active, and if there were some indifferent new appointments to chairs there were also some excellent ones, for example, that of Edmund Halley, the late Astronomer Royal, as Wallis's successor

(1703). Elections to headships of houses between 1690 and 1720 were not overdistinguished. Smooth political operators such as William Lancaster of Queen's and shady characters like Delaune of St John's hardly enhanced the university's reputation. Nevertheless much good learning, as well as some good teaching, still flourished in Oxford under the last two Stuarts – as the output of a remodelled University Press bears witness; and men who were, by any standards, professional academics played a prominent part in these achievements. For instance, the university led the way between 1660 and 1730 in the revival of Anglo-Saxon and early English studies; and at the turn of the century Edward Thwaites, Fellow of Queen's and Professor of Greek, took the lead in building up the first School of English Language and Literature. He had fifteen eager young students in 1699.

On balance, therefore, the temperate judgement of Sir George Clark on the Augustan academics still stands: that although 'towards the end of the period [before 1714] there were traces of growing laxity in the work of professors and tutors, . . . there were few signs of the torpor which spread over educational institutions in the eighteenth century'. How far this verdict can be extended to include the schools and the schoolmasters of the years 1680–1730 remains to be seen.

3

Schools and the Schoolmaster

The eighteenth century is commonly associated with the regression, or at best the stagnation, of English education; and the germs of this malaise have been confidently detected in the last forty years or so of the Stuart period. Whether long-standing impressions of a general educational decline in the eighteenth century itself will eventually be swept away by the vigorous broom of fresh research has still to be seen. What is already certain is that a number of the trends on which the theory of decline rests have been misdated to the point of distortion. Because it has become customary to look at the late-seventeenth-century scene from certain limited angles and find there an apparently drab contrast with the eighty years or more of 'educational revolution' before 1640, we have come close to losing sight altogether of some of the most basic facts about English education in the half-century after 1680: that it saw an abundance of concern, of enterprise and new ideas, and a truly substantial increase in educational provision at virtually every level, except the highest of all. In this chapter we shall try to discover what were the professional implications for the English schoolmaster, both of what survived into the period 1680–1730 of the pre-Augustan educational heritage and of the main changes and innovations in the country's schools which these five decades witnessed.

A great deal did survive and some of what survived continued to develop organically. The most influential survivors were the grammar schools. W. A. L. Vincent has revealed that the state of these institutions, taken by and large, was well short of parlous as late as Queen Anne's reign. Even if his work is often preoccupied with the search for portents of subsequent decay, it nevertheless underlines the continuance under the later Stuarts of the habit of endowing grammar schools which had been so prominent a feature of sixteenth- and early-seventeenth-century philanthropy. And wherever a careful scrutiny of the evidence at county level has been made – for example, in East Anglia, Leicestershire, Cheshire, Nottinghamshire or the East Riding of Yorkshire – a generally buoyant picture has come through. The records of the diocese of Norwich have revealed that there were twenty-seven more masters teaching classical grammar in Norfolk and Suffolk in 1700 than had been registered there in 1663. A majority of Cheshire's twenty-two grammar schools proved remarkably resilient well beyond 1700: and the fact that Ashby de la Zouche had one of the most flourishing schools in the kingdom under Samuel Shaw

between 1662 and 1696 symbolised the reinvigoration of Leicestershire's secondary education in those decades.

Since the 'grammar-school' master will figure prominently in this
chapter he requires definition, for some ambiguity cloaks the term
when we apply it to Augustan England. Relatively few of the new
schools established by private endowment after 1660 were exclusively
classical schools on the sixteenth-century model. To the pragmatic eye
of the average Restoration and Augustan philanthropist, there seemed
no strong case for multiplying strictly traditional institutions; for it
was generally agreed that most parts of the country were already
adequately provided, or even oversupplied with them. With every
decade that passed after 1660 the number of existing schools which
still regarded the preparation of boys for the universities as their
prime function shrank appreciably, and it was not only struggling
country schools which recognised this. A visitor to Doncaster in 1725
found 'a good free school here, endowed with £60 per annum and has
about forty scholars in it', with a master and an assistant to instruct
them; but that 'the last boy sent from hence to the university was
Dudgeon, the Vicar's son'. Nevertheless, 'grammar school' remained
a useful generic term to embrace not only every old school where a
classical training was still available to the minority of boys who
required it, but also every new school in which provision was made in
the endowment both for the teaching of Latin and for free places.
Nottinghamshire illustrates as well as most counties the growing and
eventually dominant trend among those new endowed foundations
that were designed to fulfil more than merely village needs. There
Tuxford School was founded by Charles Read in 1669 with the
express purpose of teaching 'reading, writing and casting accounts'
universally to its pupils, and Latin 'as the occasion should require';
West Drayton School in 1688, with a requirement laid on the master
to instruct his pupils in 'what he could of grammar learning'; Bulwell
Free School in 1669, South Leverton 'Grammar School' in 1691,
Sutton Bonington and Walkeringham in 1718 and 1719, all with a
statutory provision for Latin to be included, with other subjects, in
the curriculum.

Our criteria will be the flexible criteria of the time; and by those
standards the England of the later Stuarts and of George I had a
thoroughly respectable record as regards public 'secondary' education.
By 1685 eighty new grammar schools had been founded since the
Restoration. One hundred and forty-seven of the foundations which
were endowed in the reign of Charles II and of his three successors
down to 1714 were still in existence when the Taunton Commission
reported in 1868; and naturally there were others which had foundered
in the meantime, and more which by the 1860s had gradually sub-
sided into elementary schools. However, the new foundations of the
period from 1660 to 1714 tell us by no means everything about the
continued support given to the grammar school by late Stuart society.
In addition, an appreciable number of existing schools received either
fresh private endowments or valuable financial support from local

corporations during the seventy years which followed the Interregnum; and it can hardly be a symptom of indifference that this same period was marked by striking progress in the imaginative and coherent planning of school buildings for both old and new foundations.

What was happening to the grammar schools was only one aspect of Augustan England's educational response to the social, economic and religious climate of the day. The mounting interest of the already educated classes in 'modern' subjects in addition to, or instead of, the standard classical diet was plainly related to the employment opportunities of their sons within both an economy and a range of public services which found such subjects increasingly relevant to their requirements. The willingness of bourgeoisie and better-off gentry alike to pay for such an education where grammar schools could not provide it reflects their prosperity as well as their family ambitions. Partly linked with this development was the stimulus which the advance of religious toleration gave after 1687 to the growth of denominational education; and this, in turn, was matched at the lower level by the acute religious and social concern felt by devout Anglicans at the shortcomings of existing primary education. Out of that concern grew a determination that disadvantaged boys and girls should be equipped with basic literacy and the rudiments of Christian principles before being sent into a world seen by many laymen, as well as clergy, as grievously idle and reprobate. Finally, education and those involved in it were no more untouched than landowning, finance and much else by the greatest of all forces for change in Augustan society, war. A large navy and a growing army needed many men skilled in navigation, gunnery, explosives and fortification: and by 1715 a crop of 'mathematical schools' and numerous private ventures in the field of technical instruction testified to the answering of this challenge. For all these reasons, and for others, late Stuart and early Georgian England became a fertile provider of new kinds of educational opportunities to repair the deficiencies of the old.

It was under the encouragement and somewhat ambivalent protection of the statutory indulgence of May 1689 (sometimes misleadingly called 'the Toleration') that the Dissenting academies – a mere handful in the 1670s – grew to full bloom. Their popularity by 1730 had begun to fade to some extent; but for four or five decades the best of these academies provided a more flexible and enterprising brand of higher education than the two universities offered to the majority of their students: and it was by no means only Nonconformists who took advantage of them. In 1714 the Schism Bill was brought before Parliament. It was a pernicious piece of High Tory legislation which primarily aimed at stamping out the academies as the training ground of Nonconformist divines, but which also caught indiscriminately in its net the whole shoal of Dissenting schools which, as bigoted Anglicans saw it, now infested England. By the early eighteenth century these schools were of many different types. They might be public or private, elementary or secondary or a combination of the two, classical or 'modern', day schools or boarding schools. The Whigs and Low Church Anglicans who vigorously fought the Bill in the House of Lords lauded the achievements of Nonconformist schools since the passing of the Toleration Act as a public service of the first order. They stressed their wide distribution throughout England and Wales, their low fees and, above all, their interdenominational function. Lord Cowper, erstwhile Lord Chancellor, put their case as well as anyone when he pointed out 'that in many country towns, reading, writing and grammar schools were chiefly supported by the Dissenters: not only for the instruction and benefit of their own children, but likewise of those of poor churchmen; so that the suppression of those schools would, in some places, suppress the reading the holy scriptures'.

In a different (yet to enlightened eyes not wholly different) vein, the 1690s saw the birth of the charity-school movement, that remarkable child of the post-Revolution Anglican social conscience, so often neglected or misunderstood by modern scholars. In the face of both a moral crisis, for which Sodom and Gomorrah suggested the most appropriate parallel, and a crisis of faith, schools to furnish enough young people with the wherewithal either to pursue an honest trade or to grasp the fundamental principles of Christian teaching became a matter of obsessive concern during King William's reign. Old-style charity schools, financed by private endowments, persisted and indeed multiplied; but it was the new-model charity schools, predominantly urban foundations financed by public subscriptions, which attracted most attention and secured the prestigious support of the Society for the Promotion of Christian Knowledge (SPCK). The momentum of the movement was dramatic. As early as 1707, James Talbott, DD, writing in *The Christian School-Master*, enthused that 'progress . . . so far exceeded all human expectation that by God's blessing . . . great sums of money have been very liberally contributed towards this excellent design'.

Meanwhile over the second half of the seventeenth century social exclusiveness had become a more important consideration than hitherto in the educational priorities of parents in the wealthy and leisured classes. It would be mistaken to imagine that country gentlemen no longer sent their sons to the local grammar school by 1680. It was common practice for Leicestershire squires to do so at least down to 1700. In 1682 all four sons of one of the leading landowners in Westmorland, Sir Daniel Fleming, were attending Hawkshead Free School; while further south, Tamworth School continued to be patronised by Staffordshire, Warwickshire and Leicestershire gentry well into Queen Anne's reign, and in the 1690s counted the Earl of Huntingdon's sons among its pupils. The roll of Bury St Edmunds Grammar School after the Revolution was studded with the names of many of the best families in Suffolk. Yet there is little doubt that by then snobbery was on the march. One consequence of this, brightening the prospects of a small minority of the best-qualified teachers, was the rapid expansion of a handful of fashionable and expensive boarding schools, with Eton already standing supreme among them by 1700. It was roughly 1730 before this process was temporarily checked, by which time the phenomenon of the 'big school' had come to stay in England. By the late 1720s Eton, Westminster and Winchester together were teaching almost a thousand boys. Another consequence, both educational and professional, was that in the closing decades of the seventeenth century there developed a roaring trade in private tutors among the nobility and well-to-do gentry.

It was new economic or occupational priorities, however, rather than changing social attitudes which lay behind what proved to be, for the future of the schoolteaching profession, the most far-reaching change in the educational climate between 1680 and 1730. This was that emphatic rise in parent demand for 'modern' syllabuses at the secondary stage of schooling which has already been remarked on, and a corresponding determination to secure such an education outside the grammar-school framework, if it could not be obtained inside it. This pressure was certainly linked with the urgent needs of the armed forces after 1689; and it has also to be seen in the context of an economy and a system of public and private finance that had become strikingly more sophisticated by 1720 than had been the case in 1660. But at bottom it derived from parental attitudes that were down-to-earth and pragmatic.

These attitudes were clearly synthesised by the nonjuror, Francis Brokesby, writing in 1701. It had been a complaint of 'judicious persons' in recent years, he claimed,

> that many things in learning the grammar are imposed that are toilsome and needless, several things that may be useful are not taught in due season; ... further, that the learning which is acquired at grammar schools is of little or no use to such as are set to ordinary trades, and consequently that time might have been better spent in attaining some useful knowledge, nay much more profitably in learning to write a good hand, arithmetic, and other things of this nature.

His case was not only that for most boys a training in Greek and Latin language and literature 'tends not to improve them, or fit them for ordinary callings, except their being apothecaries, or some few such trades to which some skill in the Latin tongue is requisite'; worse still, there was 'so little need to carry [Greek or Latin] to the plough or forge, that it is rather mischievous; a smattering in such kind of learning having too often this ill effect, to make such persons more pragmatical in conversation and less mindful of their proper business, as thinking themselves above it'. Those designed for 'one of the learned professions of Divinity, Law or Physic' or those young men of good birth and property who were expected to fit themselves for public service could still be well served, Brokesby believed, by the classical education of the grammar schools; although they needed a wider range of learning than, as yet, they could normally find in such establishments. The Bishop of Salisbury, writing seven years later, was not so certain even of this:

> I have often thought it a great error, to waste young gentlemen's years so long in learning Latin, by so tedious a grammar . . . Suppose a youth had, either for want of memory or of application, an incurable aversion to Latin, his education is not for that to be despaired of; there is much noble knowledge to be had in the English and French languages: geography, history, chiefly that of our own country, the knowledge of nature, and the more practical parts of the mathematics, (if he has not a genius for the demonstrative) may make a gentleman very knowing, though he has not a word of Latin.

Brokesby had a reform scheme to suggest as well as a critical case to develop. With practical, 'modern' needs in mind he envisaged

> several of those [grammar] schools, the multitude of which in some places is complained of, converted to this use . . . and in other places such [schools] erected in which should be taught not only writing, arithmetic, the arts of navigation, surveying, agriculture, etc., but also other things to accomplish them as men and Christians, as instructions in the principles of religion, . . . some insight into the history of our own nation, so much knowledge of the laws of the kingdom as to fit them for jury men and other like offices . . .

But, in practice, he was prepared to settle for something less. Since his proposals were to be 'rather desired than hoped for', he 'could wish at least that writing schools might be annexed to grammar schools, to be under the same government and inspection'.

Brokesby's advice did not entirely fall on deaf ears, and here and there it had already been anticipated. Modern subjects had begun to make some headway in England during the late sixteenth century and the first half of the seventeenth, though by 1660 the ice of the grammar schools, as such, was still largely unbroken. Over the next seventy years there may have been relatively few ambitious conversions of existing grammar schools along the lines Brokesby recommended; but there was some experimentation in a minority of schools which were lucky enough, or could afford, to recruit suitably qualified staff. Scientific subjects were being taught to some pupils at Manchester Grammar School by the early eighteenth century and mathematics had been smuggled into the regular syllabus. In Hull a go-ahead master was allowed by the corporation after 1716 to modernise Latin instruction and to introduce a light diet of history, geography and divinity. Birmingham's large and flourishing free school had Anthony Thacker, the author of *Mathematical Problems*, as its master from the 1720s until 1746, and during the same period a specialist in mathematical geography, John Holmes, was appointed master of Holt School in Norfolk, where in 1731 he organised an end-of-term 'entertainment' on the theme of 'The Use of Globes'. In the older free schools, mathematics, not being a foundation subject, was normally only offered for a fee payable to the master or usher who taught it, and the same was true, by and large, of calligraphy, the modern subject which came nearest to realising Brokesby's hope that it 'might be annexed' to the larger established grammar schools. Wherever there were merchants or tradesmen in sufficient numbers needing clerks for their offices there was a particular need for specialised writing instruction, most of all in London; and it may have been the spectacular example of Christ's Hospital, which in 1695 acquired a new writing school designed by Wren, costing more than £4,000 and accommodating 300 boys, which Brokesby hoped many provincial schools would follow in their humbler way. Many of those who did so, as we shall see, were forced to improvise; but some were fortunate enough to be able to follow the more formal path, and indeed the pattern had been set well before the 1690s by such schools as Ipswich, where a writing master was appointed and a writing school fitted out in 1663, and Witney Grammar School, an impressive Restoration foundation whose income made possible the addition of a writing master to the staff in 1670.

How far private benefactors to public education were moving into line with educational theorists and propagandists in fostering modern subjects is plainly seen in the foundation deeds of new grammar schools in the years 1665–1735. One of the most ambitious schools set up in Augustan England, Sir John Moore's at Appleby Magna, significantly embodied a writing school from the start (Moore himself was a London merchant and a prominent benefactor of Christ's Hospital). Schools of the Tuxford type, such as Corby Glen (Lincolnshire), Sir George Buswell's School (Northamptonshire), and Risley, founded in Anne's reign by a wealthy Derbyshire widow, Elizabeth Gray, best typified the new arrivals: purveying the three Rs to the average boy, with formal teaching in accountancy possibly grafted on to a basic mathematical training, and Latin to the bright boy intended for a university or for a professional apprenticeship. At Pierrepont's, Lucton (1708), the stated aims of the curriculum were to make pupils 'fit for the university, or to be put out apprentices, services or other employment'. In at least twenty-five of the new grammar schools founded between 1660 and 1700 arithmetic was specified by the founders as a necessary part of a boy's study. Among them was Brigg Grammar School, opening in 1680, for which Sir John Nelthorpe laid down that the children of Brigg and certain nearby Lincolnshire towns and villages were to be 'taught the Latin, Greek and Hebrew languages, to write also, and arithmetic'. The first usher to serve at Brigg is described as 'William Barrett, late of Barton [-on-Humber] . . . Philomath'. That mathematics was prominent among his accomplishments is evident from the fact that he undertook land surveying and mapping for the local gentry as one way of eking out his salary, in his case £30 a year.

After the Revolution a handful of new founders appear who did envisage a more intensive specialism for their schools. Lord Harley's chaplain noticed as he rode out of Rochester along the Chatham road in 1723 'a new building, a kind of school, erected by Sir Joseph Williamson, bart., in 1707 for the teaching of mathematics: I suppose principally for the service of the Navy'. Sir Thomas Parkyn's School at Bunny (Nottinghamshire) employed a master who was required to teach 'so much trigonometry as related to the mechanical and useful parts of mathematics', while not neglecting the classics for which Sir Thomas provided his own manual of Latin grammar. Parkyn's and Williamson's were two of a select little group of special endowed schools established after 1700, a group which also included Chichester School (1702), Saunders', Rye (1708) and Portsmouth Grammar School (1732).

But despite these enterprising exceptions it had become quite clear by the later years of Anne that it was going to be left predominantly to private initiative and not to public benefactions to meet many of the new syllabus needs which Brokesby, Burnet and their like were advocating. In the last three decades of the seventeenth century private fee-paying schools, providing a post-'petties' (or, as we should say, post-primary) education became far more numerous in England than ever before; and under Queen Anne and George I they went on proliferating. Such schools generally offered either a very much more diverse fare or a far more specialised one than the vast majority of the 'free' grammar schools with which they were in competition. The number of public schools, like Williamson's, where boys could concentrate for career purposes on mathematical subjects was minimal. By far the best known was Christ's Hospital, where with royal support provision was made in 1678 for transferring forty boys at the age of $14\frac{1}{2}$ from the grammar class to a new mathematical school. On the other hand, the years 1660–1740 produced a rich growth of private mathematical schools; and while London naturally proved to be their favourite field, these schools shot up from time to time in most counties in the land. George Donn's mathematical school at Bideford; John Dougharty's at Bewdley; John Grundy's at Congeston, Leicestershire and then at Spalding; Thomas Peat's at Greyfriars Gate in Nottingham – these were just four of the many such establishments which flourished simultaneously in the early years of George II's reign. Private writing schools were in even more plentiful supply, twenty-eight of them being advertised in the pages of John Houghton's periodical *A Collection for the Improvement of Industry and Trade* in the eleven and a half years from March 1692 to September 1703.

In his research into eighteenth-century syllabus reforms, R. S. Tompson discovered only one established grammar school which had modified its syllabus to include a study of French before 1700, and no further example before the 1740s. Meanwhile, however, a variety of private establishments were giving considerable prominence to the teaching of modern languages by the early eighteenth century. Even some of the larger mathematical schools found French a necessary and, of course, a profitable accretion. In fact, the boarding school which Thomas Fletcher, a mathematician, opened at Ware in or before 1727 taught Latin as well as French along with mathematics, and employed a writing master for good measure: deservedly it remained a going concern for thirty-five years. Exemplifying better still the enterprise of the good private school was Watts's famous academy in Little Tower Street, London. Starting in 1715 in its former premises in Abchurch Lane with severely practical objectives, as a training school for counting-house clerks (a role it never abandoned), it branched out in the course of George I's reign into advanced mathematics and natural philosophy, and several other subjects of which French – the concern of a resident specialist – was one. Clare's Academy in Soho Square, which lasted from about 1718 until well into the nineteenth century, was even more ambitious: it taught seventeen different subjects, including gauging for prospective excisemen. There was a new range of vocational institutions, like Watts's original 'Accomptant's Office', in early-eighteenth-century England. They taught not only subjects of commercial relevance, such as accounting and book-keeping, but navigation, fortification and military engineering, or even, as with John Buchanan's mathematical school at Steeple Bumpstead in Queen Anne's day, quantity surveying. There were also schools (or tutors such as William Addy or John Stuart) which taught shorthand, although this was usually as an adjunct of calligraphy.

It would be wrong to think of the expansion of private education, other than that provided by personal tutors, in a purely institutional sense. A good deal of private instruction in Augustan England was hired out. John Jeffreys, a land surveyor and map-maker under the first two Georges advertised himself, for instance, as 'teacher abroad of writing, arithmetic, algebra and geography'. Peripatetic specialists were particularly useful where there were no appropriate schools. In the larger towns, especially towns with an established endowed school which lacked a writing master of its own, it usually paid professional writing masters to settle and keep a private school which grammar-school boys, as well as others, could attend at certain times in the week. But in rural areas – for example, in much of the East Riding of Yorkshire – the itinerant writing master became quite a common sight, going the rounds of the country grammar schools and of any other educational establishments or private houses where there was a call for his services.

A valuable modern study of education in eighteenth-century Cheshire concludes that the increase in educational provision which this one county experienced from the late seventeenth century onwards created 'a much greater demand for teachers than had previously existed'. Norfolk and Suffolk had 157 masters licensed to teach by the Bishop of Norwich in 1700, about half as many again as after the passing of the Uniformity Act in 1662; and when we bear in mind that with each succeeding decade it became more and more the exception for teachers outside the grammar schools and large urban public schools to seek this formal imprimatur, it can be assumed that the true scale of the increase here was a good deal greater. There was nothing untypical about these two counties. Over England and Wales as a whole, therefore, the teachers who manned all the types of academy and school mentioned so far were a numerous body in 1730: distinctly more numerous than their counterparts had been in 1680 (a difference of at least 2,000 might be a tentative guess); and of a different scale from their predecessors who staffed roughly comparable institutions in 1660. Furthermore, there were several types of school in Augustan England, mostly large categories, of which nothing has so far been said. And when we add to all the other teachers those who taught in the multitude of parish schools still functioning, many of them supported by rates or contributions, quite apart from the Dissenting elementary schools or 'meeting-house schools'; when we take account also of all the men (leaving aside the women) who found employment in the jumble of small private establishments which, along with endowed and subscription charity schools, completed the tangled thicket of Augustan primary education, it seems certain that we must think of somewhere between 10,000 and 15,000 men, all told, being involved in school, academy and private or freelance teaching by the end of our period. An accurate figure is bound to be elusive in the present imperfect state of research: and it may never be attainable. But bearing in mind the swelling of the ranks by several hundred household tutors; the existence of a quite unguessable number of itinerants who moved facelessly from town to town wherever there was a need to be met; and the fact that seventy-odd years later the number of teachers, in Colquhoun's judgement, had reached 20,500, the total may well have been closer to the upper of the two poles (15,000) than to the lower. Whatever the education of children in Augustan England may have lacked in quality, it lacked surprisingly little in quantity.

Many of the grammar schools of the Dissenters, like virtually all their elementary schools, were single-teacher establishments. The age was one in which the individual master of ability, such as John Horsley, the physicist who ran the school at Morpeth, and Isaac Antrobus of Knutsford, had great drawing-power. Yet at the other end of the Nonconformist scale there were large private boarding schools such as that kept by Issac Gilling at Newton Abbot, Devon, from 1699 to 1712, which employed several masters. At least one Dissenting school, Singleton's at Clerkenwell which had an average complement of 300 boys during the years 1673–89, must have needed five or six. However, to make even an approximate estimate of the numbers either of Dissenting schools or teachers for the country at large, at any point between the 1690s and 1730, may never be possible. It would have been otherwise if the Schism Act had ever been enforced. As it is, too many records have been lost, and those indefatigable conductors of censuses for the Presbyterians and Congregationalists in the early years of George I, John Evans and Daniel Neal, unfortunately do not appear to have sought educational information from their county correspondents. Neither can we be sure how many teachers (although clearly it was an appreciable proportion) were also ministers of Nonconformist meetings.

About the Augustan charity schools, on the other hand, we possess an exceptional amount of information down to the early 1720s. This is thanks largely to the records of the SPCK, which co-ordinated the subscription movement for new schools from 1699, the year of the society's formation, until 1724. It tried to stimulate fresh private endowments as well, vastly encouraged by what David Owen has called the 'amazing outpouring of wealth for public purposes that marked the first four decades of the eighteenth century'; and it naturally did not hesitate to include both kinds of charity school, and also mixtures of the two, in its returns. Historians have disagreed sharply both about the effectiveness of the educational leadership which the SPCK provided and the reliability of its statistics. Joan Simon's work on Leicestershire illustrates how in counties where its local sources of information were unreliable or undiscriminating, its catch-all approach to record-keeping could lead to serious exaggerations in some of the lists of new schools it periodically published. Yet there were just as certainly many new small foundations, particularly endowed foundations in country areas, which the society's officers in London never heard about; and after 1723–4 its provincial counts do not seem to have been brought properly up to date at all. So for both reasons it is fortunate that its records can be supplemented by those of the early nineteenth-century Charity Commissioners, which inquired rigorously between 1818 and 1843 into, among other things, the non-subscription charity schools of the traditional model, those endowed non-classical schools which were founded in England both before and after 1699. The reports of these commissions provide probably the most reliable statistical guide we have to any type of school in our period.

By 1724 the SPCK's published *Account of Charity Schools* was able to produce a list of 1,148 supposedly new provincial schools in England (Wales apart), including such imposing county totals as 89 for Lincolnshire, where Bishop Wake had laboured to remarkable effect during Anne's reign in whipping up subscriptions, 57 for Gloucestershire and 55 for Berkshire. By 1729 the total number of schools on the books had soared, officially, to 1,419, and the number of children thought to be attending them had reached the nominal figure of 22,203. The true figure was well in excess of that, for in many schools (over 250 in 1723) pupil numbers remained unknown to the society's officers. By 1729 the biggest stronghold of the subscription movement, London and Westminster, had 132 charity schools and 5,225 pupils. What should we make of these impressive figures? There is no reason to doubt that the society's London headquarters was accurately informed on the metropolitan situation and that it was, in general, well abreast of developments near to the capital. Its graph of progress in more distant counties, on the other hand, must not be invested with the precise, scientific aura of a modern White Paper. And although here and there it palpably over-estimated that progress – in Leicestershire, only twenty-two of the thirty-five so-called 'charity schools' listed in 1724 were post-1699 foundations – it is still quite probable that its national tallies by the 1720s erred on the low side rather than on the high. In Sheffield parish alone, five charity schools were founded between 1710 and 1724 and a sixth followed in 1729; but only the two in Sheffield town (one being, in fact, an endowed Free Writing School) appear in the SPCK's 1724 list for Yorkshire. There are, suspiciously, a mere thirteen schools in the same list for Cheshire; though recent investi-gations have uncovered evidence of twenty-nine charity schools in eighteenth-century Cheshire which were founded from 1699 onwards and which had some connection with the SPCK. Even more incom-plete was the society's information on Cumberland: its 1724 *Account* included only six charity schools for the whole county, but at least eight primary schools are known to have been founded by endowment alone in Cumberland between 1710 and 1730, while William Nicolson, who was Bishop of Carlisle from 1702 to 1718, was well known for his vigorous espousal of the subscription movement.

The Charity Commissioners' reports of 1818–43 concluded that at least 1,085 endowed schools – other than grammar schools or their equivalent – existed in England by 1730 and that 625 of those had been founded since 1698. Despite the spectacular results rightly attributed to subscriptions in the first two decades of the eighteenth century, most emphatically of all in London, the role of endowment in the charity-school movement remained crucial. In addition, a pro-fusion of new charities became attached to long-established parish schools in this same period, though falling short of endowment: 468 of these for the years 1698–1730 were still traceable by the early nineteenth century, and some certainly made possible an increase in teaching resources. The schools which benefited were not in any strict sense 'charity schools', and certainly not new schools (though some of them may have been mistaken for such at the SPCK's headquarters). Yet, however we label the new primary schools or the financially re-buttressed schools of the first three decades of the eighteenth century, there can be no doubt whatever that together they represented a wholly unprecedented increase, in so short a time, in provision for educating the children of the poor of Augustan England, and an equally unprecedented increase in the strength of the lower ranks of the teaching body.

In general, about thirty children was the most a single charity-school master was expected to cope with. When numbers got higher, at the very least a mistress was provided to teach the girls. The large urban 'blue-coat' or 'grey-coat' schools, with 50–100 pupils each, such as that at Nottingham, the four flourishing in Bristol and the two in Leeds by 1724, Blundell's Charity School in Liverpool (built from 1708–18 at a cost of almost £2,500), and those at Hull, Gloucester,

Birmingham and Wakefield, would have two or three teachers. But the bulk of all 'petty' schools in Augustan England – whether old parish schools, new endowed schools, subscription charity schools, Dissenting schools or private reading and writing schools – were at all times one-man concerns. How considerable that bulk was *in toto* one is reminded in reading the account of Bishop Nicolson, who during his first diocesan visitation in 1703, undertaken when the charity-school movement was still in the cradle, found scarcely a parish out of the fifty-eight in Cumberland without an elementary school of some kind. Francis Gastrell, Bishop of Chester, noted twenty-one schools in the twenty-seven parishes of Furness deanery in or soon after 1714. In Leicestershire, even before 1640, there had been parish schoolmasters in at least seventy villages, supported mostly out of church rates plus other contributions from the congregations; by 1730 there were, in addition, about forty parishes which now had a regular endowment to support a schoolmaster, not to mention the petty schools of the Dissenters. In Cheshire, a county of sixty-eight parishes, no child had to travel more than five miles, for much of the eighteenth century, to get basic instruction in reading and writing, and usually in arithmetic too. The more that is discovered, in fact, about basic education provision of every kind in Augustan England, the more it seems likely to bear out the truth of Francis Brokesby's words, written in 1701, 'that there are few country villages where some or other do not get a livelihood by teaching school'.

One thousand, three hundred and twenty grammar schools have been identified in England and Wales between 1600 and 1660. A parochial survey in 1819 revealed only about 700 still functioning in this capacity; but that followed some ninety years of generally declining fortunes, and the position a century earlier was clearly much healthier with numbers nearer to the mid-seventeenth-century than the early-nineteenth-century pole. The 80 new grammar schools of Charles II's reign must have been followed by at least as many again in England and Wales during the next fifty years, perhaps by a further 100. Yorkshire, Lancashire and Cheshire together had about 190 grammar schools in 1741, while the eastern seaboard counties of Kent and Essex, Suffolk, Norfolk and Lincolnshire at the same date could muster a further 91. For the whole country it would seem that the total around the end of George I's reign can hardly have been less than 1,000 and could possibly have been as high as 1,200. As well as the endowed grammar schools there were, as a leading historian of eighteenth-century education reminds us, 'the innumerable private-venture schools which honeycombed London and the towns' during the eighteenth century. One can, of course, exaggerate the number of such schools whose doors were open at any one period. The number of private classical schools which existed by George II's reign was certainly less than the 243 claimed by Nicholas Hans; and the number of writing schools and mathematical schools in the late Augustan period, though considerable in London, is not very likely to have exceeded 150 over the whole country. On the other hand, complete information on the existence of these elusive private schools is notoriously difficult to come by before the 1730s and 1740s when English provincial newspapers, with their invaluable advertisements, began to be published more widely than hitherto. The kind of impetus which had been building up during the first few decades of the eighteenth century can be appreciated from the fact that the *Northampton Mercury* alone carried advertisements for 100 private schools or academies in the forty years after 1720. It would be surprising if there were not by 1730 as many private schools teaching boys after the primary stage as there were grammar schools.

If there were indeed as many as 2,000 such 'secondary' institutions, all told, how many masters did they employ? Most of the original endowed foundations envisaged two teachers, a master to teach Greek and Latin grammar, and an usher to prepare boys for the upper school and sometimes to teach the petties. Even in the late seventeenth century, if the East Riding of Yorkshire is a reliable guide, it was only the very small or the very poor schools which did not have two teachers. When Beverley's quota of boys reached fifty in 1670 it was considered sufficient to justify the appointment of an usher. It is true that over the country at large the number of endowments which had been whittled away by sixteenth- and early-seventeenth-century infla-tion to levels that were too low to allow such a luxury, ran into some hundreds by 1700. On the other hand, some particularly large and flourishing institutions now exceeded the traditional complement. Shrewsbury School and Manchester Grammar School boasted three masters in the late seventeenth century, and Shrewsbury had acquired a fourth by the 1720s. Wakefield Grammar School, one of the best in the north (it numbered John Radcliffe, the great physician among its Augustan alumni), had over 168 boys by 1717, when a third master was appointed at £30 per annum. Newcastle Grammar School, like Witney in Oxfordshire, employed a full-time writing master as well as an usher in the late seventeenth and early eighteenth centuries, and before 1719 the Royal Grammar School, Lancaster was doing the same; while King Edward VI School in Birmingham increased its staff from two in 1676 to four by 1707.

Still better provided for were the biggest London schools – West-minster, St Paul's, Merchant Taylor's and Christ's Hospital – and a handful of élitist collegiate foundations, notably Eton, Winchester and, on a smaller scale, Charterhouse, which was still on its early-seventeenth-century site in Islington. The rising demand from well-to-do parents which led to the building of a vast new schoolroom, twice as large as the old, at Winchester College between 1683 and 1687 also called for a new level of staffing. The appointment of a second master and several ushers was necessary to keep pace with an increase in the number of boarding 'commoners' from 44 in 1653 to 155 in 1732. By that year there were 181 boys in all on the roll. By the end of the seventeenth century the college had so manifestly ceased to be a school for the local community that a new grammar school, Over's, was founded at Winchester in 1701–2 to serve the needs of the town and its hinterland. Merchant Taylor's, which had employed only a master and usher in the 1660s, at the time of the Great Fire, was on the crest of a great wave of popularity by the turn of the century and between 1700 and 1719 admitted 2,357 boys. The number of ushers was still, officially, no more than three, but they must have had further assistance to cope with such numbers. Christ's Hospital had six schoolmasters at its free grammar school in London in 1720, as well as one at Hertford and one at Ware, and according to John Chamberlayne, Westminster School had a staff of twelve in 1716. There was no danger that Westminster masters might be underemployed: by 1728 the school had 434 pupils, 80 per cent more than in 1656. Only Christ's Hospital, with 445 pupils in its writing school alone by 1709, and Eton could rival this scale of activity. For the 399 boys in the college in 1719, which was double the number it had taught in the mid-1670s and over treble its complement in James I's reign, Eton had a headmaster (the Provost being normally a non-teacher), an usher or 'under master', and possibly nine assistant masters and writing masters. In addition, there were now to be found at Eton a number of 'tutors' whom boys attended in their rooms for private tuition – as they did with the assistants – and whose remuneration depended entirely on fees. Tutors eventually appeared at Winchester, too, but not before 1738.

Most private fee-paying schools which took pupils beyond the stage of the three Rs followed the pattern of their earlier seventeenth-century predecessors and operated as one-man concerns, with a wife or female relative to look after boarders. However, a substantial minority of these schools were becoming more ambitious. Bret's Academy at Tottenham in Charles II's reign appears to have provided a teaching staff of six or seven. Some of the private London schools of the period, for example Foubert's and Banister's Academies in the late seventeenth century and Meure's Academy in Queen Anne's reign, offered syllabuses as wide, or almost as wide, as Bret's; and they can hardly have managed with fewer than three or four masters each. Certainly the celebrated Watts's Academy in Little Tower Street was employing four masters or 'professors' by the late 1720s, together with a resident French tutor and a number of part-time tutors, including Bernard Lens, who taught painting and drawing, and a music master.

While teachers' numbers rose appreciably, it was only a small proportion of those outside the swelling orbit of the private establishments whose prospects and rewards changed equally significantly. The status and social standing of the average master in the public domain was not strikingly different in 1730 from what it had been in 1680. Schoolmasters remained, as they had been throughout the seventeenth century, the most poorly paid of any large professional body in the country. The clear advance in their average earnings during the Augustan period brought uneven gains, benefiting a fortunate, growing minority of both private-school and grammar-school teachers, but probably affecting the majority relatively little. Even 'in many great towns [i.e. large market towns], and some considerable cities', it seemed to Francis Brokesby in 1701, the schoolmaster's salary remained 'mean and sordid'. In fact the normal stipends paid to many teachers in the new charity schools were appreciably higher than those which now disgraced many underendowed small grammar schools of sixteenth- or early-seventeenth-century foundation: schools whose original endowments, made in an inflationary age, had never been supplemented or perhaps (as at Malton in Yorkshire) never could be under the founder's statutes. In this miserable twilight area of Augustan education, salaries of £20 a year or thereabouts paid to sole masters of schools were commonplace, and far more abysmal depths were reached in some places.

In the new subscription schools founded from the 1690s onwards under the auspices of the SPCK the highest salaries were, in general, paid in London. For every vacant post in the capital there was normally a flurry of applications, many of them from distant provincials, whereas the country charity schools were not always so readily served. From the start the society was at pains to prescribe a minimum salary of £30 a year in London schools, the master being often provided with a rent-free house into the bargain and almost invariably with 'coals'. As the years went by, and the resources of many schools were augmented, there were incomes of £50 and even £60 a year to be earned in some of the charity schools of London by the middle of the eighteenth century. The larger provincial towns could roughly compete with London standards in the early decades of the subscription movement. The master at Reading Blue-Coat School, with his £30 yearly salary, was almost as well off, on paper at least, as his counterpart in the town's grammar school. Winkfield, also in Berkshire, offered even better terms: £30 for the schoolmaster, £20 for the schoolmistress (who could be his wife), plus a bonus of £1 10s for each boy above the number of twenty-one and £1 for every girl above the same number. The trust fund set up to finance the blue-coat subscription school in Chester yielded its master an income of £34 7s 6d in 1711, and Colchester's charity school, founded with a fanfare in 1710, paid its masters a handsome £40 a year as well as furnishing him with a house and free fuel.

Though most offered a house and garden with the job, the smaller market towns and villages could rarely hope to compete at this level; and the SPCK had perforce to comfort itself (not without some reason) that '£20 a year in the country, where living is so cheap that one can board for £10 or £12 per annum, is as good as £30 a year in Town'. Even this would not have brought much solace to the master of the Blue Cap School at Nantwich, who was said in 1718 to receive only £5 a year plus any donations made at Communion. However, even in the backwoods most charity-school subscribers would have blushed to pay their teachers the pittance of £10 a year which was all the masters of the grammar schools at Buckingham,

Wrexham and Wallingford received for teaching their 'free' pupils, or even the £12 or £13 a year paid to the grammar-school masters at Newbury, Saffron Walden, Worcester and Gainsborough. These were simply not living wages and they had either to be augmented by the stipend of a curacy or, as we shall see, in other ways.

Fortunately for the profession there were many sixteenth-century educational endowments which were not left stranded by inflation. For some schools a good reputation and a fair share of good fortune had worked wonders: as it had with Manchester Grammar School, where the high master's salary, £10 a year by the original foundation deed of 1515, increased six-fold over the next 170 years. Other trustees saw their endowments appreciate, thanks to the fortunate siting of the property which was the source of the headmaster's and usher's salaries. The most spectacular case was that of Birmingham. Here the endowed land was in the town centre; and as the metalware trades expanded after the Restoration, bringing great prosperity and maintaining a continuous demand for properties, rents rose rapidly. Even by the 1650s the original Edwardian endowment of £21 annually had become worth £73 and by 1676, £94. Thereafter, however, as various leases fell in, the governors could scarcely believe their luck. By 1700 their income had soared to £302 a year. The school-master's post here had for some time been a coveted one: in 1655 it had carried a £50 salary, and by 1676 this had been increased to £65. But the rent returns of the next twenty-five years made possible a more lavish rise still in 1702, to £88 15s, and even Birmingham School's usher at this time found himself paid £44 6s 8d a year, more than twice the salary of his predecessor in 1655. However, James Parkinson, headmaster in 1711, clearly thought that he and his three colleagues ought to have done better still; for he brought a successful court action against the governors for 'lavish[ing] away great and unnecessary sums in rebuilding'.

It was not only large urban schools whose assets appreciated. Visiting Morpeth in 1725 Lord Oxford's chaplain found 'a good free school, which by the recovery of some lands to it within these late years is worth £130 per annum, and has two masters'. The governors of Wilton Grammar School in Cheshire could pay their master, Aaron Nichols, only £16 in 1700; but by 1748 they were able to offer a newly-appointed head, the Reverend B. Shuttleworth, as much as £50. These cannot be presented as 'typical' cases, any more than the quite contrary experience of John Barber, master of the Queen Mary Free School at Ripon under George I. The nominal revenue of £40 a year which supported the school and the schoolmaster's house there was chiefly derived from house property in the town, the rents of which, Barber told his friend Timothy Thomas, were so 'very precariously paid' that he was 'obliged to keep a bailiff in constant employ for the levying of them'. There was a large element of the lottery about the grammar-school world of the early eighteenth century.

Fortunately for those schoolmasters concerned, the founders of new schools after the Restoration generally took a realistic view of basic salaries as well as envisaging the probability of their being supplemented from other sources. Most endowments of schools with more than elementary pretensions established between 1660 and 1730 sought to guarantee head teachers at least £40 a year. A few touched the heights of generosity. Lord Lonsdale's endowment of Lowther College enabled William Wilkinson to draw a salary of £100 a year from 1715 to 1740; and at Kirkleatham, a Queen Anne grammar school in North Yorkshire, Sir William Turner made a provision for a £100 salary to the master and £50 to the usher, with the stipulation that both must be graduates and the former an MA. Yet even with relatively new schools expectations could be confounded. Mismanagement of assets, defaulting on rents, deflection of income into other channels, all might cause shortfalls; and occasionally these could be serious. Sir John Nelthorpe, the founder of Brigg Grammar School, seems to have intended its master to be paid £50 per annum in salary and the usher £30. But Sir John had died as early as 1669, eleven years before the school opened its doors, and by the beginning of the eighteenth century the income from the land he bequeathed to the foundation was yielding Brigg's master no more than £36. It was as well he was allowed to take some fee-paying pupils 'in the learned tongues'; with their assistance he doubtless broke even in the end.

Private philanthropy continued to benefit some old schools as well as establish many new ones between 1660 and 1720. St Bees School, favourably placed near the swiftly growing port of Whitehaven, was fortunate in this respect. Generously endowed in the first place by Edmund Grindal in Elizabeth I's reign, it found, as an early-eighteenth-century account put it,

> the charity much increased by the late Dr Lamplugh, archbishop
> of York [he died in 1691]. The library annexed to this foundation
> is very valuable, and still increasing by several gifts daily added
> to it; and they show a list of the benefactors, in which are
> several persons of honour and distinction.

For the headmaster of St Bees, a nominee of the Fellows of Queen's College, Oxford, the library was a profitable asset, attracting fee-payers to the school, as well as a scholar's delight. The new library annexes built on to Leeds Grammar School in 1692 and at Southampton (1691–1710) similarly benefited teachers as well as pupils. In his treatise *Of Education with respect to Grammar Schools and the Universities* (1701) Francis Brokesby urged that, with pluralism forced on many schoolmasters by the level of salaries in so many of the long-established 'free schools', public-spirited gentlemen would indeed serve their country best 'not so much by founding new schools as being benefactors to old foundations'. But he can hardly have expected that any town, or any teachers, would profit quite so handsomely from such private benefactions as the inhabitants and schoolmasters of Aylesbury. At the beginning of the eighteenth century Aylesbury Grammar School was one of the most depressed in England, its endowment producing little more than £8 a year. But in 1714 Henry Phillips of London bequeathed to the school £5,000, with instructions (nicely blending the old and the new in contemporary attitudes to education) that the poor boys of Aylesbury and Walton (Bucks) were to be taught 'Latin, writing, arithmetic and accounts, so as to be fit to go and be apprentices to *good trades*' (my italics). By 1720 a new building was opened, accommodating 15 boys in the Latin school and 135 in the English school. Buckinghamshire's great historian, Lipscomb, wrote in 1847 that 'the salary of the [two] masters has varied from £100 *per an.* to £170, exclusive of a house for each [newly built in 1718]; and the respective masters are permitted to teach private pupils for their own benefit'. Thus with a few strokes of the pen one wealthy citizen, practical as well as public-spirited, had contrived almost to make a reality out of the eighteenth-century schoolmaster's El Dorado.

On the whole, however, it seems likely that rather more Augustan grammar-school teachers in the older foundations profited from the concern of enlightened corporations than gained substantially from private munificence. The city council of Coventry was conspicuously among the most provident as well as the most progressive in the country. It seemed to Celia Fiennes, as she passed through in 1697, 'a thriving good trading town and . . . very rich; they have a great public stock belonging to the corporation, above 3 thousand pounds a year for public schools, charity and the maintenance of their several public expenses'. Bristol raised the salary of its grammar school's headmaster, William Godwin, from £60 to £80 a year in 1711. The town fathers of Beverley showed their enterprise in 1736 in attracting John Clarke, a teacher of high repute, from Skipton to become head of their already admirable grammar school – 'they say the best in England [Celia had noted] for learning and care'. Three-quarters of the master's salary was already paid by the corporation; so they persuaded the two Members of Parliament for the borough to promise a supplement of £10 a year each which brought the emoluments up to £60. An additional bonus was added in the form of the Sunday afternoon lectureship in St Mary's Church, in the corporation's gift, which was worth 10 guineas. Durham and Hull represented probably more typical cases. The stipend of the master of Durham Grammar School, fixed at £30 in 1663, was allowed to congeal at that uncharitable level until 1732, when the corporation intervened to raise it by 50 per cent; even so the beneficiary remained poorly off by comparison with the master of the cathedral choir school, who by now was enjoying the luxury of £82 10s. Further south, at Hull, endowments produced under £20 a year for the grammar-school master after the Restoration. From 1670, with the help of a £6 a year reinforcement from the corporation and his half share of the obligatory fees paid by burgesses' sons, the master was able to scrape together about £38, though it is true he also enjoyed a rent-free house. By 1731, however, when the port of Hull was launched on its career of eighteenth-century prosperity, the corporation plucked up enough courage to bring his basic salary up to £50 a year, while still allowing him to retain his right to fees, which he shared fifty-fifty with his usher. A final illustration, from Nuneaton, is a reminder that a local authority's intervention did not invariably work to the advantage of schools or schoolmasters. In 1675 the town had paid the master of its free school the astonishingly generous salary of 'about £80'. But in 1694, in harder times, the governing body decided that this should be reduced to £60, or by a further £10 if the master hired an usher at £20 per annum.

The ushers (in part the apprentices of the grammar-school profession, in part the proletariat) were almost invariably poorly paid. Ironically, they could in some favoured establishments be better off financially than masters with sole responsibility for the poorest schools. But their relative good fortune was very much a matter of degree, and low degree at that. Lancaster corporation doubled the salary of the local usher by two increases, in 1709 and 1726: they brought it to £23 16s. The £28 paid to its usher in 1685 by Manchester Grammar School, a thriving institution, was infinitely higher than the average expectation in the late seventeenth century. The norm in an old provincial school was between £10 and £16 a year. The usher at Darlington had the dubious distinction of being at the bottom of the pack: in 1707 his yearly payment from the trustees sank to the deplorable depths of £6. How would he have reacted, one wonders, to the news that one of the assistant masters at Christ's Hospital (admittedly the mathematics master in a new school with a marked mathematical specialisation) occupied a post 'as well paid [so Pepys wrote in 1682] as most Professorships'?

But then, inequalities were the order of the day from end to end of the Augustan grammar-school spectrum. The successful head of a going concern, enjoying a good guaranteed salary and a fruitful supplementary income, could reasonably look for a modest affluence from schoolmastering. Such was the case, for example, with the master of King's School, Ely, in the eighteenth century. So it was, too, with the high master of Manchester Grammar School, whose salary alone had reached £60 a year before the Revolution (though fortunes, even in the best schools, were extraordinarily personalised, and proportionately precarious: so that when the Manchester school fell briefly on hard times in the 1720s, the then high master had to eke out his income by private teaching). The headship of Sutton Coldfield School was another coveted post, not only because it carried a basic £80 a year but because it conferred valuable perquisites as well. Indeed, it was the 'perks' teachers were entitled to which so often held the key to their expectations, while their salaries often developed into something rather like retainers.

For one thing, it was generally accepted that a teacher at a 'free school' was entitled to charge pupils, even foundation scholars, for giving instruction outside the statutory curriculum. Boys who took writing lessons at Lymm Grammar School were charged 4s a quarter; writing and accounts together cost them 6s. A specialist mathematician teaching in a classical school, for example John Holmes, who became headmaster of Holt Grammar School in the 1720s, was well placed to profit from this convention. Secondly, no graduate classicist with the slightest bargaining power was likely to accept a mastership unless it carried with it a rent-free house or lodging: this was reckoned to be worth at the very least £5 a year in kind, and more if the house was particularly well appointed and had some land attached to it. However, those who were likely to prosper most in the public field of education were masters who, in addition to free housing and the security of 'a good allowance', enjoyed at least one, and preferably both, of two crucial auxiliary benefits. If the conditions of their employment allowed them to take a profitable quota of fee-paying pupils in addition to the free scholars 'on the foundation', and if – better still – they were able to take in boarders and had the facilities to do so, they could be enviably placed.

Before Nicholas Burton accepted the mastership of Durham Grammar School in 1699, a post he was to hold for ten years, his father entered into strenuous negotiations on his behalf with Thomas Comber, Dean of Durham. After rehearsing his son's strong academic qualifications – 'bred almost 6 years under the famous Dr Busby' at Westminster School, 'and thence elected to Christ Church, Oxon, where [he] has been about 8 years, took his Master's degree this time twelve months and is a student of that royal foundation' – the Reverend John Burton got down to brass tacks:

> He is desirous to accept of that place . . . and does not fear to keep up the character of your school: and though the salary be but small [£30 per annum], yet with your encouragement and his own diligence the place may be made considerable . . . Eighteen boys [on the foundation] to be taught gratis is a great number: surely gentlemen and persons of ability will not grudge to give at least ten shillings a quarter, which is but half the pay allowed to Singing and Dancing Masters.

Durham, he hinted broadly, would not care to be thought more niggardly than York, where William Thomlinson, master of St Peter's School since 1679, was allowed to charge 'no less than 10s. per quarter for every boy, save only eight poor men's sons recommended by our chapter'. A majority of fee-payers, and £2 per annum a head from each of them, seemed no more than just remuneration, for 'school teaching is a laborious employment and requires both skill and industry'. It is not clear whether Nicholas's terms were granted right from the start of his appointment, but it is unlikely that he had to wait long: for quite apart from his pedagogic merits, as one who had followed closely in the footsteps of the fiery Francis Atterbury young Mr Burton's politics proved so much to the liking of Durham's Tory corporation that they appointed him to the town lectureship to make doubly certain that his pot was kept merrily boiling.

The practice of St Peter's, York, reflected the way some of the best old grammar schools in the country were moving in the last few decades of the seventeenth and in the early eighteenth centuries, often perhaps to prevent successful teachers being lured elsewhere. The level of fees varied widely according to situation and resources. Lancaster, well endowed, expected only 7s 6d yearly from the sons of non-freemen. The master of Hereford Cathedral School, 'in regard of the smallness of the annual salary', had been allowed to charge all local boys, except the very poorest, up to 20s a year, plus 5s for entrance, since 1665, and a Cambridge graduate was attracted to Dedham Grammar School in 1694 by the authorisation of a similar blanket tuition fee of 25s annually. Certainly there were no complaints from 'the reverend master' of Blundell's School at Tiverton: for as Defoe discovered on a visit to Devon in 1705, a liberal endowment ensured him 'at least, sixty pounds per annum, besides a very good house to live in and the advantage of scholars not on the foundation'. What was more, provision was made for 'the usher in proportion'. The master and usher both fared extremely well, too, at the King's School, Chester, where in 1709 there were 120 pupils and no fewer than 96 of them paid fees. And since the master, Charles Henchman, was also able to augment his admittedly low salary, £22 a year from the dean and chapter, with the stipends of a series of rectories and with the profits of a canon's stall in the cathedral, it is not surprising that he was content to stay at the school until his death in 1742.

Like all eighteenth-century headmasters at Chester, Henchman took in private pupils as boarders as well as fee-paying day boys. To keep up and improve its reputation, and also (for the two things usually went hand in hand) to attract and hold able and ambitious teachers, the good provincial grammar school in Augustan England found it hard to avoid at least a partial transition into the role of a boarding school. School statutes were revised to permit either the entrance of boarders or their increase at Dedham (1685), at Highgate (1714) and at Tottenham, 'for the better encouragement of the Master', in 1710. It was the boarding facilities it offered, in a town of excellent amenities and 'cheap provisions', that made possible the rapid rise of Beverley Grammar School to near élite status in the late seventeenth century, making it 'filled with gentlemen's sons, besides the free scholars, from all parts'. Far into the eighteenth century it kept its reputation as 'the Westminster of the North'. Richard Pocock, master of the grammar school at Southampton, was so confident of the profit he would make out of the proposed expansion of the school to take in numerous boarders that in an agreement with the corporation in 1696 he actually agreed to build a boarding-house at his own expense, on condition the town allowed him to have West Hall for a new school-house. 'Gentlemen boarders' could be good business for a provincial town which had drifted, as Southampton had, into an economic backwater. The town of Ashby de la Zouche had been enlivened by being 'continually full of boarders from London and other parts of the kingdom' during the 1670s, 1680s and 1690s, boys attracted by the reputation of the grammar school's dedicated master, Samuel Shaw; and two ushers were frequently needed to help him to cope with the demand – and share the profits. The head of a good provincial boarding grammar school, with an impressive record of preparing boys for the universities, did not sell his services cheaply by the early eighteenth century. A gentleman's son boarding at Ipswich Grammar School during the regime of Edward Leedes the younger, from 1712 to 1737, could expect to take home every half-year a bill averaging about £14 for board and tuition together, quite apart from extras such as payments to the writing master or the dancing master.

The willingness of hundreds of parents to shoulder charges of this kind, even for the increasingly questionable privilege of the traditional scholastic fare, lends credibility to some of the unlikelier individual success stories in the Augustan grammar schools. It is said, for instance, that it was mainly the rich harvests from his boarders, accumulating over a period of twenty years, which enabled Robert Jennings to pay almost £6,000 for a landed estate when he gave up the headship of Abingdon School in 1683. And it is well authenticated that Thomas Ryder, the master of Bury Grammar School in Lancashire, did so well out of his private boarders between 1717 and 1724 that he was able to give up salaried employment, come to Manchester and open a large co-educational boarding school, employing both male and female teachers. Perhaps such achievements did become more common with the rapid development of local newspapers during the first half of the eighteenth century, which gave more and more grammar-school masters a valuable new medium through which to advertise for a clientele that was potentially so lucrative. But obviously there were well-established and productive grapevines at their disposal long before the 1720s.

While enterprising old schools and the masters in them came to terms with the changing climate, new founders appear to have realised quite soon after the Restoration that the best way to lure able career-teachers to new schools, and hold them there, was to sanction the taking of boarders. More than that, their buildings were planned, where possible, in such a way as to make physical provision for these desirable 'foreigners'. When Sir John Langham, a Levant Company merchant, built a fine new grammar school at Guilsborough, Northamptonshire, he endowed it for the ostensible purpose of teaching classics and Hebrew to fifty local pupils. But it is apparent from the provision of bedrooms over the original schoolroom that the master (who had a handsome house incorporated in the block) was expected to attract boarders right at the outset; and as things turned out, partly because there was already a writing school in Guilsborough, mostly because of the close competition of Rugby School, Langham's foundation of 1670 made the complete transition within three-quarters of a century into a boarding school catering only for fee-paying boys. Lucton School, founded in 1708 by Sir John Pierrepont, and Sir

William Turner's School at Kirkleatham both exhibited a similar realism on the part of their founders. Facilities were provided at Lucton, for example, for ten 'sons of gentlemen' who would bring in £200 a year in fees. The three teachers in Sir John Moore's School, Appleby Magna, were more than usually favoured. As well as providing for salaries of £60 for the Latin master, £40 for the English master and £20 for the writing master, Moore spent £2,800 in the 1690s on building the most spectacular school of the late seventeenth century: a three-storey structure with its main schoolroom, together with houses for the two senior masters, on the ground floor, its English and writing schools on the second floor, and accommodation for some fifty boarders on the rest of the second floor and the whole of the third. A letter from Sir Christopher Wren to Sir John in 1693, on which Moore subsequently acted, crisply exemplifies the new pragmatic philosophy:

> ... I should think that a less salary with advantage of room for boarders is more considerable than a large allowance without it, and to have gentlemen's sons well accommodated is that will bring reputation to the school and a good interest to the master; for which reason you will always have choice of worthy men to succeed in the school, because it will be more desirable to any person than *a mere salary*. (My italics)

Not surprisingly, it was in London that many of the most succulent teaching plums were to be had. At Merchant Taylor's School, according to a contemporary account in George I's reign, the master and his three ushers, who were all housed, shared in the fees received from two-thirds of the school's 300 pupils, which then amounted to around £150 a year. Masters at Christ's Hospital in the flourishing later years of Charles II were comfortably off even without fees, though they worked at high pressure for their rewards. When a new head of the writing school there was appointed in 1676 his salary was fixed at £100: there were at that time sixty boys. Ten years later, when pupil numbers had quadrupled, he was voted an extra £20 a year, which was to be paid on condition that numbers remained above 250! By 1694 the boys numbered nearly 400. Not surprisingly, when Richard Gutter died in 1710 at least nine candidates applied for the vacant mastership; and George Shelley, the successful one, kept the job for the next sixteen years. But London schoolmasters, in general, Brokesby thought, were particularly fortunate, not primarily because of their salaries but because of 'the allowances and gratuities given deservedly by parents to the teachers of their children' there.

For all that, the number was rapidly increasing by the end of Queen Anne's reign who would have been loath, even on material grounds, to exchange their lot for the rigours of the great schoolrooms at Westminster or Christ's Hospital. We have seen how prosperous the Augustan age was, or became, for provincial masters as far apart as Tiverton and Appleby, Abingdon and Beverley, Ely and Sutton Coldfield, Aylesbury and Kirkleatham, St Peter's, York, and many more. How much the teachers at Shrewsbury's increasingly fashionable school made from entrance and tuition fees and from boarders is not certain; but even without these perquisites the headmaster of Shrewsbury, with £150 a year in salary alone, was observed to live like a squire, as indeed must his second master, with £100 salary and – in common with his superior – a very 'handsome house' to dwell in. Rugby could not as yet match such affluence. But from 1687 to 1731, under the distinguished rule of Henry Holyoake, former chaplain of Magdalen, it began to give strong hints of the élite status that lay ahead; and, as in so many other contemporary schools, it seems clear that the key to Holyoake's success was his ability to attract boarders, adding upwards of eighty more boys to the twenty on its foundation. Sharing with his subordinates the tuition and boarding fees that thus rolled in, enjoying a salary raised by the trustees from £50 to £70 a year and the emoluments of a succession of Warwickshire rectories from 1698 onwards (from which he appears to have met the salaries of his ushers as well as employing a curate), Holyoake reaped a just reward for his abilities and hard work in the last thirty years of his life. In fact, some of the most respected names and some of the best-lined pockets in Augustan schoolteaching belonged to men who, like Holyoake, were revivers of struggling old foundations and who became in the process lasting creators. The fact that by 1705 a school in the remote fell country of Craven had 120 boys on its roll and an unusually well stocked library to serve their needs, sprang almost entirely from the enterprise of Posthumous Warton, head of Sedbergh from 1674 to 1706, in buying a house for himself and building on to it quarters for boarders.

What the greatest 'public' school in England yielded its masters during its Augustan heyday under Newborough, Snape and Bland, when pupil numbers were mostly well over 300 and occasionally over 400, is not precisely known. Rumours that Eton was worth £1,000 a year, less outgoings, to the head of the school were most probably exaggerated, but it was certainly worth many hundreds. A memorandum survives – possibly written around 1730, just after William George had succeeded Bland and caused the 'unprecedented rebellion' of the scholars which led to a decline in the school's popularity – explaining how the rewards of the post accumulated.

> The Master of Eton School has one allocation of £50 per annum and another of £12, in all £62 per annum. Besides this he has commons of all kinds, bread, beer and easements of all sorts, without paying a single farthing. This cannot easily be computed at less than 10s per week. Besides his own lodgings which he inhabits, he has spare room enough which he lets to the boys for studies, and which brings him in usually £8 per annum. The Master receives a guinea entrance of all the boys both in the Upper and Lower School [the writer failed to mention that by the eighteenth century he received 'leaving money' as well]; but

as for annual gratuities, he receives only from those who are
under him in the Upper School. When any money is given the
known sum is four guineas per annum, and hardly ever varies by
being more or less.

N.B. No money is ever demanded, and it is supposed that one
time with another about one third of the boys pay nothing.

With his second-in-command likewise entitled to a 4-guinea gratuity
from every grateful parent of a boy in the Lower School, and
enjoying free commons by convention at the Fellows' table, it was
not surprising that a number of Eton under-masters preferred to stay
where they were rather than move to a headship. Francis Goode, a
teacher of considerable talent, remained in the post for seventeen
years after 1717.

It would be a very misleading picture of schoolteaching in Augustan
England which overlooked this grammar-school and public-school
aristocracy, for they are the reverse side of a coin whose obverse is
much more familiar. And yet, what Marchamont Nedham wrote in
1663 of the men who taught in the grammar schools of England had
by no means entirely ceased to apply to the schoolmasters of sixty
years later:

> ...no employment more publicly useful, none more toilsome and
> painful; yet no one more slighted, even to reproach, no one less
> rewarded or regarded. 'Tis a great scandal to the nation, and
> certainly as great a grievance (if rightly considered) that no one
> sort of men are greater sufferers in this kind than schoolmasters.

Even by 1730 several hundred grammar-school teachers – possibly a
majority of the whole body, unquestionably a majority of ushers –
continued to live threadbare and dispirited lives. And the number
who suffered this lot would have been far, far greater but for the
clerical pluralities which were the standby of so much of the profession.

Whatever the inequalities among masters in the 'public' schools,
however, they were surely surpassed by those which pervaded the
private sector of education. A host of itinerants and dispensers of
private elementary schooling spun out existences which were often
alarmingly precarious. Some teachers in private classical schools
prospered. Others, equally well qualified, were dogged by insecurity
and preferred the relative safety of an endowed establishment when
the opportunity offered. It is much easier to unearth information
about the successful ventures in private schooling than about the
failures, although it is hard to believe that the latter were not the
more numerous. It seems well established, for instance, that good
mathematical schools, especially those in London which offered
specialist addition to the staple fare, could be highly profitable. Their
masters were also able to pursue lucrative sidelines. William Aling-

ham, who kept one such school in Westminster in the time of William III and Anne, was a freelance surveyor and is said to have demanded (though not received) a £500 fee for a commission for restoring the sundial in the Privy Garden in Whitehall. Posts in the crack London academies of our period, such as Clare's and Watts's, were eagerly sought after, for quite apart from the rich share of fees they yielded they generally allowed time for freelance teaching as well. Peter Brown taught mathematics at Watts's Academy but also lectured privately on natural philosophy, charging his subscribers 3 guineas a course, while James Stirling, an FRS and a mathematician of European standing who owed his post at the same academy in 1725 to the influence of Sir Isaac Newton, reckoned to make at least £200 a year from the students he taught there and in his private lectures. Martin Clare, director of the Soho academy from 1717 to 1751, was a man of wealth and standing by the 1730s and 1740s: and so he should have been, as head of an establishment prestigious enough to charge, in addition to a basic board and tuition fee of £30 a year, 5 guineas 'to the House and Master' for entrance, £5 annually for such extras as a single room or the privilege of taking meals with the masters, and at least a guinea a month for additional subjects such as mathematics (other than arithmetic), merchants' accounts, drawing, dancing and music.

In prosperous provincial areas, too, private secondary institutions could sometimes turn into goldmines, especially where there was little or no competition from a local grammar school. John Rowland, rector of a parish in Kent, told how in 1675 in Eltham, 'a small town, where is no free school', there were 'no fewer than 3 free [i.e. independent] masters receiving £200 or £250 per annum by their scholars, with many gratuities and a great deal of love'. Versatility was more important to the private- than the public-school teacher. That 'dextrous' writing master, Edward Powell, was also 'a scholar, well versed in classical learning'. In 1712 he took over the highly successful boarding school in Wandsworth formerly run for many years by Richard Scoryer, and was said by his Latin usher to have cleared a cool £1,000 a year in the early years of George I's reign. Another contemporary claimed that the most celebrated London writing school of the Augustan period, in Fetter Lane, yielded to its proprietor, John Ayres, at its peak 'near 800 per annum, a fine income for a writing-master'. Among the fortunate, too, in a different line of country, were the private tutors at Eton. If William Pitt's bill from the College in 1719 is a fair guide, they might earn at least 8 guineas a year per pupil.

And so, while schoolteaching by 1730 could still with some justice be regarded as an ill-rewarded profession, the previous fifty years had seen some changes of significance, and for the better, in its remuneration. Higher prizes had become available to the élite at its head, partly through the rapidly growing popularity of private institutions offering either specialised or broad syllabuses, partly through more realistic endowments, but most of all through the broad wedge of boarders and fee-payers which had now been driven into the 'free-school' sector. With more of these prizes to go round, the élite had become merely small by 1730, rather than miniscule as it had been in 1680. Even among the swelling ranks of the elementary schoolmasters a larger proportion than in Charles II's reign could now look to make a respectable living, thanks to new and well-supported urban charity schools and the tendency for private endowments to be more pointedly directed than at any previous period towards the provision of basic instruction.

Meanwhile, a development of some note was taking place in the structure of the profession. In step with the increasing demand for fee-paying and 'modern' as opposed to 'free' and traditional schools, there was a slight but distinct shift in the balance between clerical and lay teachers, a shift towards the laity. Not that this left much mark on the grammar schools. Indeed, so far as the heads (though not the ushers) were concerned, the trend there may have been slightly in the other direction. A sample of 350 masters in 107 such schools in the period 1660–1714, analysed by Dr Vincent, reveals 74 per cent of them in orders, while a further sample taken from the years 1714–70 of 339 masters in 108 schools (most of them taken from the same group examined in the earlier period) indicates a rise in the clerical component to 85 per cent. Nonconformist pastors played a dominant part in staffing all Dissenting educational institutions, from academies and private boarding schools down to the most unpretentious reading and writing schools. All the same, the Anglican presence was still pervasive. Parish primary schools often remained in the hands of a local curate or even of the vicar of the parish, although parish clerks now figure quite frequently as teachers in these establishments. Indeed, it was becoming very much more common by the early eighteenth century for incumbents to employ lay assistants at £15 or £20 per annum to do most of the active teaching in parish schools. Where incumbents were unwilling or unable to make provision, parishioners quite often took the initiative themselves, hired a teacher and raised a subscription to support him: thus it was at Castle Carrock in Cumberland, where the bishop in 1703 found 'a few petty scholars taught by one John Green, who has no settled salary'. David Cressy has concluded that, all in all, 'the number of beneficed clergy who kept schools was fewer than might be expected'.

However, the two factors which contributed most to the slow laicisation of the schoolteaching body at large were, firstly, the rapidly rising demand for non-classicists at secondary level and, secondly, the charity-school movement, which recruited almost entirely from non-clerical sources. Most of the new specialised institutions which took boys after they had mastered the three Rs, and almost all the private academies, were staffed by laymen: some of them graduates but many, especially the mathematics masters, music masters and writing masters, non-graduates. Huguenot immigrants were prominent as masters in some areas from the 1680s onwards.

The new endowed schools of the later seventeenth and eighteenth centuries, which combined classical with modern studies, also attracted their fair share of lay career-teachers. A good example is Osgathorpe in Lincolnshire, where Cornelius Smedley, a Derbyshire yeoman's son and a Cambridge graduate, presided from the school's foundation in 1670 until his death in 1715. Guaranteed £40 a year in salary and with a house commodious enough to take in boarders, he evidently felt no pressing need to move on, and certainly no urge to take orders. However, it was the rapid spread of charity schools (not forgetting the multiplicity of small, private primary schools which dotted the towns of England by George II's reign) which most strikingly increased both the lay and the non-graduate proportion of those engaged in schoolteaching. The SPCK's requirements for charity–school masters laid great stress on excellence of character and religious orthodoxy; they stipulated the taking of frequent communion in an Anglican church as a powerful recommendation before appointment and a necessity afterwards; but apart from a sound understanding of 'the grounds and principles of the Christian religion' they required nothing more elevated on the academic side than possession of a good hand, a secure grasp of 'the grounds of arithmetic' (in effect, the first five rules), and what was vaguely described as 'a good genius for teaching'. As Dr James Talbott made clear in his treatise *The Christian School-Master* in 1707, the managers and trustees of charity schools were not looking for university-trained highflyers, with 'skill in the learned languages, poetry and oratory'. Neither were they in the market for unemployed clergymen. In fact, cases are recorded of men in orders being turned down for well-paid, charity-school posts, as at Bath in 1710, because they were considered less likely than laymen to give their full-time attendance.

We know that schoolteaching and tutoring employed a large and steadily growing number of Augustan Englishmen. (And not only men, of course: by 1730 it also provided occupation, at a rough guess, for perhaps 2,000 women, teaching in charity schools, dames' schools and private seminaries for girls.) But it is pertinent to ask, in conclusion, did it constitute a 'profession', in the sense that the Church, the law, medicine or, by our period, the armed forces, so clearly did?

If we equate 'profession' in this context with 'life vocation' the answer has to be an equivocal one. Marchamount Nedham, himself a former schoolmaster, considered it ought to be a full-time vocation, but was not: that those who stayed in it were too often 'idle, insufficient persons who have no hopes elsewhere' and for whom a school was little more than 'a sanctuary', while 'by those which have any merit, [teaching was] designed a step to some church preferment'. Even in the 1660s, when this was written, this was to paint an excessively dismal picture, though Nedham's contemporary, Charles Hoole, fully agreed that many 'judge our calling ... too mean for a scholar to undertake or desire to stick too many years'. It was accepted, then, and continued to be so (however reluctantly in many quarters) that for hundreds of graduate ushers, already in orders, teaching both in public and private schools was a stopgap: it was simply a means of earning bread while waiting, either in deacon's orders for ordination, or after ordination, for the first step up the clerical ladder. No fewer than thirteen ushers came and went at Ipswich School between 1659 and 1691, nearly all Cambridge graduates and either in orders or shortly destined for orders; and only two are known for certain to have gone on to make a career in teaching. Some governors (those of Hull Grammar School, for example) quite happily took on as ushers tyros just down from Oxford or Cambridge with a BA degree, youths designed for the ministry who were not even old enough to take deacon's orders. The headmaster at Lymm was even given authority to recruit a competent older pupil in his school to instruct the younger boys in English, while the trustees of Melton Mowbray employed as their lower-school master in 1665 a youth filling in time before going up to Cambridge.

So far as the grammar schools went, however, the most significant factor stemming from that clerical dominance which persisted throughout the century after the Restoration was the virtual certainty that not less than a third of grammar-school masters themselves, at any one time, would be 'pluralists': and while admitting its economic necessity, Francis Brokesby denounced pluralism in 1701 as fatal to the efficiency as well as the integrity of schoolmastering as a profession. He took it (not altogether justifiably) for granted that anyone who took on both a cure of souls and a school would 'do neither of them well'. The proportion of pluralists for whom teaching was a second-string occupation, undertaken out of sheer necessity to supplement a low clerical stipend, was certainly substantial. The master of Thornton-le-dale in 1743 had the care of no fewer than three small parishes in the vicinity of Scarborough. His was an aggravated case, no doubt; but there were many such men who were clergymen first and teachers second, and who, if they were lucky enough to get better preferment, often gave up their schools. John Lawson's admirable study of the endowed grammar schools of East Yorkshire names a string of East Riding schoolmasters who left even first-class schools such as Hull, Pocklington and Beverley when a really profitable incumbency came their way. On the other hand, it is less often realised that with many other pluralists the circumstances were reversed. Only the fact that they already had an unexacting benefice in the area to help to keep the wolf from the door made it possible for them to contemplate a poorly paid grammar-school post. This was true, for example, of both the long-serving headmasters at Stockport between 1704 and 1791, Joseph Dale, who served until 1752 and held the rectory of Taxall for the last twenty-six years, and William Jackson. Even a very reputable foundation, such as King's School, Canterbury, which had had a succession of lay headmasters in the seventeenth century, was compelled to revert to clerics in 1700; for the salary of £20 per annum restricted by statute from the early sixteenth century right down to 1854, could no longer, even with supplementary fees, attract teachers of quality who did not have livings or curacies to bolster them. The Canterbury chapter, however, had no thought of creating a part-time out of a full-time job: it was not to be the school that suffered from the arrangement. Darlington Grammar School, it is true, managed to keep a lay master, Jonathan Sissons, for the incredible term of sixty-six years (1668–1734), despite the fact that the salary of his post, £20 in 1654, had advanced only to £29 12 11d by 1707. But since Sissons is described in the school records as 'gentleman' it seems likely that he was a man of some private means.

Although Sissons's feat of survival was freakish, marathons of forty years' service or more in one school were by no means unknown in Augustan England, while thirty years was a milestone which possibly 10 per cent of grammar-school masters might be expected to pass. Had they known it, the fact would have brought comfort to the very large number of governing boards and trustees who by the late seventeenth and early eighteenth centuries were manifestly looking for strong evidence of commitment to a career when they appointed to a vacant mastership. Relatively few young clergymen, after all, were drawn into teaching initially by a God-given sense of vocation. With some the motives were, to say the least, mixed. When Peter Collier, curate of Warrington, solicited the interest of Roger Kenyon in 1693 to secure the vacant mastership at Clitheroe (worth £40 a year), he explained his inclination to 'take on a school' on two grounds: his stipend at Warrington was only small; and his parishioners were 'none of the easiest to please', which made him anxious for a good excuse to 'preach seldomer'. Well aware of the problems that were often created by pluralities, divided loyalties and extraneous ambitions, some grammar schools either specified that laymen must hold their posts, as Preston did, or preferred to appoint them when they could. Norwich Grammar School contrived to find two highly successful lay heads in a successful run of three from 1667 until the reign of George I (the odd man out being Samuel Hoadly, who sired the most controversial of all Low Church divines); and doubtless the fact that the school paid its master £50 per annum and gave him a commodious and well-appointed house to live in was not unconnected with its success. Other schools, which did not insist on or openly favour lay teachers, nevertheless refused to allow their masters to continue in office if they accepted a cure of souls. Such was the rule at Bury St Edmunds, Colchester, Abingdon and Hastings by the later Stuart period. Beverley was another school to follow suit, in 1717.

Of wider bearing on the quest for greater professionalism in the grammar schools was the fact that it was becoming by no means a foregone conclusion that the established clerical schoolmaster, presented with a choice of career, would plump for a living. Macclesfield Grammar School had fourteen ushers during the course of the eighteenth century; and of the eleven graduates among them several are known to have moved to masterships of other grammar schools

in the same county, while three were promoted to the headship at
Macclesfield itself. Certainly the able and energetic schoolmaster was
less dependent on private favour for his advancement than was the
divine. Increasingly he came to recognise that if he had discovered
a talent for teaching, it might prove the better financial bet in the
long run, especially if there was no obvious channel of ecclesiastical
patronage at his disposal. One of hundreds who took the gamble
during the fifty years after 1680 was Thomas Spencer who, like his
predecessor, held the curacy of Lymm in Cheshire in plurality with
the headmastership of the town's grammar school. In 1714 he chose
to resign his curate's appointment and to stay on as master alone,
which he did until 1753 to complete forty-seven years of service. At
the time he surrendered the curacy his school salary appears to have
been no more than £25, but it appreciated dramatically later and was
to reach £120 by 1818. Of course, there were clergymen who backed
the wrong horse. One can only sympathise with the affronted usher
who protested to his school trustees at Canterbury in 1721 that having
'drudged full six years at the lower end' [of the school], having 'never
undertaken a cure', and 'consequently . . . not employed myself in
making sermons but . . . conversed chiefly with the classics', he had
still been passed over for the vacant mastership.

The fact remains, however, that with or without a cure, with or
without the financial recompense which was their due, many hundreds
of graduates came out of the universities between 1680 and 1730
prepared to devote their lives to teaching in grammar schools.
Criticism of these schools at this period, whether from contemporaries
or historians, invariably overlooks one thing – the surprisingly large
number of experienced and obviously committed teachers who are
revealed when the records of individual schools are examined and
collated. When Lord Lonsdale hand picked a joint-master for his new
experimental college at Lowther ('for none but gentlemen's sons') in
1698, he chose Thomas Lodge, who credentials rested on his record
as master of three grammar schools, Heversham, Lancaster and
Preston. One of the ablest early-eighteenth-century masters of King's
School, Canterbury, David Jones (1700–13) had previously been an
assistant master at Westminster School and head of Oakham Grammar School. That same Edward Leedes, junior, who figured earlier
in this chapter as a successful master at Ipswich for twenty-five years
after 1712, had previously served a five-year apprenticeship as an
usher at Bury St Edmunds. It is interesting that his final ordination
as a priest was delayed until 1716, and that it produced no diversion
in his future career. Family tradition, in his case, did something to
condition him to the schoolroom: his father was a headmaster in
East Anglia for forty-four years and his brother Samuel master of
Woodbridge School in Suffolk from 1709 to 1727.

Masters often changed schools in order to better themselves. Not
all did so to quite such good effect as the Reverend Henry Bland, who
in 1719 exchanged the mastership of Doncaster Grammar School,
with £50 per annum and '£10 for a good usher', for the headship of

Eton. On the other hand, not many climbed up through such an unorthodox route as Thomas Dyche (later one of the best-known lexicographers and English grammarians of his day) who was promoted to Bow Grammar School in George I's reign after taking posts during the first two decades of the eighteenth century both in a private elementary school in Fetter Lane and as master of the parish school of St Andrew's, Holborn. But however and whenever they moved, these teachers took with them their valuable accumulated experience. And occasionally they took other assets as well, a point well illustrated by the case of John Clarke, an outstandingly good master of Skipton Grammar School. When, as we have seen, Clarke was lured to Beverley in 1736 he persuaded several of his profitable private boarders to migrate with him from the West to the East Riding.

It is arguable, however, that as a measure of the dedication to be found in Augustan grammar schools the loyalty of those who stayed put is at least as significant as the enterprise of those who moved on. For while some trustees were negligent or perfunctory, the majority of grammar-school governors continued to expect a great deal for very little. As Charles Hoole observed in 1660, there was little comfort for many masters in contemplating the bleak contrast between 'what good parts for learning and right qualification in all points of behaviour is required of us' and 'how small our yearly stipend is and how uncertain all our other incomes are': a point emphasised by the specifications in an advertisement for the post of first master of a newly endowed country grammar school near Northallerton in 1681. As well as 'a single man, unmarried and without children', this far from wealthy school expected

> not a man of common parts and conversation but singularly hopeful, a graduate in the university, competent in Greek and Latin, ... learned in divinity, sound in the faith, orthodox in judgement, ... sober, pious, industrious, serious, ... no raw youth, nor one that hath been debauched or was ever known to be drunk or noted for a company keeper.

Having made their appointment, governers or feoffees were not necessarily prepared to live indefinitely with an error of judgement. Some grammar schools stipulated a period of probationary service: Macclesfield, for example, placed a newly appointed usher on probation for three years from 1712 to 1715. A schoolmaster who turned out to be a misfit, idle or a poor disciplinarian or in other ways inadequate could certainly not count on survival; and when John Stevenson was found wanting by the governors of Carlisle Cathedral School in 1710, after six years as master, he was relatively fortunate to leave with a consolation pension of £4 a year. The churchwardens of Frodsham were expressly allowed by the grammar-school statutes to 'throw forth' any master who did not fulfil their conditions of 'good deportment and behaviour, diligence and industry' in his work.

With so few luxury berths to tempt the young pedagogue and not very many that were even tolerably comfortable; with no guarantee of security; and with work that was normally arduous and could be, in the words of one sufferer, 'perplexingly toilsome', it is surprising to learn that one-third of the 559 masters identified by Dr Vincent in large late-seventeenth and eighteenth-century samples held posts in a single school for more than twenty years. There seems to have been so much that militated against commitment to teaching; and yet, as Mr Robson reveals, it was staying-power (or heroism) of that order that was the rule rather than the exception in eighteenth-century Cheshire, and no fewer than five masters in this one county held their positions for forty years or more. In Leicestershire, too, long terms of service in the grammar schools were much commoner in the century after 1660 than they had been before the Civil Wars: the county even boasted a half-centurian – a master at Loughborough school whose marathon began in 1698. When, over seventy years ago, A. F. Leach wrote of the eighteenth century as 'the age of long scholastic reigns' he meant it pejoratively, conjuring up an image of grammar schools everywhere fossilising under the rods of incompetent greybeards. That long continuity often meant satisfied customers, on the one hand, and dedicated masters, on the other, did not occur to him.

Outside the grammar schools, and especially among the lay element at lower levels of education it is easier to find evidence which dilutes the impression of a vocational profession: the drifters who notoriously found their way into private schools, the 'broken tradesmen, attornies and lawyers' clerks, fit for nothing else, that set up for schoolmasters', of whom John Urmston complained in 1710, and others of similar kind. On the other hand, many of the mathematics masters and writing masters of the period, despite coming late to teaching from careers as diverse as scrivening, surveying, excise-gauging and almanack-making, remained in schools for the rest of their working lives, or at least for many years. John Bland, who became writing master in Mr Watts's Academy, in Little Tower Street in 1726, had previously been employed for nine years as a government clerk, working in the Customs department. He stayed at Watts's for the next thirteen years. Out of numerous other instances we might pick out that of John Colson, who left the sea to take up schoolmastering in Charles II's reign, kept two successful mathematical boarding schools, at Wapping and the Minories, from 1671 to 1709, and added to his income an examining fee of £10 a year paid by Christ's Hospital.

Before the 1690s few contemporaries can realistically have conceived of the overwhelming majority of teachers who staffed the elementary schools of the country or gave basic instruction elsewhere as constituting, in any sense, a profession. As a body they lacked coherence; as individuals they all too frequently lacked respectable scholarly qualifications, let alone graduate status; above all, they rarely had a full-time commitment to teaching. Admittedly there were a lot of teachers who satisfied either one or other of the last two criteria, and there were some – though the number was relatively small – who satisfied both: ushers who taught 'the petties' in the junior departments of the larger free schools; masters of decayed grammar schools which could only survive at all by dispensing primary instruction to the bulk of their pupils, while offering perhaps a little classical grammar to a handful of their brighter boys. But far more typical of the personnel involved in basic education in the 1680s, especially those involved in educating the children of poor parents, were: curates and vicars who put in an hour or two a day, or a day or two a week, in the village or parish schoolroom; parish clerks to whom the clergy frequently delegated those part-time duties; the 'dames' who scraped their weekly pennies from the village children they taught to read; even, here and there, local tradesmen or shopkeepers, for whom running the local 'common school' was a useful by-employment.

The late 1690s heralded the start of a process which over the next forty years was to inject a much stiffer dose of professionalism into lower education. There were eight endowed non-classical schools at this level by 1740 for every three that had existed in 1698; and this striking expansion of provision had far more important repercussions on both the quality and permanence of recruits to elementary teaching than is generally appreciated. Moreover, while the clergy were maintaining their hold over classical teaching in the grammar schools, lay ushers who were prepared to slog it out in the lower schools of some of the more flourishing of these foundations, specialising in the petties and aspiring no higher, were probably not such rare birds in the first half of the eighteenth century as hitherto. One non-graduate named Ashworth gave such sterling service as usher at Macclesfield from 1712 to 1748 that the governors marked his retirement with a present of £240, a remarkable gesture which underlines once more how far eighteenth-century education presents a picture of light as well as shade. As for old country grammar schools forced to abandon the teaching of Latin through lack of demand, with their established endowments they appear to have found little difficulty in recruiting, as Lutterworth School did, 'a sober and pious and diligent young man' to teach the three Rs to the poor children of the town.

However, the most radical instruments of change at the more elementary teaching levels were the new subscription charity schools. The historian of these schools has argued that 'one of the outstanding contributions of the charity school movement was the introduction of a new type of teacher into elementary instruction'. The claim may seem extravagant; yet in at least three respects it can be powerfully supported. The most important change came about through the firm expectation of the SPCK that all teachers appointed under its auspices should be full-time practitioners. By 1704 it had already become standard practice in the new London schools to require teachers to keep classes throughout an eight-hour working day in summer and a seven-hour day in winter, exclusive of the midday break. Such a regimen made demands on the masters which few but the committed, envisaging a permanent career under the new order, could cheerfully contemplate. In the second place, when filling teaching posts, charity-school governors did try to insist on the possession of a certain basic intellectual equipment appropriate to the level of work and the class of children being catered for. Very few charlatans or incompetents slipped through the net in London and the larger towns; and occasionally men turned up with specialist qualifications, such as the master who taught mensuration, gauging and navigation at Christleton charity school, near Chester, training some boys for the excise service as well as others for the merchant marine.

Thirdly, on a number of occasions between 1703 and 1736 the society toyed with the idea of establishing a training college or 'seminary' to provide vocational training for new appointees. Forced to abandon these schemes on financial grounds, it plumped instead for what has been called a 'pupil-teacher method of recruiting' – in effect, a kind of apprenticeship system, though a less formal one than that which was already in operation in certain parts of the private sector. Already in 1707 James Talbott was urging 'any newly-elected schoolmaster' in the charity-school system 'to consult with several of the present masters of these schools' in order to cultivate the 'genius for teaching'. And he went on to quote in his *Christian School-Master* the SPCK's recent recommendations to established and experienced teachers

> to communicate to every such new-elected master their art, and the divers methods of teaching and governing their scholars, according to the different capacities, tempers and inclinations of the children. And moreover it will be convenient that he should have liberty on certain days to see and hear the present masters teach their scholars, and upon occasion to assist them in teaching . . .

John Sims, master of Cripplegate School, and Henry Dixon, a master at Holborn and later at Bath, were both authors of successful books on English grammar; and they were among the select group of charity-school teachers, of proven success in method, most in demand in the early eighteenth century for taking trainee-assistants. Whether the recommended 'day-release' system was ever widely practised, even in London and Westminster, it is difficult to say.

Charity-school teaching hardly seems, in retrospect, the most satisfying of vocations. Yet once its demands and conventions were firmly defined many hundreds of men accepted them and settled down to regard such schools as an honourable source of regular employment. Soho charity school had four different masters in its first four years (1699–1702). But the fourth, Mr Ford, stayed for ten years and a successor, Mr Shanks, for twenty (1716–36). Among this new breed of teachers were undoubtedly dedicated men who left their mark on the movement. Dixon's *English Instructor* went through sixty-eight editions before 1823, and he himself appears to have spent his entire working life, from William III's reign until well into George II's, in parish schools or charity schools. John Honeycoat, who taught at Clerkenwell for many years in the early eighteenth century, was the very reverse of the plodding pedant: in fact he defied many of the canons of the society, not to mention his bishop, by such extravagances as encouraging his children to act Shakespeare in public. Bernard Mandeville's memorable picture of the charity-school teachers as 'starving wretches of both sexes that, from a natural antipathy to working ... think themselves qualified to become masters and mistresses ... ' might have been reflected here and there in some of the struggling new country schools, which found it very hard to recruit against the wealthier resources of the metropolis and the larger provincial towns. As a generalisation, however, it has been exposed as a cruel caricature perpetrated by one who was avowedly prejudiced against the whole system.

Even the old parish schools which had been in existence well before 1700 were often served in a far less hand-to-mouth way than we might imagine. Rostherne parish in Cheshire appears to have kept the same schoolmaster for some sixty years after 1709; Barthomley was tended by two men throughout the entire period from 1683 to 1770, one officiating for thirty-seven years, the other for forty-nine. However sketchy their initial qualifications, such teachers made professionals of themselves, in a sense, simply through their assiduity and vast experience. In fact, of Rostherne under Thomas Percival it was claimed that the parish school (held, like countless others, inside the church) was 'the greatest school for teaching arithmetic and mathematics in all the county', at least until the church steeple collapsed in 1741! And if parish schoolmasters were not all paragons, doubtless they learned, like Thomas Smith who succeeded Thomas Mitchell at Barthomley school in 1721, to work within their limitations; for as the historian of the parish recorded:

[he] lived at the White Lion Inn, and he was parish clerk and schoolmaster and a very industrious man. When he chanced to get half a glass too much in the morning he frequently trudged up to the steps of the school, and, as soon as he entered his first word was, Boys and Girls you must go home to tell your mothers it's St. Thomas's Day.

There is a contrast here with the early seventeenth century when the great majority of parish schoolmasters at any given time were birds of passage, young men in their early- or mid-twenties. And the new order is clearly connected with the fact that in Cheshire over four-fifths of the new parish schools founded outside the SPCK's orbit in the century after 1699 employed lay teachers in a fairly systematic way.

Schoolteaching fell some way short of being a fully fledged profession by 1730, and it was very far from being a homogeneous one. Although, within a school structure of many new dimensions and in response to a changing social climate, the functions of the Augustan school-master grew more varied and in some areas more specialised, while his material prospects became distinctly brighter, teaching, in general, still required no formal career-orientated training, as did the law or the navy. Young men training as writing masters were often bound in formal apprenticeships and so were a proportion of other special-ists, particularly those with technical or artistic subjects. But, for the most part, how to teach if not what to teach was supposed to be revealed to the new recruit by the Inner Light. Nevertheless school-teaching was much more generally regarded as a true vocation by the beginning of George II's reign than it had been during Charles II's. Under the first Hanoverian it was giving permanent employment for the better part of a working lifetime to a large number of English-men, the careerist wing of the teaching body, which may have been as many as 5,000 strong. In their own ways, these teachers were admirably if often very differently qualified. It would be perverse to regard them as anything but 'professionals'.

PART TWO

'The Great Professions':
the Church, the Law and Medicine

4

The Church

When Joseph Addison wrote in the *Spectator* in March 1711 of 'the three great professions' he referred of course to the Church, the law and medicine, or as he put it, 'Divinity, Law and Physic'. All, in his view, were 'overburdened with practitioners', too many of whom seemed to have little useful function except to 'starve one another'. But of the three it was the most ancient, the Church, that was the most thickly populated. The years between 1560 and 1640 had seen its transformation from an essentially grammar-school-educated into an almost exclusively graduate profession; so that by 1680, twenty years after the re-establishment of the Church of England at the Restoration, the Anglican clergy at all levels were overwhelmingly the products of Oxford and Cambridge. Likewise, as Dr O'Day has explained, the Church had already developed before the troubles of the mid-seventeenth century a 'career structure'; and this was to provide a pattern, albeit an eccentric one, to which the Restoration and Augustan Church to a considerable extent returned and adhered. Furthermore after the ejections of 1662, except for the 400-odd Nonjurors who suffered deprivation in 1689–90, almost all Anglican clerics, from bishops down to perpetual curates (but not assistant or other temporary curates), enjoyed effective security of tenure: in general only moral or political transgressions of the most flagrant kind could bring about their deprivation. Yet although it was the most crowded of the old professions in late Stuart, as in early Stuart England, it suffered in two obvious ways in comparison with the other two. It was not only, because of the prevalence of both private and public lay patronage over appointments, less autonomous than they were; it was also, taken as a whole, much less remunerative.

Yet it may be that modern historians (the present writer among them) in their natural preoccupation with the painful problems and dilemmas of the post-Revolution Church of England, with its internal schisms, its economic malaise, and with such wartime scourges as the high land tax levied for two decades on the tithe income and glebe lands cf the clergy, have obscured a slow but definite increase in the attractiven of the clerical profession over the course of the seventy years after 1660. The process of transition was halting. There were times when progress was snail-like, and other times when to most divines their profession seemed on some counts to be becoming less rather than more desirable. Certainly they experienced nothing under the later Stuarts or in the reign of George I that was to be comparable with the boost imparted to the incomes of several thousand parish incumbents from around 1750 onwards by agricultural changes and rising glebe values. But it is perhaps significant that even in the gruelling years of the wars against France, 1689–97 and 1702–13, when economic and financial pressures on the poorer clergy had scarcely ever been more severe, there were surprisingly few complaints that recruitment to the ministry was falling away. There were on the face of things many counter-attractions and many deterrents. Yet in spite of the sustained expansion of the medical profession and of a large part of the legal profession after 1690; in spite of a remarkable growth in new opportunities for respectable employment between 1689 and 1713, both in the armed forces and in the civil service; and in spite of the frequent lamentations of the clergy over the 'contempt' in which they appeared to be held as an order, especially after the end of press censorship, the supply of new 'subalterns' (as Mr Spectator, tongue in cheek, called them) to the clerical army was fully maintained.

Neither did it fall away in the long years of peace which followed the Treaty of Utrecht. The 1720s are often associated with the onset of an enervating erastianism, with falling congregations and low clerical morale. Inevitably they have invited unfavourable comparison with the 1680s, which stand out as the high point of Anglican endeavour in the entire seventeenth century, and as the period when the clergy's command of public and devotional support was at its height. The contrast can be exaggerated: respect for the country parson (and most Anglican ministers were still country parsons) was not dead by George I's reign, and although there were some large towns – London above all – where apathy and even downright paganism were rife, there were some, like Northampton, which were becoming recognised as 'nurseries of piety' and others where energetic and dedicated ministers could still invoke a remarkable response. On a May morning in 1725, for instance, the chaplain of the Earl of Oxford attended divine service in Thirsk parish church – 'a very large one [with] a gallery at the west end and pewed all over the bottom part' – and found that

> the best part of its inward ornament was the congregation, which was very large and well behaved. This is much owing to the diligent and exemplary conduct of the former curate there, which seems to be well followed by the present minister, whose name is Williamson [and] came hither about two years since . . . This being the first Sunday in the month was a Sacrament day, and there were a good number of communicants.

Accepting, however, that in general the Church of the 1720s had lost both in spirituality and lay esteem since the last years of Charles II and the brief reign of his brother, it is far from clear that this had had any deeply serious repercussions for the Church as a profession. Prospects had always been tough for the man with small fortune and few influential friends who trained for the ministry; and they were probably not significantly tougher by the 1720s than they had been under William III, when the Reverend John Brockbank had encouraged his son, after four years of study at Oxford, to 'consider what is that which God most of all suggests into your mind, whether divinity or physic'. Thomas Brockbank, while taking due note of his father's warning that in the ministry 'places are hard to get at present', nevertheless chose the Church. A sense of vocation, even of 'calling', continued to impel many other young men to make similar choices between 1690 and 1730, and not infrequently to make them in the knowledge that their financial advantage would not be served thereby, unless they were abnormally fortunate. Even ordination itself had become a higher hurdle than ever before. Diocesan bishops – in addition to examining candidates for full orders on their general education and scriptural knowledge (a duty rigorously carried out by the majority of them both in the 1680s and in the generation after the Revolution) – were now expected to inquire carefully into their background and capacity to support themselves. The royal injunctions of February 1694 obliged the bishops to be absolutely satisfied 'that all persons that are to be ordained [priests] have a real title, with sufficient maintenance, according to the 33rd canon'. They can only have added still further to the uncertainties of prospective ordinands, who could not, in any case, present themselves until the age of 24. For Thomas Brockbank, quite without influence at Oxford, they meant a further three years' delay in passing through the final door into his chosen profession; for, as he glumly explained, 'I find myself in a sort of dilemma, out of which it will be difficult to get, for since I have no preferment I cannot be ordained, and because I am not ordained I can have no preferment'. And yet, despite all discouragements, the numbers of young men who entered Oxford and Cambridge in the 1720s with a serious view to preparing themselves for the ministry were not, it seems, appreciably fewer than those who had done so in the 1680s. A sharp decline in general undergraduate entrants to the universities in the intervening years has been clearly demonstrated; a parallel decline in the potential clerical entry has not.* On the contrary, there are already hints well before 1730 of that overcrowding of the profession, producing a deplorable pool of unemployed or spasmodically employed clergy, which was to be one of its banes later in the eighteenth century.

---

* I base the above remarks on my own deductions from general evidence and on the impressions of contemporaries. I cannot pretend to have explored the detailed evidence of Oxford and Cambridge graduations or of ordinations in any systematic way; but the data is there and more serious research on it would be rewarding. It has been shown for example, that in the diocese of Lincoln in the course of only eighteen years (1705–23), 380 deacons and 476 priests were ordained by Bishops Wake and Gibson. Figures for much smaller dioceses, where available, bear comparison. George Hooper ordained 155 for the diaconate and 214 for the priesthood at Bath and Wells in twenty-three years (1704–27), while White Kennett granted ordination to 131 and 119 respectively in only ten years (1718–28) at Peterborough. It may be of some significance that Kennett held 11 ordinations in the last two years of his life compared with 2 in his first eighteen months as bishop, and that Hooper ordained 27 priests in the first three full years of his episcopate, in Anne's reign, but 49 in the three years 1719–21. For the above statistics, see 'Bibliographical Notes', pp. 297–301 below.

Not without some bearing on this were several factors which combined over the latter half of the period to effect a modest improvement in the economic prospects of the profession at its lower levels. The institution of Queen Anne's Bounty in 1704, slow though it was to take effect and fortuitous in operation, did result between 1714 and 1736 in the payment of more than £227,000 in grants to poor benefices, designed to ensure a permanent increase in their income. It is true, this work was to be seriously inhibited afterwards as a result of the Mortmain Act, passed by a malevolently anti-clerical Parliament in the mid-1730s. But meanwhile something concrete had been done to rectify the 'crying scandal' (as one post-Revolution bishop called it) of the failure of both Church and state to tackle the problem of clerical poverty at the Restoration; and it had been done through the medium of Bishop Burnet's cherished scheme, first broached by him to Queen Mary in the 1690s – 'a proper fund for providing better subsistence to the poor clergy; we having among us some hundreds of cures that have not of certain provision twenty pounds a year, and some thousands that have not fifty'. He was certainly not alone in judging some systematic remedy for this lamentable state of affairs to be crucial to raising the standards of the profession: for, as he frankly wrote in 1704, 'where the encouragement is so small, what can it be expected clergymen should be?'

Alongside the direct benefits of the relief fund were also to be set an almost equally plentiful harvest as a result of private benefactions, stimulated by the energy and policies of the Bounty commissioners: by 1736 £194,000 from this source had been shared among 900 of the lower clergy. The altruism of certain donors may have been questionable; the effects of their charities were not. The 631 private augmentations (none less than £200 in money) noted by John Ecton between 1711 and 1727 – all subsequently reinforced by an additional £10 a year from the governors of the fund – included, for example: Sir Edward Abney's to the chapelry of Willesley, Derbyshire (tithes worth £20 a year); the Duke of Bolton's to the chapelry of Edington, Wiltshire (£40 a year); Lord Parker's £400 to the vicarage of Shirburn, Oxfordshire; Mrs. Jane Strachey's £50 a year in lands to augment the rectory of Elme in Somerset; and Thomas Lewis's munificent gift of two rent-charges of £1,000 each to the vicarage of Radyr and the rectory of Penmarth, Glamorgan. Some of the individual demonstrations of piety and charity were quite remarkable for a supposedly renegade generation. A wealthy widow named Mrs Baron was responsible for raising the value of twenty-four separate livings, most of them in Cheshire and Suffolk; Henry Godolphin, Dean of St Paul's, contributed either solely or with other benefactors to thirty-seven livings; and that indefatigable Bristol philanthropist, Edward Colston, had a hand in the augmentation of no fewer than forty-two.

For the hitherto struggling rank and file there were financial benefits from other sources, too, as well as from royal bounty and private generosity. The remission by Act of Parliament in 1707 and 1708 of payments of first fruits and tenths for all incumbents of £50 a year or less lifted a burden of debt from many hundreds of livings. Two relatively healthy decades for agriculture after 1712 probably helped to boost tithe yields; and, as we shall see, there was even a gradual improvement in the lot of the majority of curates between 1680 and 1730, although in all too many cases it meant little more than the raising of their condition from the desperate to the merely depressed.

It is hard to believe there was no connection between the alleviation of clerical poverty in the second and third decades of the eighteenth century and the capacity of the Church as a profession to maintain and possibly increase its traditional rate of entry in the face of heavy competition: while the fact that the land tax was low for the greater part of the period from 1713 to 1739 can only have improved its economic climate. And whether for these or for other reasons (for instance, a tendency for both lay patrons and the state to pay more attention to the birth, connections and politics of candidates for preferment, especially after 1714, than to their learning or purity of life), a more marked upward shift in the social status of men attracted to the profession may also have occurred in this same period. It has to be kept in perspective. By the end of the seventeenth century it was already true that more young divines came from established clerical families than from any single background; and this seems to have been by a long way the most important factor governing clerical recruitment. Almost a quarter of the Leicestershire parish clergy of the years 1660–1714 were parsons' sons, and it is likely that by the early eighteenth century this proportion was being exceeded in some counties. Dr Pruett's analysis of the social origins of Lincoln's numerous cathedral clergy reveals a notable rise in the representatives of clerical families, from $17\frac{1}{2}$ per cent in 1642 and 22 per cent in 1670 to 42 per cent by 1750. Furthermore, while there was unquestionably a striking change between 1600 and 1730 in the ability of the Church to attract men of gentle birth, and very occasionally of aristocratic houses, into its ministry, it would be quite wrong to think of this as an eleventh-hour revolution. It was no more a peculiarly Hanoverian than it was an exclusively post-Revolution development. If we are looking for landmarks in the infiltration of the profession by the gentry, we are likely to find the major one in 1660 and a secondary one, perhaps, around 1680, the beginning of the Stuart Church's 'golden decade'. For it is interesting that Rosemary O'Day has commented on the period 1590–1630, when the great changeover to graduate recruitment was accomplished, that 'what little evidence there is of the social background of the clergy suggests no significant change other than that of the new social status conferred by education . . . The new men were but the "old" newly reformed.' And yet by the time of the Revolution a striking change had already taken place. A large sample of Anglican divines in the years 1689–90 which has recently been analysed (488 of them in all, comprising 261 displaced Nonjurors and 227 of their successors) includes no fewer than 150 whose fathers are recorded in the Oxford or Cambridge registers as 'gentlemen', at the very least. They outnumber even the 124 sons of the clergy. Even if the sample examined may not provide a wholly representative cross-section of the social structure of the late-seventeenth-century clergy – for poor and badly connected clergy could only rarely afford the luxury of refusing the oaths – the trend it highlights is unmistakable.

Naturally enough it is the upper clergy in Augustan England who display the new social habiliments of the profession most clearly. The upper clergy were the dignitaries of the Church. They formed a privileged pyramid, the apex and middle tier of which were occupied by the holders of all the chief administrative offices other than the diocesan chancellors: the twenty-six bishops, the twenty-four deans of cathedral churches and a tiny handful of deans of collegiate churches, such as Windsor and Westminster, and the sixty archdeacons. Thickly clustered at the foot of the pyramid, separated by dignity rather than by any clear-cut income line from the well-to-do parish ministers, stood the cathedral and collegiate clergy. Gregory King estimated in one of his notebooks that in the early 1690s there were some 400 canons and prebendaries in the Church of England; and in this instance he may not have been too far below the mark. For although the number of prebendal stalls approached 600 (there were 46 of these in York minster alone), 87 of them were annexed to archdeaconries and chancellorships, and a number of others to chairs or headships of colleges at Oxford and Cambridge, while some of the most desirable of the rest were held *in commendam* by church hierarchs – by deans and, very occasionally, even by bishops. The Dean of Carlisle at the beginning of the eighteenth century held a prebend at Durham worth at least twice as much as his deanery, while Samuel Bradford, who succeeded Bishop Nicolson at Carlisle in 1718, was given a Westminster prebend (as White Kennett wrily observed) 'to encourage his going into a remote and cold country'. It is difficult to categorise the cathedral clery and unwise to generalise about them. The value of canonries and prebends varied a great deal from diocese to diocese, and on a smaller scale within dioceses; so did the value of the livings or fellowships with which the holders almost always combined them; and so, too, did the obligations of residence. Of Lincoln's fifty-five prebendaries only four were genuinely resident by 1714, including the Dean and Sub-Dean. Archbishop John Sharp, who died in 1713, bestowed most of the stalls at York as a matter of policy on the hardworking priests of the main urban parishes in the county; for like the bulk of the 'simple prebends' in most other dioceses, those at York required no residence beyond what was necessary to preach a few sermons a year, and Sharp, who was a most conscientious pastor both of his lay and clerical flock, treated them as a legitimate and valuable source of supplementary income for the deserving. Of the whole conglomeration of prebends, canonries, residentiaryships, precentorships and treasurerships, a small proportion could be regarded as negligible; but most were prized, and many understandably coveted. The fifty-odd cathedral dignities in the personal gift of the sovereign yielded by the middle of the eighteenth century from £220 to £450 a year (and at St. Paul's as much as £800 a year); but the bishops, too, had many canonries to bestow which carried not only attractive incomes but the right to free houses in the cathedral close, in itself no mean consideration. In 1660 the prebend of Leighton Buzzard, in the Bishop of Lincoln's gift, was worth an astonishing £632 a year.

If even the prospect of a fat prebend was beginning to entice the scions of some of the very best families by 1700 – and such cases as George Berkeley's, an earl's son who became a prebendary of Westminster from 1687 to 1694 suggest that it was – the rewards and prestige of many bishoprics and deaneries provided them with a still more desirable target. Whatever became the case, however, in mid and late Georgian England, their attitude to such prospects in Augustan England need not be viewed with a uniform cynicism. A few of the divines of high birth who had got to the top of the profession by Queen Anne's reign may have lacked distinction but only one patently lacked vocation. This was Bishop Crewe, scandalously appointed to Oxford by Charles II at the age of 38 and soon afterwards translated to Durham. It is arguable that beyond the lure of high preferment, and the security which attended all preferment, what did most to make 'the profession of divinity' accept- able to the aristocracy and wealthy squirearchy, as well as to the lesser gentry, was the improved standing which the Anglican Church, as an institution, achieved in the eyes of the governing class between the Restoration and the Revolution.

By 1700 there was one bishop, Nathaniel Crewe, who was a lay peer as well as a spiritual lord, a second (Henry Compton) who was the brother of an earl and a third (William Talbot) who was the kinsman of a duke. Even that austere Dissenter Celia Fiennes was impressed by the splendid state kept by Lord Crewe at Durham Castle and at nearby Bishop Auckland in the 1690s. He was 'not only a baron of England but . . . a great prince, as being bishop of the whole principality of Durham, and has a great royalty and authority . . . ; his spiritual [revenue] is 5 or 6000 *l.* and his temporals since his brother's death makes it much more'. In addition to its light sprinkling of aristocratic names the bench of bishops could also boast two baronets by 1708: Sir Jonathan Trelawney, Bishop of Winchester (formerly of Exeter) and Sir William Dawes, newly appointed to Chester. If Compton was a vigorous and enlightened administrator and Talbot an elegant writer and speaker, Dawes was a preacher of high repute, destined for promotion in 1714 to the see of York. Other Augustan bishops appointed in the first two decades of the eighteenth century came of landed gentry stock; although the promotion of men such as William Wake, Adam Ottley, George Hooper and John Wynne is perhaps symptomatic of a general trend for some thirty years after 1689, when, in contrast with the pre-Revolution generation, it was the minor squirearchy and pseudo- gentry rather than the upper ranks of landed society who put their stamp on the episcopate.

To glance down the list of deans between 1690 and 1725 is more revealing. It includes a Granville and later a Montagu at Durham, a Stanhope at Canterbury and a Godolphin at St Paul's. George Verney, Dean of Windsor, was brother to the 11th Lord Willoughby de Broke and succeeded to his title in 1711. Such men had little cause to regret the choice of the Church as a career; certainly not Dr John Montagu, a son of the Earl of Sandwich, who between 1699 and 1728 harvested over £2,500 a year from a multiplicity of preferments. The wealthy country gentry, too, were well represented among the cathedral clergy. Just as one Trelawney became a bishop, so another became a dean. William Grahme, who presided over the chapter successively of Carlisle and Wells (the same Dean of Wells, in fact, whose death in 1712 stirred vain hopes in the breast of Jonathan Swift), was a brother of the first Viscount Preston, the Jacobite, and also of James Grahme of Levens Hall, a Westmorland Member of Parliament for twenty-five years (1702–27). Doubtless it was no more a coincidence that Grahme acquired his first deanery at Carlisle than that Walter Offley was promoted in 1718 from the rectory of Barthomley (in the gift of the Crewes of Crewe Hall) to the deanery of Chester; for John Crewe Offley, a former knight of the shire for Cheshire, had become one of the biggest and wealthiest landowners in the county in 1711. One would hesitate to charge as devout a churchman as the Earl of Nottingham with unworthy nepotism; but it is noticeable that his brother snapped up the deanery of York within a few weeks of his lordship's returning to court favour as Secretary of State in 1702, and also that Henry Finch was the only cleric to hold this deanery between 1617 and 1747 who was not a doctor of divinity.

And yet it is worth stressing that while the advantages of birth and connection appear to have frequently procured clergymen high preferments earlier than was normal in less favoured cases, the appointments themselves (before 1730, at least) could almost always be justified on the grounds either of pastoral energy, preaching ability or academic distinction. George Stanhope could have held his own in any ecclesiastical company; Henry Godolphin had been a notable Provost of Eton before becoming Dean of St Paul's; while Henry Egerton, the Earl of Bridgwater's brother, who became a canon of Christ Church at the age of 27 and Bishop of Hereford in 1724 when he was only 35, had studied civil law as well as divinity and was awarded an Oxford DCL in 1717. By and large, the dunces of great families had to be satisfied with a prosperous country living, and perhaps with a cathedral sinecure thrown in for good measure. Despite the influence of his father and elder brother, Hele Trelawney never rose higher in the Church than to a pair of Cornish rectories. George Fleming, the younger son of Sir Daniel Fleming of Rydal and eventual heir to a baronetcy, was a conscientious plodder at Oxford in the 1690s who failed his first examination for ordination. He did, it is true, eventually become Dean of Carlisle: but he had to wait until he was 60 for the chance.

The reverse side of the coin is just as deserving of attention. Although there is a discernible change in the social structure of the upper clergy between the 1670s and the 1720s, there was still no question at this time of the higher reaches of the profession becoming a closed shop for the well connected. Professor Hirschberg has discovered that 22·6 per cent of all bishops first appointed in the years 1660–88 had fathers who were either 'in trade' or in some lesser occupation – farmers, craftsmen, labourers or 'menials' – and the family status of a further 22½ per cent has defied discovery, not usually a pointer to a very elevated background. For those who reached the bench in the period 1689–1721 the corresponding figures (33·3 per cent and 17·6 per cent) are equally striking, even though the proportion from respectable commercial or manufacturing backgrounds had risen since before the Revolution. So long as men such as Sancroft and Nottingham, Tillotson and Tenison, Sharp and Harley, Wake and even Gibson influenced promotions, outstanding qualities of learning or spirituality would not go entirely unrewarded. Poor men's sons, therefore, could still clamber up the ladder as far as bishoprics, though they normally required a hefty shove at a crucial point of time from some patron whose high regard they had been fortunate enough to attract.

Such was the case with John Potter, the Wakefield draper's son, whose entry into University College, Oxford, in 1688 was as a humble servitor but whose scholarship earned him the favour of Archbishop Tenison and later of the Duke of Marlborough. This, in turn, was the stepping-stone, first to the Regius Chair of Divinity at his university and then, in 1715, to the bishopric of Oxford. Tenison's patronage, too, was invaluable to an even better scholar and a first-class administrator, Edmund Gibson. He had gone up to Queen's College, Oxford, shortly before the Revolution, like not a few of his fellow Cumbrians before and after him, as little more than a menial ('batteler, larder man and poor boy' was how he later described his status there). Becoming Tenison's chaplain and librarian offered him his golden opportunity; and he did not neglect it. From 1723 to 1736, as Bishop of London, he was to become the chief ecclesiastical power in the land. Gibson, in turn, played an important part in encouraging the rise of a more remarkable parvenu, Isaac Maddox. Maddox was the orphaned son of a London stationer, brought up by an aunt, sent to one of the new charity schools to acquire the basics of literacy and numeracy, and from there – after the manner of those institutions – 'put to a respectable trade', in his case as apprentice to a pastry cook. At this point Dissenting connections proved invaluable to a boy of obviously studious disposition. An exhibition from the London Presbyterian fund enabled him to take an arts degree at Edinburgh (1718–21); but after his return to London and his decision to take deacon's orders in the Church of England early in 1723, it was Gibson who sent him up to Oxford to gain the swiftest of BAs 'by incorporation', and Gibson who seems to have been behind almost every step of Maddox's rapid rise to professional prominence in the next thirteen years. Appropriately Maddox received his first bishopric, St Asaph, in the last year of Gibson's reign as 'pope' to Sir Robert Walpole: and the elevation came shortly before his 39th birthday, some fifteen years below the average age at which Anglican divines came to mitres and lawn sleeves in late Stuart and early Georgian England.

Gibson's predecessor at London for over nine years before April 1723 was Dr John Robinson; and that two such men should follow the aristocratic Compton in this important see says much for the social flexibility of the Augustan clerical profession. Robinson's story was every bit as remarkable as Maddox's, whichever of the two contemporary versions of it one cares to accept. Thomas Hearne's account of the man who as Bishop of Bristol (1710–13) helped to negotiate the Utrecht peace settlement was that Robinson had been apprenticed to a trade in County Durham and that without the charity of his master he would never have reached the university. An alternative version (while putting his birthplace, rightly, at Cleasby, on the Yorkshire side of the Durham border, rescuing him from the status of ploughboy rather than apprentice, and making his first patron a country gentleman, Sir William Wyvill, rather than a tradesman) agrees entirely on the humble obscurity of his 'first originals'. At all events, he arrived at Brasenose in the later years of Charles II, a classic case of what historians of a sociological bent would term 'sponsored mobility': certainly Oxford gave him the opportunity that must otherwise have been denied him to develop those innate intellectual gifts which were to enable him to carve out a career for over thirty years as a don and diplomat rather than as pastor and church administrator. Those contemporary prelates who were themselves the sons of clergymen had not so far to climb, but the circumstances of their families were quite often modest and occasionally less than modest. Ben Hoadly's father, though in holy orders, was teaching in a private school at Westerham when his son was born in 1676, and the headmastership of Norwich Grammar School, to which he was appointed in 1700, was the height of his professional and social achievement. Kennett and Trimnell were the sons of country rectors in Kent and Huntingdonshire, while Manningham, from a similar background in Hampshire, gained a free place at Winchester and then a scholarship to New College.

The widely discrepant rewards offered by early-eighteenth-century bishoprics are well known to historians. And they presented problems only too familiar to Augustan churchmen. Canterbury, Durham and Winchester, wrote Guy Miège in 1699, 'yield a plentiful income. Among the rest, some have but a competency, and others are not much better (some worse) than many parsonages.' To the list of those which yielded bountifully by 1730 could have been added London, Ely and York, and with less enthusiasm, Salisbury, although financially none of these sees could seriously challenge the primacy of the top three. Yet at the other end of the scale at least half-a-dozen bishoprics were so miserably endowed that 'promotion' to them had to be grimly suffered as a financial penance in order to establish a claim to greener pastures in times to come. When George Smalridge, only just comfortably established in the deanery of Christ Church, heard from Lord Oxford in 1713 that the queen had earmarked him for Bristol, the most beggarly of all English sees, he found himself 'under terrible apprehensions of a bishopric, the weight of which I have neither abilities of mind nor body, nor purse to sustain'. Early the following year, nevertheless, he bit the bullet; and alas, he did so in vain, for a change of ministry and his own political indiscretions condemned him to remain at Bristol until his death. Oxford was little better than Bristol. William Wake described it in 1699 as 'the bishopric of all England that I should the least desire to fix upon'; and he was not the only able divine to discover, when this prospect loomed on the horizon, that 'I . . . would rather enjoy my privacy and retirement than any preferment that can be given to me'. Not for the first time Wake did choose privacy in place of preferment, and it is probable that even the relatively well-to-do William Talbot would also have declined the bishopric later that same year had he not been allowed to hang on to his deanery of Worcester *in commendam*. Unlike poor Smalridge's, Talbot's reward came this side of Heaven: translation to Salisbury in 1715, and later to the pomp of Durham, with its £4,000 a year in rents, 'besides fines upon renewances which [as Sir John Perceval was told on a visit in 1701] is almost as much more'. With careful land stewardship a bishop could sometimes hope to improve his income, as William Lloyd did in the lowly see of St Asaph and George Hooper at Bath and Wells. But the great expenses involved in holding episcopal office – the inescapable duties of hospitality, the upkeep of rambling, draughty 'palaces', the painful sacrifice of the first fruits, above all the drain of parliamentary attendance when that became an annual obligation after 1688 – were normally too great to allow much latitude for good husbandry. Either pluralism or further promotion, and perhaps both, were the only sure roads to peace of mind for the man with a hopeful family to provide for.

By contrast with that of the poorer bishops, the lot of many cathedral clergy was an enviable one. While in London a prelate such as William Nicolson of Carlisle lived in lodgings for months on end, cadged lifts in friends' coaches and was forced to leave his family behind to make the best they could of the bleak inconveniences of Rose Castle. Whereas the traveller through Augustan England could pick almost at random from a dozen closes up and down the land, and there he would come across abundant evidence of the growing material prosperity and gracious living of deans and resident prebendaries. John Macky found in 1722 that 'the best houses in Winchester are the Dean and Prebends' houses' – this notwithstanding a lot of recent building in the rest of the city too, 'all sashed and adorned after the newest manner'.

> Dr Wickart, late Dean of Winchester, whom you knew chaplain to the earl of Portland at Paris during his embassy after the Peace of Ryswick, hath added a spacious garden to the old one, laid out in grass plots, grottos and evergreens, with a river running through it, which is always open to strangers. And all the prebends have neat gardens to their several houses.

It was the presence in Winchester of the higher clergy, who were 'generally speaking, very rich', which in Defoe's opinion 'add[ed] to the sociableness of the place' no less than the large number of gentry families who lived in the neighbourhood. The deanery of Winchester and the twelve prebends of the cathedral chapter, valued at £600 and £250 each respectively in 1762, were certainly among the desirable prizes of the Church in the early eighteenth century; but they were very far from being the richest of their kind. At Oxford, for example, the deanery of Christ Church was believed to be worth about £800 a year at the time Francis Atterbury moved there from Carlisle in 1711, at least half as much again as the revenue of the bishopric, and the five canonries here, yielding annual incomes of some £400 each, were actually rather more valuable than some of the poorer deaneries, such as Carlisle, Chester and Chichester. Apart from the independent deaneries of Windsor and Westminster, which were at least as profitable as Oxford, and the deanery of St Paul's, which was in a class of its own, Lincoln, Canterbury, Salisbury, Wells and York could all boast deans as affluent as most of the county squirearchy, and rich prebendaries as well. The wealth of the Durham chapter, boosted by coal revenues, was legendary.

The physical evidence of all this could not escape notice. In the fine stone houses on the battlemented crest of the castle hill in Durham 'the clergy [it was observed] . . . live in all the magnificence and splendour imaginable'. In 1692 Dean Comber spent £1,200 refurbishing the twenty-four-room deanery The Dean of Durham alone was credited with an income of £1,500 a year in 1701, and the richest prebend £500, although Lord Oxford's chaplain found it hard to enthuse about any of these dignitaries when in May 1725 he and his employer were denied a sight of the chartulary in the cathedral library because only two of the twelve prebendaries were then in residence, one short of the quorum required for the privilege. The amount of new building there by the clergy, and likewise that at Winchester, was outdone in the great walled close at Salisbury, some of it, as Defoe remarked, 'so considerable . . . , and the place so large that it is (as it is called in general) like another city'. By 1730 the denizens of 'the Closs' were running their own winter assemblies in addition to those sponsored by the city of Salisbury. At Lichfield, on a less grandiose scale, the same architectural transformation and something of the same social segregation was in progress. Celia Fiennes found the elegant houses of the clergy there impressive enough in 1697. But within the next twenty-five years, in spite of many 'pinching' years of war, the work of rebuilding and embellishment in Lichfield close was carried a good deal further. 'The palaces of the bishop and dean, and the prebends' houses in the court on the hill' were described in 1722 as 'all of them almost new' and 'very handsome'. Even in Chichester, where Fiennes could only observe 'three or four good new houses' from the top of the cathedral tower, one of them belonged to the dean.

Extensive as the variations were in the incomes of the dignified clergy – Salisbury, for example, had a wealthier deanery than Winchester but in general poorer prebendaries – it is far safer to generalise about them than about the lower clergy, the overwhelming majority of Augustan England's 'black coats'. We do not even know approximately how many ordained ministers there were at any time in the early eighteenth century. Neither did contemporaries. Between the 1680s and the 1720s estimates of the size of the entire profession varied astonishingly. At one extreme we have Gregory King's 9,500 Anglican priests and 500 Dissenting pastors, a total number tersely dismissed by one of the best-informed of Augustan politicians as 'too few'; at another, there is the 'not 15,000' of John Chamberlayne. Since he was Secretary of Queen Anne's Bounty for nineteen years down to 1723 Chamberlayne's judgement by the early years of George I was by far the more reliable of the two. He knew, for example, that although there were 9,180 parish livings in 1704 still officially subject to clerical taxation, there were also nearly 2,000 benefices too poor to have been considered taxable even at the Restoration. Most of these were curacies or chapelries in the charge of 'perpetual curates'. But how many other curates, stipendiary or temporary, there were across the country, nobody knew with anything approaching certainty. How many were officiating for pluralist vicars and rectors? How many were acting as assistants to overworked resident incumbents? How many were acting as locums for sick or senile parsons, or eking out a precarious living as lecturers, schoolmasters or tutors, or were simply unemployed rovers? A Royal Commission reporting in 1835 found that there were then 5,230 curates in England and Wales. There were fewer a century earlier: that much seems a certainty. But whether the number was strikingly lower we may reasonably doubt. To put the question of numbers in perspective, we need only recall that no less an authority than Edward Stillingfleet, Bishop of Worcester (d. 1699) was persuaded that there were at least twice as many clergymen in England in the late seventeenth century as there were benefices or preferments to accommodate them.

In a memorable passage about the eighteenth-century Church, written in 1934, Norman Sykes likened the lot of most entrants into the clerical profession, certainly of those without 'the advantages of birth and influence', to participants in a game of chance: they were involved, he wrote, in 'a lottery in which the number of blanks was alarmingly high, and the proportion of small prizes still higher'. Both the aptness of the metaphor and the general validity of the impression it conveys are indisputable. On the other hand, there is some danger of forgetting that although the extent of poverty among the parish clergy and the 'poor curates' was indeed alarming, the lower clergy of Augustan England did encompass a substantial clerical bourgeoisie as well as an exceedingly large clerical proletariat.

In 1708 the governors of the Bounty calculated that there were then in England and Wales 4,098 parish livings which yielded their incumbents an income of £80 a year or more. Some of these livings, it is true, were combined in the hands of pluralists. Others, possibly three or four hundred, were held by church dignitaries. At the same time it needs to be borne in mind that £80 a year (leaving aside the parsonage house which, of course, went with it) was more than just the figure considered by the Church's leaders to be large enough to bestow a respectable 'competency' on a divine. It was also regarded in the late seventeenth century in most of the poorer counties in England, and in some of the not-so-poor, like Devon, as an income just large enough to enable a gentleman with manageable obligations to maintain the bare substance and the minimal trappings of gentle status. And £80 marked only the basement line of the clerical middle orders. A majority of the rectories still left in clerical hands yielded appreciably more than that, long before the steep rise in land values which began in the mid-eighteenth century. Even a small minority of vicars rose above the £80 line, and a few well above it. There were 3,845 parishes in 1700 whose livings were 'impropriated': that is to say, they had lay rectors and their cures were served by vicars, most of them with no more than the small tithes to supplement their yield from their glebe lands and the dues paid to them for christenings, marriages and burials. The author of *The New State of England* wrote in the 1690s that by and large 'the condition of vicars is much the same with that of curates, if not worse'. But there were fortunate exceptions, and they were to be found both in towns and in country parishes.

In the provincial towns the patronage exercised by certain corporations, the benign influence of some bishops and chapters, and a tradition of congregational support for incumbents inherited from a Puritan past were the three main factors creating a small élite of favoured vicars. One Mr Mudge, elected in 1732 vicar of St Andrew's, Plymouth, a populous urban parish in the gift of the corporation, could look forward in the estimation of the *Gentleman's Magazine* to 'upwards of £300 p. an.' to reward his labours; though he could also expect to earn every penny of it in this dockyard town, which had grown so rapidly over the previous forty years that, as Macky had noticed soon after the French Wars, 'the [parish] clerks are obliged to be in deacons' orders, in order to assist in baptising, marrying, burying and administering the Sacrament'. The vicar who officiated in Plymouth's other church, 'a fine modern pile' dedicated to Charles the First the Martyr, appeared to the same visitor to be at least as well provided for as his neighbour. Far to the north-east, in the diocese of Durham, the wealthy corporation of Newcastle upon Tyne was expending £900 annually by the mid-1720s on the maintenance of the vicar of St Nicholas's and the curates who served the rest of the town – four of them in 1698 but probably six or seven by 1725. In Yorkshire, at much the same time, the vicarage of Thirsk, a cure of the Archbishop of York, was said on the clerical grapevine to be worth about £180 a year and that of Northallerton, in the patronage of the chapter of Durham, £300. At Rochdale the Archbishop of Canterbury was both patron and impropriator; and Bishop Gastrell noted that with 'a large glebe, and all the houses of two of the best streets in the town belong[ing] to him – 130 houses', the vicar here, too, could probably depend on an income of £300. The vicar of Leeds was still more fortunately circumstanced. His income was supplemented by a voluntary offering of twopence from every communicant in this great, seething parish which had nine chapels of ease in addition to its mother church. The Reverend Timothy Thomas valued the incumbency in 1725 at around £400 a year. Contributions were also crucial at Doncaster, where Thomas found that 'the settled income of the vicarage is but £80 per annum, but by the help of subscriptions and a lecture, commonly amounts to £200, in which I include £10 a year which is paid him for reading prayers and preaching once a month in a chapel near the town'. In rural or semi-rural parishes, on the other hand, vicars' prospects were heavily, and often almost exclusively, dependent on the charity of those who held the great tithes. When exceptional generosity and agricultural prosperity went hand in hand, as they occasionally did, those prospects could be bright. The vicarage of Eye in Herefordshire was valued by repute in 1732 at £200 a year and that of Hellington in Huntingdonshire at half as much again; while even seventy years before, William Beaw (later Bishop of Llandaff) had ensconced himself in the vicarage of Adderbury – in the gift of New College, Oxford – 'happy in my privacy, and as I judged, a competency' on its income of £330. Even if he paid good allowances to the curates in his parish's two dependent chapelries, he was still as comfortably placed as most rectors in the profession.

The country rectory was for many Anglican parsons the height of their ambition. If its rewards were as high as its demands were low, what more could a pastor of average gifts desire as age began to take its toll? Those lucky enough to get a presentation of this kind early in their careers normally sat tight thereafter. Not untypical was John Thomlinson, the eldest son of a Cumberland yeoman or pseudo gentleman, who spent three years after being ordained deacon in 1717 serving as curate to his uncle at Rothbury, but was soon afterwards presented to the rectory of Glenfield, Leicestershire. There he took root, married a country gentleman's daughter and died still in the same incumbency forty years later. By 1730 it seems probable that the bulk of such rectories brought in between £80 and £200 annually. But £300 was not exceptional – even though Thomas Baskerville thought it worthy of special remark in Gloucestershire, when he met the rector of Bourton-on-the-Water in 1682 – and on £200 a year, it is worth noting, the rector of Croft in north Yorkshire, Mr Bell, was able to build himself 'a good new brick parsonage house' in the early 1720s. The Earl of Oxford's chaplain, with a keen eye for such matters, noticed that there was 'a great deal of lately improved ground on both sides' of the road between Denton and Croft village: so it may well be that Bell had profited accordingly.

There were lean kine, inevitably, even among country rectors. In the county of Essex, outside the town of Colchester seven-eighths of all the rectories continued to be charged to first-fruits and tenths from the later years of Queen Anne, as having a 'clear yearly value' of more than £50. But thirty-two Essex rectories, almost all of them in rural parishes, were discharged; and although official figures produced for the Bounty office revealed that the vast majority of the poorer brethren in possession of them could depend on between £40 and £50 a year, the rector of Hareleigh was reduced to £30 and the rectors of Braxted and Birch Parva to a pittance of £2½. In fact, most counties had their black spots. It was no surprise to the new Bishop of Carlisle to find the rectories of Beaumont and Kirk Andrews in 1703 united and held in plurality by one of the masters at Lowther College; for their combined value was no more than £25 to £30, Beaumont had a church but no rectory, and Kirk Andrews had a rude clay parsonage house but no church.

The other end of the scale was at least as notable, however, and unquestionably a great deal more noticeable to those anti-clerical Whigs who belaboured the Church in the House of Commons in mid-Walpolean England. Almost every diocese had its share of incumbent rectors whose sleek prosperity belied their professional label as 'inferior clergy'. Celia

Fiennes, travelling the Hemsworth to Rotherham road in 1697, was grateful (good Dissenter though she was) for 'the hospitality of a clergyman, one Mr Ferrer', probably rector of the valuable living of Darfield, 'which was a very genteel man and gave us a civil entertainment and good beds'; 'he has [she noted] a very good house and genteelly fitted, good hall and parlour and the garden very neat'. When Fiennes enthused about a private house it was a near certainty that it was a new one, and the notable building activity of many parish clergy between the 1690s and the 1730s – a lot of the evidence for which still survives – was something on which travellers, well-wishers and critics of the Church all agreed, though historians have tended to ignore it. Timothy Thomas, for instance, observed with approval two new clergymen's houses in the vicinity of Thirsk in 1725, as well as Mr Bell's at Croft. The rectory at Burford, Oxfordshire, was rebuilt by one of Sir Christopher Wren's master masons about 1700, a model of small-scale Augustan sophistication. The better-off vicars were not to be outdone. The Reverend Samuel Dunster, recently appointed vicar of Rochdale, pulled down the old thatched vicarage there in 1725 and built in its stead a carbon copy of the house his father, a London merchant, inhabited in the Savoy; while in the diocese of Oxford, Chalgrove parsonage, erected in 1702 with a seven-bay facade, cocked a snook, albeit an elegant one, at war, taxation and all their attendant problems. Ironically Bishop Nicolson found gentleman rectors, like the incumbents of Bowness, Kirkbridge and Castle Carrock, a mixed blessing in the north-west. They preferred to live in their family houses and were inclined to let their parsonages fall down – and, in the case of Hall of Kirkbridge, his church too: 'I never yet', wrote the bishop, 'saw a church and a chancel, out of Scotland, in so scandalous and nasty a condition'. In Cumberland it was mostly worthy curates, as at Wetheral and Cumwhitton, who were undertaking new building in Anne's reign, with grants from the dean and chapter. But in most counties it was the rectors who naturally did most to satisfy the wish of every good bishop that his clergy should, wherever possible, provide well not only for themselves but for their successors. Bishop Gastrell, for one, was gratified to find early in his regime after 1714 that among the Cheshire rectors occupying 'good new houses' were those of Christleton, Waverton and Barthomley, none of whom could count on more than £140 – £150 a year.

Those were not princely livings by rectorial standards in Augustan England. Over the country as a whole a sizeable cohort of rectors (many of them with aristocratic patrons, like the Earl of Carlisle at Morpeth) mustered incomes of from £300 to £400, while in exceptional cases the returns could be much higher still. The richest livings, generally speaking, were to be found either in London and its environs or in some of the great sprawling parishes of Lancashire and the north-east. It took fifteen years to persuade William Wake to forsake the lucrative rectory of St James's, Westminster, for a bishopric; and in the end it was only the offer of Lincoln that lured him away. The recory of Lambeth was thought to be worth 'three or four hundred pounds per annum' to George Hooper, when, on promotion to the bench, he unwillingly disgorged it in 1704 – Edmund Gibson being the lucky recipient; but Henry Sacheverell's yearly harvest from St Andrew's, Holborn, was generally put at nearer £700. Two London rectories, Bow and St Anne's, Soho, were lucrative enough to be later annexed to poor bishoprics to be held *in commendam;* and so, a little further afield, were the vicarages of Twickenham and Greenwich. Populous country or semi-urban parishes in the neighbourhood of the capital, whose farmers never lacked a ready market or the incentive to improve, often yielded appreciably more by the 1720s and 1730s than they had done thirty or forty years before. Among them was the large parish of Barking in Essex, where Defoe observed 'by the improvement of lands taken in out of the Thames and out of the river [Roding] which runs by the town, the tithes, as the townsmen assure me, are worth above £600 per annum'. Even if there were three chapelries to be served out of the income, it was still an enviable harvest. London was unique, too, in the plentiful opportunities it offered to the able preacher to add a second string to his bow. Francis Atterbury's first appointment there was to the afternoon lectureship at St Bride's, Fleet Street, and he continued to hold it after becoming minister of Bridewell Hospital, one of many lucrative chaplaincies in the capital. A few years earlier, in 1688, Wake had been made 'Preacher to the Society of Gray's Inn', a post which brought him a stipend of £200 a year on top of the income of his rectory.

In the north, Sedgefield in Durham had long enjoyed the reputation of being the richest cure of souls in England. Defoe, in his travels to Scotland, had heard the figure of £1,200 a year mentioned with bated breath in this connection, 'besides the small tithes, which maintain a curate, or might do so'. But this, he was told, was but one of the thirteen livings in the same county in the bishop's gift valued at over £500. It is clear that, among them, Houghton-le-Spring was at least as valuable as Sedgefield and probably more so. The grass was scarcely less green in Lancashire, where Fiennes perceived that 'most of the parishes are a great tract of land and very large, and also as beneficial, for all over Lancasterhire the revenues of the parsonages are considerable, 2 and 300£, 500 and 800£ apiece'. Apart from Liverpool, two of the most coveted prizes in Lancashire were the rectories of Prestwich and Winwick (near Warrington), both of them being said at times to guarantee incomes of £800. Between gross and net income, however, there could be a big difference, and rumour frequently ran well ahead of fact. In the case of Winwick there was no exaggeration; with its glebe lands leased out at high rents and renewal fines alone calculated at £1,000 in the 1720s, it was every bit as valuable as it was reputed to be. But William Asheton, as rector of Prestwich from 1685–1731, reckoned his income at nearer £400 than £800, although having inherited the advowson from his father he was able eventually to make a further £100 a year for ten years from its sale in 1710, as well as pocketing a down payment of £1,000 from the purchaser, Thomas Watson Wentworth. When Edward Finch, one of Lord Nottingham's clerical kinsmen, was presented to the rectory of Wigan in February 1707 some estimates put his annual expectations on that account as high as £600; but Bishop Nicolson's careful inquiries about the living at this time elicited from the Archbishop of Canterbury a 'clear' income figure of only half that sum. The far-flung parishes of Lancashire (Rochdale, for instance, was forty-six miles in circumference) usually contained many chapelries: 4 or 5 was common, Manchester had 9, Blackburn 7 and Whalley, technically, 16, although some in that parish were unserved. Each, therefore, had its clutch of curates, among them men so inadequately or precariously maintained from settled revenues that a conscientious rector might feel some obligation to contribute to their provision. Thus William Asheton supplied the entire salary of the curate of Oldham and made generous supplementations to the other two chapelries in Prestwich parish. And when Bishop Francis Gastrell inquired, seven or eight years after William Nicolson, into the value of Wigan he concluded, significantly, that is was 'above £300 p.an. clear, *all curates paid'* (my italics).

All the same, the prosperity of many of these north-country parish ministers was plain for anyone to see. Even the rectors of the new urban parishes of St Peter's, Liverpool (1704) and St Anne's, Manchester (1712) were guaranteed at least £100 a year from either pew rents or an assessment on houses and clearly received a good deal more in practice. Pound for pound, moreover, the northern clergyman was a good deal better off than his southern counterpart because he could live so much more cheaply. Robert Wake, coming into the rectory of Buxted, in Chichester diocese, in 1720 and finding it 'with the hop gardens, . . . worth *communibus annis* at least £300 per year, with a most excellent house, garden, stables and fishponds' thought his condition paradisal; and he felt he could well afford to pay the curate of Buxted's associated chapelry of Uckfield as much as £40 in stipend. But, as the Earl of Thanet (who held advowsons both in the south-east and the north-west) had reminded Archbishop Sharp at the turn of the century, 'a man that has no exception to so cold a remote country' as Westmorland could take a living there of rather more than £200 a year, furnish from his income two chapels of ease, 'which are fit to have £50 a year out of it', and still expect to 'live as plentifully there . . . as one worth 400 pounds a year' in Kent. By the same token the rector of Stockport, enjoying an annual income of more than £500 in the period 1714–24 had no cause, on financial grounds at least, to feel envious of the holders of the richest parish livings in London.

About the size of the clerical middle class in Augustan England, even in very round figures, it is impossible to be dogmatic. So many questions about church history between the Restoration and the early nineteenth century will only be conclusively answerable when many more individual dioceses or counties have been investigated in depth, and into this category fall most of the statistical aspects of the development of the clergy as a profession. But there is enough evidence to suggest that not far from a quarter of the 'inferior clergy' were able to achieve a comfortable prosperity on a par with that enjoyed by the solidly successful of every other major profession of late Stuart and early Hanoverian England; and it is clear that they even had a very few highly privileged representatives in the professional luxury class. Looking at the group as a whole, as men who had achieved professional success in worldly, if not necessarily in spiritual, terms, a small proportion can be distinguished as private chaplains, employed in the households of bishops or lay peers or by a handful of the very wealthiest gentry. Rather more, as we have seen, were successful schoolmasters, either first and foremost or purely and simply. But the overwhelming majority were parish clergymen, varying from those in modestly easy circumstances to the patently well-to-do.

Private patronage contributed most to their good fortune as a group. Government patronage was certainly a powerful influence, too, for of more than 1,050 livings, including chapelries, in the Lord Chancellor's gift many were valuable. At the same time the Church of England hierarchy itself did retain some control over preferment and promotion, as we have seen, through the many advowsons in the hands of bishops and chapters: one year with another, around a quarter of all pastoral appointments were internally made. On the evidence of such dioceses as Durham, York, Chester and Canterbury, the succulence of the fruits which could be distributed by the bishops should not be underestimated. Of course, no bishop ever had half enough parochial (or, for that matter, prebendal) preferment at his direct disposal to enable him to satisfy the just claims of the able or deserving, and some were exceptionally handicapped in this respect. Shortly after taking possession of Carlisle in 1702 William Nicolson reported to his metropolitan that 'The best living in the diocese of Carlisle (and in the bishop's gift) is the vicarage of Torpenhow, worth about £140 per an. It's now enjoyed by (my brother-in-law) Mr Nevinson, who is about 40 years old. The rectory of Calbeck is the next in value . . . the rest are not worth naming to your grace.' George Hooper, who made a particular point at Bath and Wells (1704–27) of rewarding worthy men within his own diocese wherever he could, was rather better equipped to do so than Nicolson. But according to one of his parsons, Thomas Coney, Hooper was always acutely conscious of how insufficient his patronage was for, in his own words, 'a numerous, an indigent and a deserving clergy'. On the other hand, for much of this period, and certainly in the years between 1689 and Lord Chancellor Cowper's resignation in 1718, holders of the Great Seal frequently took advice from diocesans before making their recommendations; and, in addition, a strong-minded bishop could use the power of institution, at least in a negative way, to influence lay nominations. If he had the happy gift of securing the confidence, or enjoying the friendship, of many of the leading private patrons in his diocese, as John Sharp did at York from 1691 to 1713, such influence could be turned into more positive and constructive channels.

The influence of the universities, too, had important professional implications. In the first three decades of the eighteenth century many Oxford and Cambridge colleges appear to have embarked on a systematic spending spree, picking up the patronage of livings where and when they could in order to be able to place their Fellows advantageously and ensure a steady turnover in the senior common rooms. St John's College, Cambridge, acquired no fewer than thirty-eight advowsons between 1690 and 1736. Lincoln was well behind in the Oxford queue, but invested £1,735 in the years 1726–35 in the livings of Great Leighs, Winterborne Abbas and Winterborne Steepleton. It is little wonder that college fellowships were eagerly sought after by young scholars who had no family influence and little opportunity to catch the eye of a private patron. For these were by far their best hope of achieving a reasonable professional return on an investment that, without a scholarship, rarely amounted to less than £30–£35 a year for five or six years and could be as high by the reigns of Anne and George I as £80–£100 a year.

One other factor determining the brightness of many a parish minister's prospects, a factor of unquestionable importance in the eighteenth century, was pluralism. Apart from the two or three thousand clergy who could subsist without difficulty on the proceeds of a single benefice, hundreds more managed, sooner or later, to haul themselves up to social respectability and some degree of material comfort by securing two neighbouring livings of average value (£40–£60 a year each) and holding them in plurality. Gregory King calculated at Michaelmas 1695 that there were then about 200 'double-beneficed clergymen of £120 per annum' or more who should pay at the £5 rate for the poll taxes; and most of his estimates were conservative. Those whose combined livings brought them in between £80 and £120 must have been much more numerous. Only pluralists can have brought the proportion of Leicestershire incumbents enjoying incomes of £100 a year or more to 45 per cent by 1714. It was often said by the Church's apologists, and with some justification, that pluralism at parish level existed more to alleviate poverty than to create morally unjustifiable prosperity. This applied not only to much double beneficing but to less publicised forms of pluralism, such as the combining of a small living or the curacy of a chapelry with 'keeping school', or with an appointment to one of those readerships or endowed lectureships which (even in an 'age of reason') were still surprisingly numerous in early-eighteenth-century English towns. Nevertheless, the fact that generations of reforming ecclesiastics, from Whitgift to Gibson, could find no effective substitute for the right of priests to hold (under dispensation) more than one cure of souls simultaneously, did leave the door open for hardened accumulators. And there were too many of these for the health of the profession at large. Henry Pigot, rector of Brindle in Lancashire, was in this company neither an unduly scandalous nor a venial offender. But his case illustrates well enough how even the unequal rewards that were available were often still more unequally shared out. Pigot had acquired the rectory in his early twenties, had added to it the vicarage of Rochdale in his thirties, and held them both until the day of his death in 1722 at the age of 94. Their combined value was certified in 1707 at about £350. That Pigot was also chaplain to the Earl of Derby proved too much even for one of his friends, who wryly described him as 'a doubly qualified Peter, both for souls and fishes, and a complacent associate to the gentry and to all learned persons'. In the circumstances, it is not surprising to find that late in life Pigot joined the numerous band of clerical builders of the early eighteenth century, 're-edifying' Brindle rectory with 'a fair, stone building'.

For perhaps two-thirds of the Anglican clergy who were drawers of blanks or meagre prizes in the lottery of the profession, for the shabbily genteel, the straitened, the depressed and the submerged, there was no dramatic change of fortune between 1680 and 1730. Every diocese abounded in hard-luck stories, some of which improved in the telling as they were recounted to solicitous bishops and sympathetic visitors but most of which had, and still have, a depressing ring of authenticity. Paradoxically, while leading churchmen from Sancroft to Wake and Gibson deplored the 'irreligion' of their countrymen, the established Church remained everywhere under steady pressure during this period to lay on services and to provide a regular, if not a permanent, professional presence in numerous long-neglected corners of the land. It was anxious to respond, and likewise to maintain existing services even in places where the number who attended them was paltry. But whether adequate means would be forthcoming was a wholly different matter. All too regularly the unlucky clergymen who were thrust into these bleak situations for want of anywhere better to go were prey to heedless landlords, greedy lay rectors and harassed farmers; or, alternatively, they were at the mercy of subscriptions, the frequent inadequacy of which was often as much the result of the poverty of their parishioners as of their meanness.

The variations on such themes were legion and the handful of illustrations which follow do them imperfect justice. 'Churches are very thin in this part of the world', observed a traveller up the Great North Road beyond Alnwick in the 1720s; and yet when he did come across one, at the village of Belford, he found that the vicar, Mr Hunter, was only 'allowed £10 per annum by Mr James Montagu for serving the cure'. At Todmorden, a perpetual curacy, it was the encroachments of Dissent which almost led to disaster in the early eighteenth century. At the end of Queen Anne's reign the curate, John Welsh, found himself struggling to survive on about £16 a year, some £14 of which came from contributions and £1 from a charity sermon preached annually in Rochdale church. 'The chapelry formerly paid £20 p.an., and thought themselves bound by custom so to do', churchwarden Wroe had explained some years earlier, 'but now they are most Quakers'. The owner of Todmorden Hall had long paid £3 8s towards the incumbent's maintenance, but a new Quaker landlord refused to pay a farthing and 'the curate [it was said] is not able to sue him'. As a result of these tribulations Welsh's predecessor was starved out, the cure lay untended for seven months in 1713 and Welsh himself, though ensured £20 a year in subscriptions as the result of a public meeting in 1719, must have been very hard pressed until he became a most deserving recipient of the Bounty in 1724. Close-fisted Dissenters (a third of his entire tally of parishioners in 1703) were a grievous problem too to the 'honest poor curate' of Grisedale in Cumberland. The parish of Harwood in Yorkshire acquired a new incumbent in the early 1700s who was promised that 'the vicar's ancient pension' would be more than doubled out of the patron's own pocket to bring his income up to a comfortable £55–£60 a year. But not liking the cut of the parson's jib, the squire in question, John Boulter, flatly refused to honour his pledge. Lastly, we may note Bishop Gastrell's comments on the maintenance of just two of his Cheshire curates, those serving the chapels parochial of Pott and Poynton, near Macclesfield The curate of the former had a certified income of £22 10s 0d, but only 10 guineas of this was endowed or came from guaranteed fees: the other £12, the bishop tersely noted, was due 'from the inhabitants for seats [pew rent], but *part not paid'*. As for Poynton, he 'certified there is no certain endowment. There was anciently a pension paid out of the tithes, but this hath for a long time been unjustly detained. Voluntary contributions, £11, viz. £4 by Mr Warren [lord of Poynton manor], £1 by Mr Downes, £6 by subscription of the inhabitants.' It would have been of some comfort to conscientious bishops if they could have been assured that no cases of dire clerical poverty could be blamed directly on the shortcomings of the Church's own hierarchy. It is clear that such cases were diminishing between 1680 and 1730, but even at the end of the period the record was not without blemish. To find the dean and chapter of Durham paying a pittance of 20 marks (under £14) to a curate to tend St Bede's, Jarrow, while drawing a small fortune, believed to be £1,800, from the impropriated tithes was singularly shocking even to a clergyman like Timothy Thomas, well acquainted with the vagaries of his profession.

Of course, the problems of the lower clergy were not always created by the negligence, selfishness or malice of others. Many of them were simply the result of historical accidents or the legacy of the Church's own chaotic and outmoded parish structure. Some of the poorest livings in England were to be found not in remote, economically backward rural outposts of Anglicanism but in the small, huddled parishes of old city or town centres, especially in places where once-flourishing urban economies had fallen on hard times. Lincoln's 13 parishes were so meagre in value that by 1728 only 5 had an incumbent and only 2, St Peter's by the Arches and St Mary Magdalen, could offer a clear yearly return of over £30. In Worcester only 2 livings, those of St Peter and St Martin, were worth more than £50 a year; the other 7 were valued at pitiful amounts ranging from the rectory of St Nicholas's £23 13s 7d to that of St Alban (£3 6s 8d). Exeter (with its 18 parishes), Colchester, Ipswich, Bristol, York and Norwich (the last two with over 50 parishes between them) were similarly afflicted. Even the widespread pluralities which were an absolute necessity in such circumstances left many of these city incumbents still far short of an adequate maintenance, and small prebends or lectureships were quite frequently used to bail out the worthiest of them. On the other hand, there were dozens of single-parish towns whose vicars were also disadvantaged, as John Ecton explained:

Whoever will compare the greatness of the duty in many market towns . . . with the smallness of the recompense for performing such duty, will from the great disproportion of one to the other be easily convinced of the necessity of establishing some method for the better support of persons officiating in such cures.

There was, as we have seen, no sudden, spectacular turn of the tide for the clerical proletariat of Augustan England. And yet, almost as a backwash from the great 'Church in danger' waves in Parliament and the country in the years 1698–1715, some economic benefits did accrue to them. They did not eliminate that truly desperate poverty at this level, the sheer volume of which in the 1690s and early 1700s had led to the consideration of parliamentary remedies and, above all, to the genesis of Queen Anne's Bounty. But they did reduce it; and by the first half of the 1730s, the later years of the Walpole–Gibson church alliance, this reduction had become significant.

The Bounty Act itself was, in the long run, the most decisive step forward; and some of its effects, especially in stimulating private philanthropy, have already been referred to. Many hundreds of vicars and perpetual curates who in the first fifteen to twenty years of the eighteenth century had lived perilously close to the bone were ensured, at worst, a status midway between penury and decent respectability. The curate of Upper Darwen in Blackburn deanery, who in 1704 received only £24 18s 4d for serving the two charges of Darwen and Tockholes (an area twenty-one miles in circumference and containing 175 families) must have been well pleased to find his income almost doubled by 1720, thanks to the augmentation of Darwen. There was a further large group of parish clergymen, however, who benefited more emphatically, partly because their circumstances were less appalling to begin with, partly because their livings enjoyed private benefactions which outstripped their public augmentations. The parochial chapelry of Billinge, for example, was yielding its curate annually just over £34 at the time the Bounty Act was passed, £15 of which was income from an estate bequeathed in 1672. In 1705 the £10 per annum left in the same bequest to support the chapel school was made over by the feoffees to the curate. Twelve years later James Seabrooke, a Liverpool merchant, largely financed the reconstruction of the chapel building itself, and in 1720 a £200 contribution from Thomas Bankes of Wigan towards the improvement of the endowment entitled Billinge to an augmentation from the governors of the Bounty. Thereafter its curate, with some £65 a year guaranteed, could count himself among the more fortunate of his kind. One benefit which the Bounty brought to the clerical rank and file is easy to overlook. As well as succouring existing incumbents it created between 1715 and 1736 numerous new opportunities of settled employment for clergymen hitherto without any. Chapelries like Heywood or Horwich in Lancashire, and Wetenhall or Woodhead in Cheshire, which for lack of adequate endowment had never in living memory been more than occasionally tended by neighbouring vicars or curates, became full-time cures: if necessarily near the bottom of the clerical scale and lacking the full legal security of a freehold incumbency, they were now at least viable. Woodhead, indeed, was one of several brands plucked from Nonconformist burning, for its chapel had been occupied by a Presbyterian congregation for about twenty-seven years before the augmentation in 1723.

Queen Anne's Bounty, however, profited only poor incumbents and perpetual curates (those holding cures of souls without institution). Except for the new cures it effectively created, it had no direct relevance to the most intractable problem of an overcrowded profession, that of its stipendiary curates. Some aspects of this problem were to remain irremediable not only up to 1730 but long afterwards. The uncertainties bred both by insecurity of tenure and by the fact that neither merit nor conscientious service in a curacy could guarantee promotion to a living in the fullness of time, were perhaps the deepest of all the flaws in the career structure of this most haphazard of professions. When Thomas Brockbank, a man without influence, was seeking to establish himself in his native north-west after taking priest's orders in 1697, he served his second assistant curacy, at Garstang, assiduously from 1699 to 1701, only to be told by the vicar that he 'found Garstang not sufficient to maintain two, and therefore all on a sudden told him they must part . . . ' At least, however, his former employer promised him 'he would serve him in seeking out a place'; and eventually such a place was found at Sefton, near Liverpool, where the curate received '£35 per annum, besides weddings, churchings, burials and funeral sermons', not to mention an unfurnished room in the parsonage house. Both then and subsequently Brockbank, in fact, was a good deal luckier than many of his kind. Sometimes such men lurched from one temporary post to another for an intolerable span before finding a patron willing to hoist them on to the lowly but firmer ground of a free chapelry or perpetual curacy. A minority of them never put down roots, even ill-nourished ones.

While the uncertainty and insecurity of the stipendiary curates' lot defied solution, however, the economic aspects of their position were not quite so resistant to reforming endeavour. It was Queen Anne's last brief Parliament – what the Tories later nostalgically recalled as the last 'Church of England Parliament' of their lifetimes – which finally addressed itself to them, by putting on the statute book a measure much urged of late in Convocation. The 1714 Act stipulated a £20 minimum annual stipend for an assistant curate and a maximum of £50. Achieving the absolute maximum, persuading either lay rectors or clerical employers to pay as much as £50 to officiating curates, was a pipe dream so long as several thousand vicars and rectors themselves earned less. Yet it has been shown that by the time of the Gibson regime in the 1720s and 1730s a very high proportion of the curates in the diocese of London were in fact being paid between £30 and £45 per annum. Canterbury diocese under Wake (1715–37) had an equally impressive record: of the 66 stipendiary curates whose salaries were noted in the Act Books for that period, only 3 were receiving as little as £20–£29 a year, and at the other end of the scale 29 enjoyed £40 and 6 were allowed the maximum of £50. Even in the affluent south so many such payments would have caused astonishment in the later seventeenth century.

The deep concern of successive primates from Sancroft to Wake, and most of all that of Archbishop Thomas Tenison, was at least as instrumental as praliamentary intervention in improving the economic position of the stipendiary curate between 1680 and 1730. There were, of course, variations from diocese to diocese, depending on the vigilance of individual bishops, and likewise within each diocese, depending on the circumstances of individual vicars and rectors. Even by the end of the eighteenth century almost three-quarters of the assistant curates in the diocese of Worcester (where there were more than 150 of them) were still struggling along on stipends of between £30 and £50 – incomes which, by then, were worth a good deal less in real terms than earlier in the century. Not every Augustan bishop had managed to extract a formal promise from pluralists of the kind Wake institutionalised at Lincoln from 1705 to 1715, where before being licensed to his second benefice the applicant was pledged *in verbo sacerdotis* to 'have under me in the benefice where I do not reside a preacher lawfully allowed, that is able sufficiently to teach and instruct the people; and [to] allow him such a competent salary as the bishop of Lincoln for the time being shall direct and appoint'. White Kennett at Peterborough, however, was among those who would not ordain for the priesthood in his own diocese until he had satisfied himself of the salary as well as the nature of the intended curacy in each applicant's title.

Most diocesans probably shared Gibson's view that the pluralist, providing for the parish in which he was not resident, should be expected to pay a higher stipend than 'he who was absent on account of ill health or other necessary avocations, and had nothing but a single benefice to maintain him and his family'. But it had to be recognised that even pluralists were far from equal in their capacity to pay, and that this was not simply a question of what their benefices were worth. Archbishop Sharp was as anxious as any of his colleagues in the early eighteenth century to see his Yorkshire curates properly provided for. But whereas he was not disposed to regard the vicar of Huddersfield as particularly generous in paying £40 a year to his curate at Kirkheaton, where the rectory was worth four times as much, what could he say to Timothy Ellisonne when he applied in 1702 to retain the living of Haworth for a year or two after accepting 'two small places in Lancashire near to Liverpool' and proposed to put in an assistant there with an allowance of £20 a year? After all, Haworth was worth only £31 all told to him, and in addition Ellisonne could justly plead 'straightened and mean circumstances . . . the greatness of my family, six hopeful children' and debts incurred both through inordinate family sickness and 'disposing of three of my children'. In the event, Sharp solved this particular dilemma by insisting that Ellisonne should resign Haworth and leave it open to a straightforward incumbency.

A brief glance at how the Anglican clergy 'disposed' of their sons provides an illuminating final commentary on the profession, and in particular on the often bizarre inequalities of opportunity and achievement which it presented in this period of slow and uphill change. Firmly implanted by 1700 was the tradition that one son, at the very least, should follow his father into the cloth if there was the slightest possibility of maintaining him through the inevitable five, six or seven years at university. In 1698 Timothy Ellisonne had calculated that, despite his then meagre £30 a year as vicar of Colley, he could, with some financial help (a small prebend from his archbishop would have met the case nicely!), contrive to give a classical education to his two youngest sons, exploit their natural aptitude for scholarship and 'do what I can to fit them for the university'. A hard-up but well-read parson could naturally tutor his sons at home, and many did so. On the other hand, there was much to be said for getting them in, even at the price of a small fee, to one of the many grammar schools which offered closed scholarships or exhibitions to Oxford or Cambridge colleges, as Manchester Grammar School did to Brasenose or Sedbergh to St John's, Cambridge. The better-off might send their boys to Westminster School, that great forcing-house of the Augustan clergy, whose scholars dominated Christ Church, Oxford. That they should pick up some award was, in most cases, more than desirable. For although the Church remained the most accessible of the traditional professions for families of modest means and plebeian origins, very few prospective ministers could hope to scrape a training on less than £30 a year by the early eighteenth century. It cost a fairly poor Lancashire parson £278 to keep his son at Oxford from his matriculation in 1687 until 1695, shortly before he was ordained deacon. In the view of the author of a comprehensive guide to careers, written in 1747, the sacrifices so many parents were still prepared to make in such a cause were ill-judged. The soundest advice he could give to them was

> to bring up as few of their children as they can to this profession . . . The education is expensive, and many accidents may fall out to make the fruit miscarry, even when it is almost brought to maturity. The friends you depended upon for a living at first setting out may die, circumstances of families may alter, and the young gentleman, after he has passed many years in the expectation of a comfortable living, may be obliged to put up with some paltry curacy.

It was shrewd worldly counsel; but worldly considerations, as we have seen, were by no means the only ones, even in the prosaic climate of the early Hanoverian Church, which counted or prevailed.

Although the overwhelming bulk of clergymen's sons who went to the universities did so to train for the Church, a few, mostly from relatively privileged backgrounds, chose instead careers in 'physic'. One of the most successful London physicians of the 1720s and 1730s was the son of Bishop Manningham of Chichester. To train as a doctor, or alternatively to read for a qualification in the civil law, were both paths that had been trodden with some regularity for a long time past. But thanks to the rapid expansion and development of other professions than their own in the half-century following 1680, by the early 1700s Augustan divines found several attractive options open to them in 'breeding up' their sons which two or three generations earlier would scarcely have been contemplated at all, or at least would have been available only to a very small number of the higher clergy. The armed services claimed a few recruits from this quarter during the long wars against Louis XIV, occasionally with remarkably successful results, as the case of General Cornelius Wood illustrates. But the chief flow was into the common law and into the lesser branches of medicine.

In the second half of the seventeenth century, as in the first half, the inns of court were dominated (so far as their students were concerned) by young men from the landed and leisured classes. They, together with the sons of men already established in legal practice, regularly accounted for as much as 90 per cent of all admissions; and as time went by, as we shall see (below, pp. 145-6), reading systematically for the bar became an increasingly daunting prospect for any but the affluent or the generously patronised to contemplate. In these circumstances, none the less, 21 clergymen's sons entered the Middle Temple in the 1670s, 29 in the 1680s, 38 in the 1690s, 33 (out of a smaller intake) in the first decade of the eighteenth century, 49 (out of an even smaller one) between 1710 and 1719, and 51 in the 1720s. There was a trend here too pronounced to be accidental. The Inner Temple may well have seen a similar rise (it is worth remembering that one of the leading Tory lawyers of this period, Nathan Wright, who became Lord Keeper of the Great Seal from 1700 to 1705, was a Leicestershire county rector's son who began his legal training at the Inner Temple in 1677). At Lincoln's Inn, whose student numbers in the early eighteenth century were much less than half those of the Middle Temple, the number of clergymen's sons (nearly all eldest sons) called to the bar rose from a mere two in the decade 1695-1704 to six (1705-14), then to eight (1715-24) and finally to ten – or 8 per cent of all the inn's bar calls – in the years 1725-34. An equally popular route into the legal profession by this time, and one that was in general much easier on the clerical pocket, was through the articling of boys as clerks to attorneys or solicitors. An analysis of the apprenticeships served by the sons of Anglican ministers between 1710 and 1720 reveals that exactly one-tenth of the 610 whose names are recorded in the Stamp Office registers for those years entered lawyers' offices. By doing so, they were by this time certain of preserving or achieving gentle status, provided they became at the end of five or six years properly qualified (see below, pp. 154-5); but the outlay in which their parents were involved varied considerably. Most provincial five-year clerkships cost between £60 and £100 down. But in 1715 Samuel Jacques, the son of an Uxbridge parson, was articled to Henry Cranmer of Furnival Inn for only £32 5s, and for a seven-year period into the bargain; whereas Francis Brooke, rector of Kersey in Suffolk, could afford to place his son George in the office of Thomas Mayhew of Colchester, a prominent attorney of the common pleas, and pay £150 for the privilege.

Premiums as high as £60, or even £50, though representing only a fraction of the normal cost of a bar training were, of course, beyond the horizons of thousands of needy parish priests, without the timely assistance of a well-breeched relative. Even clergymen who were by no means destitute could frequently afford only to train one son for a respectable, gentlemanly profession. For the rest, some loss of status was often inevitable. Francis Cruso of Mautby, Norfolk, whose rectory was valued at over £50 a year and may have yielded much more, apprenticed one of his sons to a Norwich worsted weaver in 1712. The Reverend William Morris's rectory of Lyme in Cheshire was worth 'about £80 p.an . . . and a good house'; yet in April 1712 he was reduced to sending his son Richard to Manchester to learn barber surgery for seven years under William Lawrinson, and only £14 changed hands with his indentures.

Provincial barber surgeons were by now no more than clinging by their finger tips to the fringe of a medical profession which had been changing more rapidly than most since the Restoration. And as the status of true surgeons steadily rose, along with that of apothecaries, it was not surprising that through apprenticeships to these practitioners the age-old links between the Church and medicine were reforged in a new way. Except for the minor gentleman's country house or town residence, and perhaps the yeoman's farm, the parsonage supplied more recruits to medicine at this level by the early eighteenth century than any other source. No fewer than 112 of the 610 sons of the clergy apprenticed in the second decade took up either the apothecary's profession (for it had now ceased to be a 'trade' in the estimation of its own members) or surgery. It was not always certain what status they would ultimately achieve by doing so. The range of premiums asked and paid was even wider here than in the case of lawyers' clerks and reflects the extraordinary divergencies of opportunity which the middle and lower reaches of medicine might offer. The number of clergymen who could contemplate the £150 to £250 premiums demanded by a handful of the London surgeon princes by the early years of George I was infinitesimal; but a few are to be found paying the highest provincial prices in the early eighteenth century. In 1719, for example, Francis Bere, the well-to-do vicar of Prescot (£140 a year) disgorged £105 to a surgeon in distant Guildford, Thomas Howard. Howard must have had an outstanding local reputation, for the sum involved was over £30 more than the still considerable outlay incurred by the Reverend Thankful Frewen, rector of Northyam, Sussex, in placing his son Thomas a few months later with a successful surgeon in Sevenoaks. Yet right at the other end of the scale, poor parsons such as the Londoner, John Altham, or the Sussex curate William Griffith, were able to find members of the London Barber Surgeons' Company, practising minor surgery, willing to take in their boys for as little as £15–£20. The £40–£50 which was the fairly standard price of an apothecary's training in London or an important provincial town by Queen Anne's reign was understandably attractive to many clerical parents; although here, too, there were many who could only wait in the hope of snapping up a bargain – such as Thomas Miller of Hale in Cumberland (who paid only £30 to John Pennington of Kendal) – while others were able to afford the very best on offer. Henry Pugh, an Essex country parson, for instance, entrusted his son's 'education' to Richard Chapman, a prominent member of the London Society of Apothecaries, for £105.

However, the most significant fact about the way the ministers of the Church of England were providing for their sons by the early eighteenth century is the very high proportion of boys who were apprenticed to minor tradesmen, small manufacturers, shopkeepers and craftsmen of all kinds. Roughly two-thirds of the entire 1710–20 cohort of apprentices from clerical families were disposed of in these – on the face of it – generally unprepossessing backwaters. Between £8 and £20 was as much as most of their fathers (or their widowed mothers) could scrape together. Some could not even manage to find that. In 1711–12 Joseph Clemencon, one of the none-too-hopeful progeny of a Worcestershire cleric, and Ephraim Holmes, the son of a deceased Cumberland parson, were indentured to London barbers for £3 4s 6d and £5 respectively. It must have been small comfort to them and their like, yet entirely appropriate to the lottery of their fathers' profession, that while they could only go 'into trade' with a whimper, some of their privileged cousins do so with a resounding bang. The articles of Thomas Hayley, the Dean of Chichester's son apprenticed to a prominent City of London merchant in May 1715, cost his father £350.

And yet very many of the thousands who had been bound in recent decades to respectable small tradesmen and shopkeepers ought at least to find solace, the author of *The London Tradesman* reminded them in the 1740s, in the thought that their clerical fathers had *not* been able to scrape up enough to send them to Oxford or Cambridge. For if, after so much hard-earned money had been invested in his education, the student of divinity found himself, as too large a proportion still did,

obliged to live upon a very trifling curacy, there is nothing more despicable; a journeyman tailor can afford to live and bring up his family with more decency than such a man; yet he has all the notions of a gentleman, and there is not a more helpless thing in nature than a poor clergyman. How strange is the pride of parents, then [the writer went on to reflect] that beggar themselves to thrust some unthinking creature into the ministry, where he must live contemptible and mean all his life-time! Whereas, if they had laid out one tenth of the money to make him a tailor, or some less ingenious handicraft, he might have earned a much more comfortable living. Though he might have remained a fool, yet a foolish tailor is not half so contemptible as a poor, ignorant and perhaps profligate parson.

Any picture of the ministry as a profession in Augustan England, and more specifically of its thronged lower ranks, would be incomplete without taking in the Dissenting ministers – legally tolerated under licence after May 1689 and numbering well over a thousand by the early years of the eighteenth century. At the time of the Toleration Act a surprisingly high proportion of the pastors who had been preaching openly since James II's Declaration of Indulgence in 1687 were still many of the same men who had been ejected from former Anglican livings in the years 1660–2; although relatively few of them (unless they had private means) seem to have found it very easy, even with rising congregations in the early years of the new era, to live comfortably on the allowances made to them by their 'hearers'. The contrast is pointed by the cases of Peter and William Aspinwall. Peter, ministering to the Presbyterian congregation in the busy Lancashire linen-manufacturing town of Warrington, had '3 or 400 hearers, require[d] no salary, [had] an estate . . .' But the unfortunate William, preaching in the north of the same county in the small community of Cockerham, was only 'reported to have £14 a year and £4 more from Sir John Thomson'; with some further supplementation after 1690 from London he was to battle on in the same place until he died in 1702. He did not lack companions in distress. William Becket, the Congregational minister at Stroud in Gloucestershire after the Revolution, 'finding the people poor and not able to raise above £10 a year', had to remove to Winchcombe and Cleeve in order to make ends meet, while Giles Firmin eked out his sparse subscription income from the Presbyterians of Ridgewell in Essex by practising physic.

Among the Presbyterian and Independent (or Congregationalist) clergy cases of extreme hardship became uncommon after the 1690s, though much less exceptional among the Baptists whose flocks were usually of a lower social standing. The various central relief funds set up after the institution of the Toleration – the Common (later the Presbyterian) Fund in 1690, the Congregational Board Fund in 1695, the Particular Baptist Fund in 1717 – played an important part in creating the conditions in which a subprofession could firmly establish itself. Clearly they did something to iron out the more extreme differences in the circumstances of the clergy, as well as providing invaluable financial support for candidates for the ministry unable to pay for their own higher education. So far as stipends went, however, in a system of remuneration which relied so heavily on the local subscription, the nature of each congregation, both its size and its wealth, was bound to remain the basic determining factor. A congregation of as many as 500 in a town such as Deptford could yield its minister a 'competency' (as it was then considered) of £40 a year; at Reading, Thomas Juice was more happily placed with '4 or 500 hearers, the people considerably rich'; whereas at Halstead, Essex, 'a large but poor people . . . 600 hearers' could muster only £30 for their pastor, Abel Collier.

The Congregational Board regarded an income of £50 per annum as unusually high for an Independent minister, although both they and the managers of the Presbyterian Fund often paid small additional allowances to clergy whose subscriptions hovered around the £40 mark and correspondingly more to the less fortunate. There had emerged by the early eighteenth century, however, a small élite of Nonconformist divines, perhaps thirty to forty at most, who earned from £80 to £150 a year and lived like gentlemen, irrespective of private means. Generally this was because they ministered to either very large or singularly affluent congregations, notably in the City or the west end of London or in great provincial strongholds of Dissent like Bristol, Manchester, Sheffield, or Norwich. In Norwich, for example, the well-to-do pillars of one meeting house, even in the early 1690s, were not only able to pay the Reverend Martin Finch £130 a year but to provide the same allowance for an assistant. The wealthiest congregation in England outside London by the time of Queen Anne's death was probably the 1,600 or so gathered round the Presbyterian preacher Michael Pope in Bristol. Isaac Noble's 'Account of the City of Bristol', written to John Shute Barrington the year before Pope's death in 1718, stated that some of the latter's hearers had 'been sheriffs of the city and put themselves out of the council because of the Occasional [Conformity] Act; several others persons of condition, divers very rich, many more very substantial, few poor. The whole congreg[ation] computed worth near £400,000'. Noble himself, a Congregational minister in the same city, had less than a third of Pope's number of hearers, but he was plentifully supplied by a congregation whose combined property he reckoned at £100,000 in value.

Like the Anglican Church, moreover, the Nonconformist ministry contained many pluralists. By far the commonest kinds of pluralism were hardly sources of great profit: the teaching in Dissenting schools, for instance, that was carried on as a by-occupation by a large number of ministers – perhaps as many as 200 – and the lectureships in small meetings supplied by neighbouring pastors, as that at Godalming was held by Roger Foster, Independent minister at Guildford. Yet there were a few select corners of the vineyard where the pickings were more promising. A handful of learned and active men were clearly able to prosper by combining a flourishing ministry of the gospel with the mastership of a Dissenting academy. Timothy Jollie, for example, had over 1,100 hearers in his Presbyterian congregation in Sheffield in 1715 (though it is true there was an assistant, John Wadsworth, to share the maintenance), while a few miles away, at Attercliffe, he ran one of the most successful academies in the country. Yet other fine scholars, such as Dr Caleb Rotherham, minister of Kendal, gave courses of subscription lectures on a variety of secular as well as religious subjects (in Rotherham's case as far afield as Manchester): potentially a lucrative activity. And not least, in an older tradition, there were several qualified doctors of medicine with Continental degrees – among them, Adam Holland at Macclesfield, Jonathan Harle at Alnwick and John Gyles at Shrewsbury – who combined spiritual and bodily healing to advantage.

In the years from 1715 to 1717 John Evans, minister of the Hand Alley Presbyterian meeting in London and secretary to the Committee of Three Denominations, compiled a list of Presbyterian, Independent and Baptist congregations in England and Wales along with their ministers; and from 1718 to 1729 he kept the list as up to date as he could, adding new names whenever he had news that a preacher had died or moved elsewhere and that his successor had been appointed. In these fourteen years he noted the names of 1,451 Dissenting ministers, 318 of whom are known to have died in the course of that time – a great many of them between 1727 and 1729, which were years of exceptionally high mortality in most parts of England. This would appear to suggest that by the early years of George I the Nonconformist clergy made up a professional group between 1,100 and 1,200 strong. In fact, their numbers were higher than that; for Evans ignored foreign Protestant ministers almost entirely and those of the lesser sects totally; in the case of an appreciable number of Baptist congregations – five in Sussex, for example, and four in Pembrokeshire and Glamorgan – he failed to find out the name of the presiding minister; and there were in any event ninety-nine congregations in England alone, most of them probably with a resident pastor, which were not known to him but which were picked up in another Dissenting census (exactly contemporary with his own) undertaken by Daniel Neal, minister to London's Aldersgate Street Congregationalist meeting.

By the mid-1720s the 1,400-odd men who made up this important adjunct of the 'great profession' of divinity were in some respects more rationally organised professionally than their Anglican brethren. Although only a small minority had degrees, from Scottish or Dutch universities, the vocational training which most of the third generation of Dissenting preachers had received was normally very thorough. It was acquired at one or other of the twenty to thirty academies which flourished at various times in the early eighteenth century: and among them were institutions such as Manchester, Moorfields, Hoxton, Tewkesbury, Exeter and Warrington academies which became theological seminaries of distinction. Once trained, moreover, the newly ordained Dissenting clergyman could generally be fairly certain that 'promotions' from a small to a larger and proportionately more profitable charge and to a respected place in local society would come sooner or later to reward preaching flair, scholarship and energy. There were, by now, probably relatively few Presbyterian or Independent ministers of ability who could not reckon in the course of time to achieve 'a competent supply'. None of them would become rich men; but none of them had hoped or expected to.

5

The Lawyers and Society in Augustan England

Despite the brightening economic prospects of many Anglican clergy during the early decades of the eighteenth century and some improvement in the social standing of all but the irredeemably 'poor and ignorant' of the black-coated army, even the most euphoric prelate in 1730 would scarcely have claimed any primacy for his order. Among the three learned professions the law still stood supreme: indeed its primacy was now far more secure in many respects than it had been fifty years earlier. The past half-century had been one of great importance for the common lawyers. Legal historians, and even more constitutional and political historians, have naturally found more excitement in the activities of the bench and the bar during the late Elizabethan and early Stuart periods. But it remains a puzzle why the broad advance of an entire profession in the late seventeenth and early eighteenth centuries, and the social changes which both conditioned and accompanied it, have attracted such very limited attention. The statute of 1731, insisting that all legal proceedings from then on should be in English instead of in law-French and law-Latin, fittingly crowned two generations of notable development. It was not, after all, so very long before that Roger North had written in all seriousness, in the course of a manual packed with shrewd advice for the contemporary law student, 'I should absolutely interdict reading Littleton [still the first priority text for every serious entrant to the inns of court], etc, in any other than French . . . For really the law is scarce expressible properly in English, and, when it is done, it must be Francoise, or very uncouth'; while in 1660 the lawyers had easily reversed a recent attempt by republican reformers to impose the vernacular on the courts. Yet there was not even much token opposition, and certainly no uproar or palpable sense of professional outrage, when Parliament struck its blow for rationality and intelligibility early in George II's reign. Four or five decades, in the course of which the common lawyers had become much less like a private sect practising its peculiar mystic rites and more and more closely integrated into the fabric of society at large, had, it would seem, already prepared the way.

In this process of integration the extensive lower reaches of the profession played a very full part, as we shall see. But it was the rise in public esteem of the judiciary and the bar which brought about the most basic change in the relations between lawyers and society in Augustan England. By George I's reign the *cachet* conveyed by the judge's and barrister's status had become irreproachable, reinforced as it was by its most recent and valuable acquisition, relative imperviousness to the favour of kings or political parties. Lawyers during the first half of the eighteenth century rightly began to value themselves on their 'independence', and others began to envy their profession this quality. By the beginning of George III's reign Lord Hardwicke was to take it for granted that the law was 'the most independent' as well as 'I think, the most advantageous profession in England', echoing the assurance with which Lord Chesterfield had written some years earlier: 'I wish that my godson may take a liking to the Law, for that is the truly independent profession.'

This 'independence' was a legacy of Augustan England. It was not a word that any objective observer would have applied to the common lawyers in the late 1670s or in the 1680s. Then their public image had been far from good. Their vulnerability to the political influence of the monarchy and the Stuart Court had become increasingly debilitating in the course of the constitutional conflicts of 1673–87. Wealthy clients complained of their chicanery (the second Earl of Clarendon could recall 'only two honest lawyers' among his acquaintance) and Members of Parliament of their mercenary conduct in the House of Commons, where Roger North was disturbed to find in 1685 that the saying 'the lawyer speaks for his fee' had become a commonplace. As for the opinion of common people, this was tersely summed up in the words of the old woman who stood watching the workmen strenuously rebuilding the Middle Temple after the devastating fire of 1678: 'I see ill weeds will grow fast!'

Whether the professional morality of the common lawyers had in fact declined further since the time of James I, when it had been widely deplored and the king himself had expressed the view that barristers were spawned in corruption, was of less account than whether the public thought it had. When all who plied or served the courts – not only pleaders – stood to profit financially from the abuses of a system which had a built-in capacity for procrastination, the temptation to play that system must have been hard to resist. Dishonesty did not have to be flagrant. The tricks of the trade were many; and there were wily foxes, to most appearances models of probity, who were up to all of them. It was, for example, 'credibly reported' of the great John Maynard, at the time North was learning the ropes of the profession in the 1670s, 'that being the leading counsel in a small-feed cause, [he] would give it up to the judge's mistake, and not contend to set him right, that he might gain credit to mislead him in some other cause in which he was well-feed'. Far more damaging, however, than dubious standards of professional conduct was the political pliancy of too many leading members of the legal hierarchy. By 1687 both the manipulation of the judiciary by the royal brothers and the judges' own conduct in the courts were threatening near-disaster to the whole fraternity. The coarseness and gross partiality of a Scroggs or a Jeffreys, the ignorance of a Wright, even the trimming of a Pemberton, not to mention the unscrupulousness of those aspiring counsel who fawned upon such men in the courts, had gone far within a decade to cast a deep shadow over what good repute the profession had earlier contrived to muster.

That it not merely recovered its standing over the next thirty years, but substantially improved it, was naturally due in part to the Glorious Revolution: in particular, to the fact that the post-Revolution monarchy exhibited a respect for the judiciary which had been all too lacking from Charles II and James II. After 1688 the twelve judges in the three main common law courts ceased to be appointed, by and large, with political ends mainly in view; at the same time they acquired a rock-like permanence in office which for all practical purposes was shakeable only on a change of monarch and which contrasted vividly with the constantly shifting sands of the late 1670s and 1680s. The whole profession rested on stabler foundations thereafter, for judges could still exert enormous influence on the careers of young barristers, encouraging or depressing them in the courts, and it was both unhealthy and publicly damaging for the currying of political favour to be a factor of importance in the professional rat race. The restoration of the common lawyers' self-esteem also owed a great deal to the personal example set to lesser lights in the profession by one great judge and two great Lord Chancellors. The incomparable Sir John Holt brought a rare combination of integrity, humanity and wisdom to the office of Lord Chief Justice of the King's and Queen's Bench from 1689 to 1710, while John Somers and William Cowper, two of the brightest ornaments of the bar in the late seventeenth century, held the Great Seal between them for sixteen out of twenty-five years after 1693 and brought lustre to their uniquely influential office. The commitment of many common lawyers to politics, through parties, certainly continued long after the 1690s. It may well have influenced the outcome of particular causes in the courts. But politics never again came near to imperilling the general course of justice, as it seemed to many to have done in the 1680s. Neither could those unfortunate appointments to judgeships, or even to the woolsack, which inevitably took place from time to time throughout the eighteenth century endanger the repute of the bar and the bench at large.

One indicator of the common lawyer's enhanced prestige by the early eighteenth century is that the barrister's claim to be ranked as 'esquire' by virtue of his call alone and irrespective of his social origins had finally been established beyond refute. It was a privilege which seems to have been assumed by the majority of ordinary counsellors-at-law since early Stuart times but which was still not wholly secure after the Restoration. In fact it was challenged by the College of Arms as late as 1681 when Sir Henry St George, Clarenceux, insisted in his visitation instructions to the heralds that although barristers of three years' standing in the Westminster courts were

entitled to be considered for arms, neither they nor their seniors at
the bar were to be accredited with any higher rank than 'gentlemen'.
Only a serjeant-at-law, at the peak of his profession, should be
ranked equal 'in quality' with an esquire. The College was an
immensely conservative institution, it is true: but its attitude is a
reminder that in the unfavourable public climate of the 1680s the
common lawyers were still finding it difficult to persuade social
sticklers that five or six years at one of the inns of court, followed
by a call to the bar, warranted the same degree of social recognition
as a university doctorate conferred on a civil lawyer. In the very
different climate of the 1720s there was no longer any question that
this particular battle had been won. Among many other indicators
of a change of climate, perhaps the clearest is the substantial increase
in the salaries paid to judges after 1714 and likewise the ability of
many leading counsel to raise their fees between the 1680s and the
1730s without undue consumer resistance from litigants. The question
of fees and rewards is one that will recur (see below, pp. 121–9,
130–2). But what is especially noteworthy in the present context
about the upward trend of the late seventeenth and early eighteenth
centuries, as compared with pre-Civil War conditions, is that it
coincided with many decades of comparative price stability (there
were exceptions, but they do not materially affect the case); and
also that it took place when the bar was more heavily populated than
it had ever been, and when both the country's population and the land
market were stabler than they had been between 1540 and 1640 – in
short, at a time when 'market pressures' might have been expected to
work against rather than in favour of higher earnings at the bar.

'The law' in Augustan England was a complex as well as a large
profession. Yet in various ways its structure was less amorphous and
correspondingly more rational and functional by 1730 than it had
been in the mid-seventeenth century. The civil lawyers apart (see
below, pp. 147–50), by the early eighteenth century three broad differences of function had created three distinct categories of professional
men: those who either judged or pleaded cases in the courts; those
who practised the forms or 'mechanics' of the law, from the drawing
up of pleas and the preparing of briefs down to a variety of non-
litigious work, such as executing deeds and conveyances; and those
who staffed the law courts in clerical or other capacities. The second
and broadest range of functions – Coke's *officium laborii* of the law –
was mostly discharged by thousands of attorneys and solicitors: officially distinct from each other right to the end of our period (for
example, in the terms of the Lawyers' Act of 1729) but by then
increasingly difficult to disentangle in reality. In 1700 their numbers
were still augmented by far smaller groups with narrow specialisms,
such as notaries (deeds and contracts) and scriveners (conveyances).
But by 1730 such groups were shrinking rapidly.

The major compartments of the law were not entirely distinct,
even by 1730; and between their subcompartments, too, lines could

be blurred. The 'Justices of the Great Sessions in Wales', for example, though judges on one of the four Welsh circuits, practised at the bar in the Westminster courts in term time and quite often contrived to work an English circuit as well. Civic or manorial courts were regularly presided over by both barristers and attorneys. A small proportion of men called to the bar never practised there, but either from necessity or choice set up as attorneys. The latter, and the solicitors, year by year gobbled up ever more of the work traditionally earmarked for notaries and scriveners; and a variety of posts in the multi-ramified bureaucracy of the law courts were coveted as lucrative 'perks' by men in private practice. Nevertheless the structural changes that had taken place since Charles II's reign were highly important. There were still barristers in the post-Restoration generation who were carrying out Lord Keeper Littleton's instructions to the serjeants in 1640 to 'take not briefs of ordinary solicitors, but draw the briefs yourselves'; even so distinguished a doyen of the bar as Sir John Maynard was doing this regularly on the western circuit as late as the 1680s. But, by then, such all-rounders were a dying breed. For the leading barristers the sheer weight of cases handled made a division of functions inescapable. Indolence or self-importance influenced the rest. The inexorable consequence was that 'the business, of course, falls to the attorneys'. Even in his *Autobiography*, one of the last works of his long retirement, Roger North's advice to 'young gentlemen' aspiring to good practice as counsel was not to be too proud to 'set pen to paper and be mechanics and operators in the law as well as students and pleaders'. But by the time he died in 1734 those qualified barristers who, like 'lawyer Starkie' at Preston, were prepared to take such advice were few indeed; and it seems that it was far less palatable to students at the inns of court than it had been during the years of North's own training in the 1670s. Increasingly, they were prepared to accept the insecurity of the bar as a worthwhile price to pay for membership of an élite professional body.

As for the 'mechanics' themselves, they drew closer together as their independence of the barristers became increasingly secure. Solicitors had originated essentially as assistants to attorneys, soliciting business from prospective litigants and picking up such lesser scraps of business as the attorneys could not be bothered to deal with. By the early seventeenth century, though still the target of dismissive comments (to a contemptuous William Hudson solicitors were 'a new sort of people' as late as 1635), they had begun to carve out a special place for themselves in the prerogative courts and in the courts of equity, where their role was broadly comparable with that of attorneys in the common law courts. The years 1640 to 1660, however, had been disturbing ones for them. Both Star Chamber and the Court of Requests were abolished and the Restoration rapidly confirmed that they had gone for good. *The Compleat Solicitor* of 1668 suggests that an important reappraisal of functions was taking place, since it was 'not enough for the solicitor to be, as it were, the loader to the attorney, or the intelligencer to the client'. He had to pick up all the non-litigious business that was going and try to make his position in Chancery cases, often so lucrative, as near to a monopoly as possible; but he also had to make certain that his toe-hold in the courts of King's Bench, Common Please and Exchequer, the simple right 'to be able to breviate his client's cause', was made into a firm foothold.

Although the immediate consequence of these readjustments was to widen the gap between attorneys and solicitors, by the 1680s bridges between them were going up, and over the next fifty years there was a growing amount of two-way traffic across them. Attacks concentrated on attorneys and solicitors without discrimination, like those in the House of Commons in 1672, in 1700–1 and again in the late 1720s, had the predictable effect of drawing them together and breaking down the remaining prejudices of the former against the latter. Sworn attorneys had always claimed, and been accorded by the courts, the right to practise as solicitors if they so wished. The Act of 1729 made it easier than ever for them to do so by abolishing the extra fees payable in such cases. The solicitors, for their part, established their right to practise as attorneys provided they had five years' standing in the courts. Although they were not given by statute unrestricted access to the attorney's preserves in the common law courts until 1750, the barriers between the two groups had effectively disappeared well before then. So when the attorneys of London and the adjacent counties formed their first professional organisation in or shortly before 1739, it was natural for them to admit their solicitor brethren on perfectly equal terms.

In terms of worldly success, an attorney 'in great practice', even outside London, could comfortably vie with the majority of barristers by 1700. Likewise, among the fortunate holders of plum offices in the legal bureaucracy were a handful, like the Prothonotary of the Common Pleas, who ranked with the wealthiest professional men in the country. However, in trying to understand more of the development and growth of the Augustan legal profession, to examine its recruitment and training, and above all to appreciate its rewards it makes sense to consider the lawyers within the functional framework we have just sketched out, even though lack of space prohibits any detailed consideration of the legal bureaucracy. And if some of the remarks which follow have to be hedged round by reservations, that is because there is an astonishing amount of evidence, on the judges and barristers, in particular, that historians of this period have still to explore.

The legal profession by the early decades of the eighteenth century had an upper crust which was not only less thin than that of a century before but, overall, far richer. Its constituents were the judges, the law officers and high legal officials of the Crown, on the one hand; and, on the other, the leading practitioners in the courts of common law and Chancery. Some of the latter combined private pleading with official appointments (Welsh judgeships, for example, or King's Counselships); many combined both with parliamentary politics; but a very significant minority were able to prosper handsomely in a purely private capacity as serjeants- or counsellors-at-law, their careers often embroidered with Recorderships or other local dignities, but remaining essentially 'independent' professional men.

There were three major political appointments in the Crown's control which invariably assured their holders a lofty place in the common law élite: the offices of Lord Chancellor (or Keeper of the Great Seal), Attorney-General and Solicitor-General. Their profits ranged from at least £3,000 a year for the most unenterprising Solicitor-General to around £7,000 for the most scrupulous holder of the Great Seal. An office of securer tenure, but comparable prestige and profit, was that of Master of the Rolls, the Lord Chancellor's chief assistant in presiding over the Court of Chancery. Between 1693 and 1738 two men, Sir John Trevor and Sir Joseph Jekyll, held this office for forty-five consecutive years, the former surviving even the disgrace of expulsion from the House of Commons in 1695 for taking bribes as Speaker. The 'twelve men in scarlet', the judges of the common law courts, of whom the senior was the Lord Chief Justice of the King's Bench and the next in the hierarchy the Chief Justice of the Court of Common Pleas, were conclusively rescued after the 1688 Revolution from the precariousness which had beset them in the previous decade. With their value correspondingly enhanced, their offices represented thereafter a more permanent passport to professional and social eminence. Their security was at some risk on the death of a sovereign, as three judges found to their cost in 1714; and the incomes of most of them could not match those of many barristers who practised under them; but their prestige and social standing, underlined by the splendid rituals and gastronomic excesses of their assize progresses, was assured.

Other places of a judicial character in the legal hierarchy which were much coveted were the Masterships in Chancery (twelve in all, of which Master of the Rolls held one):

These Masters [wrote John Chamberlayne in a brief contemporary sketch of the judiciary] do sit at Westminster Hall, with the Lord Chancellor or Keeper, three at a time in term-time, and two at a time out of term, when the Lord Keeper sits to hear causes at his own house. And to these Masters the Lord Keeper does often refer the further hearing of many causes. They have also a public office, where one or more of them do constantly attend to take affidavits.

Their medieval predecessors had been clerics or civil lawyers (or both); but by the late seventeenth century, although a few Masterships still fell to 'civilians' they were increasingly being treated as appropriate prizes for barristers of good and, usually, long standing. Thomas Gery, who held a Mastership in Chancery from 1700 to about 1719 and was knighted by Queen Anne, had been a barrister of the Middle Temple since 1687; and James Medlicott, a Master from 1706 to 1717, had practised with considerable success at the bar for over twenty years before his appointment. Although they carried an official salary of only £100 a year, the Masterships were regarded as exceptionally lucrative. Medlicott sold his for £3,000 early in George I's reign, applying this and the proceeds of eleven years' profits towards the cost of lavishly reconstructing the already fine new house in Somerset which he had built for himself between 1698 and 1700. Indeed, well before the early eighteenth century a brisk trade in these offices was developing. The traffic became a public scandal in 1725 when Lord Chancellor Macclesfield (the former Sir Thomas Parker, LCJ) was impeached for accepting bribes from contenders for vacant Masterships. At his trial it transpired, among other things, that whereas he had taken a 'present' of 1,500 guineas from Thomas Kinaston, a seasoned barrister, when the latter became a Master in 1721, his price for promoting Francis Elde, a young man of 32 with only six years' bar experience, was '5,000 guineas in gold and bank notes'. The Elde transaction throws an extraordinary light on the value attached to these appointments. Its sequel is no less instructive: Macclesfield was disgraced – a victim of Whig faction feuds; but Elde was allowed to enjoy his investment undisturbed for thirty-six years and, what is more, was called to the bench of the Middle Temple after only four years in his office.

The judicial patronage of the Crown by the late seventeenth century also included eight appointments as 'Justices of the Great Sessions' for Wales. Their holders, as we have noted, were part-time judges only: they presided over the king's courts in Wales and Cheshire only on assize, returning to London to ply the common law bar for the rest of the year. They did not share the new immunity enjoyed by judges in the Westminster courts after the Revolution. In fact their posts were generally reshuffled whenever there was a significant change of ministry and it became common, though not universal, for them to be filled by party stalwarts. By 1715 unsuccessful aspirants to such patronage had cause to feel disappointed, for the original small patent fees paid to Welsh judges were heavily supplemented towards the end of Charles II's reign and again at the beginning of George I's. The total salary paid to the Chief Justice of Chester was raised to £530 in 1680 and to £730 in 1715 – extremely high in view of the small amount of work involved. The other seven judges appear to have drawn £250 a year from 1681 to 1715 and £450 from 1715. In addition to those who became Welsh judges, a few of the most successful practising barristers were eligible for appointment as King's Serjeants or as King's (or Queen's) Counsel. The latter prizes represented a notable *coup* for the barristers since the order of KC had been heavily neglected by Charles II. From 1685 to 1714 the recipients hardly ever exceeded six at any one time; but they had increased to eleven by 1736. Apart from the business of the Crown which came their way through assisting the Attorney-General, 'His Majesty's Counsel learned in the law' enjoyed precedence in the courts and, as Roger North pointedly commented on his own promotion in October 1682, were 'let . . . in to advanced fees'. After the Revolution their appointments quickly came to be regarded as another legitimate area of party political patronage and by Anne's reign were almost invariably confined to Members of Parliament.

The alluring prospect of such a prize thus became a powerful additional incentive to the talented and aspiring barrister of Augustan England to embark on a political career. Few were as lucky as Thomas Lutwyche, the son of a former judge of the Court of Common Pleas, who was made a QC immediately after his first election for Appleby in the Tory landslide year of 1710. He profited as much from his party's relative scarcity of top-class legal talent as from his own felicitous progress at the bar since 1697. Even Spencer Cowper, whose brother was made Lord Keeper just before his own arrival in the House of Commons in 1705, had to wait for another ten years before joining the ranks of the King's Counsel: he was then 45 and had been practising for twenty-two years. Although there were those, as we shall see, who had cause to regret it, such waiting-time, for this or any other party perquisite in the legal field, was usually time well spent. During William III's reign alone, twenty-four barrister-MPs picked up either legal posts in the royal gift or appointments as King's Serjeants and King's Counsel. Even if no office accrued at all, the enterprising barrister could always turn his membership of the select club in St Stephen's Chapel to good professional account. The productive contacts he made there usually more than repaid any outlay necessary to get himself elected. The supply of lawyers in the House of Commons had always been plentiful since the late sixteenth century. By the early eighteenth century the demand for seats had become remarkably sustained, with 62 qualified lawyers, including 2 civilians, elected to the short Parliament of 1701–2, 76 sitting in the Parliament of 1715–22, 73 in that of 1722–7, and 74 in the first Parliament of George II's reign. For many such members their seats simply reinforced an existing place among the wealthy bar élite. But, just as frequently, the Westminster ladder materially helped others to reach such a place.

Since the mid-sixteenth century the judiciary, legal office and the bar had together supplied easily the most productive professional channel of upward mobility in English society. In 1684 Henry Philipps published a book entitled *The Grandeur of the Law*, the subtitle of which was self-explanatory: 'An exact collection of the nobility and gentry of this kingdom, whose honours and estates have by some of their ancestors been acquired or considerably augmented by the practice of the Law, or offices and dignities relating thereunto.' It was an awesome compilation. Even the names and achievements of those whose professional origins went back no further than a century furnished a catalogue of impressive substance. During that century lawyers had vied with, and probably surpassed, the wealthy merchants of London as the most voracious group of land buyers in the country outside the ranks of the established gentry. The most celebrated of them in each generation had, in Dr Edward Chamberlayne's words, 'purchased estates fit for lords'. Not least was this so after the Restoration when the tendency for the truly grand rewards in the law to be concentrated 'into a few hands of those which are most renowned' was much less in evidence than when Sir Thomas Wilson had detected it at the end of the sixteenth century. What effects, then, did the development of the profession at its higher levels have on these coveted avenues of advancement in the half-century after 1680?

It is safe to say, in the first place, that in no other profession in late-seventeenth and early-eighteenth-century England did so many men make so much money, or make it so quickly, as in the law. It may have been the case by the second half of Anne's reign that a dozen or so army officers or admirals, perhaps half that number of fashionable physicians, and three bishops could match the incomes of the top lawyers. But the law's combination of spectacular peaks with solid rewards in depth was unique. The custody of the Great Seal might well be thought to have guaranteed access to one of the very highest, if not the highest peak of all; and so it did. It is all the more striking, therefore, as a reflection of the profits of the most successful private practices of the early eighteenth century (especially when they could be combined with the less elevated, but more flexible, law offices) that after 1700 Lord Keepers were not always easy for governments to come by. Admittedly, when they accepted their appointments all holders of the Great Seal, like judges after the Revolution, effectively turned their backs for good on a private career. Yet the compensations were many and enticing. Both the Lord Chancellor and Lord Keeper enjoyed a basic salary of £4,000. A generous pension could be anticipated after retirement or removal; in fact, after the Revolution it was usually promised as a matter of course on appointment, as it was to Lord Cowper in 1705 – in his case an annual £2,000, duly paid after his resignation in 1710. There were also delectable perquisites during tenure. The most important, before the trade in Masterships began in earnest, were the 'New Year's gifts' which realised anything from £1,500 to £3,000 each year until they were discontinued by the scrupulous Cowper in 1706. Few holders of the Great Seal by the late seventeenth century, therefore, had to budget for less than an income of £7,000, even in a modest year: Lord Cowper, even without his New Year's gifts, accumulated over £41,000 in slightly under five years to September 1710. Even so, the dismissal of Lord Chancellor Somers in 1700 had created a most frustrating situation for the Crown, one that was only resolved at the eleventh hour by the somewhat desperate appointment of Serjeant Wright (subsequently Sir Nathan Wright), who was widely considered an unworthy choice. Among the refusers in 1700 were Holt, who declined to leave the King's Bench, and Sir Thomas Trevor, who had become Attorney-General in 1695 after fifteen years at the bar and was considered a far abler lawyer than Wright. Trevor made the same decision ten years later, after Cowper's departure, earnestly pleading the precariousness of his health – which proved to be good for another twenty years. Subsequently, Sir Simon Harcourt held out for several weeks that same autumn against the combined blandishments of Harley and the queen, plaintively offering his 'innumerable defects' as his excuse for seeking to evade the Lord Keepership. In complete contrast to these embarrassed shufflings there were at least five top-flight Tory contenders for the Attorney-Generalship in 1701, when the disappointed included two barristers in the very highest flight, Harcourt and Sir Thomas Powys, and two others, John Conyers and Sir Bartholomew Shower, whose reputations were scarcely less formidable.

Why this post and its junior counterpart the Solicitor-Generalship were in such demand appears plainly from a string of late-seventeenth-century success stories. John Somers began his career at the bar in 1676, when he was 26 years of age, with few connections and little save his own shining talent to depend on. Within a decade, according to his contemporary biographer, his earnings had risen to £700 per annum. This was a fine achievement for a young man – it was, after all, £100 more than Parliament ruled as the minimum qualification for a knight of the shire in 1711 – but it was not yet enough to lift him into the ranks of the common law élite. The Seven Bishops' case (1688) opened the golden gate for him; for apart from enhancing the value of his private services it paved the way for the start of a brilliant parliamentary career in 1689, and that, in turn, brought him the Solicitor-Generalship almost at once and the Attorney-Generalship early in 1692. As these offices did not close the door on private practice – in fact, we hear of Somers himself proposing to go on circuit in 1690 – they were invaluable to him. How valuable we can judge from the examples of some of his predecessors. Francis Winnington was earning well over £2,000 a year in private practice in the early 1670s; but in his first year as Solicitor-General, 1675, his income soared to £4,066. Sir Francis North kept up his business in Westminster Hall after becoming Attorney-General in 1673, and earned £7,000 a year over the next two years. Even sixty years before this Francis Bacon had valued the post itself 'honestly' at £6,000 per annum. It is little wonder that Sir Thomas Powys, at the age of 61, saw the Tory victory of 1710 as an opportunity to regain this coveted prize at last, 'and be thereby something freed from the constant attendance at the bar, which I have so long now laboured under'. He was even prepared to promise the new ministry of that autumn to apply himself 'wholly . . . to the execution of that office'. He was passed over, however, in favour of a former incumbent, Sir Edward Northey, whose political stance was much more moderate and whose 'great abilities in the law', as Cowper testified, commanded general respect.

Unless they were unusually fortunate, most barristers in private practice, aiming at big money, had to be prepared to work every bit as hard as Powys's plea implied. Except for the equity specialists in Chancery, hard work usually meant being prepared to ride the circuits assiduously twice a year, often an immense drain on physical stamina. In 1671–2 Francis Winnington earned £1,791 in fees in the Westminster courts, with a peak of £521 in Michaelmas Term, 1671. He had then been eleven years at the bar, but he still went on the Oxford circuit as usual that year, being no more willing to sacrifice so rich a source of present profit than he was to spurn his less spectacular earnings, such as the £120 in fees he picked up during the Long Vacation of 1676. Serjeant John Maynard, that acknowledged master of 'the special plea' who remained in the top flight of advocates even in the Restoration period, had reputedly reaped £711 from a single circuit as long ago as 1647, when he was 45; yet he was still plying the same circuit thirty-five years later, long after he had accumulated princely wealth. Between £200 and £300 'clear of charges' for a circuit, and some £400 or £500 a year if he rode both Easter and Summer circuits was a more realistic expectation for the average member of the bar élite early in Charles II's reign. It is true that there was often a striking difference between the earnings of the undisputed 'cocks' of a circuit, like Erasmus Earle and Francis North in Norfolk in the 1660s, or Maynard himself in the west, and the ordinary run of their fellow barristers. Nevertheless, even those who had to play second fiddle for years to the men in possession would generally have agreed with Roger North that 'the circuit found [them] business for the town, and the town for the circuit'.

Although the acquisition of a law office proved to be, for some, the crucial bridge between prosperity and really great wealth, careers like that of John Maynard did teach the able barristers of Augustan England that a gentleman of the gown could make a fortune from advocacy without office. 'Some lawyers gain in fees £3,000 and some £4,000', remarked Dr Edward Chamberlayne in 1694. As a 'civilian', trained at Oxford at a time when there was no love lost between civil and common lawyers, Chamberlayne injected more than a drop of bile into his accounts of the latter profession in some of the many editions of his *Angliae Notitia*. But on the subject of incomes and fees there are few grounds for believing that he overstated the case; and in some respects he understated it. Somewhere between the first four decades and the last two or three of the seventeenth century a sea-change unquestionably took place. In a recent study of counsellors' earnings between the 1580s and the 1640s, Wilfred Prest has produced some solid evidence to suggest that they may have been very much lower than some well-known contemporary estimates imply. All the lawyers whose incomes he scrutinised were regarded as professional successes, at the least benchers of their inns and Recorders, in some cases future serjeants-at-law or judges. Yet one of them only three times surpassed £200 a year in a career lasting from 1582 to 1632, and only the eminent Sir James Whitelocke of those in practice down to 1650 touched the dizzy heights of £600 (this in the last four years before 1620, when at the age of 50 he was appointed a serjeant and a Welsh judge). On the basis of this sample it is incomes varying from £150 to £450 which, in general, predominate under the first two

Stuarts and, despite the great resurgence of court business after the first Civil War, it appears that Arthur Turnour, though a serjeant and a pleader of thirty years' experience, only twice did more than £400-worth of business between 1646 and 1650.

Was there a watershed in the expectations of successful barristers some time in the 1650s? Thin and scattered though the evidence is that has so far come to light, it does seem a fairly strong possibility that the inflation of counsellors' and serjeants' earnings to which Chamberlayne drew his readers' attention, however much further it had gone by the 1690s, had begun some forty years before. For almost the first time surviving fee books of the republican period begin to reveal here and there four-figure returns for single years. Arthur Turnour's son, Edward, who had begun his career in the most difficult circumstances in 1640 and whose income by 1643–4 had struggled up to the meagre sum of £36 18s was able eleven years later (1654–5) to achieve £1,076. By Michaelmas 1660 he was making almost as much in a single term as Whitelocke had made in a whole year forty to forty-five years earlier; and although elected Speaker of the House of Commons in May 1661, which severely limited his practice at the bar from then on, he recorded a total for fees and retainers of £1,353 for 1660–1, 'notwithstanding the loss of my practice at the bar and circuits the half of the year', and of £2,022 in 1663–4, 'though the Parliament sat all Easter Term'. 1663 was the year that John Archer, an Essex lawyer who had practised with distinction for well over thirty years, was made a judge. No information survives on his earnings after the Restoration, but Archer is known to have enjoyed a golden year in 1658 when his income from four terms and two circuits totalled £1,257. It was at the end of that year that he was appointed a serjeant-at-law.

Despite the jibe of a retired barrister in the early eighteenth century that the serjeants were 'an order of persons full of avarice and deal in small profits, all which depend upon their monopoly of the Common Pleas bar', many of them are still to be found by 1700–30 very much in a van of the profession so far as profits were concerned: but the sums involved are now of a different order altogether. Sir Thomas Powys, for example, who was marked out as a coming man at the bar well before the Revolution and was appointed a Queen's Serjeant in 1702, had built up by 1713 a comprehensive practice valued, in the expert judgement of Lord Cowper, at almost £4,000 a year. First-class though this achievement was, it is hard to believe that it was not equalled and probably surpassed by more silver-tongued Augustan advocates than Powys, such as Heneage Finch, Sir Simon Harcourt, Sir Thomas Parker or Sir Peter King. It may be thought that because these were all men who combined practice at the bar with prominent political careers, they enjoyed an advantage over their non-parliamentary professional colleagues which put them in a special category of those enjoying ultra-inflated rewards. A brief glance at the experience of one leading counsellor who never sat in the Commons at all, Sir John Cheshyre, and another, John

Comyns, who always maintained that his parliamentary career had for many years reduced his earnings, is enough to expose that fallacy. Cheshyre was made a serjeant in 1706 and promoted Queen's Serjeant in 1711; he developed, like Powys, a many-faceted practice which was far from being confined to the Court of Common Pleas. It yielded him an average of £3,241 a year from 1719 to 1725. What is striking about his fee book is that it shows a steady drop in earnings every year from £3,805 13s 0d (Michaelmas 1719–Michaelmas 1720), when Cheshyre was 57 and still relatively vigorous, to £2,246 15s 0d (1724–5). It was only after Michaelmas Term of 1725, at the age of 63, that he decided to draw in his horns and settle for an average of £1,320 per annum thereafter in the Common Pleas, 'contenting to amuse myself with lesser business and smaller gains'. John Comyns was three years younger than Sir John Cheshyre but of much the same professional seniority. After eleven years at the bar he was persuaded by Lord Halifax, against his own inclinations, to stand for Parliament towards the end of King William's reign. From January 1701 until May 1715 he spent all but two and a half years in the House, only to be 'by every ministry successively treated with disregard, not to say despite'. It was only when out of politics again in the years 1715–22 that he was able, as he later told Lord Hardwicke, to go 'quietly on in my business till I gained by my practice about £3,000 a year'.

The fortunes to be made at the equity bar by the late seventeenth century not infrequently exceeded what was possible in the common law courts. Roger North recollected in his retirement having 'heard Sir John Churchill, a famous chancery-practiser, say that in his walk from Lincoln's Inn down to Temple Hall, where in the Lord Keeper Bridgman's time causes and motions out of term were heard, he had taken £28 with breviates, only for motions and defences for hastening and retarding hearings'. North's own early career, of which he has left us a vivid and detailed record, is as revealing as any on the rewards that could now fall in Chancery to a young barrister of unexceptional talents, provided he had energy, determination – and, of course, luck. North, on his own endearing admission, was no ball of fire: his 'first flight in practice', the purely formal opening of a declaration at *nisi prius* in Guildhall, was, he confesses, 'a crisis like the loss of a maidenhead', only struggled through 'with blushing and blundering'. It was a long time before he could pluck up enough courage in court to ask a witness a question. Yet his sheer pertinacity and commitment, plus the abundant interest that accrued to him from his brother Francis's high reputation, soon made him a 'judges' favourite' and brought him in a mere eight years of practice an enviable income. At this point, in the autumn of 1682, he was made a KC and, both in 1683 and 1684, he made over £4,000 a year from his Chancery practice. After the Revolution this court continued to yield astonishing dividends to some of its most assiduous practitioners. Although he never held office, nor even bothered himself with a parliamentary career until he had reached the age of 60, Thomas Vernon of Hanbury cultivated his equity practice so single-mindedly that in some thirty years afer his first appearance at the

Chancery bar in 1679 he raised its annual yield (on Sir Richard Temple's estimate) to no less than £5,000.

With such a bountiful harvest to be reaped at the bar, the prospect of promotion to the common law bench often presented a dilemma by the early eighteenth century. As Lord Cowper explained to the incoming monarch in 1714, Sir Thomas Powys had, from a purely professional point of view, made an astonishing decision the previous year when he had 'laid down his practice . . . to be a judge, not worth £1,500 a year', accepting a cut in income of some 60 per cent. His motives, Cowper thought, could only be construed as political; 'if the Pretender had succeeded he would have made, and that very justly, a merit of this step'. Until 1714 the basic salary of a King's Bench or Common Pleas judge, or of a Baron of the Exchequer, was a mere £1,000. Perquisites and fees might occasionally bring in half as much again; but only the Lord Chief Justice, to a much lesser extent the Chief Baron of the Exchequer, and above all the Chief Justice of the Common Pleas could expect handsome returns from that quarter. Chief Justice Trevor made no secret in 1710 of the fact that he preferred the 'certainty [and] profit' of his present position, together with its guarantee of 'some ease and leisure' to the rigours of the Lord Keepership. It was widely believed that Trevor received a 'consideration' of £4,000 in 1711 when he allowed George Cook to succeed his father as Prothonotary of the Common Pleas. But even for the presiding judge of the Court of Common Pleas windfalls of this size were extremely rare: significantly, the elder Cook reached 82 before he accepted that the time had come to think about resignation. Offered a rank-and-file place on the bench, therefore, the energetic barrister who was still in high demand had to balance against a sure fall in income the new security which, as a judge, was his by convention from 1689 and by law from 1701. Hitches could occur. But, generally speaking, after the Revolution the scarlet robe became a sound insurance policy, often taken out in one's fifties, looking towards a ripe old age. The duller men could accept with little hesitation; Littleton Powys, one of nature's plodders, who had bored the courts to tears for twenty-one years from the bar before he even found a berth in a serjeants' inn in 1692, was well content to survive over thirty years on the bench (1695–1726) before retiring with a handsome pension. But for the able pleader at the height of his powers acceptance of a judgeship – unless, like Sir Thomas Parker in 1710 or Sir Peter King in 1714, he was offered the presidency of a court outright – could only be a gamble on achieving fairly swift promotion. If the gamble came off, as it did for John Pratt when he succeeded Parker as Lord Chief Justice in 1718 after a polished bar career and just four years as a puisne justice, all well and good; if not, it could be a very expensive mistake. It was partly to make this gamble seem more worthwhile that the government raised the salary of puisne judges to £1,500 and those of the three chiefs to £2,000 from the beginning of George I's reign.

Although serious work on the wealth of the lawyers is still in its infancy, so that most generalisations have to be tempered with caution, there are many indications that by 1700 the cream of the rewards of bar and bench was not only far thicker at the top but more generously spread across the profession than it had been in 1600. One reason for this was the mounting volume of cases, particularly long, difficult and expensive cases, coming before the courts during the years 1680–1730. Edward Hughes described the second half of this period as 'a great age of litigation in the north', citing as one example the twenty-one suits in which William Cotesworth was involved in the course of ten years as lord of the manor of Gateshead. And witnesses before a Commons' committee of inquiry under Sir William Strickland's chairmanship in 1729 emphasised the general increase in Common Pleas business over the early decades of the eighteenth century. A much more important factor than the greater demand for barristers' services (though obviously linked with it to some extent) lay in the rise in fees charged by most barristers between the mid-sixteenth and the early eighteenth centuries, and the fact that the fees of the élite, especially, went on rising steeply long after prices had levelled out in the mid-seventeenth century. The readiness, and the capacity, of a more affluent society by the second half of that century to pay more for the best professional services was something from which the lawyers benefited in full measure. Although barristers' fees were never subject to the fixed tariffs of the courts which (officially) applied to attorneys, solicitors and clerks, they had kept for the most part within a framework of conventions adjusted during the Tudor period in response to price inflation but, in general, maintained at least down to the Interregnum. Conventions still existed between 1660 and 1730, but there are many signs that they were in a state of flux; while the free market in fees for the more successful practitioners achieved by the end of the sixteenth century – by when, Dr Prest has observed, 'barristers were at liberty to charge for their services whatever their clients might be prepared . . . to pay' – became progressively freer, and wider, after 1660.

'Angels work wonders in Westminster Hall', wrote Brant in his *Ship* of *Fools* in 1509, reminding us that an angel (a gold coin worth 6s 8d), and quite often half an angel, remained the standard fee charged by serjeants-at-law simply for giving counsel in their chambers. But during the second half of the sixteenth century fees of under 10s became increasingly unacceptable to many lawyers, serjeants or no, and during the seventeenth century the asking price gradually rose, first to 10s or half a guinea, then with growing frequency to £1 or a guinea. All the same, fee books examined by Prest for the first half of the seventeenth century lead him to the firm conclusion that 'the fee most frequently paid to both barristers an serjeants [on all accounts] was between 10s. and 20s.', with 10s fees still extremely frequent. A not untypical instance was that of Arthur Turnour, serjeant-at-law, who took twenty-two 10s fees in the Court of Common Pleas in Hilary Term 1642, ten of a £1 and nothing higher. General fee levels, in other words, had no more than kept pace with inflation since the late fifteenth century. However, it is notable that, even in his early days as a barrister in the 1670s, a 1-guinea fee is the lowest Roger North mentions; while in the books of a far more experienced practiser, Edward Turner, the

10s fee figured so rarely by 1660 that in the middle of Michaelmas Term 1663 he abandoned the traditional 10s unit of calculation and henceforward entered all his fees simply in pounds. Turner's standard fee 'pr advisaments' in the late 1650s was either £1 or £2, but £3 figures with some regularity from Michaelmas 1660 onwards, and numerous larger sums are received for advising on cases: £5 from Mr Gardiner and Lady Capel in Easter Term 1660, and in the following Michaelmas £10 and £20 from Sir Anthony Browne and no less than £40 from Alderman Warner. In Turner's book for Trinity Term, 1662, £10 fees for advice occur four times and a £20 fee once. In 1668 one wealthy client, Sir William Drake, paid him £10. No wonder that by Anne's reign a pamphleteer bitterly complained of 'golden counsellors that hardly in a year have a fee in anything but gold, and would throw a 10s. fee at a man's head if he should offer it 'em'.

The inflation of counselling fees was fully matched by the charges made by successful barristers for their services as advocates. Edward Chamberlayne, who had himself sought legal advice from Turner as early as 1661 and twice in one term had been stung £5 for his pains, sourly reminded his readers in the 1690s that 'anciently the fee expected by a serjeant from his client . . . for pleading in any court of judicature was no more than 20s and the fee of a barrister 10s (which yet is much more than is usually given in any of our neighbour countries at this day); but at present it is become almost ordinary to give some serjeants £10 and some £20 and to a barrister half as much, at the hearing of any considerable cause . . .' Such a situation represented an emphatic change even since the early decades of the seventeenth century when just a handful of serjeants and barristers were so sought-after that they were able to charge £10 for a single day's advocacy. Chamberlayne was certainly not exaggerating. Roger North, who practised in the 1670s and 1680s and was moderate and scrupulous in his charges, prided himself on never once having taken a fee above 20 guineas: he expected, he tells us, 'in very great causes ten guineas, with a huge breviate . . . and five in the better sort of causes'. In ordinary cases he would take 2 or 3 guineas, and one for simple motions and defences. Turner's fee books in the 1660s show a similar flexibility but rather less moderation: with him £5 became almost as standard a fee as £2 or £3. Turner took £20 for appearing for the plaintiff in *Roberts v. Wynne* in 1663 and a further £10 for pleading in the same cause in Hilary Term 1664. Later that year he received £45 for making five appearances for Colonel Arundel, plaintiff in a case in the Court of Exchequer: that, however, was most exceptional. Although Chancery and Exchequer, and the King's Bench, too, at times, proved rich in pickings for the Augustan lawyers, the House of Lords over time became the happiest hunting ground of all for the bar élite. To plead a case before their lordships in the winter of 1707–8 the Marquess of Annandale employed Serjeant Pratt and Sir Peter King. For giving advice in chambers before the first hearing they twice received 5 guineas each. For attending four hearings in the Lords they each charged 5 guineas for one and 10 guineas for each of the remaining three. Both, therefore, made 45 guineas out of this single case.

The rampant prosperity of the Augustan common law élite, a prosperity that was the envy of all other professions, cannot have gone unrecognised by the layman, if only because it was still very much reflected in the fundamental lineaments of seventeenth- and eighteenth-century England. It was earlier observed that the well-rooted, pre-Civil War tradition that the aristocracy of the law translated their glittering wealth into social status by buying great estates and frequently erecting a fine new mansion on their acres continued to flourish after the Restoration. The old pattern was spectacularly reset in 1663 when Maynard completed the purchase of the Gunnersbury estate in Middlesex and moved into the imposing pile which John Webb, the pupil of Inigo Jones, had been building for him there since 1658. Appropriately enough, Maynard's 'palace' was to become a residence for royalty in the eighteenth century. A generation later, Roger North was to find that even a short career at the bar, provided it was studded with briefs, could be enough to establish landed independence. On the proceeds of a mere dozen years (for his Chancery practice was shrivelled by the bleak Jeffreys wind between 1686 and 1688) he bought Rougham in 1690, built a comfortable mansion-house there a few years later and, helped by a lucrative marriage, proceeded to live out the rest of his life as a non-juring country gentleman.

The quarter of a century which followed the Glorious Revolution, coinciding with two great wars, much agrarian depression and the coming of an institutionalised land tax, partially – but only partially – quelled the hunger of thriving lawyers for land and park, brick and stone. Research into Lord Cowper's estates has revealed that he spent only a tiny percentage of his earnings from the Great Seal between 1705 and 1710 and between 1714 and 1718 on land. He preferred far more profit-able stocks and government funds as a source of investment in the war years, and only launched out into major purchases in the last few years of his life. In 1704 he did have a house built at Coln Green in Herting-fordbury parish, on farming land which he had acquired in 1694, and had it enlarged in 1710–11; but even with its two wings it was modest in size and cost only £3,020. Otherwise his interest in real estate was for many years minimal, and on the eve of the South Sea Bubble he had holdings of Bank and East India stock valued at £24,757. P. G. M. Dickson's analysis of public creditors in England between the reigns of William III and George II shows that Cowper was far from being alone among major lawyers in his partiality for paper investments, though he does seem to have been the biggest operator among them. Lawyers were well represented in the first Tontine and Bank subscription lists of 1693–4 – John Blencowe, Gilbert Dolben and Sir George Treby among them; even after the war, and before the Bubble fever, eleven London lawyers, among them five Chancery Masters, held over £10,000 each of the 5 per cent government stock issue of 1717.

To draw extravagant conclusions from these facts would be unwise, however. Chancery Masters, in the nature of their office, did not always invest on their own accounts. It may also be significant that some of the biggest investors were not ordinary career lawyers. Cowper certainly could not be described in those terms. He was the eldest son and heir of a baronet, who succeeded his father in 1706 and could afford to support the grant of a peerage in the same year; he had no need to buy status for himself and he had no surviving sons to provide for until Queen Anne's last years. Sir Littleton Powys, who dabbled in short-term government securities and owned £15,000 of Bank stock in 1723–4, was likewise the heir to a substantial landed estate. Another Bank investor, Robert Eyre, was equally fortunate with his family inheritance near Salisbury. But even when attitudes to the post-Revolution land market have been closely studied it is quite possible that no very clear or logical pattern will emerge. Lawyers, by and large, were certainly more discriminating in their attitudes towards land in the quarter of a century after 1689 than had been the case in the previous thirty years. Yet it is also clear that for many leading barristers, judges and law officers 'a stake in the English hedge' proved difficult to resist even in wartime England. And it may well have had particular attractions for those who, in contrast to the Cowpers and their like, came of urban, professional or small gentry stock, were younger sons of larger landowners or even the eldest sons of financially embarrassed ones.

As the son of a Leek attorney, Sir Thomas Parker, who succeeded Holt as Lord Chief Justice in 1710, was one who understandably felt the need for *terra firma* under his feet. From his father he had inherited some property in Sneyd Hamblett, Staffordshire, and 'coal mines therein', but before he was raised to the peerage in 1716 he had begun to lay the foundations of a major landed estate. However, the timing of some of his early acquisitions is uncertain and it is possibly significant that his most important purchase, the Shirburn estate in Oxfordshire, was not made until July 1716, and that even on that he only laid out the fairly modest sum of £11,350 plus a further £7,000 for Shirburn Castle. A huge present of £14,000 from George I in 1718, when Parker became Lord Chancellor, may have encouraged further sallies into the market: at all events, by 1725 the then Earl of Macclesfield was drawing close on £3,000 a year from his rentals in Oxfordshire and Staffordshire and owned other lands in Berkshire, Wiltshire, Cheshire and Warwickshire. Richard Wynn did not quite rise to Parker's heights in the profession. Nevertheless, as a barrister in great demand, and later as a serjeant (and for a while a Welsh judge), he prospered rapidly; and though a London merchant's son who had twice married into trading families, he had no doubts as to how to dispose of his gains. After less than fourteen years at the bar, and in the middle of the Nine Years' War, he was able to lay out nearly £25,000 on two of the embarrassed Clinton family's manors in Lincolnshire. Not satisfied with this major investment and with the parliamentary seat at Boston which it earned him, Wynn moved into Hertfordshire in 1701 to buy the Bidwell Park estate and establish his main residence there. Yet he kept his town house in Charterhouse Yard and was still busily practising in London in 1711. An even bigger investor in the wartime land market was Sir Nathan Wright, a Leicestershire rector's son who was Wynn's senior at the Inner Temple in the 1670s. Wright severed his connection with the law in 1705 at the age of 51, when he was dismissed from the Lord Keepership. Until then he appears to have been content with the small property he had inherited from his father in 1668 and with his marriage into a Midland gentry family. But within the space of three years thereafter, at the height of the War of the Spanish Succession, he spent almost £50,000 on three estates in Leicestershire, including the ancient Villiers patrimony at Brooksby, together with Caldecote in Warwickshire. At the same time he seriously contemplated buying the Caryll family manor at Winchelsea in Sussex, with an eye to the election interest in the town.

It was more common, all the same, for the lawyer with a full purse and landed ambitions to accumulate his estates, as Wynn and Parker did, while still active in the profession. Sir Thomas Trevor, who had a heady early career at the bar as well as twenty-two years as law officer and judge, poured much of his great wealth into broad acres in Bedfordshire and Northamptonshire in the early eighteenth century; his most important purchase – Bromham and three other manors in Bedfordshire, which cost him £21,394 2s 6d – was made in 1708. Trevor was a younger son, though he did come of a substantial Welsh landed and political family. The career of Sir John Pratt, Lord Chief Justice under George I and the father of Lord Camden, provides a variation on a similar theme. He, too, came of a landed family, but one whose Devonshire estates had been ruined in the Civil Wars; so that from 1682, when he became a barrister at the age of 25, he had to live almost entirely by his professional wits. When he was 48, and had been a serjeant for five years, he purchased the manor of Hidulfe's Place in Kent and settled his large family there in a country house which he oddly called 'Wilderness'. He was already a very wealthy man when he first came into Parliament in 1711; and he extended his landed estates still further just after the end of the war by buying Baynham Priory.

On the other hand, land did not invariably prove an irresistible magnet even to those whose careers began without it. Until the very last of his thirty years of bar practice before succeeding as Master of the Rolls, when he inherited the Somers properties, Sir Joseph Jekyll resided in London; and to the end of his life, when he left £20,000 of East India stock to help to pay off the National Debt, he continued to favour government securities and Bank or Company stock as sources of investment. Philip Yorke, finding suitable residential estates in short supply in Kent, waited until 1740 before plunging deeply, and then in Cambridgeshire. Lawrence Carter, who had been a Member of Parliament both in William III's reign and Anne's before becoming a KC in 1715 and a judge in 1726, based himself all his life in a house in the lawyers' colony at Leicester, in which his father had practised as a solicitor. There is also the case of John Comyns, a barrister's son, who had been practising with notable learning and distinction for twenty-five years when, in 1715, he was turned out of his parliamentary seat at Maldon for not having the minimum qualification of £300 per annum in real estate. He owned a house at Highlands, not far from his native town, but even this had possibly been inherited from his father as long ago as 1686. Most of his eminent colleagues, however, were already fortified against electoral embarrassments by the time the Qualifications Act was passed in 1711. Sir Peter King, for instance, who was the son of an Exeter grocer, was already something of a marked man in politics and was not disposed to gamble too far on an uncertain future. In 1710, the year of the Whig Party's Sacheverell débâcle in which he had been involved, King had bought the manor of Ockham in Surrey, complete with Jacobean manor house. This was after little more than a decade at the bar and two years as Recorder of London. It was not, however, until 1725, presumably to celebrate his appointment as Lord Chancellor, that King commissioned Hawksmoor to begin work on the grandiose pile which was to dominate Ockham Park for more than two centuries.

The itch to build continued to afflict denizens of Westminster Hall periodically throughout our period. John Ward of Capesthorne, barrister and Tory politician, consoled himself for the misfortunes of his party by employing John Wood and Francis Smith to design him a fine early Georgian residence, with detached wings and a family chapel to boot: it was built on his Cheshire estate between 1719 and 1732. Long before this, Thomas Trevor's predecessor at the head of the Common Pleas, Sir George Treby, had begun the erection of a princely mansion in the Palladian style near his Devon birthplace, though it was left to his son George to complete it. For sheer splendour, however, Plympton House was outdone by Hanbury Hall in Worcestershire, that remarkable monument to the lucrative possibilities of the Court of Chancery. Thomas Vernon, its owner, had inherited a small estate in the county in the same year that he was called to the bar, 1679. Under William III and Anne he accumulated extensive lands in Worcestershire. After completing the building of Hanbury on the site of his family house he embarked with equal lavishness on its embellishment, employing, among other fine craftsmen, James Thornhill to paint the grand staircase walls and ceiling, and embodying in the latter in 1710 (like the good Whig he was) a picture of Dr Henry Sacheverell pursued by the Furies. Even his exceptional income was strained to support such an orgy and perhaps it was not, as Cobham later suggested, to indulge a ruling passion alone that having retired for a while to live on his fortune, Vernon then 'return[ed] to the Chancery to get a little more when he could not speak so loud as to be heard'.

We have been much concerned so far with the glittering prizes of the legal profession in Augustan England. Of course, for a large majority of those who stayed the normal seven or eight years' course of a training in one of the inns of court to qualify for a call – usually between the ages of 23 and 26 – there were no such prizes ahead. The prospects for many were very far from bleak, as we shall see. But there can be no doubt that the bright vision of almost limitless opportunity which the bar and the bench appeared to offer the successful did have, as Campbell lugubriously observed in 1747, 'a dark and dismal reverse'. Prospective barristers were warned not to forget that, while 'the expense of their education was great and certain . . . it is almost impossible to form a judgment of the genius of the student till he has gone through every branch of his studies; at which time it is more than ten to one but some wants, some natural impediments then appear which were not dreamed of before'; and furthermore that

> after he has finished his studies, and the fond parent believes him possessed of all the qualifications fitting the bar, all his trouble is lost unless he has a fortune to support him in the character of a gentleman till he gains practice; which he never will attain to, let his merit be never so conspicuous, without a large acquaintance, a great number of friends, and some eminent personage to countenance and patronize the young barrister.

Later in the century Adam Smith was to present a more vivid picture still of the 'lottery' of legal practice: 'Put your son apprentice to a shoemaker, there is little doubt of his learning to make a pair of shoes. But send him to study the law, it is at least twenty to one if he ever makes such a proficiency as will enable him to live by the business.' Smith's statistics can be discounted; but there was a valid point behind the hyperbole. The same may be said of the brilliant twenty-first issue of the *Spectator*, in March 1711, where Joseph Addison painted the law with his satirical brush as one of those professions 'overburdened with practitioners, and filled with multitudes of ingenious gentlemen that starve one another'. Few of his readers can have met a starving lawyer. But overdrawn though it was, his portrait of London practice, where the stakes were highest and the competition fiercest, was not unrecognisable:

> This prodigious society of men may be divided into the litigious and the peaceable. Under the first are comprehended all those who are carried down in coachfuls to Westminster Hall every morning in term-time. I must, however, observe to the reader that above three parts of those whom I reckon among the litigious are such as are only quarrelsome in their hearts, and have no opportunity of showing their passion at the bar. Nevertheless, as they do not know what strifes may arise, they appear at the Hall every day, that they may show themselves in a readiness to enter the lists whenever there shall be occasion for them.

But were things strikingly different in 1711 from what they had been seventy or eighty years before? Certainly there had been dilettantes in the profession in Charles I's reign; there had also been destitute barristers then who had drawn from time to time on the charity of all the inns; and an inquiry among Middle Templars in 1635 had brought to light several qualified barristers among the thirty-two members found to be practising as 'common attorneys'. So the situation was not a novel one; but it may well have been aggravated from around 1680 because of the pressures of a profession that was, by then, expanding over fast. These pressures could be felt by barristers of long standing, such as

Richard Chamberlaine, an Ancient of Gray's Inn, whose practice had dwindled virtually to nothing by 1695, or Francis Atterbury, called in 1683 but 'reduced to want' and voted £5 by the benchers of the same society in 1725. But, in the main, it was the young, inexperienced and unsponsored who were most vulnerable to them. The fact was that the upper branches of the law, laden enough before the civil wars and the Interregnum, were by the time of William III's and Queen Anne's reigns weighed down by the teeming produce of the inns of court. The common law's most dynamic and productive period, in terms of bar calls at least, was not the thirty years before 1640 (as we have been accustomed to believe) but the thirty years before 1690. Between 1660 and 1689, 1,996 young men were called at one or other of the four inns, 623 more than in the years 1610–39. Sir Henry Chauncy, who was Treasurer of the Middle Temple in 1686 and had then been in practice for thirty years, stated bluntly that the influxes of his generation had begun to 'overstock the profession'. The output of the inns did fall away to some extent during the war-dominated years from 1689 to 1713, which was natural enough in view of the expansion of both the armed and civil services of the Crown and the unprecedented scope for alternative careers thereby created. But it recovered again in the 1720s and remained more than enough between William III's accession and George II's to maintain the strength of the bar at the peak levels it had reached by the early 1690s (see Appendix, pp. 288–9 below).

What those levels were it is not possible to say with any real precision. By no means every law student who was called to the bar went on to practise at it. In addition, there were always young barristers, particularly eldest sons of good family who inherited their patrimony quickly, who were too prosperous on their private incomes to need to drudge away at building up and maintaining a law practice. Robert Raikes was a not untypical case: living a country gentleman's life in Northallerton under Queen Anne, 'a famous jockey' (as a government tax collector observed to Harley in December 1710) and 'some say more conversant with ladies than law books'. And it is certain that the drop-outs, from choice or necessity, were more numerous still. We can be confident, therefore, that Sir Thomas Wilson's contemporary calculation that in 1600, judges and court officers apart, there were 'in number, of serjeants[-at-law] about 30, counsellors about 2,000' was a massive exaggeration. A more convincing modern estimate is that the strength of the entire 'higher degrees' of the law probably rose from little more than 200 in 1574 to at least 700 by 1616; so that by the eve of the Civil Wars there were perhaps around 1,000 serjeants and counsellors who were either in practice or – and the distinction is a most important one – entitled to practise. With 3,783 newly qualified men being turned out by the inns in the course of the seventy years after the end of 1659, compared with 2,463 in the years 1580–1639, it would seem that in trying to envisage 'the barristers' as both a professional and social phenomenon in the early eighteenth century we ought logically to think of a group at least half as large again as its predecessor in Charles I's reign. But without reliable knowledge of the true extent of 'wastage' in a profession where it was notoriously rife, it is impossible to equate logical deduction with reasonable assumption.

Just as we can be sure many of those called to the bar never became career lawyers, so it is equally certain that only a minority of career lawyers – well under half if early Stuart indications are any guide – practised at all regularly in the Westminster courts. A recent estimate by Prest puts the strength of 'the practising bar' in the late 1630s at no more than 400, while Duman suggests that a century and a half later its strength was even lower. London business was clearly the hardest of all for the tyro to get a foothold in: many of those who tried did not succeed, and many more never tried at all. Success, if not survival, in Westminster Hall mostly went either to the fittest or to the luckiest; and even the most talented might need the smile of fortune. To catch the eye and eventually gain the favour of one of the judges, as the young Philip Yorke did with Lord Chief Justice Parker early in George I's reign, was of great importance. Even more likely to make or break was the attitude of the select 200–300 attorneys and solicitors who monopolised so much Westminster business. Only the manifestly able or the fortunately connected of the novices would appeal to this discerning aristocracy of the courts, so long as there was an abundance of established counsel to be had and clients' pockets could afford their fees.

In such circumstances it may seem that the Parliament of the Inner Temple was being disingenuous, to say the least, when it registered a complaint in November 1683 against members called in recent years to its bar, that 'many of them so soon as they are called immediately leave the society and seldom appear again'. Of 'twenty-seven called not having chambers', they were horrified to discover, 'two only have bought chambers'. But this was not a lament against a large number of young barristers neglecting their careers: the sore point was that, in the majority of cases, they were taking indecently early opportunities of pursuing them elsewhere, furthering their own interests but depriving the inn of revenue. The fact was, however, that by the end of the seventeenth century the pressures on the man who had worked hard for years to qualify for the bar, driving him even harder to make at least a modest success of it, were more severe than they had ever been; and the strongest pressure of all was financial. Training was now a costly business, as we shall see – already much more expensive than fifty or sixty years before – and it promised to become more so. And it was by no means only younger sons whose fortunes were committed to it. Indeed, the most convincing evidence that a fair return could generally be expected on the investment is the number of eldest sons on whom these sums were staked. Research into Lincoln's Inn career admissions has revealed that an astonishing 65 per cent of all new barristers called there between 1695 and 1704 were eldest sons; and although the proportion fell in subsequent decades, it was still as high as 50 per cent between 1715 and 1724. What, then, were the options open to the young barrister where the door to a prosperous, full-time metropolitan practice was closed?

One option was to combine, from a London base, a spasmodic business in the Westminster courts with circuit business, until such time as connections or persistence landed one of the host of offices in these courts which could be combined with a modest practice. In time, there was the hope of a full-time place in the legal bureaucracy. As well as clerkships of all kinds, general and specialised (and running into hundreds), the Westminster courts yielded a luxuriant crop of filazers, exigenters, cursitors, prothonotories, chirographers, examiners and registrars. Some posts required no specific legal training. For many of the rest, barristers competed with attorneys and solicitors. But for others the former were given preference: we know this because barristers are normally identifiable in contemporary lists by the suffix 'Esq.'. Cursitorships, for example, were seemingly their preserve; whereas filazers were drawn from the full range of 'persons in the law'. Quite apart from the bureaucracy of the courts most large, and some small, government departments in London had at least one legal adviser. He was by no means always an attorney or solicitor, despite his designation; the post of 'solicitor' to a department could go to a barrister, and the recipient was not precluded from private practice.

Failing London, what else? By the end of the seventeenth century a high proportion of the solid bread-and-butter majority of the profession was provincially based. Here a wide range of opportunities beckoned the barrister of average talents, enabling him to build, at worst, a modest prosperity on the foundation of his professional qualification. To begin with, no duchy or palatine town was without its clutch of resident barristers, and few assize towns or substantial commercial centres lacked at least one. Coventry in the 1680s, for instance, had the irascible Edward Palmer. Manchester, in William III's reign, had Edward Herle, 'an ancient, though no eminent lawyer [in Roger Kenyon's view], not well to pass in the world, though he hath been much better', and the more recently qualified John Walmsley. In 1698, when Celia Fiennes visited Leicester, which had two assizes and four sessions a year, she found that within the wide confines of the Newarke, 'encompassed with a wall of good thickness, there were 'several good houses, some of stone and brick, in which some lawyers live franck [free]'. In early eighteenth-century Chester, lived, among others, Roger Comberbach and Hugh Foulkes. Comberbach came of an old Nantwich family, had become a barrister of the Inner Temple in 1694, some years after his marriage to the daughter of a prominent Chester alderman, and had served as Town Clerk of the city before becoming Recorder from 1700 to 1720. Foulkes, the son of a Deputy Baron of the Exchequer in the Palatine Court, studied at Gray's Inn and was called in 1698, but he practised in Chester and lived in a house in Castle Lane. Foulkes became Vice-Justice of Chester in 1717, while Comberbach enjoyed the distinction of having a flight of steps built in the city wall for his convenience by the corporation, since known as 'the Recorder's Steps'.

Resorts and spa towns, with their concentrated gentry clienteles, understandably proved to be magnets for barristers as well as attorneys. Bury St Edmunds, 'the Montpelier of England', was especially attractive. Yet there were many settlements of provincial lawyers which cannot be explained away by special circumstances. For instance, when Gregory King and his colleagues in the College of Arms, Thomas May and Henry Dethick, carried out their visitation of Warwickshire in 1682 and 1683, they discovered thirteen barristers resident in the county. Two lived in the growing manufacturing town of Birmingham (in fact, there had been three until the recent death of George Palmer) but others were country dwellers: William Knight of Barrells, for one, lived near the village of Ullenhall, ten miles from the nearest town of any size. There were analogous cases in many other counties. John White, the barrister father of Gilbert White, the naturalist, resided in the early eighteenth century in the small Hampshire village of Selborne, roughly mid-way between the market towns of Alton and Petersfield.

How, then, did these provincials make a livelihood and, more than that, in many cases patently flourish? It is said that Knight was one who operated mainly within the parochial confines of quarter sessions and manorial courts; but since he seems to have had rich connections it may be that he was under no necessity to be more enterprising. For the more ambitious or needy a tempting field was the small provincial legal bureaucracy existing separately from the teeming officialdom of the capital. The Duchy of Lancaster courts at Preston, for example, had a well-heeled permanent staff of their own. There was a smaller one to serve the palatine and grand sessions courts at Chester and the special courts at Durham. At Durham in 1733 the Solicitor-Generalship of the County Palatine fell into the grateful lap of Thomas Gyll, the only son of a small North Riding squire, who had been called as recently as 1725 and had decided to make his base in the old cathedral city. The staple diet of the provincial barrister was giving 'counsel', for which his usual charge was half a guinea a time in the seventeenth century, though attorney's bills of the early eighteenth century show that the £1 or guinea fee was becoming more commonplace. He could normally expect to have a steady succession of problems referred to him by the local attorneys for an opinion. Early in his remarkable career, Isaac Greene, the south Lancashire attorney, passed on some of his thorniest problems, involving complex titles or the tying up of family settlements, to the Prescot barrister, Edward Blundell. But undoubtedly there were local barristers who relied heavily on assize causes too, for in his own 'country' a man who would have been swallowed up in the vast London sea was often a big-enough fish, with sufficient contacts, to become the centre of a small shoal of local attorneys, and share their feeding grounds. Even so brilliant a prospect as Francis North chose at the start of his bar career in the 1660s to cultivate the Norfolk circuit, 'where he was best known, and that by employments and performances, as well as family and acquaintances'. If the barrister was wise, he kept to one circuit; and this was one powerful incentive, quite apart from cheapness of living, to base himself locally. The other incentive lay in the fact that assize business, being of its nature infrequent, had to be combined with other provincial business. And of this business, the commonest and not the least remunerative was 'court-keeping'.

Augustan England, like sixteenth- and early-seventeenth-century

England, was still blanketed from end to end with a multitude of local courts. Some were important. Duchy courts, the courts of the Stannaries in Cornwall, and the Royal Franchise Court of Ely all in their different ways transacted major business. Other types of court varied greatly in scope and reward – forest courts, for example, and the complex network of municipal courts exercising civic jurisdictions; and some, including most of the bewildering profusion of manorial courts, courts leet and courts baron which still functioned, after a fashion, in the late seventeenth and early eighteenth centuries, were petty or negligible. But all had to be presided over. For many, perhaps for most, local attorneys and solicitors were once again in competition. But if a barrister was interested (and it is clear that many were) in taking such pickings to augment his fees from circuit cases or from giving legal advice, his superior status could give him valuable pull. 'As fellows of colleges in the universities get pensions and benefices', wrote the author of a seventeenth-century tract deliciously entitled *The Art of Thriving,* 'so barristers and counsellors of the inns of court advance their means by keeping of courts . . . and by places of judges of inferior courts: as London and other like corporations . . . ; the Tower of London; St Katherine's, near the Tower; borough of Southwark; the Clink'. Ambitious young lawyers with bright futures still regarded 'court-keeping' as necessary preliminary experience. Well-established practisers, like Sir Edward Turner (who continued to preside over the Franchise Court of Ely and Sir John Barrington's Essex courts even when Speaker of the Commons) and William Jessop (who kept the Duke of Newcastle's courts in Anne's reign), were quite prepared to supplement their incomes from such sources. But for the run-of-the-mill provincial barrister court-keeping could be at least half a living. When the Westminster courts had ground to a halt in the early stages of the Civil War, local courts had kept the wolf from many a young barrister's door: Edward Turner, for one, made well over half his meagre income in 1642 from court fees. The diary of Walter Powell of Llantillo, a shrewd and indefatigable Welsh attorney, shows how earlier in the seventeenth century such men as he had brought the keeping of courts almost to the status of a full-time occupation, and certainly to a fine art. By the end of the century the opportunities had barely diminished and the provincial barrister was often ideally placed to exploit them.

A versatile barrister could find other places, too, in the attorney's territory in which to pitch his tent. Peniston Lamb, who died in 1735, was considered a successful 'pleader under the bar'; but he was also recognised by his peers as a lawyer 'skilled in weaving settlements and ravelling threads of adverse wills' and became the indispensable legal agent to the Fitzwilliams. Since the middle of the seventeenth century it had become customary for big landed families to retain a counsellor-at-law on a permanent, feed basis as well as to employ an attorney-agent. Turner, in the 1660s, had received 'retaining fees' from the Marquess of Worcester, John Danvers, and Lords Salisbury and Carlisle: the latter's half-yearly fee alone was worth £25 to him. Provincial counsellors picked up the tail-end of this business, sometimes to their great profit. The favour of corporate bodies could be as valuable to them as that of private families. Town clerkships were normally engrossed by attorneys, but there were plenty of exceptions. Warwick was one town which had a barrister, Thomas Newsham of the Middle Temple, as its Town Clerk for many years under the later Stuarts: it owed him a particular debt during its rebuilding after the fire of 1695. The biggest local prize most barristers could land, however, was the Recordership of some incorporated town, borough or city. The bigger or more ambitious the borough, of course, the more likely it was that its worthies would look for some eminent barrister, preferably a Member of Parliament, on whom to bestow their Recordership, if only because of his capacity to do them favours. So it was with Sandwich and Sir James Thurbane; with Maldon and John Comyns; or with Derby and Sir Thomas Parker. Yet, with well over 200 Recorderships available and the more important corporations long accustomed to retain at least one feed counsel (as Newcastle upon Tyne had retained Sir Edward Turner) in addition to their Recorder or Deputy Recorder, there was no lack of scope for favourite local sons or for provincial barristers of no particular eminence.

Four out of many examples, taken from a span of more than fifty years, will serve to illustrate that scope. Henry Chauncy, having involved himself actively in Hertford's affairs for two decades, became the town's first Recorder under its new charter of 1680. On the other hand, Lawrence Carter, with his father's great local influence behind him, scooped the Recordership of Leicester after a mere three years at the bar, long before he had made his name. George Kenyon, who owed his appointment as Recorder of Wigan in 1697 to the patronage of Sir Roger Bradshaigh of Haigh, is a particularly good instance of a 'native heath' barrister who took all the local opportunities that were going after he had begun to practise around 1680. He kept courts for the Shakerleys and for the Earls of Derby (at Salford), he became Clerk of the Peace for Lancashire; and eventually he was appointed Vice-Chancellor of the Duchy of Lancaster. When in 1733 the *Gentleman's Magazine* reported the death of Samuel Gatwode, counsellor-at-law, its readers were informed that he had held the Recordership of the town of Cambridge for the previous thirty years. There is nothing to suggest that Gatwode had ever had a scintillating career as a pleader. But his local office, retained for so long a period in a place of some 8,000 inhabitants, and in a university centre, was a little goldmine of lasting value. In all probability, it also conferred on Gatwode a secure standing in the Cambridgeshire community.

The place of the lawyers in the society of their day and their relationship with that society is in some respects not difficult to gauge. But in other respects, so far as the barristers of Augustan England are concerned, placing them in their social context raises questions that require research beyond the pretensions of this chapter. Was the period between the reigns of Charles II and George II a transitional one in the social composition of the bar? Did the surging growth of the profession at this level under the later Stuarts entail a corresponding broadening of its social base? There are hints in some modern work on both the seventeenth and eighteenth centuries which might seem at first sight to point this way. One is Dr Prest's belief that 'under the later Stuarts the Inns gradually ceased to play the part of academies and finishing schools for "gentlemen of the best qualitie" [a major part of their Tudor and early-seventeenth-century function] and largely reverted to their former role of associations for practising and would-be lawyers'; that the inns, in short, became a great deal more professionalised after 1660. Paul Lucas has suggested, as a complement to this, that there was a corresponding decline, not reversed until early in George III's reign, in the proportion of entrants of high birth or of well-to-do gentry backgrounds. There are contemporary pronouncements, too, from time to time which seem clear enough in their implications. In the Middle Temple the 1680s saw 233 of its students called to the bar, easily breaking its own record of the previous decade. Yet the year 1686 found its Treasurer, Sir Henry Chauncy, in no self-congratulatory mood. Nostalgically he recalled the days when all the inns had served as 'nurseries' for sons of noblemen and country squires, not only grooming them for the law but preparing them for taking on their responsibilities to the state and to their local communities. But 'now', he mourned, 'mechanics, ambitious of rule and government, often educate their sons in these seminaries of law'. After the Restoration, students were still able, on occasion, to short-circuit the lengthy standard route through the inns by serving as attorney's clerks, thereby mastering legal forms and picking up invaluable practical experience well before they began formally to read for the bar: a few, such as Saunders and Trevor, actually reached the peaks of the profession from such backstairs beginnings. It is possible that the practice became less common after the 1680s; but William Blackstone, significantly, thought it necessary to make a special point of condemning it as late as 1758 and on the ground that it attracted social undesirables into the law and repelled men of stainless credentials. 'Few persons of birth, or fortune, or even of scholastic education', he declaimed, 'will submit to the drudgery or servitude and the manual labour of copying the trash of an office.'

The picture conjured up, both by these historical arguments and contemporary lamentations, is of the bar playing its part along with many other professional avenues as one of the thoroughfares of an increasingly mobile society. It should be viewed with caution. Even at the apparently simple level of entry there are many pitfalls in attempting, on the basis of descriptions of status in the admissions registers, to compare the early seventeenth century with the early eighteenth; for by the latter period the inns had become much less euphemistic, much more ready to call a spade a spade, or a merchant a merchant. Their Elizabethan and Jacobean predecessors had been excessively sensitive about any possible dilution of the social status of barristers and consequently concealed many a rough diamond behind the decent screen of a 'gentleman's' suffix. In reality, the representatives of the *landed* gentry, men of armigerous backgrounds, who practised at the bar probably made up well under two-thirds of all counsellors, even in the decades before the Civil War.

We must be equally wary of exaggerating the decline in the social function of the inns of court. Gray's Inn, once *par excellence* the place for the socialites, unquestionably put on a more serious face in Augustan England; but there was a particular reason for that. A series of disastrous fires between 1680 and 1687 meant an acute shortage of accommodation there, and it was well into George I's reign before rebuilding was completed. As purely social institutions the inns of court in general, however, experienced no dramatic 'flight of the gentry'. The first flutterings of a migration were detectable as early as 1630; yet a century later most of the birds had still not flown. Well over two-thirds of the students admitted to Lincoln's Inn in the 1720s were never called to the bar. Charles Worsley, Treasurer of the Middle Temple, was right to comfort himself, even in George II's reign, that the old notion of the inns as 'places designed for the education of the sons of the gentry and nobility' was 'not yet wholly eradicated out of the minds of our gentry'. Out of all the students admitted to the Middle Temple during the 1620s 21 per cent had eventually been called. In the 1690s the proportion of calls to admissions was virtually unchanged; to be precise it had fallen by 1 per cent. By the 1720s the situation appears much the same, with 810 students admitted and 167 of them subsequently emerging as English barristers; but in one respect there had been a change. For this decade saw the beginning of the great influx of Irish students into the Middle Temple, more than 200 of them, and the great majority went back to Ireland for their calls. By and large, however, the social attractions of the inns remained strong in the half century after 1680, and especially powerful during the long war years, when for most young gentlemen the Grand Tour was scarcely feasible.

As for the recruits to the bar between 1680 and 1730, as distinct from the general entry of the inns, four generalisations about their social background do seem permissible on the basis of the printed records of the societies. The first is that the landed gentry remained an indispensable source of supply. Their sons did not dominate the Augustan bar, but they were amply represented both there and on the judges' bench. Of those 167 students admitted to the Middle Temple in the 1720s who were subsequently called to the bar, no fewer than 90 were the sons of 'esquires'; and as many as 68 of them were eldest sons. The attractions of the profession to the landed classes is nowhere more sharply illuminated than in the very large number of their heirs who were not only sent to the inns but studied seriously and stayed the course; and it was by no means only minor families such as the Kenyons of Peel or the Gylls of Barton who provided them. In the second place, the flow of intending barristers from well-to-do professional or business backgrounds was increasing during the century following the outbreak of the Civil Wars. By 1730 considerably more clergymen's sons and attorneys' sons were practising at the bar than a hundred years earlier, and probably more sons of merchants, tradesmen and manufacturers also. In the three decades between 1695 and 1724 the sons of Anglican divines accounted for 16 out of 164 calls at Lincoln's Inn. Eighty-two clergymen's sons and nineteen doctors' sons were accepted as students at the Middle Temple between 1700 and 1719. They proved to have rather more staying power than entrants from a commercial or industrial background. Had all or most of the fifty-eight sons of overseas merchants, tradesmen and manufacturers who became Middle Templars in the 1720s been seriously intent on a legal career, the alarmists' case that the social traditions of the bar were being undermined might seem more plausible; but, in the event, only a third of them stayed long enough to qualify themselves for practice. Two further features of the early-eighteenth-century bar and judiciary ought to have comforted the traditionalists. One was that, in common with the Church, the law was becoming an increasingly inbred profession in the Augustan period. The rising output of qualified lawyers from the inns between the 1660s and the 1690s was matched by a rising intake of lawyers' sons, then and over the next three decades. It was much greater, in fact, than the records superficially indicate, since attorneys' sons (a major source of recruitment) were rarely differentiated from those of 'gentlemen' at large. Lincoln's Inn, where in each of the periods 1695–1704, 1705–14 and 1715–24, 22 per cent of the calls involved the sons of barristers or attorneys, exemplifies the general trend. Decade by decade after 1680 more and more legal dynasties were being consolidated or taking shape. On the other hand, the genuinely plebeian entry to the inns of court was assuredly no higher in 1730 than it had been in 1630. Indeed it is clear that it was, if anything, even more difficult for a poor man's son to fight his way to the bar by the age of Walpole than it had been in the age of Clarendon and Finch. And the surest protection for the bar against the spectre of social dilution was that 'great and certain' expense of a professional training to which Campbell rightly pointed in the 1740s.

There was no question that since the Civil Wars the normal cost of a barrister's training had risen steeply. The abandonment of formal readings and mootings at Lincoln's Inn in 1677, and elsewhere at much the same time, far from checking this process was partly responsible for accelerating it. For, being thrown back on his own resources, the keen student often had recourse to an informal system of tutoring and 'guided reading', a system in which the London attorneys or Chancery solicitors came increasingly to play a key part. Unless he undertook clerical labour as a *quid pro quo,* this could add considerably, among many other factors, to the expense of his long endurance test. Many earnest students had contrived to struggle through their long apprenticeships in the early seventeenth century on allowances of £40 or even £30 a year; £80 a year in the 1620s enabled a young man to study in comfort and to live quite luxuriously. Even from 1669 to 1674 Roger North, whose family was hardly penniless but who was kept short by a tightfisted grandfather, 'jogged on for divers years' at the Middle Temple with £10 to fit out his chamber, a gift of £30 from his 'careful mother' to start a small law library, and a regular annual income of only £40. It was touch and go, however, and he reflected in later years that 'without the aid I had from my brother [Sir Francis North], I could not have subsisted, and must have fallen'. His successors two generations later were to be in no doubt that they were in a different world. In 1718 Charles Saunderson, a top-flight attorney of thrifty Northumberland stock, cautioned a friend that it could well cost him £200 a year to maintain his son at the Middle Temple. Saunderson, like his countryman Charles Salkeld, who coached Philip Yorke when the latter was at the Middle Temple between 1708 and 1715, attached great importance to both the pastoral and professional advantages of persuading a string of eager young students to read regularly in his chambers. Small wonder attorneys in such prestigious practice were now prepared to pay high rents to have chambers conveniently sited in one of the inns of court. The sons of some of the cream of the north-eastern gentry were sent to the Inner Temple to be under Saunderson's wing: William Cotesworth, junior, and his brother Robert, sons of the wealthy squire of Gateshead; Edward Heslop Cotesworth of the Hermitage, their cousin; Henry Liddell, Henry Ellison and Robert Ord.

Long gone were the days when an Essex squire's son of Queen Elizabeth's day had paid his tutor at one of the inns 5s for 'reading law to me'. And gone, too, were the days of the shoe-string budget. Under George I, while a tradesman's or clergyman's son could afford to dispense with the 39 guineas for music, dancing and French masters allowed for by Saunderson in a young gentleman's budget in 1720, he might have to pay up to £20 or £25 a year for chamber rent and £70 or £80 a year to eat and dress as well as many of his fellow students were now accustomed to do. Tuition fees could be a major item. By comparison, the £5 annually which Saunderson expected his pupils to spend on law books was a drop in the ocean. The entire seven- or eight-year investment might amount to anything from £1,000 to £1,500.

In Restoration England there were at least a handful of cases of astonishing social mobility via a barrister's gown. The most spectacular was that of Chief Justice Edmund Saunders, who ran away from an unhappy home in a Gloucestershire village, came to London and took shelter in Clement's Inn, where he ran endless errands for the attorneys' clerks and lived on such scraps as they procured for him. One of them provided him with a makeshift desk; he learned legal hands, and by copying documents earned enough to feed and clothe himself respectably. He was an avid borrower of books and, having taught himself Norman French and law-Latin, concentrated on mastering two skills, conveyancing and special pleading. Some leading attorneys were so impressed that they encouraged him to enter the Middle Temple as a student, which he duly did in July 1660. Saunders qualified four years later and from then on his rise was meteoric. By the 1730s such 'rags to riches' stories are very hard to uncover. And the chief obstacle, beyond doubt, to the entrance into the profession of men without means or substantial patronage was not any social barriers raised by the inns themselves, though these were not entirely fictional. It was rather the all-but-inescapable expenses of a barrister's training, which had risen so much over the past seventy years, and with such particular effect since the Revolution.

The legal profession and the common lawyers were not synonymous in Augustan England. Although in numerical terms those who practised in the courts of common law and equity, together with those who served those courts as officials and clerks, overwhelmingly predominated, some of the most respected and prosperous legal practisers in the country were still 'civilians'. The civil lawyers, many of them university-trained, were those who specialised either in Roman and maritime law, for the most part managing cases before the admiralty courts, or in canon law, handling the business of the courts ecclesiastical. In addition, a handful of civilians remained in demand as advisers to successive governments on questions of international law: Humphrey Henchman and Sir John Cooke made themselves particularly useful in this field under the last two Stuarts.

For this branch of the profession, by contrast with the dynamic experience of the common lawyers, the years 1680–1730 proved an uneventful, relatively static phase in its long history. The civil lawyers had never been a large battalion, even in their heyday. There were still throughout the country well over 150 courts in which the civil law held sway, of which 7 were major courts sitting in London, 26 were bishops' (or consistory) courts and 21 others were vice-admiralty courts for the seaboard counties. Most of these courts had a presiding judge, variously designated, and each had at least one registrar and a number of proctors specifically allotted to it. But so rife was pluralism that no calculation of numbers is possible from these premises. In the early 1700s the chief metropolitan courts, excluding those of the diocese of London, were probably served by fewer than ninety active civilians. And it seems very unlikely that there can have been, at any one time, more than 500 men, other than apprentice clerks, regularly involved in the work of the whole bewildering complex, the length and breadth of England and Wales. Their total was probably nearer 400. The impression they often gave of belonging to a more than usually tight, exclusive and ritualised sect was enhanced during the years from 1660 to 1720 by the tendency of a handful of Oxford and Cambridge colleges, notably All Souls and New College in Oxford and Trinity Hall in Cambridge, to become acknowledged nurseries of civil lawyers.

It is an impression that is not altogether misleading; but it would be wrong to assume from it that this was a sect which had already drifted into redundancy and was exhibiting every sign of fossilisation. In a valuable study of the civil lawyers under the early Stuarts, B. P. Levack has explained how their strongly loyalist affiliations at that time undermined the popularity and prospects which they had enjoved in Elizabeth I's reign. Although they managed to survive the threa of extinction during the Interregnum and enjoyed a brief reflowering of former glories in the early Restoration years, their history subsequently is represented as one of lingering decline lasting until the reforms of the mid-Victorian era. Taking a long perspective across two centuries this is not a generalisation which can be quarrelled with. Undeniably, admissions to the Court of Arches (one yardstick of the profession's health) fell away badly after 1720. But in Augustan England the practice of the civil law was still a long way from the 'cosy, dosey, old-fashioned, time-forgotten, sleepy-headed' Dickensian picture of 'private theatricals, presented to an uncommonly select audience'.

Various circumstances combined to ensure that the profession suffered few anxieties on the score of recruitment in the later seventeenth century or in the first two decades of the eighteenth. In the 1680s the civilians profited from Archbishop Sancroft's reinvigoration of the church courts before James II's Indulgence of 1687. In this decade, too, one prominent civil lawyer, Sir Leoline Jenkins, became a Secretary of State after representing the Crown at the peace congress of Nijmwegen, while another, Sir William Trumbull, was made envoy to Versailles and ambassador at Constantinople. By Anne's reign the business of the High Court of Admiralty had probably reached its highest peak yet, thanks to the twin stimuli of the Nine Years' and Spanish Succession Wars. The activities of the church courts may, indeed, have been contracting, yet they still enjoyed a monopoly of a wide range of business. Probate (the administration of wills), the hearing of all matrimonial causes except those initiated by parliamentary Bill, tithe suits, clerical discipline, cases of blasphemy and bastardy were only the most notable areas of their authority. Despite the fact that their competence over the full gamut of moral offences, a source of great unpopularity in the past, was now being undermined, there is no doubt that the professional pickings to be had in the church courts were still far from negligible. And once again, by the early 1700s leading civil lawyers – men such as Hedges, Henchman, Cooke, Henry Newton and George Clarke – were for one reason or another in the public eye. Sir Charles Hedges, for instance, punctuated a long career as an Admiralty and Prerogative Court judge with two spells as a Cabinet minister; Cooke took part in the abortive Anglo-Scottish Union negotiations of 1702; and Henchman was consulted by Harley's government in the framing of the Treaty of Utrecht.

Only doctors of law, armed with a higher degree from one of the universities, were allowed to serve as advocates or officiate as judges in the High Courts of Admiralty and Chivalry and in the five central courts of the province of Canterbury. They presided over most vice-admiralty and commissary courts as well, and in 1704 were filling all but seven of the twenty-six diocesan chancellorships. For them the path to the threshold of the profession was a costly one to tread. Nevertheless there were few signs before the 1720s of the supply of recruits from Oxford and Cambridge running dry. The social kudos of a doctorate was enviable, carrying 'esquire' status automatically and precedence equal to that of serjeants-at-law. Although the big prizes of the profession were relatively few they were well worth having and could often be secured more quickly than those of the common law. Henry Penrice, having made a reputation for outstanding ability in his early appearances at the bar, succeeded Henry Newton as Judge of the Court of Admiralty in 1715 although it was only nine years since his first admission to Doctors' Commons. The rise of John Bettesworth was even more meteoric. He became Dean of the Arches in 1710 at the age of 32, a mere three years after beginning his career as an advocate; he then spent the next forty-one years demonstrating that his durability was even more remarkable than his precocity. When Bettesworth drew up his will in 1749 he could dispose of a manor and farm at Crowle, an estate at Littleheath in Berkhampstead, £1,500-worth of stock in the Million Bank, in addition to South Sea and Bank of England stock and Bank annuities of an unspecified amount, a moiety of fee farm rents in Warwickshire and Worcestershire, and the annual income on four 'Exchequer orders of long annuities'. The fact that so much valuable patronage was in the hands of the Archbishop of Canterbury instead of being controlled by the Crown may help to explain why the careers of the civilian doctors sometimes appeared more open to talents than those of the common law barristers. They certainly drew fewer of their recruits from the armigerous gentry. Bettesworth's dazzling progress is the more remarkable because his father was a Hampshire saddler and his school an insignificant grammar school at Baddesley.

Meanwhile apprentices (frequently from good families, prepared to pay premiums which, by the years 1710–30, usually ranged from £70 to £150) continued to come forward to train as proctors – their pre-requisite a classical education, though not necessarily beyond the level of a good grammar school or private academy. Some proctors did hold bachelor's degrees in civil law; and graduates were particularly prominent among the élite group of thirty-four proctors of the Arches Court in 1723. But an academic training alone was of dubious relevance to what was, for the most part, a 'practic' function akin to that of attorneys in the common law courts.

> The proctor, like the attorney [wrote Campbell in 1747] must be acquainted with all the writs and different forms of proceedings in the several supreme and subordinate courts; takes information from the client, puts the suit in motion, and prepares briefs for the counsel when the cause comes to a hearing, and conducts the whole till it comes to a final issue.

The desirability, if not necessity of the newly qualified proctor setting up in practice with a firm financial cushion at his back meant few opportunities in this area for poor men's sons, regardless of whether they had passed through a university or not. But once they were established civilian proctors of more than common ability often did better for themselves financially than their supposed betters, the doctors. The proctor's fees, 'though not large', according to *The London Tradesman* in the 1740s, 'are yet so frequent that a spiritual suit is near as bad and expensive as one in Chancery'. One late-seventeenth-century proctor, George Smith, married his daughter to Sir Charles Hedges; another, Everard Exton, married his into the thriving Sayer family, which produced both advocates and proctors well into the Hanoverian period. The system being what it was, the highest returns often went to those who played the accumulation game to good purpose. George Sayer, for instance, was Lord Admiral's Proctor in the 1720s as well as being a dominant figure among the proctors of the Arches Court; but he was outdone by Henry Farrant who in 1723 held down simultaneously the posts of King's Proctor, Register and Actuary of the Arches Court, Register of the High Court of Chivalry and Deputy to the Principal Registers of the Prerogative Court of Canterbury. Nothing, however, underlined more emphatically the status of the most flourishing London proctors by the end of the seventeenth century than their admission to the civilians' holy of holies, Doctors' Commons, where in 1696 they were already occupying five of the nineteen houses or sets of rooms available.

On a tiny scale the invasion of Doctors' Commons by the proctors mirrored a roughly parallel but far more significant trend among the common lawyers. Papers laid before the House of Commons showed that by the end of 1729, of the first 601 men enrolled under the recent Regulating Act as solicitors in Chancery and Exchequer or as attorneys of the King's Bench and Common Pleas no fewer than 38 gave addresses in the inns of court. Richard Eadnell, James Mundy, Charles Rochester and John St Elay, attorneys specialising in criminal cases, were among eighteen leading London practisers who had chambers, and in some cases lodgings, in the Inner Temple. By the time Parliament's information was complete in 1731, however, these denizens were revealed as only the tip of a very large iceberg. Over 240 rooms or sets of rooms in the four inns were found to be occupied by lawyers who had never been called to the bar. Such chambers, often highly rented and well furnished, were appropriate symbols of the continuing advance of the attorney, and of his associate the solicitor, in late Stuart and early Hanoverian England.

This rise was a general seventeenth-century phenomenon, not a purely Augustan one. Indeed, it was the most remarkable single development in the whole professional sector of English society between 1600 and 1680. Yet over the next fifty to sixty years the respectable, qualified attorney not merely improved and consolidated his social status but extended his range of functions and, in many cases, greatly enlarged his income. Likewise, after 1680 the numbers engaged in this branch of the profession continued to grow unchecked, and (if we take account of the shadier elements, a most extensive periphery) quite probably at an accelerating rate. In the middle of Elizabeth's reign it is unlikely that there were in the whole country as many as 500 qualified attorneys, properly trained in one of the (then) eight inns of Chancery. But as the land market seethed with activity and litigation multiplied, attorneys and solicitors, no less than barristers, found an open-ended demand for their services. Parliamentary alarm, which was to erupt periodically over the next 150 years, is in evidence as early as 1605. Under Charles I the Privy Council ascertained that the number of attorneys formally enrolled in the Court of Common Pleas, their commonest habitat, had risen from 313 in 1587 to 1,383 in 1633. The fact that they were registered there did not mean, even in the early seventeenth century, that the great bulk of them had their principal practice in London and Westminster. On the contrary, between the reigns of Charles I and

James II it was the spreading rash of provincial attorneys which increasingly attracted notoriety. In this connection the comments of John Aubrey, recorded at two points in the 1680s, are highly revealing, even if the precise figures accompanying them should be regarded with caution.

> Mr. Baynham of Cold Aston, in Gloucestershire, bred an attorney, says that an hundred years since there were in the county of Gloucester but four attorneys and solicitors; and Dr Guydot, physician, of Bath, says that they report that anciently there was but one attorney in Somerset, and he was so poor that he went afoot to London; and now they swarm like locusts.

> Fabian Philips tells me (1683) that about sixty-nine years ago there were but two attorneys in Worcestershire, sc. Langston and Dowdeswell; and they be now in every market town, and go to markets; and he believes there are a hundred . . .

Local opinions such as these, impressionistic as they usually were, suggest that Aubrey's own conjecture towards the close of Charles II's reign – 'tis thought that in England there are at this time near three thousand [attorneys]' – may have been more conservative than he imagined.

The total number of attorneys who were officially on the rolls of the Westminster courts on the eve of the Revolution, together with *bona fide* solicitors who regularly practised there or in Chancery, must itself have approached 3,000; for even fifty years before, the attorneys' rolls alone had mustered 1725. However, there were now so many unsworn or unregistered practitioners in the provinces that these rolls had become a very unrealistic gauge of the size of this part of the profession. A Bill introduced by Lord Rochester in 1697, aimed at prohibiting any person from acting in legal proceedings unless he had been admitted and sworn in a court of record, fell by the wayside. It was especially difficult to keep track of solicitors. Chancery, in the main their preserve, was still not formally an enrolling court. Technically, the fact that equity suits were not heard in local assize courts ought to have greatly inhibited the spread of solicitors into country towns; but the reality was very different. It had long been the practice for defendants living out of London to be allowed to have their answer to a plaintiff's bill in Chancery heard by commissions sitting locally and attended by solicitors; witnesses, too, could be heard at the same time. Of the early-seventeenth-century Monmouthshire solicitor, Walter Powell, whose diary has been printed, Mr Birks has written that 'much of his recorded work consisted of commissions'. Except when they were sent down to the assizes, where there was less punctilio, cases in common law courts involving solicitors' clients were normally handled by attorneys acting as agents for the provincial practisers. In such circumstances it was not difficult for solicitors, like attorneys, to put down strong roots in every county.

During the reigns of Charles II and his brother cases of provincial solicitors achieving considerable local standing, as well as building up tidy fortunes, began to multiply. The father of Lawrence Carter, the Whig barrister and judge, had made himself one of the most influential men in Leicester before the Revolution; among many civic services, then and later, he played a major part in organising the town's first regular water supply. Of comparable weight in south-east Kent was Philip Yorke, senior, who flourished in Dover well before the end of the century, acquiring a formidable reputation as an 'obstinate executor, well versed in the knavish part of the law, and very resolute to insist upon it'. But for every Carter and Yorke there were now scores of men of small reputation (or none) calling themselves 'solicitors', many justifiably, many not, but all busily at work in the great provincial ant-heap of the law.

Neither the 1688 Revolution nor the war in the 1690s had any discernible effect in stemming the advance of the attorneys and solicitors, whose numbers were said in the House of Commons in 1700 to have reached 'exorbitant' proportions. Attempts to do so by legislation in 1701 and 1706 both foundered. The second failure was especially notable for the powerful pressure group of lawyers and legal officials who obstructed it. When a wideranging law reform Bill, sponsored by Lord Somers, was sent down to the Commons it was very evident to its supporters, among them Bishop Burnet, 'that the interest of under-officers, clerks and attorneys, whose gains were to be lessened by this bill, was more considered than the interest of the nation itself: several clauses, how beneficial soever to the subject, which touched on their profit, were left out by the Commons'. By this time it was the 'knavish' element in the profession that was causing most alarm, 'now indeed swarming', as John Evelyn wrote, shortly before his death, 'and evidently causing suits and disturbance, by eating out the estate of people, provoking them to go to law'. And yet, after Parliament in 1729 had at last decided that it could ignore the unacceptable face of the profession no longer, it was to discover that even the nominally acceptable face had grown disconcertingly larger in recent decades. Some 6,000 names were returned to the House of Commons by March 1731 of attorneys and solicitors sworn in the four parent courts at Westminster (including Chancery), and in certain provincial courts of recognised standing, since the Regulating Act was first applied in May 1729. Even though around a quarter of them (overwhelmingly the names of Chancery and Exchequer solicitors) appeared on more than one roll, this still represented a major change since the Revolution, let alone since the 1630s. About the attorneys alone we can be more precise. So far as the court rolls are concerned their numbers had risen over the past century by roughly 150 per cent. There were 1,157 attorneys of the King's Bench (compared with 342 in 1633), 2,677 entitled to practise in the Court of Common Pleas, and a further 418 enrolled with either the Courts of Great Sessions in Wales, the Courts Palatine of Lancaster and Chester, or the King's Court of Record at Newcastle-upon-Tyne: in all 4252. A high proportion of these men must have had articled clerks – apprentice attorneys – in their offices: and since many of these clerks would expect to qualify for independent practice within little more than the five-year minimum period which Parliament was now insisting on it seems clear that further reinforcements were still coming in at an appreciable rate. Over 1,150 new apprentices had been recorded by the officials of the Stamp Office in the ten years from 1711 to 1720, and it is well known that there was much evasion of the statutory duty. How numerous the 'rogue' element among the attorneys had been before the passing of the 1729 Act, or how large it remained after 1730, we can never hope to know with any certainty. A general estimate for England and Wales made long afterwards, in 1759, put the number of men practising as attorneys, many of them unsworn, before the Act came into force at over 6,000. Whether it was more than a plausible guess it is impossible to say.

While the numbers of attorneys had been expanding apace so, too, had the bureaucracy of the law courts. In 1732, for instance, the Wyndham Select Committee reported to the Commons that since Queen Elizabeth's later years 'the officers of the Court of Chancery are exceedingly increased . . . by patents and grants, and many secretaries and clerks, and other honorary attendants upon the judges of that court, appear now to claim large fees, whose services were unknown to the ancient practisers of the fortieth of Elizabeth'. More insidiously, a whole new substratum had appeared in the profession, emerging from comparative unimportance in the early seventeenth century. Its constituents were the 'entering clerks'. According to Sir George Cook, then Chief Prothonotary, roughly a thousand entering clerks were formally accredited to the Westminster Court of Common Pleas alone by 1729; but many more – probably at least twice as many more – were functioning by this time who had never been formally sworn in any court, or worse still, were in no sense qualified to be sworn by having served out their articles. By 1729 no one knew even approximately how many practising clerks there were in England and Wales. William Tullie, an experienced lawyer giving evidence before a Commons' committee of inquiry, would venture no more than that 'he believed there were some thousands'.

Finally, there was the proliferation of the 'solicitors'. This was something all contemporary observers were unanimous about but to which no one could begin to attach precise figures. This was partly for technical reasons (essentially, the lack before 1729 of any formal solicitors' roll). But what chiefly bedevilled the issue was the difficulty of drawing a clear-cut line between the legitimate element in the profession and the semi-legitimate or illegitimate practitioners, something that plagued the law increasingly between the 1680s and the 1720s. It was this, more than anything, which precipitated the full parliamentary inquest into the lower tiers of the profession and led ultimately to the legislation of 1729 designed to impose order and control upon them. In the case of the entering clerks, the anarchic situation which had been developing over the previous fifty or sixty years would have mattered much less if they had been content simply to do the hack work for attorneys and solicitors. But, in practice, many hundreds of them – it may be, even a majority of them – assumed the functions of formally qualified attorneys themselves, taking out and prosecuting writs in the courts (connived at by judges and officials, so long as there was an attorney's name appended to the writ), as well as involving themselves directly in a wide selection of non-litigious activities on behalf of 'clients'. Many, it seems, had little conscience about openly calling themselves 'solicitors'. When *The Compleat Solicitor, Entring-Clerk and Attorney* first appeared in 1668 its author, while conceding that 'the licentiousness' of the years 1642–60 had 'introduced disorder and confusion' into the profession, could 'see no reason, as the case stands, why a man of brisk parts (though formerly, against his inclination perhaps, or by some cogent necessity, put to a trade) may not as well set up for a solicitor . . .' A formal training was, of course, to be preferred; but the writer flattered himself that, armed with his treatise, 'no man needs to despair whom God and Nature have blessed with a competency of wit, memory and judgement, and inclinations and industry suitable to his profession'. By the time its second edition was published in 1683, however, *The Compleat Solicitor* was losing its faith in Providence. In fact, it had so far changed its tune that it was even advocating a Chancery roll of properly educated and sworn solicitors. But before this finally came about forty-six years later, the author's complaint that 'now every idle fellow whose prodigality and ill husbandry hath forced him out of his trade or employment, takes upon him to be a solicitor' had taken on further substance, as the Strickland Committee discovered to its consternation soon after George I's death.

By 1759 Joseph Massie believed that a further 2,000 could reasonably be added to the 10,000 'persons in the law' calculated by his predecessor, Gregory King, in 1688. Taking account not only of judges, barristers and court officials but of attorneys, solicitors (legitimate and otherwise), notaries and entering clerks, his guess is likely to have been closer to the mark than is sometimes thought. At least half the whole number, at all events, must have practised as attorneys and qualified solicitors. And yet, by a curious paradox, what is already striking by the reign of Anne and the early years of George I, when poll books for some of the larger cities and towns began to be published, is the difficulty of identifying these very lawyers who played such a vital part in the life of their communities. The same can be said of similar lists (tax assessments, for example) which attach occupations or status to the names they contain. In the fifteenth century and long into the sixteenth, when all attorneys were still members of one of the inns of Chancery, the new profession had been conceded 'gentleman's' status. Its rapid expansion after 1580, accompanied by a significant decline in the remuneration of many attorneys so that far fewer over the next three-quarters of a century were able to 'live like gentlemen', placed them in a more equivocal social position. However, as the economic prospects of the profession in turn revived in the late seventeenth century, so, too, did its social pretensions. On the face of things it would appear from a 1715 poll book that the 3,000 voters at the Norwich election included 42 'gentlemen' but not a single attorney or solicitor and only one solitary notary. It is utterly incredible that the kingdom's second city and the heart of a notoriously litigious county where the farmers were said to 'carry Littleton's Tenures at the plough tail' should have been so bereft of legal services. The 1790 Law Lists for Norwich were to name thirty-two attorneys in a city not much larger than its early-eighteenth-century predecessor. In 1730 the small borough of Brecon, perhaps a fifteenth of Norwich's size, is known to have had ten attorneys living in it. The message of the poll books is unmistakable: prosperous colonies of attorneys are plainly subsumed there under the 'gentlemen' whose votes are recorded. Long before the middle of the eighteenth century, as was argued in the Court of Common Pleas in 1741, the sworn office of attorney-at-law had indisputably conferred this rank. For the attorneys and sworn solicitors of the Home Counties to name their first professional organisation in the late 1730s 'The Society of Gentlemen Practisers' was therefore entirely proper.

Facts like these can serve as a useful qualification to the view advanced in Robert Robson's admirable study of the eighteenth-century attorneys, which is that as a professsion they only achieved respectability during the second half of the eighteenth century, and then only very slowly. It is tempting to be seduced by the wit of Dr Johnson, to whom Boswell attributes the choice remark (c. 1770) that 'he did not care to speak ill of any man behind his back, but he believed the gentleman was an attorney.' And yet for all the profession's many faults and shortcomings, even by the beginning of the eighteenth century the attorneys could claim a very substantial top layer of able, honest and socially acceptable practitioners, now fully assimilated into the ranks of the town gentry if not of the country gentry. What is more, this large 'liberal and reputable' body in the legal profession (as Lord Mansfield later distinguished it) enjoyed a growing *esprit de corps*. No group that could muster 1,169 signatures on a petition to the Treasury in 1707 on behalf of attorneys threatened with prosecution for non-payment of stamp duties can be said to have justly merited Michael Birks's scathing description of them at this date as 'collectively . . . a rabble'. It was unfortunate, of course, that the 1729 Act fell a long way short, in practice, of the aims of those who looked to it to sweep the stables entirely clean. Its stipulations were stringent enough. Yet the author of a 1759 pamphlet contended that very few attorneys and solicitors, however ill qualified, who had been in practice thirty years earlier had, in the event, been forced out by the Act. Neither had the door been firmly closed since then against dubious newcomers. Why this was so can be understood, partly, in the light of the predicament of the judges, who were under great pressure to enrol and could hardly institute an examination in every doubtful case. But it becomes even more intelligible when we realise the extraordinary range of functions performed by the Augustan attorney and solicitor, and how little many of them needed to come into direct contact with the king's courts while making a perfectly adequate living.

We have seen how between 1660 and 1690, as front-line barristers conclusively restricted their involvement in law suits to pleading and counselling, the attorney and solicitor had finally made themselves their indispensable agents. By this time the body of case law and precedent was already so vast and complex, and a knowledge of the minutiæ of legal forms such a specialism, that a proper and lengthy training had become almost inescapable for anyone wishing to practise exclusively, or largely, in the Westminster courts. Likewise, for the much greater number who handled a lot of circuit and sessions work while relying on London agents to handle their clients' Westminister business, success had almost always been prefaced by an orthodox training. A very small and ever-dwindling minority of Augustan attorneys and solicitors still acquired this training in the traditional way, at Clifford's, Clement's, Staple or one of the other Chancery inns. Already by 1680, however, the vast majority were learning the ropes through apprenticeship to practising attorneys and solicitors for a period that varied between four and seven years, but was normally five years. This norm was made compulsory by statute in 1729. The training was frequently gruelling. Yet the pressure on apprenticeships remained strong throughout these fifty years. In the first three decades of the eighteenth century the number of youths and young men (most of them between the ages of 16 and 23) who were in articled clerkships at any one time can rarely have fallen far below 1,500.

The reason is not far to seek. For densely populated though it was, 'the practic part of the law' now offered ample scope for any skilful or hardworking lawyer to make good. The expansion of court business in the late seventeenth and early eighteenth centuries must certainly have played an important part in sustaining demand and in swelling profits. It was sometimes said that there was not enough business to go round even for the London attorneys, and one writer wrote scathingly of them in the 1740s that 'the legal fees of their profession are so small that without tricking and low arts it is morally impossible for any one of them to live like a gentleman merely as an attorney [that is, through the fair profits of litigation]'. To judge, however, from the experience of many of those who regularly plied the Westminster courts and the lesser courts of the City, this was palpably a wild exaggeration. Sir George Cook bore witness in 1729 to the increase of business in the Common Pleas in the twenty years since he had become Prothonotary. John Croft, Deputy to the Master of the Middlesex Office, admitted at the same time that he had known as many as 1,000 writs issued in that office alone in a single vacation, and around 3,000 in a year. And although fees in the overworked Court of Common Pleas had not, it seems, been raised for a long time, it would have startled most litigants to hear that they were 'low'. In fact, it had become conventional for attorneys and entering clerks alike to charge £8 in costs for all uncontested actions – 'whether for 40s. or £50 damages', according to Cook – and it was agreed to be 'a certain rule' for the officers of that court to allow costs of at least £14 10s whenever a cause went to trial. Much the same tariff for judgements by default held good in the Courts of Great Sessions for Wales and in the Court of Exchequer; and, in the latter, it was observed by one of the sworn attorneys in the Office of Pleas of that court, Richard Marriott, that 'where the judge, in case of a trespass or for battery, certifies for under 40 shillings, the costs [were] usually taxed at £16 or £17' and had been known to amount to £30.

What is so interesting, however, about much of the surviving contemporary evidence on individual attorneys and solicitors of the seventeenth and eighteenth centuries, whether it comes from fee books, notebooks, diaries, letters or memoirs, is the surprisingly modest contribution which litigation fees, from any source, made to their income. In the income of the country attorney, especially, such fees were often no more than a marginal element. And it was the massive inflation of non-litigious business in the second half of the seventeenth century and the early eighteenth century which more than anything else explains why so much of the profession's expansion at this time was concentrated in the provinces. A good deal of the country attorney's profit came from straightforward documentary work: drafting and executing wills, drawing up deeds and settlements of every nature. The established local man with clients among the gentry or among urban business or professional families could do very well out of winding up a large estate or negotiating a marriage settlement. Property was a major sphere of activity. Ambrose Holbech, who lived at Mollington in Warwickshire and has been described by a modern historian of the county as 'perhaps the most successful Warwickshire lawyer of his time', was commemorated in his epitaph in 1701 as 'very eminent in the law, particularly in the art of conveyancing which he practised with great integrity'. When Gregory King came to Warwickshire on behalf of the College of Arms in 1682 Holbech had been practising for some thirty years, and against his name Rouge Dragon wrote simply 'Attorney very rich'. Even for the workaday attorney small conveyances came along regularly; but the richer the client and the better the connections, the brighter was the attorney's chance of handling substantial deals in real estate, and perhaps participating in them himself. Isaac Greene, who had half the merchants of Liverpool and half the gentry families of south Lancashire among his clients before he was 40, developed an uncanny knack of picking up windfall land in this way. Among the fellow attorneys of the Chauncys in Hertfordshire before the Revolution were two, Joshua Lomax and Stephen Ewre, 'who dealt much in buying and selling of lands, by which this Joshua Lomax obtained a fair estate'. Lomax, who died in 1685, was a dissenter from Lancashire who had made enough money by 1666 to buy an estate near St Albans (a borough his son was to represent in Parliament), and later he acquired the manor of Bovington and set up his younger son there.

By the late seventeenth century, when a client employed a local lawyer in property transactions he often expected him not only to examine titles and draw up conveyancing deeds, and perhaps survey the property, but arrange for a mortgage. Thus it came about that the provincial attorney or solicitor, at a time when the private country banker was almost unknown, became – sometimes *par excellence* – a handler of money. He not only negotiated loans for his clients, drawing fees for preparing the bonds; he also accepted deposits from them, paying 3 or

4 per cent interest, putting some of the money out on loan and collecting both interest and principal when due. Not least, he lent a good deal of money on his own account, charging 1 or 2 per cent more interest than he himself paid on deposits. The debt book of Joseph Hunt (1688–1725), a rich attorney in Stratford-upon-Avon with a number of prominent local clients, lists 193 persons who owed money either to him or his clients in one year alone. In the more sophisticated commercial or manufacturing communities this kind of function was already developing into something very like investment consultancy. Isaac Greene provided a regular investment service for clients in what was, by 1720, the third most flourishing port in the land.

Another service the attorney commonly performed for his property-owning clients was to collect their rents (Hunt, for example, charged them $2\frac{1}{2}$ per cent on takings for the service); and this, in turn, led the successful attorney, with clients among the landed gentry, across the open frontier into the field of regular stewardship or estate management. After that it was but a short step for some to doing brisk business as an election agent, especially during the frenetic period of electoral activity in England from 1689 to 1715. The height of his ambition was to become the fully-fledged 'agent' or man of affairs of a great landlord, perhaps even of a group of landlords, as Alexander Leigh of Hindley watched over the interests of the coal-owning Bradshaighs of Haigh, or as Matthew Lamb of Southwell served the Cokes of Melbourne, and Joseph Banks of Sheffield, the Howards, Osbornes and Pelham-Holleses. Isaac Greene's services to the Molyneuxs of Croxteth culminated in what his biographer justifiably calls 'a remarkable letter' written to the fifth viscount in 1726 setting out proposals to take over that peer's entire estates and guarantee him a fixed annual income out of their rent yield! The multifariousness, and profitability, of the attorney's functions in Augustan England was thus the result of a seemingly endless series of chain reactions. And to help him in many of these capacities, though most of all in comprehending (as the *The London Tradesman* put it) 'all the windings, shiftings and turnings' of pursuing cases through the courts, he could stock his shelves by 1730 with a row of well-thumbed manuals. *The Compleat Solicitor* now had numerous companions, among them *The Attorney's Academy* (frequently re-issued), *The Practick Part of the Law* (1678), *The Practice of the Courts of King's Bench and Common Pleas* (1696), *The Practical Register in Chancery* (1716) the second edition of William Bohun's *The Practising Attorney: or Lawyer's Office* (1726), and West's *Symboleography*, which was the bible of the eighteenth-century conveyancer.

It is not difficult to see, therefore, why there was no overpowering incentive before 1729 for even a trained articled clerk to get himself on the attorneys' roll, especially when he had to pay for the privilege. It is also plain why hundreds of men with no more than a perfunctory training were able to set up as solicitors, and quite often (in small market towns especially) as self-advertised 'attorneys'. Quite simply there was no lack of business for such men, the 'pettifoggers' of popular contemporary parlance. It did not require formidable expertise to take on bread-and-butter suits in local courts: small actions for trespass or nuisances, for example, which still kept many manorial courts busy, or even cases of small thefts and assaults at the quarter sessions. The bolder brethren would involve themselves with gusto in the recovery of debts, even though these had normally to be taken to the king's courts and required the help of an accredited attorney or solicitor to act as agent. The pettifoggers, who picked up a lot of their custom in inns and coffee houses, could also rely on much small business as 'writers' (some would charge 3d or even 6d a letter). Simple wills and settlements were also within their competence. Above all, they could merrily involve themselves in the money-lending and broking functions of the country lawyer. Nothing did more to jeopardise the repute of the profession at large in Augustan England than the financial machinations of the provincial factotum; and, in particular, the foxy activities of that notorious fringe element, the pseudo-'solicitors'.

There was, however, one range of functions open to attorneys and solicitors, presenting a whole area of lucrative opportunities, to which only the properly qualified could aspire. There was an abundance of public offices in Augustan England, local as well as central, which were regarded as the preserve of lawyers and were usually compatible with private practice. Possibly a fifth of the whole profession found grazing in these pastures where even the relatively thin grass was tolerably nourishing. In some corners attorneys were in danger of being nosed out by enterprising or needy barristers; but there were many other parts, with crops ranging from coveted clerkships in Chancery or solicitorships of Excise to circuit clerkships or country clerkships of the peace, where the succulent shoots were usually theirs alone (not invariably: when a Bolton attorney named Morton became Clerk of the Peace for Lancashire in 1694, he displaced the barrister son of Roger Kenyon of Peel). An assiduous attorney who took pains to master the business of one of these local clerkships could reasonably hope to make his tenure impervious to shifts of political fortune. Thus Lancelot Simpson of Allesthwaite became Clerk of the Peace for Cumberland in 1690, when he was 47, and retained the office for the next twenty-one years until his death, despite acting as a local agent for the Whig magnate Lord Carlisle.

The office of Town Clerk, too, was becoming increasingly sought after by provincial worthies of the profession, sometimes as a stepping stone, sometimes as a coping stone to local prominence. John Chauncy, who was Town Clerk of Hertford from 1663–70, at a relatively early stage of his career, later progressed to being clerk to the justices and finally to becoming a magistrate himself in William III's reign. Two Town Clerks of King's Lynn under the first two Georges, Edward Bradfield and Robert Underwood, lived in impressive style, while Helston's Town Clerk, Henry Tremenheere, was also Deputy Recorder of the borough on behalf of the Godolphins. Like so many other offices in Hanoverian England town clerkships were prone to become family concerns. The Leigh family had to wait a long time for the office in Wigan; but when Alexander Leigh finally acquired it in 1732, five years after he had been mayor of the borough, he made sure it was passed on, first to his son John and then, in 1741, to his former clerk John Wiswall. Some boroughs, like Leicester and Oxford, employed town solicitors as well as town clerks; and, indeed, there was work enough for them all in a period when corporations were increasingly involved with litigation, petitions and even private bill legislation. The creation of new parishes in expanding towns, as at Manchester, Liverpool, Birmingham and Sheffield, and the river navigation schemes which absorbed so much interest, time and money from the 1690s onwards, were just two examples of fresh activities which involved Acts of Parliament (there were thirty-one river Acts alone between 1680 and 1730) and which called for the advice and piloting abilities of shrewd lawyers. Isaac Greene made himself invaluable to the corporation of Liverpool in handling the Weaver Navigation Bill in 1719–20, as on many other matters; while as Town Clerk of Wigan in the early 1730s Alexander Leigh was a moving spirit and a heavy spender in the protracted campaign to make the Douglas navigable from Wigan to the sea. The careers of both men also illustrate admirably one further aspect of the attorney's official opportunities, court-keeping. To have acquired the stewardship or clerkship of seventeen manor courts, as Leigh had by 1733, including Sir Roger Bradshaigh's courts at Wigan and Haigh and Lord Derby's at Knowsley, must have constituted some sort of record even for the avid eighteenth-century attorney. Greene, for his part, contrived to combine the stewardship of five or six courts, mostly for the Molyneuxs and Cases, with his plethora of other activities: indeed he throve on it all, and had reached the age of 71 before an apoplexy finally carried him off.

It is no coincidence that travellers in Augustan England often found the most striking physical evidence of the prosperity of attorneys in towns or areas where the opportunities for local office-holding were especially plentiful; in Preston, with its duchy courts; in Chester and Durham, with their courts palatine and consistory courts, or in the stannary towns of Cornwall. In Preston, Ralph Asheton, Thomas Seed and three other attorneys were paid officials of the Duchy Court of Chancery in 1723. Not surprisingly, when Celia Fiennes had arrived there in 1698 she had found

> at the entrance of the town . . . a very good house which was a lawyer's, all stone work . . . and high built according to the eastern building near London The ascent to the house was 14 or 15 stone steps large and a handsome court with open iron pallasadoes in the gate and on each side . . . which discovered the gardens on each side of the house, neatly kept flowers and greens; there was also many steps up to the house from the court. It was a complete building.

Preston seemed to Defoe to be 'full of attorneys, proctors, and notaries, the process of law here being of a different nature than they are in other places'. About the attorneys, at least, he was right. There were twenty-eight of them resident there by 1731, just two less than in the city of Chester; and as in so many other congenial provincial towns of the period which were increasingly becoming residential centres for the urban gentry and resorts for the country gentry, the Preston and Chester lawyers enjoyed a rich diet of private business quite apart from official duties and litigation. Defoe also found 'a pretty many attornies' at Launceston in Cornwall. There, as at Liskeard, Helston and Truro, lawyers such as Philip Welch, Nathaniel Carpenter and Samuel Lyne were in great demand as agents for the owners of tin and copper mines, as well as doing regular business in the Stannary courts. The Treasury found to its consternation as early as 1698 that there were in Cornwall 'rich attorneys in great practice' who in the assessments for the quarterly poll tax had either escaped their contributions altogether or had been taxed 'at only 4s.' – the rate designed for plain gentlemen; and indeed at Helston, where eight attorneys were entrenched by 1730, a whole dynasty of interrelated legal families established its hold on the town and, according to H. S. Toy, 'formed a sort of lesser aristocracy' there. Some of the choicest surviving provincial town architecture dating from the Augustan period can be traced back to the prosperity and good taste of successful attorneys: a splendid house in High Street, Burford, for instance, and the rich-fronted residence later called 'The Ivy' in Chippenham, built in 1728 by an attorney named Norris, which has been described as 'a very remarkable specimen of regional baroque'.

Before the passing of the Qualifications Act in Anne's reign a small handful of these professional representatives of the new pseudo-gentry of the towns made brief appearances in Parliament, representing their native boroughs: the elder Laurence Carter (Leicester) and Thomas Christie (Bedford) both did so under William III. After 1711, however, such ambitions could only be legally satisfied by translating wealth into land and founding squirearchical families, and in 1731 Parliament placed even the less exalted target of the country magistrates' bench out of the range of the provincial lawyer unless he was prepared to invest in real estate of a minimum value of £100 a year. But a marked trend in this direction had, in any case, set in during the previous three decades. In the years of war after 1702 no less than in the long period of peace after 1713 provincial lawyers emerged as an exceptionally active group of buyers. The majority favoured marking their success by the acquisition of a country house with a small estate within easy commuting distance of their place of business. Typical of many in this respect were John Starky of Rochdale, who bought Heywood Hall from the Heywood family in 1717, and William Hopwood, one of the most prosperous Halifax attorneys of the day, who after living for some years at Rastrick bought Hopwood Hall near Halifax in 1710, but continued to build up his practice for another twenty years and trained up his son Richard to carry it on. Similarly Thomas Wright, attorney of the King's Bench, while still making money rapidly amid the grime of Sheffield in the mid-1720s, was able (as a travelling parson observed) to enjoy the amenities of 'a new built little box, very pleasantly situated in a grove of five young thriving oaks', close to the Sitwell estate at Renishaw.

A prominent minority, however, were more ambitious. Men like William Plumbe of Liverpool and Thomas Becke of Lincoln typify their aspirations. Plumbe, who figures frequently in the diary of one of his clients, Nicholas Blundell of Crosby, was transacting business in his Liverpool office as late as 1727. But well before this he had built a country house at Wavertree, bought land from Sir Cleve Moore and in 1718, the year in which he drew up a new settlement of the Blundell lands, purchased the estate of a leading local squire, Richard Hesketh of Aughton. Becke was a younger man who began practising as an attorney in Lincoln in 1711 and became city chamberlain in 1720. Not content with the urban society in which his family had quietly prospered during the seventeenth century, he laid out most of his profits on a landed estate at Cherry Willingham, acquiring the advowson and building a new church for the village. The Hawkins family of Pennance and Trewithen owed their great estates to the 'pains, care and skill in that profession' of Philip Hawkins, reputedly the wealthiest of the hundred or so Cornish attorneys at the beginning of the eighteenth century; and one of his county contemporaries, Edward Hoblyn, moved into the country during King William's War at a time when neighbouring squires were groaning about the land tax, and built a handsome mansion house at Croan. More spectacular still were the operations of the Liverpool comet, Isaac Greene. In 1712, at the age of 34 and only twelve years or so after setting up in practise on his own, he bought his first manor, Eltonhead, in the parish of Prescot where his family had held a copyhold for several generations. Four years later he acquired the manor of Wavertree from Lord Strange, along with the estates of Everton and West Derby. They cost him £3,611 5s 3d, but they did not appease his hunger for he was ready to lay out a further £4,600 in 1718 on two estates of the Legay family, on one of which, Childwell, he built a new country seat. Other wealthy attorneys invested further afield. Joseph Banks, a Sheffield attorney of the previous generation (b. 1665), bought heavily in Lincolnshire and Nottinghamshire after the turn of the century, set up his son, William, as a country gentleman at Revesby Abbey and left him estates of more than £3,000 a year in 1727. His grandson became a baronet, as did the grandson of the Wigan factotum, Alexander Leigh, and the second son of Matthew Lamb of Southwell.

There were some persuasive seventeenth-century precedents for the activities of local lawyers in the land market. One of the most notorious was set by Robert Benson, senior, whose son (b. 1675) was to build a superb pile at Bramham Park in Yorkshire in Anne's reign on land which he bought in 1699. The elder Benson was a slick and none-too-scrupulous York attorney. He had purchased a manor and country house at Wrenthorpe and had left his infant heir an estate thought to be worth £1,500 a year in 1676. Robert Benson the younger became a peer of the realm in 1711. Yet his father, as Sir John Reresby sourly records in 1673, was 'of no birth, and . . . had raised himself from being clerk to a country attorney'. The family case history over fifty years highlights the very rapid social mobility which a successful attorney's career could engineer from the Restoration onwards. Here the contrast with the bar was sharp and important. The chances of the son of an obscure man establishing himself in one of the 'lesser degrees' of the law and achieving social respectability through his profession, as John Round, a Warwickshire innkeeper's son did at Stratford in the 1680s, remained relatively bright for much of the Augustan period. With uncommon ability, and luck, he might even attain great wealth: Isaac Greene, after all, was the son of a bankrupt merchant who appears to have fled abroad to escape his creditors, while Thomas Brereton, whose father Lord Egmont described as 'an ordinary fellow who kept an alehouse', made use of an articled clerkship in Chester as the first rung on a ladder that was to lead *inter alia* to marriage to a brigadier's daughter, a landed estate at Shotwick Park and £500 a year in the Victualling Office for almost two decades.

All the same, it would be a sorry distortion to suggest that the Augustan attorney or sworn solicitor was generally a man of lowly origin. His social background was exceptionally varied. It is transparent in the Stamp Office registers, which provide unique insight into recruitment to the 'practic part' of the law after 1710, that by Anne's reign there was quite stiff competition among men of good social standing to article their sons to soundly established local attorneys, as well as to leading London practisers. No one was surprised by now to find a Sitwell practising in Sheffield, a Mosley near Manchester, or a Bradfield at King's Lynn. A sure pointer to the attorneys' rising star and to the growing number of sons of gentle birth who followed its beckoning light is the general level of premiums which those in good practice expected with an apprentice-clerk. Despite the sullying of the profession through the activities of the 'pettifoggers' this level rose steadily and appreciably from the late seventeenth century onwards. Not until the 1730s was there a startling upward surge; yet even by the years 1712–30 it was not unknown for top-flight London attorneys to charge, according to the purse or status of applicants, as much as £200–£220 for taking youths into their offices for five years. In 1716, for example, one of the knights of the shire for Gloucestershire, Thomas Stephens of Upper Lypiatt, paid a £200 premium to have his son George trained in London by Nathaniel Hickman, a successful King's Bench attorney. A few leading Chancery solicitors, such as Thomas Paratt, William Bedford and John Mills, were already in a position when taking pupils to set their sights still higher, at around £250. These were great sums; and they foreshadowed the years after 1735 when even £500 was not unknown. While it must be appreciated that they were some leagues above the London mean, which by the same period, 1712–30, was closer to £100 than to £200 or £250, they do illustrate (as does the increasing tendency for fashionable provincial attorneys in the south of England to require premiums of £100, £105, in a few cases as much as £120) the undoubted vocational attractions of the articled clerkship in late Augustan England.

Yet the norms are just as significant in their own way as the ceiling.

Even by 1730 over much of the country the price of a five-year training, while it did not often fall below £60, very rarely exceeded £90. The contrast with the cost of reading for the bar, which by now could quite easily prove ten or fifteen times as expensive, was vividly apparent. The fact that such an outstandingly successful local lawyer as Isaac Green asked only £80 with a Lancashire squire's son in 1712, or that John Borlase of Pendeen, a Cornish Member of Parliament, was able to article one of his sons to a St Austell attorney three years later for £75 7s 6d helps to explain why the law remained accessible as a career to hundreds of men of far less favoured origins who could reasonably hope for a cheaper deal still. A sizeable minority of country premiums fell as low as £30–£50 in the early decades of the century. For men whose fathers were at least as far down the social scale as tradesmen, superior craftsmen and yeomen, and occasionally lower, the attorney's or solicitor's office continued to provide a serviceable ladder for scaling the lower ramparts of a major profession; and from there, provided they were able to lift themselves subsequently above the journeyman status of the lawyer's clerk, to the achievement of a secure social respectability.

On the other hand, for every tradesman's or shopkeeper's son articled to a London attorney by the early eighteenth century there was at least one whose family was already engaged in one of the professions, as well as another who came of landed gentry or town gentry stock. The commonest professional background, naturally, was in the law itself, though the Church was not far behind as a supplier. John Cooper, who practised in Salisbury in the mid-eighteenth century was no rarity at this date in having both a father and a grandfather who had been attorneys before him. Indeed by the 1720s and 1730s it was already possible to find whole clusters of attorney families in county after county whose extensive networks of fathers, sons, brothers and nephews were playing a vital part in the consolidation of the legal profession. There were the Fearnleys, Radcliffes and Skeltons in and around Leeds, the Mosleys and Byrons in the Manchester area, the Peterses of Liverpool, the Pottses in Newcastle, the Bucks and Aslabees of Rotherham, and dozens of others like them elsewhere. In Cornwall there were times when it must have seemed that half the plentiful legal business of the county was being engrossed by cliques of Rawlingses, Sandyses, Polkinhernes, Lynes and Tremenheeres. The widow of George Warburton, who was Town Clerk of Newark until his death in 1706, predictably articled her only surviving son to an attorney at East Markham from 1714 to 1719. However, as events turned out it was not as a lawyer but as a writer and divine that William Warburton was to leave his rumbustious mark on the eighteenth century. The links between the Augustan parsonage and attorney's office were close. The Archdeacon of Lincoln's son and at least five other clerical sprigs entered attorneys' offices in London in the year ending in November 1712. In all 10 per cent of the 610 children of the cloth apprenticed between 1710 and 1720 were articled to lawyers.

Noting in 1683 that many attorneys of his day 'will take a hundred pounds with a clerk', John Aubrey mused that 'they do now rule and govern the lawyers [barristers] and judges'. There is no doubt that at the start of our period many barristers resented their growing dependence on attorneys and solicitors and it was not uncommon, even in the early eighteenth century, for some of them, in defensive reaction to this and to growing public concern at the ailments of the 'lesser degrees' of the legal profession, to resort to contempt or even abuse in their attitudes to the latter. But right through the Augustan period many circumstances were working together to repair this division and bring a greater degree of unity and common identity to the lawyers as a whole. Mutual dependence for the bulk of their income, especially between the élite practitioners on both sides, was clearly one such unifying factor. Also barristers and attorneys were increasingly closely associated in local communities: in towns such as Preston, Leicester and Chester they lived cheek by jowl with little, if any, difference in their style of life. The growing importance of the London attorney's office in the training of young aspirants to the bar was yet another force pulling in the same direction. Not least important, it had become by no means unusual by the late seventeenth and early eighteenth centuries to find both sides of the law represented in one and the same family at the same time. 'John Chauncy, gentleman', the younger brother of Serjeant Chauncy and uncle to Henry Chauncy, junior, barrister of the Middle Temple, was still tending his attorney's business in Hertford in the 1690s. While the elder Matthew Lamb, grandfather of the first Lord Melbourne, was cultivating his Nottinghamshire practice in the early years of the new century, his brother Peniston was on the way to making a fortune of £100,000 at the bar. The elder brother of Charles Salkeld, the eminent London attorney of Great Brook Street, was an equally distinguished barrister. Under the first two Georges the Starkie family of Preston was represented in the town by an attorney, Thomas, and by two barristers, Nicholas and his son Edmund. The cross-flow between senior and junior branches was all the time increasing. Philip Yorke senior was still pursuing his solicitor's calling in Kent when his son was first setting the bar alight in Westminster Hall in 1715. And while attorneys and solicitors such as Yorke of Dover, Thomas Parker of Leek, Robert Raikes of Northallerton and John Brace of Bedford were busy grooming their eldest sons for the bar, barristers in growing numbers were happy to send at least their younger sons into attorney's offices. The profession was closing ranks. Once the attorneys and solicitors had clearly shown, as they did with the foundation of the first embryonic 'Law Society' in the 1730s, that they were determined to set their professional house in order, the day was not many years ahead when Hume Campbell, the barrister, would assure that same Society of Gentlemen Practisers that 'he considered the worthy part of the profession, whether attorneys, solicitors, or counsel, as one body'.

6

The Coming of 'the Doctor'

By the late seventeenth century the third of 'the great professions' of Stuart England, the practice of medicine, was conferring on a select few at its peak a status that was roughly comparable with that enjoyed by the far larger élite of the legal profession. But it was a status still resting uneasily on the great wealth of its most successful members. Whatever prestige came the way of those who did not share the dazzling success of this small minority depended much on the social cachet which a liberal education, crowned by the award of a university doctorate, imparted to those who practised 'physic' in the traditional way. It was not yet based squarely on a general respect for the doctor's strictly professional qualities, or for his medical as opposed to his academic qualifications. The arrogant pretensions of London's Royal College of Physicians not only offended the men engaged at other levels of medical service, of whom there must have been at least 3,000 by 1700; they also cut little ice with lawyers or with able, learned clergymen, who were disposed to judge them by the unvarnished professional yardsticks they applied to their own colleagues. As late as 1716 Dudley Ryder, then in the middle of his law studies at the Middle Temple after having already passed through Edinburgh and Leyden universities, recorded this conversation with his cousin Nathaniel Marshall, an accomplished young curate at the church of Kentish Town:

> He talked in general about the practice of physic and said that *materia medica* lay within a very narrow compass and that the business of a physician required the least time to be perfect in of any profession. He talked also about empiric medicines, ... for he recovered his daughter by one of them given by a gentlewoman, when all that the doctor could prescribe had proved useless and ineffectual.

The physicians, for whom these strictures were mainly reserved, alone had, in their own eyes, an unimpeachable claim at the start of our period to professional standing. Technically, and to some extent in law also, there was still a very rigid functional hierarchy in late-seventeenth-century medicine. In this hierarchy the physicians, who diagnosed diseases and prescribed remedies, occupied the higher planes (and graduate 'doctors of physic' the highest of all); while below them the apothecaries, who traditionally made up and supplied the prescribed medicines from their shops, had since the early decades of the century usurped the middle ground from the surgeons. The latter were theoretically expected to confine themselves to treating the external conditions of patients with the knife, the leech, the plaster and the bandage. It was physic, therefore, rather than medicine at large which the purists envisaged when they referred to the third of 'the great professions'.

However, during that very period when men such as Ryder and Marshall were growing up, going through their training and beginning to establish reputations in their own vocations, fundamental changes were taking place in medicine. No Augustan profession was in a more active state of flux. Some of the solvents that were responsible had been at work for many decades. Even on the eve of the Revolution the anonymous writer of 1687 who referred to 'physicians, chirurgeons, apothecaries and *men of that profession*' (my italics) had not been entirely unrealistic in envisaging a single, if loose-knit, profession, with three main branches. At least he was closer to the mark than the pedantries and arcane posturings of some of the leading members of these branches might suggest at that time, if taken at their face value. By 1730, however (and even more by 1740), the process of fusion had gone so much further that here and there some of the vague outlines of a modern medical profession are already beginning to be discernible. In fact, I shall suggest in this chapter that it is between the years 1660 and 1740 that 'the doctor' truly arrives in English society. His coming was perhaps more readily recognised by the patients than by the medical men themselves. And he came, though increasingly within certain common professional parameters, in a variety of guises. But come he did, none the less; and essentially as a result of three great changes which transformed English medicine in the fifty to sixty years after 1680. One was a basic change in its professional structure, made inevitable by a crumbling of the ancient frontiers within the tripartite federation of medicine: a change which affected London most particularly since in the provinces, outside the main towns at least, it had been anticipated by trends which went back many years. The other two changes were the very marked advances that had been made by the 1720s, 1730s and 1740s in the professional training and competence of medical men, and the status revolution in the hitherto 'inferior' branches of medicine to which those advances made their contribution. Here, too, it is important to envisage developments throughout the period taking place at two levels: events in London, the principal bastion of tradition, proceed on one plane, and those in the provinces, where pragmatism and experimentation had a longer history, unfold on another.

Medicine was beyond comparison the most pamphlet-ridden of the late-seventeenth- and eighteenth-century professions. From the avalanche of writings issuing from the leading polemicists among the physicians, apothecaries and surgeons of Augustan England, one might well conclude that the pen was considered to be far mightier than the prescription, the powder and the poultice. Much of this literature, focused on particular or recurring controversies, makes repetitive and tedious reading. But sifting through the best of it (and even some of the worst of it) from the 1670s to the 1740s can be revealing and rewarding. In 1735 there appeared in London a pamphlet entitled *A Dialogue concerning the Practice of Physic*. Its author, an MD, expressed his grave concern that many men who were now being addressed as 'doctor' by their patients and their neighbours had started as mere 'raw unlettered lads', whose only formal training had been to be placed 'for two or three years under the care of some apothecary'. While the author libellously misrepresented both the rawness and the lack of education of such practitioners, his concern was not synthetic. In fact, he put his finger on the most basic structural and functional change which medicine had undergone in the previous few decades, of which the new nomenclature was simply a public recognition.

It is clear that by 1730 a large number of apothecaries, whether in London or elsewhere, were now accepting or using the title of 'doctor' because that was precisely what they were: they were being consulted by patients and were treating them entirely on their own initiative. One London physician, the author of *Reflections on a Libel*, had foreseen this with foreboding as early as 1671. 'The sick call the apothecary, doctor', he wrote in consternation; 'if allowed to do so, they will soon think him a fit and lawful practitioner.' He was quite right. It transpired, for instance, during assize proceedings in Lancashire in 1694 that in the far south of that county few folk had cavilled at the strict qualifications of a certain 'Dr. Bromfield, as they call him', although in sober fact he had been an apothecary in Warrington in the late 1680s. It is also beyond question that the same social courtesy title was being widely accorded by the early 1700s to many surgeons and to the new breed of surgeon-apothecaries, most particularly in the provinces in areas where the man in question was regarded as the leading practitioner in the neighbourhood, or in the numerous cases where he was the only one. The convention extended well beyond the poor and the sick. Squire Blundell of Crosby wrote in his diary on 2 July 1703: 'I came from Cole Brook, baited [took refreshment] at Warrington, was met by Doctor Latham and treated by him in the road'; but 'Doctor' Richard Latham, who was (or had been in the late 1680s) a Roman Catholic, was licensed only to practise surgery in this neighbourhood.* Similarly in January 1704, when

---

*The surgeons themselves were probably more scrupulous. Richard Kay of Bury was meticulous in his usage in his private diary. While staying with his cousin Joshua Taylor's family, 'they called in Mr. Fletcher, an apothecary, but we differing in our opinions, they sent for Dr. Watson who ordered him to be bled'. He was summoned to London by 'Mr. Stead . . . Apothecary to Guy's Hospital'; 'drank a dish of coffee with Dr. Fenwick a physician's pupil to St. Thos.'; saw 'Mr. Belchier, one of the surgeons to Guy's, cut for the stone'; 'attended [while] . . . Mr. Girle, one of the surgeons to St. Thos. lectured us from a slink calf'; and so on. W. Brockbank and F. Kenworthy (eds), *The Diary of Richard Kay, 1716–51 . . . a Lancashire Doctor* (Chetham Society, 1968), pp. 33–4, 61, 87, 80, 71.

Blundell's good lady suspected she was pregnant, 'my wife sent for Doctor Fabius, he said she was with child'. Fabius was a Liverpool apothecary, albeit a man of some classical education; for his real name was Bean but for professional purposes he chose to practise under the Latin name for that humble vegetable.

A string of entries in the town accounts of Torrington, Devon, in the late seventeenth and early eighteenth centuries illustrate how misty in the provinces the old distinctions had become. In 1692 'Dr. Potter' received £3 10s for providing medicine for poor people. In 1707 'Dr. Brad[ford]' was paid 3 guineas for 'the cure of John Welsher's thigh, being broke'; while, to quote just two more extracts, in 1727 and 1731 'Dr. Craddock' earned 3 guineas for 'churgring [performing surgery] and physic to the poor people not under relief' and 2 guineas for 'salivating and curing Mary Dulyn of the pox'. Philip Potter was the town apothecary, who had inherited the business of his father in 1688. Bradford and Craddock were patently surgeons (no genuine physician would now have deemed a case of venereal disease within his proper province). Not one of the three, it seems, had a licence to 'practise physic', yet Craddock obviously did so, and Potter almost certainly did likewise. The town fathers of Torrington clearly did not care a jot about the legal position, even supposing they were aware of it: and they paid all three men the mark of respect due, in their eyes, to full professional status. Overseers of the poor in many parts of England had now adopted the same convention in their dealings with whatever medical practitioners they appointed, though the 'doctors' in question were normally apothecaries or surgeon-apothecaries.

As we shall see in due course, it was the apothecaries and surgeons who supplied many of the dynamic elements of professional change in Augustan medicine, at least before the early part of George I's reign. Yet even in the 1730s the only medical men who were strictly entitled to the prefix 'Dr' were the qualified physicians. We must first establish, therefore, what had been happening since Charles II's day to the professional structure of 'physic' and to the recruitment and training of physicians. The short answer is, a great deal – including much that was distasteful to the powerful conservative faction in the Royal College of Physicians.

I The Physicians

It is hardly surprising that as late as the reign of Anne the Royal College was still taking an official view ranging from the patronising to the derogatory of those 'craftsmen' and 'tradesmen', the surgeons and apothecaries. For the many traditionalists among its members, clinging to the College's right ever since 1518 to restrict closely the number of practitioners of physic in the London area, were still struggling to impose on physicians themselves a notional table of precedence and to consign to inferior if not downright dubious status all who (in their eyes) occupied the lower rungs of the ladder. With every decade that passed, however, particularly after 1700, the absurdity of such attitudes became more apparent.

By the terms of the College's charter no physician was allowed to practise within a radius of seven miles of the centre of the capital unless he had either been elected a Fellow or held the College's licence – the latter being a privilege granted only by examination and subject to a stiff fee. The legal position outside the London area was that only Oxford and Cambridge doctors of medicine had the right to practise physic without licence, but that bachelors of medicine from the universities, Continental MDs, and others without any degree could do so with the benefit of a so-called 'extra-licence' from the College or, in special circumstances, by licence from the appropriate diocesan bishop. Although the College had resented and resisted these 'bishops' doctors' for a long time, the pass in the provinces had been effectively sold before the mid-seventeenth century. But in London the Fellows understandably clung on with far more determination. Episcopal licensing was no real problem in the city and inner suburbs; and after the *comitia*, in a sudden fit of common sense, was persuaded in 1687 to accept a doubling of their Fellows' numbers to 80, there was a time in William III's reign when the College did appear, briefly, to have an outside chance of recovering its control over graduate freebooters. Together, Fellows and Licentiates numbered 136 in 1695, and few though this may seem to serve the sick of more than half a million inhabitants, it was a vast improvement on the 46 of twenty years before. Not all currently practising London physicians who were of fellowship calibre had become Fellows in 1687. But at least a respectable and justifiable proportion of the city's doctors had now been elected; most of the new appointees were eminently worthy; and a few – Hans Sloane and John Radcliffe, for example – were of exceptional gifts.

Unfortunately for the Royal College – though happily for the profession and for the patients of the metropolis – in the first two decades of the eighteenth century most of the ground that had been regained was lost, and lost beyond reclaim. It was simply not worthwhile for a physician with a vast urban market awaiting exploitation to pay expensively for a licence to practise, a piece of paper which to his patients was the merest technicality. Had Licentiates enjoyed substantial extra privileges it might have been a different story, but they did not. The price for what Bernice Hamilton has called 'journeyman' status in the College, without voting and other rights, was a high one, with admission fees alone coming to £33 6s 8d; so it was only in the late 1680s and 1690s, when the Fellows were experiencing their transitory mood of realism, that numbers of Licentiates reached for the first and about the only time acceptable levels. By 1695 there were forty-one of them. At least in the mid-1690s the College could reasonably argue that its old claim to control and regulate the practice of medicine in the metropolis was being backed up by determined recruitment, by a resolve to proceed against illicit practitioners there, and a meaningful attempt, by its own lights, to maintain the standards of the profession of 'physic'. But from that time onwards the story, from its point of view, was one of steady, sorry deterioration. By 1719 the number of properly validated physicians in the capital, Fellows, Candidates and Licentiates, had fallen away to a miserable 78; and the list of widely consulted and prosperous defaulters who had cocked a snook at the College in the intervening years included one of Queen Anne's own physicians, Sir John Shadwell, until he was offered a fellowship in 1712. Once defiance became widespread, as it unquestionably was by the 1720s, there was very little that the College, for all its displays of ritual ferocity, could do about it. The 41 Licentiates of 1695 had become 25 by 1730 and reached the deplorable eighteenth-century nadir of 21 by 1738–9. By 1764, when the College made the most determined drive since the Revolution against the pirates on its doorstep, it was able to produce a list of almost forty unlicensed London physicians who held doctor's degrees and it was certainly aware of many others with lower qualifications then busily practising within its supposedly sacred precincts. Clearly the distinction between licensed and unlicensed physicians mattered very little to Londoners by the early eighteenth century; while neither the professional distinction between Fellows and Licentiates, so long and stubbornly maintained by the former on the strength of the spurious claims of Oxford and Cambridge, nor the foolish social distinction which was erected alongside it meant anything at all to the layman.

In theory, the structure of the profession of physic was completed (in the Fellows' eyes) by a provincial base made up, like the London doctors, of two tiers. One was occupied by MDs of Oxford, Cambridge and Trinity College, Dublin, who were free to set up practice at any time after graduation outside the London seven-mile limit; the other by those with English bachelor's degrees in medicine, foreign degrees, or lesser qualifications who could practise in specific areas with the authority of the College's 'extra-licences'. If theory had borne any resemblance to reality there would probably have been no more than 300 doctors of physic and extra-licentiates in the provinces at any one time, even by the early eighteenth century. Yet J. H. Raach has claimed to have identified 814 country physicians in England as early as the years 1603–43, of whom only 158 were found, for certain, to have died in the course of that period. This figure may be suspiciously high, but it is still impressive enough to leave no doubt how far the Royal College had lost, or abandoned, any genuine control of the situation in the provinces long before our period opens. Although in periods of relative vigour after 1680 it took a token interest in the state of the profession in the provinces, this rarely went further than attempts to toss a periodic spanner into the works of the other medical licensing authority in Stuart and early-Hanoverian England, the Church. It was happy enough to pocket the fees which its extra-licences brought in – and the £11 15s 6d charged to one especially distinguished candidate in 1702 was said to be 'the lowest that ever

was paid' in order to tempt him to take the College's examination –
but it had too many problems on its own doorstep to concern itself
unduly about the paucity of applicants from the provinces. Neither
does it appear to have agonised greatly over the very low, and declining, success rate in the examination. Fewer than eighty provincial
physicians passed the examination for an extra-licence in the sixty
years from 1691 to 1750, and this was little more than half the
number of successful candidates in a roughly comparable period
before 1690.

    Who, then – other than empirics – treated the sick in the provinces?
During the reign of Elizabeth I and under the early Stuarts the
graduate physicians had been compelled, in practice, to accept the
blunt fact that the shortage of qualified medical men of all kinds was
so grievous, and was so far aggravated by chronic difficulties of
travelling, that it was futile to try to maintain a strict division of
labour throughout the country between physicians, apothecaries and
surgeons. Likewise the Royal College had had to abandon its insis-
tence that all provincial physicians other than the MDs of three
universities must be validated by its *comitia*. As a result, it is possible
to detect the phenomenon of 'general practice' (though not the term)
already beginning to take shape in places before the Civil Wars.
It was a simple matter of supply and demand. Not just in the first
half of the seventeenth century but in the first twenty years after
1660, in large market towns or cathedral cities, especially in centres
which held particular attractions for the local gentry, a reasonable
measure of specialisation had often been possible; and where there
was no exceptional population growth there was no great pressure to
abandon it. Such was still the case, for example, in early-eighteenth-
century Wells, as Dr Claver Morris's diary reveals. On the other hand,
where no qualified physician was available, or where urban growth
was presenting impossible problems to those who were, it was inevitable that either an apothecary or a surgeon would try, and for
that matter, be expected, to assume their functions.

    When the provincial apothecary or surgeon of the early seventeenth
century moved across the physician's frontiers it is clear that in
numerous instances he did so without any formal authority. At the
same time, a growing number of men who were also apothecaries or
surgeons by training became qualified to practise as provincial physicians and legally entitled to call themselves *medici* – 'doctors' – by
assuming the decent fig-leaf of a bishop's licence. And for at least
half a century after the Restoration these 'bishops' doctors' continued
to increase in numbers and became an integral part of the structure
of the profession with an accepted place in country society. The
Church's right to authorise medical practice originated in an Act of
Parliament of 1511. A large majority of the bishops' licences issued
during the seventeenth century were granted only to intending surgeons, over a thousand of whom are known to have successfully
sought such qualifications before 1700. But well before the collapse
of the established Church in the 1640s the pressure was building up

on bishops (or rather on their chancellors) to meet the demand for physicians. Resort to the ecclesiastical authorities may have been greater in the remoter dioceses, but it was by no means confined to them. When episcopal licensing was revived in 1660 so was the call for bishops' doctors. By the 1680s pressure on the Church authorities was probably higher than it had ever been. In Norwich diocese, for one (despite its proximity to Cambridge and to London), more physicians were licensed in the last few decades of the seventeenth century than at any time before.

The facts of the medical market guaranteed that 'doctors' for the provincial sick would go on being produced in this way, though at a diminishing rate, well into the eighteenth century: they remained a part of the professional landscape at least as late as 1750. The shortage of graduate or College-licensed physicians was still acute in many counties in the years 1700–20. In Bedfordshire it was said that one might have to go fifty miles to find one. In Essex the inhabitants of Harwich complained in 1715 that there was no graduate doctor of physic nearer than Colchester. When William Blundell of Crosby was taken fatally ill in July 1702, his son, Nicholas, first sent a messenger hot-foot to Preston, twenty-three miles distant, only to discover that Dr Valentine Farrington, the standby of the local gentry, 'was not to be found'. He himself then rode to Wigan, twenty miles in another direction, where there were two physicians – the Worthingtons, father and son – and returned with young Dr Francis Worthington; and finally, on 1 August, when there was no improvement in the patient's condition, he dispatched his father's butler to Whitchurch in Shropshire, forty miles away to the south, in a fruitless quest for a Dr Bostock.

So although the Royal College of Physicians had never pretended to like the system of episcopal licensing, and after the Restoration periodically expressed alarm at the 'ignorance' of the men whom the Church of England was foisting on a gullible public in this way, there was little the Fellows could do except huff and puff. In 1687, ostensibly with James II's support, they tried to bully the bishops into resigning their powers completely; but only one prelate, Cartwright of Chester, is known to have capitulated. They renewed their efforts, though in a milder form, in 1713. It would be uncharitable to assume that these outbursts of alarm were entirely synthetic; but a lot of the concern being expressed by the late seventeenth century was exaggerated, and some of the grounds for it were irrelevant.

Admittedly, only a small fraction of episcopal licencees in the seventeenth century could boast degrees: Archbishop Sheldon's request in 1665 for returns of all the practitioners in physic in his province produced the information from Exeter diocese that only eleven out of the forty-two physicians resident there were graduates of any description, even arts graduates. Yet by this criterion the record of the College's own extra-licentiates was not at all impressive either. The whole situation was to change emphatically after 1700 as the supply of non-English graduate physicians increased, first slowly, then dramatically. But, in any case, the non-graduates who got bishops' licences under Charles II, James II and William III were not necessarily any the worse for their origins – usually as apothecaries or surgeons; indeed, as practical medical standards rose during the second half of the seventeenth century, as anatomical knowledge improved and the range of drugs employed vastly increased (see pp. 184–5, 190, 205), men who had served a long apprenticeship with an able master, and who had then accumulated years of experience and armed themselves with a reasonable library, were often very much better equipped by their background for 'the practice of physic' than many (perhaps even than most) holders of English university degrees in the subject. Some were even able to demonstrate this academically in impressive style. Richard Russell was apprenticed to his father, a surgeon-apothecary of Lewes, just after the turn of the century; by 1724 he was so experienced after over fifteen years of general medical practice, and so knowledgeable, that he was able to go to the University of Leyden and take his MD degree there by dissertation in the extraordinary time of two months. Thomas Dale, who took only one month longer to achieve the same qualification at the age of 23, did so with a training as an apothecary (under his father at Hoxton) behind him.

One 'bishops' doctor' about whom we know a great deal, thanks to the survival of his journal, is James Yonge of Plymouth. He was possibly the best-known surgeon in the west country under the later Stuarts. He had begun botanising, studying healing herbs, at the age of 13. He not only acquired ten years' invaluable practical experience in general medicine as a ship's surgeon between 1660 and 1670, and a year's training under a Wapping apothecary learning how to make up medicines; he also spent a lot of the profits of his voyages before his marriage building up a medical library and worked hard to improve his theory. Only his father's parsimony had thwarted his ambition to study in Leyden in 1665. Yonge, it is true, was something of a herculean figure in his day, a fact the Royal College itself ultimately recognised; but his type, the gifted all-rounder, was not freakish in the English provinces at the beginning of the Augustan period, certainly not in country districts. At least it bore more resemblance to reality than the College's crude caricature of the ignorant sawbones, granted by a careless Church authority a licence to poison his patients in addition to a licence to torture them.

Much the gravest charge against the bishops, could it have been sustained, was that they or their officials failed to show adequate care in scrutinising the non-academic credentials of the men they validated. As late as 1747, in *An Address to the College of Physicians*, a pamphleteer of the Oxford and Cambridge establishment was still claiming that the Church authorities had consistently ignored the legally imposed safeguard that an applicant's qualifications should be vouched for by four existing physicians. Most successful licensees, he believed, were supported by the opinions of men of no better medical standing than themselves – apothecaries, surgeons, Scotsmen or, worse still, parsons and churchwardens – to the perpetuation of a vicious circle and to the great prejudice of 'fair practitioners'. It is probably true that many bishops, especially in the generation after 1660, did set a lot of store by evidence of personal integrity and loyalty to the Anglican Church. But that does not mean that they carelessly debased the medical coinage. James Yonge, a seasoned campaigner as we have seen, seems to have been well satisfied with the standing of the physician's licence he himself received from the Bishop of Exeter. The College's extra-licence, he told its president, Sir Thomas Millington, in 1702 'would be but a feather in my cap, would cost more money than worth'; his bishop's licence, he hastened to assure the College, had made him 'very safe'.

If Exeter custom followed that of London we can understand why he thought so. A careful study has been made of licensing practices in London diocese between 1660 and 1725. It shows that tougher standards were applied to intending physicians than to surgeons, to compensate for their lack of any formal apprenticeship in 'physic', and that chancellors and their officials looked for testimony from several well-informed professional sources, either of many years of private study by the applicant or of very considerable practical experience. They were impressed in 1699 by the qualifications of Charles Wilcox, Surgeon to His Majesty's Garrison in the Tower, backed by a certificate from three physicians (who included a Licentiate and a 'practitioner in physic') and two chemists. The successful application of Richard Strutt, gentleman, to practise in Chelmsford in 1705 rested, securely enough, on a certificate from three MDs to the effect that he had been 'educated and practised as a surgeon for these thirty years last past', and that he was 'a skilful person and fitly qualified to practise physic'. Applications from experienced surgeons were the commonest of all; and the bishop's officers would not be unaware of the big advance which the surgeon's craft and status had made since the days, just before the Civil Wars, when John Symcotts, MD, of Huntingdon could write contemptuously of the treatment dispensed by a local 'doctor' one of his own patients had been consulting: 'I like it not. Such vowelling, drawing and slabbering smells too much of his barber's shop, from whence he came out doctor.' Of a different sort of pedigree was Edmund Belson's licence to practise physic at Edgworth in 1673. It was supported by a certificate from two MDs, one Licentiate of the Royal College and one apothecary, 'who assert[ed] that for many years past he has assiduously studied the art of medicine'.

To procure testimonials such as these, especially in counties like Essex where fully qualified physicians were so far scattered, was no mean achievement in itself. For instance, the certificate of fitness on behalf of Joshua Draper of Braintree was signed by only two MDs, but it arrived at the Registry with this covering letter:

Mr. Butler,

Mr. Draper of our town, Bachelor of Physic, was promised by my Lord of London a certificate at the Visitation, whenever he should send up a certificate according to law, in order to it. He hath not been unmindful ever since, but was unwilling to request a testimony of any practitioners below him, and Doctors of Physic are not so plentiful hereabouts. He had the hand of one with whom he was joined in consultation, and because it was required to speed up his certificate, he hath now sent to a physician in London for his [signature] with whom he hath often been in consultation.

In such circumstances it would have been needlessly obstructive for diocesan chancellors to insist on the precise letter of the law. Yet in London diocese, at least, they used their powers to license physicians with discretion. In fact, in the later years of Henry Compton, bishop from 1675 to 1713, they were so sparingly employed that his lordship's successor, John Robinson, was strongly urged from Harwich to issue more physicians' licences to experienced surgeons in order to ease the pressing difficulties of that unusually isolated area.

Fortunately, both the dilemma of conscientious bishops and the problem of ill-served counties were in sight of some relief by George I's reign. Right through the seventeenth century there had been a fair smattering of academically trained physicians practising in England whose qualifications had been obtained at one of the leading Continental medical schools, such as Paris, Rheims, Utrecht or Padua. Most were English by birth but they included a few foreign immigrants. In the decade which followed 1712, the year fighting ended in the Spanish Succession War, the inflow of British-born medical graduates from foreign universities assumed a far larger scale than ever before. The University of Leyden had been establishing some claim to primacy among the Continental training schools even in the late seventeenth century, when it began to attract, especially, the sons of prosperous English Nonconformists with professional ambitions, and also many Scots. Under Hermann Boerhaave, *lector* from 1701 and professor of medicine from 1709 to 1738, and with Bernard Albinus, the leading anatomist of his day, in its chair of anatomy, Leyden advanced its reputation much further. Only the medical faculty at Rheims (another regular producer of British doctors at this time) could remotely rival it in the early eighteenth century. And since a hardworking young man without previous academic medical training could hope to proceed to a doctor's degree at Leyden, as at Rheims or Utrecht, in an average time of around eighteen months and an appreciable number of Leyden students actually graduated in from eight to twelve months from matriculation, the lure of such a training was all the stronger. The contrast with the bachelor of physic's qualification in Oxford, which normally took three years to acquire after a previous MA, and with the Oxford doctorate which required continued membership of the University

(though not necessarily residence) for a further four years, was a
stark one. Without exceptional dispensations, over and above those
that were common form for arts graduates, the whole process of a
physician's training at Oxford from the time of matriculation could
technically take twelve years. In Cambridge it might be less protracted
and expensive; even so, the statutes did not officially permit a student
to take even his MB in under six years from matriculation.

In all, 746 English-speaking students of medicine, including some
360 of English birth and 244 Scots, were trained at Leyden during the
period of Boerhaave's teaching career. One hundred and fifty-nine of
them had already matriculated before 1713, but in the eight years
after the Peace of Utrecht they were followed by another 175, and
by a further 212 from 1721–30. These are spectacular figures; but
they conceal an enormous variety of educational patterns. For example 64 of the students, mostly Scots from Rheims and Englishmen
from Cambridge, already had bachelor's degrees in medicine. Over
200 others went to Leyden for courses of lectures and demonstrations
but took no degree there, or, so far as is known, anywhere else: some
of them were already in unqualified medical practice and were content
to go back to it with their added experience, while others, going to
Holland in their late teens or early twenties used their Leyden training as a passport to a bishop's licence on their return to England and
practised as *medici* in the provinces. One who took the latter course
was Charles Morton, a later FRS and curator at the British Museum,
who set up as a physician at Kendal. More extraordinary is the fact
that of the 468 genuine Leyden 'undergraduates' who did take
degrees, less than a third stayed there to receive their Leyden MDs.
No fewer than 175 went, or returned, to Rheims or Utrecht to
graduate, 34 to the Scottish universities, and 42 to Oxford and
Cambridge.

In the light of such data an elastic construction must obviously be
placed on 'the late swarms' of 'Leyden physicians', of whom the
author of *An Address to the College of Physicians* was still pointedly
complaining almost ten years after Boerhaave's death. But this should
not belittle the major influence exerted on the development of the
English medical profession in the first half of the eighteenth century
by the Leyden medical school. Neither should it obscure the personal
influence on the advance of the English doctor of Hermann Boerhaave
himself, *communis Europae praeceptor.* Ashworth Underwood, to
whose work we owe most of our statistical knowledge of Boerhaave's
English-speaking pupils, has called him 'probably the most successful
medical teacher who ever lived'. Leyden-trained doctors left a very
marked imprint even on London, the profession's least yielding area.
Well-known physicians such as Edward Hody, David Ross, who was
appointed one of the physicians to St George's Hospital on its
foundation in 1733, and Richard Conyers of Dover Street, an expert
in children's diseases, practised for years in London on the strength of
their Continental training and their subsequent reputations. Hody
(Leyden and Rheims, 1719–23) was a physician in the capital for

some seventeen years before he bothered to apply to the Royal
College for a licence; Ross, with an MD from Rheims in 1726,
practised for about twenty years before he was licensed in 1749; and
Conyers for roughly thirty years before, very late in life, the College
elected him a Fellow. Others, like Drs Mortimer and Porter, con-
formed much sooner, and Robert Nesbitt, a Dissenter's son who set
up in London after studying at Leyden from 1719 to 1721, thought
it prudent after five years there to seek a licence. On the other hand,
there were some who never did so, and at least one for whom the
mountain came to Mohammed. Following his Leyden training (1714–
16) John Birch built up a successful practice as a fashionable
accoucheur in Bow Lane, inheriting to some extent the lucrative
mantle of Sir David Hamilton (see below, pp. 182, 220–1). After ten
years the College took the now uncommon step of electing him an
Honorary Fellow.

It was outside London, however, that the great majority of Conti-
nental-trained physicians settled between 1690 and 1740; and the
second generation of incomers did so thickly enough to constitute the
most important reinforcement the provincial profession had ever
received. Many of these men became doctors of great local reputation. Among the trail-blazers were Gilbert Heathcoat (Leyden and
Padua) in Middlesex, Simon Brown (Utrecht, 1695) in Shropshire,
John Milner (Leyden and Utrecht, 1711) at Leeds, and Thomas
Attwood, another Utrecht graduate of the war years, at Worcester.
In the years of peace after 1712 scores followed their example.
George Bailey quickly established himself as the leading practitioner
in and around Chichester, and remained so, a county institution, for
fifty years; and what Bailey was to that part of Sussex, William
Chambers became to Hull, Michael Lee Dicker to Exeter, Cuthbert
Lambert to Newcastle upon Tyne, and John Huxham to Plymouth.
All had sat at the feet of Boerhaave and taken their doctor's degrees
at Leyden, Utrecht or Rheims between 1715 and 1724. Some settled
closer to London: Thomas Hadfield and Richard Russell at Peckham
and Ware, and Nathaniel Cotton at St Albans. Others, like William
Brownrigg, who became Whitehaven's principal physician after graduating at Leyden in the 1730s, Thomas Glass of Tiverton and Henry
Bracken of Lancaster followed John Milner of Pudsey in choosing
to return to their native parts. Nor were all these men simply big
fish in little pools. Huxham, Brownrigg and Russell were three who
achieved a national standing through their research and publications.
So, too, did Dr William Hillary who took his doctorate at Leyden in
1722 and subsequently punctuated a career in practice at Ripon, Leeds
and Bath with a long spell in the West Indies, becoming one of the
leading eighteenth-century experts in epidemic diseases.

Beginning later than the influx from the Continent, but continuing
for longer and achieving, in the long run, more dramatic proportions,
was the invasion of the Scots. Although it was some years after the
Union of 1707 before the movement of doctors southwards attracted
serious notice, and it was not until the full flowering of Scottish

medical education in the middle decades of the century that it reached its fullest scale, the advance guard of the Scots was already on the move in the reigns of William III and Anne. It was in the 1690s that John Arbuthnot, William Cockburn (later Swift's doctor) and David Hamilton joined George How in establishing themselves in London practices that quickly flourished and brought them fame. But apart from Arbuthnot, and also Charles Oliphant who prospered in London during Anne's reign having published a treatise on fevers in 1699, these early immigrants took care to strengthen their credentials with doctorates from Leyden or Rheims. They had counterparts in the English provinces, too, among them Archibald Adams who began practising at Norwich under Queen Anne. Switching to medicine after taking his MA at Edinburgh in 1695, he was probably able to take advantage of the facilities for serious medical study which the city, if not yet the university, was just beginning to develop. The Edinburgh Royal College of Physicians had been founded in 1681. It was barred by its charter from creating a 'school' of medicine, but it kept a library and imposed a stiff examination for its licence. The much older Edinburgh 'Incorporation' of Surgeons built an anatomy theatre for dissection and demonstration in 1697. No doubt Adams acquired clinical experience in Scotland as well; but he still took the precaution, before making the permanent move to England, of taking what today might be called a 'crash course' at Leyden in 1705 and successfully submitting a thesis, *De secretionibus*, for a Utrecht doctorate in June of that year.

It was a precaution that within two decades was to become unnecessary. The Scots were catching on in the English provinces in their own right. Whereas Robert Taylor, possessing a Glasgow MA but no medical degree, secured an extra-licence in 1721 to follow his profession at Boroughbridge, James Mackenzie's Aberdeen MD, acquired in 1719, caused no raised eyebrows in Worcester where he practised happily for much of the next thirty-two years. It was predictably in Edinburgh, however, that the important watershed had been passed. In 1705 the city's university arranged for the Edinburgh College of Physicians to examine a 'student of physic' on its behalf, and as a result a Mr David Cockburn was awarded the university's first MD degree. A handful of others followed, by the same method, later in the reign, and after the university had appointed the young Edinburgh physician, James Crawford, as its first Professor of 'Physic and Chemistry' it was able from 1718 to conduct examinations of its own by co-opting members of the college to assist Crawford. Before the end of 1719 four successful candidates in these examinations had taken their doctor's degrees. And so, while Alexander Monro senior's great Edinburgh medical school officially dates from 1726, its foundations had been firmly laid by the beginning of the new decade.

It was in 1720 that Monro, a brilliant young surgeon-apothecary of 23 who had completed his education by studying under Cheselden in London, in the medical school at Paris and for ten months under

Boerhaave, was appointed 'Professor of Anatomy in the City and College of Edinburgh'. The appointment was jointly made by the city council and the Incorporation of Surgeons. From the early winter of 1720 Monro organised the first coherent set of medical lectures in Scotland, apparently in conjunction with the university. There was his own course on anatomy, Dr Charles Alston's on *materia medica* and Professor Crawford's on chemistry. It was the beginning of a staggering teaching career in the course of which, on his own claim, 4,464 medical students passed through Monro's hands. It was also the true beginning of the 'Edinburgh school'. By 1725 Monro had been formally inaugurated to a chair in the university and in the following year, after further appointments, a fully fledged university medical faculty came into being. Over the next twenty-five years, as its reputation first equalled, then surpassed that of Leyden itself, Edinburgh attracted more and more students until it was eventually handling almost 200 annually; and since many of the products of the Edinburgh school from the start took the broad road south almost as soon as they were qualified, the English medical profession had received such a transfusion from this source by the late 1730s and 1740s that it was never to be the same again. By George III's reign Scottish-trained doctors were dominating English medicine. In the six widely scattered counties of Somerset, Sussex, Warwickshire, Staffordshire, Nottinghamshire and Yorkshire, 90 graduate physicians were practising in 1783; at least 48 of them (and probably several more) held MDs from Scottish universities, overwhelmingly from Edinburgh; and of the rest, 6 were products of Leyden and 5 more had trained in other Continental medical schools.

From the early years of the Edinburgh school the traffic had by no means been solely from north to south. Englishmen themselves intent on a career in medicine, especially those barred from their own universities by the religious tests, were soon making the return journey for their physician's training. Among those who from a fairly early stage chose Edinburgh rather than Holland or France was the Lancashire Dissenter, Samuel Kay, the uncle of Richard Kay of Baldingstone who figures elsewhere in this chapter (see below, pp. 201–18 *passim.*). He went to Edinburgh about 1729, at the age of 20 or 21, took his MD there in 1731, and after that returned to England to practise almost continuously in or near Manchester for most of the next fifty years – though with a spell of postgraduate study in Leyden in 1733. Another who took the same route shortly after Kay was John Fothergill, a young Quaker from across the Pennines. He was sent to Edinburgh after completing a full apothecary's training in Bradford, fell under the spell of Munro, Alston, Rutherford and Sinclair, graduated in 1736, and coming to London as a physician at St Thomas's Hospital, launched himself on a career of exceptional prosperity.

Had Oxford and Cambridge been able to copy the example of Leyden and Edinburgh in the first thirty to forty years of the eighteenth century, it is just possible that the onward surge of the apothecaries into the territory of the physicians, to which we shall shortly turn, might have been partially checked. But the English universities, hampered admittedly by their collegiate structure, showed little inclination to change their anachronistic approach to medical training: a method whereby a man could receive a doctor's degree essentially for book-learning, after having, unbelievably, witnessed no more than two anatomical dissections and participated in none. Indeed, the career of Thomas Clayton showed that it was perfectly possible to hold a chair of medicine in Oxford in the seventeenth century despite being 'possessed of a timorous, effeminate humour' and being 'unable to endure the sight of a mangled or bloody body'. Thomas Sydenham had told John Ward long before the 1680s, partly on the strength of his own Oxford experience and partly after observing over some years the book-bound diagnostic bankruptcy of many of his London colleagues, that 'physic is not to be learned by going to universities'; rather he was 'for taking apprentices, and says one has as good send a man to Oxford to learn shoemaking as practising physic'. After 1700, however, as the stars of Leyden, Rheims and Edinburgh rose through the creation of recognised medical schools, the medical reputation of Oxford and Cambridge declined still further and their capacity to attract recruits fell away alarmingly in the eighteenth century, especially from the second decade onward.

Yet, in spite of this, the standard of professional training of academically qualified physicians, taken as a whole, was unquestionably higher in 1740 than it had been in 1680, and so was their general level of competence. It is true, there are plenty of indications – in the correspondence or diaries of the county gentry, for example -- that country physicians, in particular, could be very reluctant to depart from stereotyped, traditional treatments. The prolonged and puzzling illnesses of two members of the Blundell family in 1724–5 conjured up nothing more imaginative from Dr Francis Worthington of Wigan, Drs Broomfield and Dickens of Liverpool, and Dr Philip Fernihough of Chester than a relentless regimen of 'purges', 'vomits' and bloodletting, supported by occasional 'blistering plasters' from a Liverpool surgeon-apothecary. Nevertheless, standards were rising and for this the often-abused Royal College could fairly claim a certain share of the credit along with the Continental universities and Edinburgh. Its examinations in this period were a searching test of knowledge: even the immensely experienced surgeon, James Yonge, who was promised an easy ride if he agreed to be examined for an extra-licence in 1702 (he had told the President he was 'too old to be catechized') found himself hard-pressed in the course of a ninety-minute *viva*. But given that fewer doctors, in proportion to the size of the profession, were willing to submit to these rigours by the early eighteenth century, it was fortunate that something of the philosophy of Sydenham, the greatest name in seventeenth-century clinical medicine after Harvey, continued to percolate through the profession of physic after his death in 1689. London medicine, especially, benefited over the next fifty years from the slow absorption of Sydenham's message that at the start of a career there was no substitute for practical bedside experience and careful clinical observation of symptoms in the company of a seasoned practitioner. Most of the biggest names on the physicians' roll by the first half of the eighteenth century were men who had served an assistantship of this kind. Thomas Dover, the patentee of 'Dover's powders', was one of those fortunate enough to begin his long career, stretching well into George II's reign, under the wing of Sydenham himself. It must have been a bracing experience. Sydenham's remarks to the most famous of his protégés, Hans Sloane, when he came to the great man in search of such an assistantship flourishing an impressive set of theoretical qualifications, were redolent of the pragmatism he fostered:

> This is all very fine but it won't do: anatomy, botany – nonsense, sir. I know an old woman in Covent Garden who understands botany better, and as for anatomy, any butcher can dissect a joint just as well. No, young man, all this is stuff: you must go to the bedside. It is there alone you can learn disease.

A further sign that the physician's knowledge was slowly advancing and that his skills were becoming more refined was the limited trend towards specialisation that became discernible from around 1700. The first oculists make their appearance, not all as lacking in formal qualifications as Queen Anne's oculist, Sir William Read; and so, too, do the first paediatricians, such as Richard Conyers. Midwifery had become a standard part of every good surgeon's training by the 1720s; but some prominent London physicians practised now as *accoucheurs*. Sir Richard Manningham was one, as well as Sir David Hamilton and John Birch (whose careers have already been mentioned). By George II's reign it was not unknown, even in the provinces, for graduate physicians to specialise as 'man-midwives'; indeed, one of them, John Burton of York, was cruelly captured for posterity as 'Dr Slop' in the pages of Sterne's *Tristram Shandy*.

We might well wonder what qualities were called for in a physician of the Augustan age to secure the astonishing rewards reaped by such professional tycoons as Sloane, Richard Mead or John Radcliffe? For we know that in some respects (though by no means all) their treatments, in common with those of their humbler provincial brethren, were still based on horrifying ignorance of the true causes of disease; and the sly old paviour's riposte to Radcliffe on being accused of covering up his poor workmanship – 'Doctor, mine is not the only bad work the earth hides' – came very close to the bone. Good connections were certainly useful, particularly in making a successful start; and they were no more despised outside London than in it. 'There is a gentleman at Manchester (one Dr Buck) that designs to set up, either at Manchester or at Warrington, in the practice of physic', wrote Sir Thomas Gipps to Roger Kenyon in April 1691.

'He has a letter from some of your friends, recommending him to your favour and countenance to promote his interest...' Buck was also lucky enough to be able to flourish another testimonial 'from a special friend and kinsman (a doctor in physic) of the first rank'. Such connections, lay and professional, could get a man so far; but not to the very top either of the local roost or of the élite who gobbled up the guineas from the fashionable sick of London. One might be tempted to think that two of the main essentials were good public relations and a great deal of luck. Radcliffe certainly had both in full measure, as did Mead; and it is quite plausible that in Radcliffe's case even his epic outbursts of rudeness towards some of his patients was part of his appeal, given the emollient approach of the standard physician's approach. What is easily overlooked is that the aristocrats of London medicine often worked extremely hard. At least in their practice-building years, most of them probably worked as hard in their own way as the popular country physician with his countless hours in the saddle: the favourite picture of bewigged and pot-bellied doctors lolling at their ease with their pipes in the London coffee-houses, doling out prescriptions by the score to attendant apothecaries on behalf of patients they had never bothered to see, is a gross caricature. Above all, the Radcliffes, Sloanes and Meads of Augustan London possessed great instinctive ability, based on observation and experience. They did not neglect book-knowledge; even Radcliffe, who loved to pooh-pooh the old Latin classics, was a devotee of the works of Thomas Willis. Those who had studied abroad, as Mead had, valued the lecture courses of the great Continental professors. But, in general, the great ones subscribed to the Sydenham doctrine that the best teacher of all was the bedside.

Physicians who could not get all the experience they needed at the private bedside discovered, especially from the 1720s and 1730s onwards, that 'walking the wards' of the London hospitals, the fifth of which had opened its doors by 1734, could offer a more-than-useful substitute. Later we shall notice what golden advantages accrued to both surgery and pharmacy from the opening of sixteen new hospitals in England between 1719 and 1755, including the first twelve infirmaries or hospitals, in the modern sense, ever established in the provinces (below pp. 199–202). However, they also afforded precious experience to the younger generation of physicians, as men such as Stuart, Oldfield, Fothergill and William Wasey were able swiftly to demonstrate. The major benefits from this development, obviously, still lay in the future in the 1730s. Even before 1740, however, it had already served quite significantly to advance the knowledge of 'general medicine' and, what was equally important alike to patients and the profession, to foster the habit of co-operation between medical practitioners of whatever pedigree. In the wards and demonstration rooms of Bart's and St Thomas's, the Westminster Hospital, Guy's and St George's by the early years of George II, the coming of 'the doctor' was a manifest reality. For the working hospital physician (there were a few ornamental ones), for the man who was daily in contact with the often eminent apothecaries and surgeons who were his colleagues, the ideal of a true medical fraternity, a common profession united by a common purpose, was not difficult to sustain.

The Apothecaries

Although by the 1730s the standards of academically trained physicians were rising, their supply remained limited. Thanks, in the main, to Boerhaave's Leyden, it did not fall so woefully short of demand as it had in 1680 or 1700. But outside London it was still acutely inadequate in many places at the beginning of George II's reign, before the influx of Monro's men from Edinburgh had properly begun; and in the capital itself, housing 10 per cent of the entire population, resources were heavily overstretched. It was partly for this reason, and partly because physicians' fees had lost contact with the capacity of ordinary pockets that by 1730 the transmutation of the apothecary into the family doctor had become irreversible. For the average English household below the gentry and above the poor, the apothecary had now become the practitioner who was turned to first when sickness struck. Increasingly the gentry family, too, had recourse to him for its less serious ailments, and his status as 'doctor' was as unshakeable by now in London as it had been for many years in country districts and in the majority of towns outside the capital. In this last respect, above all – that of status in the community – there had been a striking change in the situation since the Restoration.

The claim of the apothecaries, traditionally no more than dispensers and vendors of medicines, to be what Dr Hamilton has called 'the ancestor of the G.P.' rests initially on circumstances which can be traced back three quarters of a century before the 1680s. The chronic scarcity of university-trained physicians by the end of the sixteenth century had first opened the door, and a Star Chamber judgement of 1607 by Sir Edward Coke in favour of provincial apothecaries propped it ajar. The long apprenticeships of the seventeenth-century apothecaries; the abundance of practical experience in the observation of symptoms which both training and subsequent business frequently brought them; the fact that their pharmaceutical knowledge was often superior to that of the physicians at a period when the range of medicines in use was being rapidly extended: these were all advantages which had given the public confidence to invite the apothecaries in and consult them directly. Most influential of all in the long term in recommending them to patients were the remedies and, in particular, the pain-killing palliatives now at their disposal. When the new 'exotic' drugs began to be imported into England from the East after the conclusion of the Anglo-Spanish war in 1604 the apothecary was presented with a unique opportunity to steal a march over his medical associates by making himself expert in their compounding and use; and especially after the 1660s, when opiates and other 'exotics' figured increasingly prominently on the bills of lading of most East Indiamen sailing into London, a generation less tolerant of pain than its predecessors grew heavily dependent upon them. In 1665 a standard pharmaceutical guide was listing some 240 exotics, and it has been estimated that the import of drugs was at least twenty-five times greater in 1700 than it had been in 1600. By 1680 it seems clear that their use had become widespread even on the periphery of the provinces, yet evidence of any serious competition for patients between provincial apothecaries and physicians by the late seventeenth century (except occasionally for the better-off ones in country areas) is hard to come by. With the call for medical services of all kinds wellnigh limitless, this is not perhaps surprising. In London, on the other hand, the prospects for the development of a rational and harmonious medical profession still seemed far from bright at the close of the seventeenth century; for one old issue and two relatively new ones continued to keep apothecaries and physicians there seriously at odds.

The old issue went back at least as far as the second and third decades of the seventeenth century. By the early 1640s the London apothecaries had appeared to be losing their running battle with the Royal College over this problem, the basic question of their right to practise medicine without reference to the physicians and to make a concealed charge for their consultations. But their situation, which improved during the Interregnum only to deteriorate again immediately after the Restoration, was transformed by the last great English outbreak of bubonic plague in 1665. All but two dozen of the London physicians, three of whom were to meet honourable deaths at their posts, followed their well-to-do patients out of town to escape the terrible pestilence; and into the breach stepped the apothecaries, gaining in abundance both patients and general admiration – commodities the physicians on their return found it desperately hard to regain. When, thirty years after the Plague, a Bill was brought into Parliament to exempt apothecaries from jury service and from appointment to ward and parish offices, its supporters assumed that it was, by then, 'supposed to need no proof that the apothecary's attendance on the sick (in all cases considered) takes up much more of his time than the physicians spend upon the like occasions'.

The London apothecaries' assumption of the physicians' habit, however, remained uneasy on one vital score. Since they had no legal right to charge a consultation fee, a tacit understanding developed between them and their patients that the charge for advice would be subsumed in the final bill for 'physic supplied'. But it remained a precarious position, vulnerable to legal process by the Royal College of Physicians. By the time of the Restoration the College had tacitly accepted that no London apothecary would be prosecuted for unlicensed practice if he confined himself to treating minor ailments without calling in a physician. But the apothecary's metamorphosis from shopkeeper to bedside consultant would remain only half accomplished until he had established beyond all challenge his legal right to diagnose disease and prescribe remedies, even in cases of the most serious illness. And in the last resort this right hinged on the delicate question of payment. The trouble here was that conventions which had begun in mutual good faith could easily degenerate into artful dodges.

> Compositions... are to be minced and subdivided [sneered the Censor of the College early in Anne's reign], and (which is mysterious) each part valued at the price of the whole. Decoctions and juleps are put into small glasses, for each draught of the patient. The electuaries are transformed into 10 or 20 boles. By this artifice, a quart of bitter decoction, or such like, well paid for at a shilling, will fetch 8 or 10...

And just as the inflation of bills was open to abuse, so it left those forced to resort to this stratagem exposed to the risk of harassment or prosecution for overcharging. The hawks of Warwick Lane were never loath to pounce on any dubious case brought to their notice. It was for this reason that the year 1704, when the London Society of Apothecaries won a famous victory in the highest court in the land over the Royal College of Physicians, seemed at the time the critical one in determining that the apothecaries could wear the doctor's mantle thereafter with perfect propriety.

The events leading up to that victory began early in 1700 when William Rose of St Nicholas Lane, a London master-apothecary of some seven years' standing, was consulted – as some hundreds of his contemporaries were being consulted every day – by a sick patient. Having no physician's licence he could not charge for his advice, but he prescribed medicines and supplied them and in due course sent the man his account in the now accepted form. Only two features marked out this case from countless others in recent years. One was that Rose's charge was exorbitant. Though setting no record in this respect (Sir Gideon Harvey had claimed, more than thirty years before, to have 'known an apothecary's bill so extravagant that the sum at the bottom of his account amounted to fifty pounds in the space of thirty days, when the ingredients of the whole course could not be computed to stand him in forty shillings'), Rose's bill of £50 for twelve months' treatment was, by any normal standards, excessive. The other special feature of the case was that the patient, a butcher named John Seale, finding himself no better in health and very much worse in pocket for all Rose's 'boluses, electuaries and juleps', proved less resigned to his lot than many other Londoners in similar circumstances. He went to a physician early in 1701, was sent to the Royal College's own dispensary, cured in a few weeks' time at a cost, so he said, of rather less than £2, and (just possibly at the physician's instigation) brought his grievances against Rose to the notice of the College.

To the *comitia* of the College this seemed an open-and-shut case for a prosecution for unlicensed practice; and the Court of King's Bench duly found against Rose and fined him, though not without a heavy hint from Lord Chief Justice Holt that the prosecution was mean-spirited and that a statute which had so many 'inconveniences arising from it' for those treating the sick in good faith badly needed to be clarified by a definitive interpretation. Encouraged by this, the Society of Apothecaries prompted their liveryman to appeal to the House of Lords on a writ of error, and in March 1704 the peers declared for Rose and, in principle, for all 'practising' apothecaries. We do not know what swayed them most: whether it was the skilful pleading of Sir Thomas Powys on technicalities, designed to demonstrate that the College had not established the nature of Seale's illness and whether it had been serious enough to call in a physician in the first place; or whether it was Samuel Dodd's emotive plea that he was 'not only for the apothecaries but for all the poor people of England' [provided, one must presume, the poor had £50 to spare]. In any event, the decision was a historic one. As Sir George Clark has written, 'one of the pillars of the professional structure which the College of Physicians had been shoring up since 1614 had fallen'.

To put its fall in perspective, however, we have to see it in the broadest context. For one thing, other pillars, large and small, had already gone: the biggest of all had been undermined by the Plague in 1665–6; and the original Company of Apothecaries' decision to appropriate the respectable title of 'Society' around 1680 had knocked another prop away. On the other hand, since the Revolution the College had embarked on some vigorous repair work. In fact for the London apothecaries the relief afforded by Rose's case was the more timely because the optimism induced by their successes since 1665 had suffered two jolts in the 1690s. The more severe came when a sector of the Royal College, not without humanitarian motives, set up a novel Dispensary for the Sick Poor near the College building in Warwick Lane. This not only made a bid for public sympathy and strove to counteract one of the apothecaries' chief advantages, their cheapness (real or supposed), but also infringed the dispensing monopoly inherited from the old Company by the new Society. When the opening of two branch dispensaries quickly followed, many apothecaries foresaw a serious and sustained threat to their business. In the savage pamphlet war which ensued Samuel Garth published a best-selling poem, *The Dispensary*, mutual insults were freely exchanged, and the resultant atmosphere, heavy with the distrust and recrimination in which Rose's case was fought out, was slow to clear. This particular bone of contention was not finally removed until the Warwick Lane dispensary, after a chequered history, closed its doors in 1725. And it was only shortly before this that the College ceased to aggravate the Society with the remaining aspect of its harassing tactics since the 1680s, the exercise of its provocative right of search over any premises where drugs were sold.

There is a further and more important respect in which the significance for the medical profession of the legal events of 1701–4 has to be qualified. We are now aware that outside the London area the victory of 1704 in the House of Lords caused little stir. It was not only that unofficial usurpation of the physician's role by the apothecary had a far longer history in the seventeenth-century provinces than in the capital, but also that outside London, the country and market-town physicians never had the slightest chance of checking it. Some, indeed, boldly championed the activities of the 'pothecary-doctors, and Henry Stubbe, a highly cultivated Warwickshire physician who died in 1676, went into print in *Lex Talionis* (1670) with good, detailed advice to apothecaries on how best to brush up their reading in order to keep abreast of the physicians: for diagnosis the works of La Framboisière (pre-Harvey) and Willis were most strongly recommended, and for therapeutics the *Praxis Medica* of Riverius and James Primrose's *Enchiridion Medicum*. In contrast to the more cloistered denizens of the College, men such as Stubbe plainly recognised that an absolutely basic change in the structure of the profession was already well advanced in the English provinces by the middle years of Charles II, and they were anxious to accommodate it as helpfully as possible. Nothing seemed as important to them as the provision of more skilled labourers for a lamentably undertended vineyard.

Doubtless there were many provincial physicians who, at times, shared the anxieties articulated by one apologist for the Royal College around 1704, that some apothecaries used their pharmaceutical power – and especially their command of the new drugs – injudiciously: that too many of them, called in to treat a serious disease which at first exhibited 'seemingly inconsiderable symptoms', were inclined 'at first dash to give one of their cordials, wherein there never fails to be a good store of opium, whereby whilst they please their patient and his friends with giving him some present rest and ease, they...so far confound the symptoms as to make it difficult even for a well skilled physician to distinguish truly the species and genius of the distemper'. But, on the other side of the coin, Stubbe was prepared to argue that those of his fellow-physicians who preened themselves on making up their own medicines were often venturing into waters too deep and dangerous – deep for them and dangerous for their patients. His *Lex Talionis* bore the pungent subtitle *Sive Vindiciae Pharmacop[oe]rum:...Wherein may be discovered the Frauds and Abuses committed by Doctors Professing and Practising Pharmacy.*

The provincial apothecary still kept his shop in the early eighteenth century; and notwithstanding the claim made on behalf of his London colleague in 1695 that he 'often...attends the greatest in quality when sick', the country apothecary's clientele usually contained a far higher proportion of lower bourgeoisie, tradesmen, yeomen, craftsmen and artisans than that of his neighbour, the physician. Unlike the latter, he could not take fees merely for diagnosis and giving advice. But in the essentials of practice there was often little to distinguish the two; and whatever feelings of social and professional superiority country physicians may have cherished towards the local apothecaries, there appears to be extraordinarily little evidence of animosity between them. The position in Wells at the beginning of the eighteenth century, where the leading physician, apothecary and surgeon of the city co-existed and co-operated harmoniously, relying on each other's special skills and knowledge but with no jealous regard for lines of demarcation, probably followed a pattern that was common enough in places of similar size and professional resources. Claver Morris, the physician, sent his patients to Mr Lucas, Wells's surgeon, for operations – the removal of tonsils, for example, or the opening of abcesses. At the same time, Morris raised no objection if patients, especially of the poorer sort, consulted Mr Cupper the apothecary in the first instance, knowing that the latter could be relied upon to pass on to him any case that was not straightforward. Cupper, for his part, accepted that Morris, one of a small minority of physicians who kept up a keen and active interest in chemistry and had a laboratory in his house, would often dispense drugs; indeed, he was glad to have the doctor's own preparations regularly supplied to his shop.

In the end the professional development of provincial medicine was governed by one fundamental fact. Whether the apothecaries were practising general medicine themselves or were confining themselves mainly to dispensing physicians' prescriptions, in a society where disease was rampant and pain inseparable from everyday life there was ample scope for both them and the physicians to co-exist. More than that, they were in normal circumstances assured a living that was, at worst, adequate and, at best, handsome. After the 1720s there were still apothecaries ambitious enough to acquire formal licensed status as medical practitioners. John Lambert of Melton Mowbray, determined to arm himself at all points, described himself in 1712 to an official of the Stamp Office as 'apothecary and licensed practiser in physic and surgery in the archdeaconry of Leicester'. For much of the eighteenth century, however, the majority preferred to treat their patients in the capacity of courtesy 'doctors' from their traditional base, the shop. Not until late in the century did this distinction between physicians and apothecaries also begin to disappear with a fairly large-scale exodus of the latter from their shops and an unequivocal cession of the retailing of medicines to chemists. Even in the late Augustan period, however, it was frequently remarked how the shop came to be left more and more in the charge of the apprentice or journeyman, and already by 1730 some wholesale druggists, by turning retail 'chymists', had started to grasp the resulting opportunity.

At that time the apothecaries everywhere were still riding too high to be seriously alarmed by this new pressure from below. It was now thirty-five years since spokesmen for the London Society of Apothecaries had explicitly described their members' vocation as 'a profession instituted for ... most noble and inestimable purposes', at least as worthy of public esteem as the lesser degrees of the law, since they were dedicated 'to remove sickness and pain (two adversaries more dreaded by, and hurtful to mankind than any the attorneys can defend us from)'. Their prospects early in George II's reign had never seemed brighter. Standards varied from place to place, as with all apprentice-based vocations, but, in general, were unquestionably rising; and to the Society of Apothecaries, which administered the obligatory examination for London apprentices stringently, standards were crucial to making good their claim to the status both of a profession and of a liberal art. Quite apart from the vastly wider range of drugs available by 1700, as compared with 1600, knowledge of *materia medica* advanced considerably in the late seventeenth and early eighteenth centuries. The establishment of the Botanical Gardens at Chelsea (1680) and Kew (1730) helped to push out the frontiers and so, too, did the notable private researches of leading apothecaries such as Samuel Dale, author of the influential *Pharmacologia* (1693), James Sherard, Fothergill and Cruickshank, as well as those of physicians such as Cockburn and Sloane.

Even within the London medical profession, right through the second and third decades of the eighteenth century more and more physicians had come to terms with the inevitable. There had never been as much hostility between rank-and-file physicians and apothecaries, even at black periods like 1697–1704, as the bad blood between the College and the Society suggested. On the physicians' side, the number of liberals inside and outside the College who accepted that many apothecaries were well qualified to practise and that both sides must learn to work together in reasonable amity had never been negligible. At the time the 'Apothecaries Bill' was before the Commons in 1695, the Society publicly acknowledged its debt of gratitude to 'some of the learned'st and eminent'st physicians [who] knowing the grounds of this bill to be true, have industriously promoted the passing thereof'. The influence of these sympathisers increased significantly after 1700, gaining strength from the co-operative attitude of such leading figures as Sir Richard Blackmore, Sir Hans Sloane and Richard Mead. And their efforts to win over their more doubting or truculent colleagues were greatly assisted by the large number of the Freemen of the Society itself who had continued to cultivate their contacts in the physicians' circle and to profit from them. After all, in the fashionable London of 1680–1730 the lucky apothecaries who were satellites of a Radcliffe or a Garth were assured of a good living on that count alone; and by the early eighteenth century, in many a corner of the city, the friendly division of the spoils which Dudley Ryder observed in 1716 in the practice and business of his cousin, Mr Watkins, was daily going on:

When I was in his shop Mr Budget came in, who talked with my cousin about the course of physic he put him in and how much harm he had done him and rallied him upon his pressing physic upon him. And indeed this seems to be very much his fault. He is very apt to overload his patients with medicines, and besides, the doctors themselves are privy to it and act in concert with

them. Dr [Edward] Hulse came in while I was there about a
patient of his. He said he was pretty well and in a fair way, but
he would write him some little thing, which he puts into the most
advantageous form for the apothecary. This has made me almost
resolve to be my own physician, at least to come as little into
their hands as possible.

Above all, the apothecaries had risen in status without losing what
had long been their greatest strength, numbers. A responsible source
maintained at the time the dispensary war broke out in 1698 that the
apothecaries of London and Westminster had multiplied roughly
eight-fold in the previous sixty years; and that there were then (including, it would seem, 'journeymen' not in independent business) 'about
eight hundred, and a great many of them not of the [Apothecaries]
Hall'. Only three years earlier the Society of Apothecaries itself,
preparing its *Reasons on behalf of the Apothecaries' Bill*, found that
the number of master-apothecaries with their own premises within the
city and its sixteen inner suburban parishes was 188, a rise according
to its own records of just over 80 per cent in the past seventy-eight
years. Some idea of the continued rate of increase between 1695 and
1783 can be gauged from the fact that at the latter date Samuel Foart
Simmons MD, in the third and last edition of his *Medical Register*
named 367 master-apothecaries in business or resident in London, of
whom 242 were members of the society. This was only part of the
story, however; for Simmons's London roll did not include practitioners
in the capital's now sprawling outer suburbs, and even in 1695 it had
been conceded by spokesmen for the Society that the tally of master-
apothecaries in London and the traditional 'outparishes' had already
reached 337. As for apothecaries' shops in the same area – many of
them manned by journeymen – there were, according to one estimate,
almost treble that number. Dr Robert Pitt was to complain in 1704 that
the point had been reached in London 'when the shops of medicine are
increased to fill the town . . . and no alley or passage without the
painted pot, and that every village [round London] which formerly had
their physic hence has now two or three'. There is no doubt that much
of the London physicians' alarm, and the grudgingly defensive posture
which they appeared to strike on so many occasions through the
seventeenth century, is to be understood in the light of the sheer
numbers of potential competitors who seemed to be besetting them.

We can get a very conservative idea of how numerous apothecaries
were in parts of the provinces in the latter half of the Augustan period
by taking note of the numbers who voted in parliamentary elections in
those cities and boroughs for which there is detailed poll-book evidence.
(These numbers can be very roughly adjusted by bearing in mind that
an 80 per cent turn-out of voters at an average contest was a very high
one.) In Norwich, whose 30,000 inhabitants made it the country's most
populous urban centre outside London at this time, ten apothecaries
voted in 1715. The same city, according to L. A. Clarkson, had contained only two apothecaries in 1569 and none at all less than fifty

years earlier. There must have been a far higher proportion of absentee voters than usual at the Norwich election of 1715, for most other English towns on which we have information housed by this time considerably more than one apothecary for every 3,000 of their population. At the same general election eight resident and four country apothecaries turned out in York, a city little more than a third the size of Norwich. Fifteen Bristol apothecaries cast votes at the contest there in 1722; and once again a city's reputation for turbulent elections must have deterred a fair number from venturing from their shops to the polling hall, for a reliable local source in 1754 states that Bristol had by then twenty-nine apothecaries in business and practice, roughly one to every 1,200 of its inhabitants. There is no reason to doubt that there was expansion on a similar scale in most of the smaller provincial administrative and market centres, especially in those towns with an established gentry clientele. Even on the incomplete evidence of the guild rolls there were at least two apothecaries in Preston by 1702, three by 1722 and five by 1742.

By 1754 Bristol had five resident physicians to its twenty-nine apothecaries. Preston – a town on a smaller scale but with a fashionable clientele – had two 'doctors of physic' on its roll of resident burgesses in 1742 along with five apothecaries, and it is very likely that there were several more of the latter in business and practice there who were not on the roll. As for the general run of market towns, as late as 1700 only a small proportion could boast a university-trained physician. Yet a majority, and perhaps a substantial majority, did now have a medical practitioner of some description: and this represented a notable change since the first half of the seventeenth century. In the years between 1650 and 1699 there were only eighteen out of the forty-seven towns in Norfolk and Suffolk which were not served either by an apothecary or by a 'doctor', and many of the neglected ones were small places such as Dunwich, Loddon, Watton, Ixworth, Debenham, Wickham Market and Needham Market, with populations of between 350 and 700 or 800. Far to the north-west, even a place the size of Kendal, the county town of Westmorland, whose population was enumerated in 1695 and found to be 2,159, appears from the tax assessments of that year to have still been without a resident physician. By 1783 Kendal was to be served by two MDs and at least four surgeon-apothecaries in recognised general practice. But in the middle of William III's reign the work of tending the sick not only in the town itself but in much of its extensive hinterland was principally in the hands of its five apothecaries; and as in numerous market towns with between 1,000 and 2,500 inhabitants in the early part of our period, the latter's only reinforcements were provided by those who described themselves (as no fewer than ten did in Kendal in 1695) as either 'barber-surgeons' or 'chirurgeons'.

III   The Surgeons

The difficulty of disentangling surgeons from barber-surgeons in some contemporary lists relating to the late-seventeenth-century provinces is a reminder that there, at any rate, the status of the surgeon had traditionally been dubious. And, indeed, for at least thirty years after the Restoration most country surgeons, and for that matter many in London also, seem to have rated little higher in common esteem than good craftsmen, if as high. A fair reflection of contemporary attitudes is the salaries paid to surgeons in the armed forces. As late as the Austrian Succession War the surgeon at the average military garrison was only paid £45 12s 6d a year, although this admittedly was not the limit of his earnings. The Royal Navy was regarded as a much better training school for surgeons than the army. It had established this reputation in the 1650s, and between 1660 and 1700 several hundred naval surgeons were able to make a good living on their return to civilian life on the strength of the experience they had gained at sea. But while they were in the service the Admiralty itself for a long time thought relatively little of them They were warrant officers and, as such, except in fourth-rates and below, were paid less than pursers and bosuns; less, too, than the rawest young lieutenant. In fact, at the start of William III's reign the surgeon even of a first-rate of ninety-eight guns had a meagre salary of £2 10s a month or £30 a year. During King William's War, however, the London Barber Surgeons' Company seems to have finally convinced the Admiralty of its right to act as the certifying body for ship's surgeons and of the necessity of having every surgeon submit to an examination by the Company before being furnished with a certificate. At much the same time, and possibly not coincidentally, the surgeon's remuneration was suddenly doubled (1694); and that was only part of this story of his improving fortunes. As was said in 1747,

> Besides the allowance by the government, he has two-pence for every man on board the ship [the 'surgeon's twopences' had a long history]: he has forty shillings for every clap or pox of which he cures them, which is stopped out of the sailors' pay: he has a chest of medicines at the government's expense [from £8 5s to £30 depending of the rate of ship he served in]; and is allowed for slops, that is, linen rags, rice, spices and some other articles allowed the men in their sickness. All which put together make a surgeon's place in a sixty-gun ship to be worth near two hundred pounds per annum in time of peace, besides his share of prizes in time of war, in the division of which he is ranked as a lieutenant.

On shore establishments naval surgeons were being paid a fixed salary of £150 a year by the early eighteenth century, significantly only £50 less than the salary paid to physicians with comparable appointments. The change in the ship's surgeon's standing and prospects was partly related to a general improvement in naval pay; yet it also reflects the wider change which had come over the position of surgeons at large, both within the medical profession and in the estimation of society, in the years since Pepys's early naval reforms in the late 1670s. It was a radical change and was to prove irreversible.

It was their line of descent from the barbers which the English provincial surgeons of the seventeenth century had found so hard to live down. And even in the capital the status of surgery had suffered for similar reasons, though to a lesser extent. Where surgeons were organised at all in guilds or companies, as at Salisbury and Newcastle upon Tyne, it was with barbers that they were still associated. Even in London they did not finally emancipate themselves from the old 'Company of Barber Surgeons' until 1745, whereas the city's apothecaries had made their break with the grocers in James I's reign. Medieval barbers had found it a natural progression from shaving, polling and delousing their customers to venturing on minor surgery, such as setting broken limbs and opening abscesses. As bloodletting became a standard part of the treatment for almost every illness, it was the barbers – some of whom increasingly called themselves barber-surgeons – who did the 'cupping'. When toothache became unbearable and domestic implements failed it was to the barber-surgeon, also, that men and women betook themselves to have the offending object drawn. It is true that there had emerged in London as early as the fourteenth century, well ahead of the provinces, a specific group of 'surgeons', distinguishable from barbers and barber-surgeons; and by 1435 they had formed a small 'craft' within the Barber Surgeons' Company, with seventeen members. By the reign of Henry VIII such practitioners had been effectively segregated in most respects from the barber-surgeons, who still (among other reminders of their origins) displayed poles outside their shops. Surgery nevertheless continued to carry with it something of the taint of the shop. Under the Surgeons Act of 1540 every surgeon in London was still required to display a sign of some kind on the street side of his house. Nor, with some notable exceptions, was the Tudor and early Stuart surgeon normally a man of education. He was still a world away from his descendant, the London surgeon of George II's reign, who was expected as a matter of course to be thoroughly versed in both theoretical and practical anatomy; who was recommended to equip himself with an 'education . . . as liberal as that of the physician's' and who can have found nothing in the least incongruous in the description of his vocation in a popular guide to the London trades and professions in the 1740s as 'the second branch of the medical art; very little inferior to the first [physic] in point of utility, but founded upon principles much more certain, and less precarious in its success.'

Few, apart from the very best surgeons themselves, would have argued as late as 1660 that surgery, as generally practised, warranted the accolade of either an 'art' or a 'science'. In the previous 160 years, except for one profitable interlude, serious anatomical study by surgeons had made only slow progress. In 1540 the London Barber Surgeons' Company had acquired the legal right to the bodies of four hanged criminals each year for purposes of dissection and the next two decades had seen a considerable advance in knowledge. By Elizabeth's reign, however, able anatomy lecturers were in short supply, and for some forty or fifty years – the very decades when the London apothecaries were beginning to make their presence strongly felt – neither the anatomical training nor the practice of surgeons was able to make much headway. As late as Charles II's reign John Locke, who had taken a bachelor's degree in medicine in 1674, thought the advantages of a study of anatomy distinctly limited 'for removing the pains and maladies of mankind'. Even as he wrote, Locke was being proved unduly pessimistic. By the second half of the seventeenth century the top London master-surgeons were growing steadily more ambitious and their skills, by earlier standards, relatively sophisticated. The work of Richard Wiseman, who died in 1686, proved that there were here and there surgeons capable by now of contributing with distinction to the medical literature of the time. All the same, it was only at the beginning of the eighteenth century, when the London surgeons themselves captured the drooping initiative in anatomical teaching from the physicians that its great revival truly began. In two to three decades after 1700 the study of the human body by dissection took major strides forward, from which surgeons benefited by the hundred rather than by the score. It was a revival that succeeded in defying the persistence of traditional mob hostility to the removal of bodies from the gallows although it was not until 1746, in William Hunter's private medical school in London, that individual students of anatomy in England were for the first time given their own subjects for dissection.

Whatever the problems of status or education afflicting the rank and file of their Company during the century from 1580 to 1680, the leading master-surgeons of London had continued to take conscious pride in their knowledge and dexterity. Significantly, too, by the beginning of the seventeenth century the generality of London surgeons had begun tentatively (a good deal more tentatively than the apothecaries) to edge into the periphery of general medicine. After all, many patients in need of surgery suffered from other conditions – fevers, for instance (or if they did not, they very soon developed them!). Physicians had usually neither the time nor the wish to concern themselves in such cases, and in 1627 the Royal College of Physicians began to issue licences to surgeons to practise medicine so far as was necessary in the normal course of surgical treatment. Some doctors began the convention of selling 'covering prescriptions' to their surgeon acquaintances. Dr Roberts has found a case, probably not exceptional, of a surgeon paying a physician 10s for such a prescription and then charging his patient four times as much. Most surgeons under the early Stuarts and during the Interregnum, even in London, needed some latitude to make a decent living; and the wealthy City physicians did not find it difficult to be indulgent to a body which in 1663–4, for instance, when the College was self-importantly seeking legislative sanction for its new charter, announced that its members would acquiesce provided only that 'they were allowed to practise their art within the old limits and were allowed the cure of tumours, fractures, dislocations, ulcers,

wounds, syphilis and diseases of women'. As one physician compla-
cently remarked, 'we granted all this easily and willingly enough'. It is
clear that the apothecaries, who in the past sixty years had overtaken
and passed the surgeons of London in prestige, were by now seen as by
far the greater threat to the physicians' supremacy. Between the Restoration and Queen Anne's reign the Royal College was never locked in
ferocious conflicts with the Barber Surgeons' Company, like those
which disfigured its relations with the Society of Apothecaries. Its
interests and that of the Company were more easily demarcated and as
late as 1680 even the most sought-after London surgeons could not
hope to rival the most fashionable physicians in wealth and status.

But the day when they would do so was not as far off as it must have
seemed. The seventy years after the Restoration, and most particularly
the years after 1690, were to see the function and image of the surgeon
and his place within the medical fraternity transformed. The role of
the capital city in this process is easier to delineate than that of the
provinces. Outside London, conditions and levels of competence varied
hugely from place to place and from person to person, at least to the
end of the seventeenth century; but except in one respect already
noticed – his quite rapid intrusion into 'general practice' under the later
Stuarts wherever the supply of medical practitioners was under pressure – the provincial surgeon rarely proved as active a catalyst of
change as his neighbour, the provincial apothecary. A thorough training in the basic traditional skills could probably be had in most of the
larger towns by the end of Charles II's reign, and elsewhere there were
individual practitioners of high local reputation who were much sought
after by parents with sons to apprentice. On her visit to Newcastle
in 1697 Celia Fiennes was taken

> to see the Barber Surgeons' Hall which was within a pretty garden
> walled in . . . a good neat building of brick. There [she records]
> I saw a room with a round table in it, railed round with seats or
> benches for the conveniency in their dissecting and anatomising a
> body and reading lectures on all parts. There was two bodies that
> had been anatomised, one the bones were fastened with wires, the
> other had had the flesh boiled off and some of the ligaments
> remained and dried with it; and so the parts were held together by
> its own muscles and sinews that were dried with it.

But only a very small minority of students outside the capital were
fortunate enough to enjoy facilities such as this before 1700. In fact, a
very much larger minority were to be found at the opposite pole. As
late as the 1720s and 1730s it was possible to find some good, as well as
many indifferent, provincial surgeons who had served their time under
one of the hundreds of old-style barber-surgeons who still populated the
foothills of medicine quite thickly towards the end of the seventeenth
century. And this was not a phenomenon peculiar to distant market
towns, such as Kendal; for even in flourishing cities and ports the old
connection with barbery died hard. William Thornhill, for example,

who was appointed one of the original surgeons to Bristol's new infirmary in 1735, had been apprenticed to 'Old Rosewell', who kept his
pole at his door, along with the sign of the porringer and a red garter,
to the end of his life. Under him, so one local newspaper reported,
Thornhill had learned to shave customers, let blood and extract teeth,
'his master being so celebrated that on a Sunday morning there were
swarms of persons to be bled, for which each paid 6d to a shilling'
(which was about half the going rate in ordinary London practice at
this time); and Rosewell's habit was frequently to ply these customers
– they were scarcely regarded as 'patients' – a quart or two of ale to
recruit their strength for the journey home. By 1750 there was still a
place left in provincial society for these curious hybrids, though it was
a shrinking one. The same count of Bristol's medical practitioners in
1754 which, as we have already seen, discovered 5 physicians and 29
apothecaries also revealed 19 surgeons in the city, but only 13 barber-
surgeons. When Samuel Simmons compiled his first *Medical Register of
England* in 1779 he excluded barber-surgeons totally as being unworthy
of professional consideration.

What was it, then, which revolutionised the true surgeon's place in
the medical profession and in society in late Restoration and Augustan
England? Four circumstances, in the main, brought this major change
about. To begin with, an important part was played by the wars of the
1650s and of 1665–7, and a vital one by those of King William's reign
and Queen Anne's. In fact the wars against Louis XIV's France probably had a more far-reaching effect on the structure of medicine than
they had on any other profession outside the armed services themselves
and the civil service. It was Cromwell who first exempted surgeons who
had served in the New Model army and in the republican navy from
the licensing authority of the local companies. Many successful provincial surgeons of Charles II's reign were men who had profited from
this exemption or who, like James Yonge at Plymouth, had picked up
invaluable experience in the expanding merchant fleet as well as on warships after the Restoration. But much more spectacular were the effects
on civilian medical practice of the flood of demobilised ships' surgeons
and army surgeons from the vastly larger forces of 1689–97 and 1702–
13. Many were men of wide experience in treating all manner of complaints. Indeed, the rigorous examination which intending naval surgeons had to undergo by the early eighteenth century before they were
ever taken on a ship (carried out by the Barber Surgeons' Company
and the Physician to Greenwich Hospital by arrangement with the
Navy Commissioners) tested their knowledge of the nature and treatment of all common diseases, especially fevers and 'scorbutic diseases',
and their proficiency in *materia medica* as well as their strictly surgical
qualifications. Even more, perhaps, than the London apothecaries'
triumph over the College of Physicians, the return of the army and
navy surgeons into civil society after the two French wars of the years
1689–1713 was the most important stimulus to the spread of general
practice in the whole of our period. And as well as greatly hastening the
coming of 'the doctor', it more specifically encouraged the advance of

the surgeon-apothecary (see below, pp. 202–3), so that a type of practitioner who had been a relative newcomer to provincial medicine in
1700 became in the space of fifty of sixty years its bedrock.

'The physician should know something of the surgeon's business',
wrote Campbell in *The London Tradesman*, 'and he of the doctor's . . .
But there is one branch belonging to the doctor which the town surgeon has almost monopolized to himself; that is, the cure of the
venereal disease'. Herein lies a second explanation for the new prestige
the surgeons acquired between 1680 and 1730 and for the increasingly
heavy, and to them profitable, demands made on their services. The
use of mercury ointment for the treatment of syphilis had been recommended, with reservations, by Paracelsus before the middle of the
sixteenth century, but late Tudor and early Stuart physicians generally
preferred the infinitely safer, if relatively ineffectual, guaiacum or 'pock
wood'. The dangers of mercury, especially when employed for 'salivation' as well as 'inunction', were still recognised as acute in the 1660s
and 1670s: even the eminent Richard Wiseman frankly admitted in his
classic *Severall Chirurgical Treatises* (1676) that his experiments with
one new mercurial treatment of congenital syphilis had been disastrous.
Once, however, the value of carefully prepared mercury compounds
had been generally recognised, and their risks, in normal cases, substantially reduced, it was the surgeon – who at one time had only been
called in to treat the external symptoms of syphilis and, in dire conditions, to amputate – who, as Campbell later said, 'usurped the place of
the doctor, and monopolized this odious distemper to himself'. 'Whore
houses increase', wrote Anthony à Wood, the Oxford antiquary, in
1686; 'surgeons have work and great salivation used.' Learning carefully how to treat venereal diseases became an indispensable part of
their training, and on the prevalence of such diseases alone (it was
being said of London by the 1740s) 'the subsistance of three parts in
four of all the surgeons in Town depends'.

Meanwhile, a third development of the previous sixty to seventy
years had had the effect of vastly improving the general quality of
the surgeon's 'art' and of ensuring his acceptance as a professional
man. His whole training, and not just his education in the use of a
single specific, had become more rigorous and more ambitious; and the
key to this was the much fuller and sounder anatomical knowledge on
which increasingly it came to be based. This was most evidently true
of London, where Surgeons' Hall blossomed as a teaching centre of
great merit from around 1700 until at least the 1740s, and where
private lecture courses, initiated in 1701, proliferated in response to an
avid demand. Foreign immigrants settling in the capital, such as Paul
Buissière, Peter Lamarque and Nathaniel St André, played a part in
this revival, as did John Douglas and other Scots. But its most striking
feature is the swelling confidence of English surgeons in their own
native skills and in their capacity for imparting and improving them,
together with an infusion of the entrepreneurial spirit which was
characteristically Augustan. In all these respects the renaissance was
perfectly epitomised by the contribution of William Cheselden, who

embarked on private tuition at the age of 21 or 22 when with almost incredible aplomb he printed, in 1711, his *Syllabus of Anatomy, in 35 Lectures, for the use of his Anatomical Theatre.* From 1713, at the latest, to 1731 Cheselden delivered four courses a year, each course lasting up to two months; and almost at the outcome his rapacious enterprise in procuring bodies to dissect on his own premises earned him a rebuke from the elders of the Barber Surgeons' Company for '[drawing] away the members of this Company and others from the public dissections and lectures at the Hall'.

It is clear that in the provinces, also, determination to learn and to profit from new techniques, together with a striking camaraderie among committed surgeons was fostering a new sense of professional pride and corporate feeling. Many examples could be given. The king's Serjeant-Surgeon, spending two days at Plymouth in 1677, not only put James Yonge in the way of £50 worth of business among the royal entourage but passed on to him some valuable 'secrets in chyrurgery'. In 1681 Yonge travelled all the way to Oxford to discuss professional matters with Roger Fry, the University anatomist and with a well-known city surgeon, Mr Poynter, who told him 'freely the way of making a skeleton, at which he is excellent'. Within a few months Yonge was off again, this time to Richmond at the invitation of another surgeon named Rossington, from whom he 'pumped some practical things'. And it is well known that Yonge himself, provincial as he was, was responsible for devising around 1679, and subsequently making popular, an important refinement of the art of amputation whereby the stump was padded with the patient's own soft tissue. It was in London, however, between 1719 and 1726 that the two success-ful new techniques of 'cutting for the stone' were perfected; and good provincial surgeons – among them Claver Morris's friend Lucas, in Wells – were at once eager to learn them. 'Mr Lucas and Mr Pye of Bristowe came and desired me to see the operation', Morris wrote, on 22 August 1723, 'being to take out a stone from the young fellow by the new [Douglas] method of cutting through the belly, which I did. Afterwards I went (with many spectators) to Mr Lucas's and prescribed for the patient.' The perfection of this technique, the 'supra-pubic' method, by the London surgeon John Douglas in 1719 earned him not only a glowing testimonial from Sir Hans Sloane and other royal physicians, and a letter of congratulation from Boerhaave, but the coveted appointment of lithotomist at the new Westminster Hospital. Cheselden, however, pioneered an even more successful alternative method, the 'lateral' operation, at St Thomas's Hospital in Southwark in 1726 and improved on it in 1727. He performed it with lightning speed so as to minimise the shock to his patients and from the first hundred lithotomies he performed at St Thomas's by his improved method only half-a-dozen fatalities resulted.

These circumstances point directly to a fourth development which did so much to advance surgery and the status of surgeons at this time. This was the sudden multiplication under the first two Georges of the London hospitals; the new importance which these hospitals acquired as teaching centres (a process in which their own surgeons were well to the fore); and finally the fact that by the 1730s and 1740s the provinces were beginning to follow London's example. As late as Queen Anne's reign the only two institutions in London which were 'hospitals' in something remotely like the modern sense were the long-established St Thomas's and St Bartholomew's. The latter was sited in West Smithfield, but it had two small offshoots, one at Kingsland and the other across the river at Southwark. Together they then employed nine Master-Surgeons and three Assistant-Surgeons, to which were added at St Bart's in the mid-1720s '2 Surgeons for cutting for the stone'; and some of the greatest names in the early-eighteenth-century medical profession – Cowper, Cheselden and Edward Greene, for example – were closely associated with them. So, too, was Robert Gay of Hatton Garden, to whom Claver Morris once sent a Somerset patient for the removal of a breast cancer. But as late as 1718 these two establishments, medieval in foundation, were still tiny oases in a vast desert; and that desert extended throughout the provinces where they were, as yet, no 'general infirmaries' at all, though a small naval hospital existed at Plymouth by the 1680s and later expanded to accommodate hundreds of sick or injured seamen.

In 1719 a charitable society in Westminster, established three years earlier, founded an infirmary in Petty France from which developed a third metropolitan hospital, the Westminster Infirmary. It admitted its first patient in May 1720. From then on the London voluntary hospital movement gathered a remarkable momentum, giving the lie by its achievement to the facile writing-off by some historians of Walpole's England as a complacent and uncaring age. By 1724 the building of Guy's Hospital, thanks to the munificence of a London bookseller of exceptional wealth, was almost complete. Sadly, its founder did not live to see it open its doors in the following year. St George's Hospital was opened eight years later, the London Hospital (the closest to the now densely populated 'east end') in Prescot Street in 1740 and the Middlesex, off Tottenham Court Road, in 1745. In addition to all this, the complete rebuilding of St Bartholomew's Hospital, financed by a public subscription, began in 1729 and was to result at length in what Dr Samuel Simmons later described as 'a large and handsome square, in which are airy and spacious wards for the reception of upwards of four hundred patients'. By 1780 there were to be about 1980 beds provided by these seven hospitals – nearly 860 at St Bart's and St Thomas's combined, and 430 at Guy's – and the small Lock Hospital, founded in 1747 'for the cure of the veneral disease', had 40 more. Altogether there was provision on their various foundations for twenty-seven surgeons.

All these London hospitals, the old and the new, became crucial vehicles for the improvement of surgical skills and training. In 1702 the governors of St Thomas's formally regularised a practice which had been creeping in for several years and causing friction with the Barber Surgeons' Company. They amended the hospital's regulations to permit its surgeons to take pupils, though stipulating that 'none shall have more than three cubs at one time, nor take any for less than one year'. The 'cubs' referred to here were not formal apprentices, who were taken on in the surgeons' private capacity and rarely for less than seven years, but their 'dressers': young pupils already 'bound to another [London] surgeon', as the St Thomas's men explained in 1695, 'or such as had served a considerable time to a surgeon in the country and for bettering their judgement in the art came to London to see the practice of the Hospital'. The precedent thus set was to be of prime importance. Although until 1742 only St Bartholomew's and St Thomas's taught formally, medical students appear to have had no difficulty in making private arrangements to take advantage of the facilities offered by the new hospitals founded from 1719–40. One of many who did so was Richard Kay, apprentice-surgeon of Baldingstone, near Bury, Lancashire, who wrote in his diary on 1 August 1743: 'This day in the morning after breakfast and prayer . . . I set out upon my journey for London, where I am entered pupil to Mr Steade, Apothecary to Guy's Hospital for a year.' Guy's did not officially begin surgical teaching until 1769, but among Benjamin Stead's prescribed duties as house apothecary was the supervision of students and apprentices, and he drew up a programme for them which ensured them the best relevant instruction available at his own and other city hospitals, and elsewhere, on virtually every major aspect of contemporary medicine. On 10 August Kay had his first day 'attending business in Guys and St. Thos Hospital, was present at the amputation of a thigh, saw some other curious operations, heard Mr Sharp's anatomical lecture'. It was the beginning of a crowded twelve months, during which he attended two courses of lectures (on anatomy and the circulation of the blood) from Samuel Sharp, senior surgeon of Guy's, and two from John Girle, junior surgeon to St Thomas's which ranged from the alimentary canal, through specialist instruction on the eyes, ears, cranium and teeth to bandaging. He went to a variety of demonstrations and lectures at Surgeons' Hall, and from May 1744 followed two short midwifery courses 'with Mr Smedley, the man midwife in Gerrard St'. He walked the wards of the two Southwark hospitals at least three days a week, and he witnessed scores of operations, from abdominal surgery to a girl being 'cut for a hare lip'. It was an unforgettable experience. 'Seldom a day but something remarkable happens,' he wrote at one point; '. . . I believe being here is being at the fountain head for improvement.'

It was less than fifty years earlier that one anonymous London physician, writing with some weight of Royal College opinion behind him, had deplored the widespread credence given in the later seventeenth century to the mistaken view that 'we have no good chyrurgeons in England; and that if a cataract is to be couched, a Frenchman must be sent for over: or if one is to be cut of the stone, a Dutchman must be employed'. By 1740 this self-deprecation has gone. There were, it is true, plenty of surgeons in London and some in the provinces who were ready, by then, to sing the praise of Edinburgh University as well as the Hotel Dieu in Paris as finishing schools for their profession. Yet few of the 'young pupils' and apprentices whom Richard Kay met in the wards, theatres and lecture rooms during his year in London, those who 'walked in the square' at Guy's with him and talked medicine day in and day out, would have questioned his conviction of London's now established excellence in the field of surgical training. For them it was indeed 'the fountain head for improvement'; and so it was for the master-surgeons in almost every part of England who sent them there to drink deep at its waters.

The new English provincial infirmaries of the 1730s and 1740s could not, of course, hope to match as training centres such major hospitals as St Thomas's or Guys's. Nevertheless there were twelve of them in existence by 1755, the first six – at Winchester, Bristol, Exeter, York, Bath and Northampton – being founded in a sudden spurt between 1736 and 1743; and their appearance on the scene does, in a sense, symbolise the physicians' final acceptance of the skilled provincial surgeon as an equal on professional terms, if not as yet a full equal on social terms. These new foundations represented one more blow, perhaps the ultimately decisive blow, against those barriers which had traditionally maintained the old tripartite segregation of England's medical practitioners. The first dozen provincial hospitals provided around a thousand beds and were served by almost a hundred doctors. Almost all maintained a resident house apothecary (in the case of Manchester a house surgeon-apothecary), and their patients were attended by some forty surgeons and roughly the same number of physicians. These men worked together in tending the sick poor of their provincial towns and cities, and it is worth observing that around three-quarters of the surgeons, as well as of the physicians involved, gave their hospital services free. On the evidence of Kay's diary, the co-operative spirit of the infirmaries is appropriately matched by the easy intimacy which existed in the London hospitals between medical students of all kinds, whatever branch they were intending to specialise in.

Apart from the invasion of the Leyden doctors and the emergence in the first four decades of the eighteenth century of the London hospital surgeons as an élite breed within the medical profession, perhaps the most interesting new phenomenon to appear among the personnel of medicine in the Augustan period was the 'surgeon-apothecary'. He epitomised that broadening experience of general medicine which good surgeons all over the country were adding to their rapidly improving technical skills in order to meet a need that was only too evident, especially away from the larger towns. It was a process in which, as we have already seen, the wars played an important part and it was yet another aspect of that levelling and merging trend which I have called 'the coming of the doctor'.

It will not have escaped notice that Richard Kay's principal teacher and mentor in London was Guy's house *apothecary*. Although the young man was sent up to town primarily to enlarge his surgical experience, he had every intention and every opportunity to further his general medical education at the same time; and when he returned to south Lancashire and began his dedicated, all too short, career in partnership with his father, he was to all intents and purposes a general practitioner. 'Lord . . . own and prosper me,' he wrote in April 1747, 'whether I be employed as surgeon or physician.' As well as attending to innumerable wounds, abscesses and broken or diseased limbs, removing cancerous breasts and small tumours elsewhere, and in addition to dentistry and midwifery, he was called on to treat pleurisy, gravel, quinsy, tuberculosis, smallpox and all manner of fevers. 'We seldom have a leisure hour', he found; though he rarely failed to find some time each day to thank God for 'daily business' and 'daily success'.

So far as we know, Kay never formally described himself as a 'surgeon-apothecary'. The local Unitarian minister, in the funeral sermon he preached in 1751, described 'his profession as a surgeon and an administer of physic'. But he was clearly of the same *genus* as those surgeon-apothecaries who first made their entry towards the end of the seventeenth century. One of their very earliest precursors in the London area was probably Robert Hitchcock of Ware, 'apothecary and chirurgeon', whose referees at the time of his application for a physician's licence in 1662 deemed him 'skilful in the art of an apothecary and painful in his office of a surgeon, in the same art initiated at Surgeons' Hall, London, and known by our experience to be fit and able to practise physic'. In 1693 George de Folleville of Cheshunt, describing himself as a 'surgeon-apothecary' applied to practice physic and surgery. John Harris was practising in Whitechapel for some years before 1700 as 'surgeon and apothecary'. Mostly such men trained first as a surgeon's apprentice, and then spent a year or two with a qualified apothecary learning the drug business from the inside. In Aylesham, Norfolk, in 1733, for example, lived a doctor named Benjamin Taylor. Normally he described himself as a surgeon, but as the only practitioner in this little township he also kept an apothecary's shop there and advertised its 'fresh stock of drugs'. It is probable that many who set up as surgeon-apothecaries in country districts during William III's reign and Anne's were ex-naval surgeons who had had some training, and a great deal of practical experience, in dispensing. On the other hand, Edward Jacob, who had a flourishing practice in Canterbury under Anne (asking £100 for taking on one of his apprentices in 1712), was styled 'apothecary and surgeon' – with the clear implication that the former was his original vocation – and this was certainly true of John Lambert who practised in Melton Mowbray at the same time. A certain rapacious 'Dr' Horseman, who was twice complained of to the Royal College for making excessive charges to his London patients, claimed to have served his time in both branches of medicine and to have a formal qualification in each. But birds of his precise feather must have been exceedingly rare.

It is not difficult to understand how even in London, with its bottomless demand, such 'doctors' were ready to undertake every kind of practice, medical, surgical and dispensing. Although the leaders of the surgeons' profession sometimes frowned on these hybrids, they were swimming against too powerful a tide. 'The chyrurgeon-apothecary' was already commonplace in Scotland by 1730, as carefully trained in anatomy and chemistry as he was in botany and compounding; and before the middle of George III's reign his counterpart was to dominate much of country, and not a little urban, practice in England. Even when a town was important enough to accommodate a physician, it was becoming increasing common by the 1730s to find, as in White-haven, a surgeon-apothecary as his second string. In rural districts, where it was often impossible to make an adequate living by surgery alone, the surgeon-apothecaries met a crying need. And if such all-rounders were looking for the entrée to an upper-class clientele, they were clearly better placed than unvarnished surgeons to collect a bishop's licence as a physician or, more exceptionally, to take the Royal College's examination for an extra-licence. Even more than the 'pothecary-physician – even more, one might say, than the family doctors of our own day – they were truly *general* practitioners.

The presence of surgeon-apothecaries in growing numbers by 1730 served to emphasise still further the two deepest impressions left on the personnel and practice of medicine during the previous fifty years by the needs and expectations of Augustan society. For one thing, it underlined the growing unwillingness of many Englishmen of the day to surrender passively to pain and sickness. That their attitude was different from that of their early Stuart forebears there is little doubt, and it prompted them not merely to look for more doctors (and be pre-pared to pay for the services of those doctors) but to expect higher standards of professional training and skill at all levels of legitimate medicine. At the same time, it was inevitable that in a disease-ravaged land, despite the steadily increasing flow of young men into medicine, demand should still far outstrip supply. Apart from the unprecedented opportunities this presented to quacks, whose blandishments few were able completely to resist, this meant that the needs of the great majority of patients, outside London, at least, could only be met by 'general practice' or by the nearest possible approximation to it. The 'pothecary-physician and the surgeon-apothecary were thus merely different aspects of essentially the same response in the years 1680–1730. But the effectiveness of the response was of course made much easier by the slow fusion of the old disparate elements within the medical profession which was taking place at the same time.

Only when the frontiers of medical knowledge (and, above all, knowledge of sepsis and anaesthesia) had been pushed very much further out than had been possible by 1730 would the needs, even of those who could afford to pay for orthodox treatment, be close to satisfaction. But at least in the meantime the advent of a new breed of medical men had achieved something of not negligible importance towards bringing satisfaction within sight. The physician whose know-ledge before practice was derived only from books; the apothecary who was no more than a dispensing shopkeeper; the barber-surgeon or surgeon who kept firmly within the narrow territory of tradition – each was still a commonplace of medicine in the first half of Charles II's reign. By the 1730s each was a comparative rarity. Into their place had come 'the doctor'. Moving with the times, the Ulverston apothecary Henry Lampe made provision in his will in 1711

> that in case my son, Ephraim Lampe, when he cometh to years of discretion, incline to betake himself to the study and practice of physic, that he be put betimes to a good apothecary, in a country town . . . where they have a deal of business for making up of doctors' bills and for visiting of patients, for three or four years, after which time I would have him to frequent some good hospital, where he may see and learn surgery and the different operations belonging to it.

However 'the doctor' of 1730 was formally labelled, he was by and large far more versatile than his predecessor two generations back, less hidebound by the old circumscriptions and prejudices and more responsive to change. He was likely to be more receptive to the virtues of what we now call 'preventive medicine';* and he was furnished with laudanum, with specifics such as mercuric oxide, cinchona ('Jesuit's bark', a close relative of quinine), calomel and ipecacuanha, and, if not equipped with then often backed by, surgical skills of no mean order. If he was a trained surgeon or surgeon-apothecary even the instruments he used were better, more sophisticated and varied than those of sixty years before, and provincial as well as London craftsmen had begun to produce them. And how far the services of the best 'doctors', at least, had come to be valued in their local communities by George II's reign may be not unfairly judged, in conclusion, from part of the obituary of one of the best documented provincial predecessors of the modern GP, Richard Kay, struck down in his prime in 1751:

> He was well skilled in his profession . . . He had a sagacity in discovering the grievances of his patients, knew the common methods of treating them and sometimes struck out into uncommon but successful way of managing them. The tenderness and humanity wherewith he treated his patients, the concern he showed for their welfare, the success that generally attended him in all curable cases, the lamentation that is made for the loss of him shows how useful and serviceable he was.

---

* Achievements in this area since the Restoration ranged from a growing realisation of the merits of ventilation, 'fresh air' and exercise, and greater knowledge of dietetics, to the introduction on a small scale of inoculation against smallpox in the years 1721–8.

7

Society and the Medical Profession, 1680–1730

The doctor's coming, and the accompanying transformation in the structure of medicine and the training of its practitioners, were momentous changes in themselves. They represented over the eighty years or so between the 1660s and the 1740s the rise of a true medical profession, and one that already had a measure of homogeneity, by contrast with the motley association of professionals, quasi-professionals, tradesmen and skilled craftsmen which had uneasily occupied the world of legitimate medicine at the time of the Restoration. Every bit as striking, however, were the changes in the social standing, status and economic prospects of medical men which these processes entailed; and so were the enhanced opportunities for advancement and freer mobility in English society which they made possible. By the middle decades of the eighteenth century there was no longer the immense cleavage in social terms between the graduate doctor of physic and the rest of the world of medicine that had existed a century earlier. As for the distribution of material rewards, the geographical division of the profession into those who practised respectively in London, in provincial cities and towns of importance, and in small market towns and country parishes had become a more evident source of inequalities since the later seventeenth century than the old functional divisions. By 1730 his location and the quality of his clientele were at least as likely to determine a doctor's financial prospects as whether his official training was as physician, apothecary or surgeon. In other respects, too, there were far-reaching changes over the course of half a century. How the place in society of medicine and of those who practised it was transformed along with the rise and consolidation of the profession is the theme of this chapter.

Physicians as a body came from rather too diverse a range of social backgrounds in Augustan England for the peace of mind of the Royal College. The College maintained throughout our period, and well beyond it, a stereotyped image of itself as the guardian of a gentry preserve and, in particular, of a traditional refuge of country gentlemen's younger sons. Francis Brown, one of the pamphleteers engaged in the Rose case, rejected out of hand the right of apothecaries to practise. The grounds of his argument were essentially social: a limited right could only open the door to universal practice, and this would automatically depress the study of physic in the English universities and strip the gentry of one of the few honourable and lucrative vocations that were open to younger sons bereft of landed patrimony. Not a little of the disquiet voiced by Oxford- and Cambridge-trained physicians at the inflowing tide of Dutch and Scottish graduates into the profession from the 1720s to the 1740s appears, at root, to have been of a social nature. There were those who firmly believed, with Thomas Withers, MD, that 'the character of a physician . . . cannot be maintained with dignity but by a man of literature'; and on this score at least, if on no other, Leyden and Edinburgh, Utrecht and Glasgow were found wanting – or so it was said. What was palpably true was that a high proportion of the students who went to those universities to train, or to others in Scotland, Holland or France, were not gentlemen by birth: and there were traditionalists who hastened to damn the medical schools of those institutions on this ground, above all.

That there was a good deal of cant about all this goes without saying. On the score of gentle birth the antecedents of a large minority of the Fellows and Licentiates of the Royal College would not bear searching examination. As for the extra-licentiates, with so few applicants coming forward the *comitia* could hardly afford the luxury of social discrimination: one of the very few extra-licences granted in the early 1720s, for instance, went to George Lock, a Northumbrian who practised in Alnwick, had no degree and was the son of the Duke of Somerset's local bailiff. There is no reason to believe that entrants to the medical profession by the traditional route were more exclusively of gentry stock than any other groups of professional trainees at Oxford and Cambridge; and it is fairly plain that to the younger sons of the landed squirearchy, at least, the appeal of the physician's profession could not match that of the law, or indeed of the army, by the early eighteenth century. At the same time, on financial grounds, minor gentry with sons who were university material were more likely to consider training them for the Church than encouraging them to become doctors.

Of course, there were prominent physicians in Anne's reign and George I's who did conform, more or less, to the theoretical social norms. Two such were Henry Plumptre and Tancred Robinson, younger brothers of well-known Whig Members of Parliament. The Plumptres of Plumptre House were a Nottingham family of long and honourable pedigree, while Robinson, though only one generation removed from a wealthy merchant house, had a Yorkshire landed baronet for a brother. Edward Norris, who took his doctorate in physic at Oxford in 1695 and became an FRCP late in life – though he practised mainly in Cheshire – was a fifth son from a south Lancashire gentry family, the Norrises of Speke. Another younger son, Charles Cotes, who became Physician to Westminster Hospital in 1733, had impeccable social credentials, for he boasted a Shropshire squire on his paternal side and a peer's daughter for a mother. Nor was it too difficult in Queen Anne's London to live down the professional stigma of a Scottish education and find an easy route into fashionable practice if, like Charles Oliphant, one happened to be the descendant of a lowland baron and the client of a highland duke. On the other hand, many of the biggest names in late-seventeenth- and early-eighteenth-century London medicine were misfits in any gentry-orientated view of the physicians. The great Hans Sloane, it is true, had a fairly orthodox background in one sense, as the seventh son of an Irish gentleman, although the purists would have preferred him not to have procured his medical education at the universities of Paris, Montpelier and Orange. But in any social anatomy of the leading London practitioners, what was to be made of Radcliffe, whose father had been a none-too-successful attorney and overseer of the house of correction in Wakefield, or of Sir Edward Hannes, whose father probably kept a herb shop in Bloomsbury market? Radcliffe went up to Oxford as a Freeston exhibitioner and could never have afforded to stay on and study for his first medical degree from 1670–5 without a fellowship at Lincoln College. For obvious reasons Oxford and Cambridge had no place, as students, for Richard Mead or Richard Morton, both the sons of Nonconforming pastors. Samuel Garth's lineage was respectably if not impeccably rooted in the well-to-do yeomanry of the border country between Yorkshire and north Lancashire, where he attended the small grammar school at Ingleton. But Shadwell's background, as the son of a supremely undistinguished poet laureate and opium addict and the grandson of a struggling barrister, was eccentric; while that of Richard Blackmore, a one-time schoolmaster who after leaving the 'whipping trade' had practised as an empiric before picking up a belated MD from Padua, was barely reputable. Blackmore's fellowship, more than any other conferred in the great augmentation of 1687 (see above, p. 170), was thought by many of his colleagues to demean the College of Physicians.

The connection between the parish clergy and medical practice had long been a close one. By the end of the seventeenth century it was not being maintained as closely at the most prestigious level of medicine as among the surgeons and apothecaries, yet a number of Augustan physicians came from prosperous clerical families. One was Sir Richard Manningham, the second son of the Reverend Thomas Manningham who became Bishop of Chichester in 1709. Another was John Freind, one of the arch-Tories among the London doctors of the early eighteenth century, who had first made his name by going to Spain as chief physician to Peterborough's expeditionary force in 1705 and writing a vindication of that controversial general's conduct in the Peninsula. Less affluent clerics could not finance a full-scale university medical education; yet, like Robert Munsey, a Norfolk rector deprived as a nonjuror in 1690, they might still contrive to provide their sons with the training necessary to secure a physician's licence or extra-licence. As family traditions became more solidly established in medicine, however, the profession of physic became to some extent self-generating in Augustan England. Certainly medical backgrounds became far commoner among physicians than clerical ones. Phineas Fowke, a Fellow of the Royal College from 1680 to 1710, Edward Hulse, elected in 1717, and Gideon Harvey junior, Registrar at Warwick Lane in the 1720s, were just three examples of sons following fathers as MDs, while Henry Plumptre was both the grandson and the father of a physician.

Whatever their social origins, one thing was now apparent to all intending physicians: a formal university training for the profession, in England especially, usually cost a great deal of money. It could be just as expensive at Utrecht, Leyden, Paris or Rheims, although in general it was less so and in some cases appreciably less. Much depended on how much previous experience the student going to a Dutch or French university had under his belt, for example through apprenticeship; and, in practice, the average period of full-time study for a coveted Leyden doctorate during Boerhaave's reign was surprisingly short – around eighteen months. The difference between such flexibility and the conventions of Oxford and Cambridge was particularly important in diluting the social exclusiveness of the English physicians after 1700. It is hard to see, for instance, how John Huxham, whose practice and research in Devonshire became perhaps the most distinguished of any provincial physician of his generation, could ever have afforded an English 'liberal' and medical education of the orthodox brand. His father was a Totnes butcher; and even if the local patron who underwrote his apprenticeship and presumably paid subsequently for his year's intensive training at Leyden and Rheims (1715–16) had been an Anglican parson instead of a Nonconformist, it would have been heavy odds against his being able to send Huxham along the standard route to a doctorate at Oxford or Cambridge. Even the very last stage of that route, the ritual of taking the doctor's degree, was exceedingly costly. In 1691 Claver Morris, who had been practising with good reputation in Wells for six years with a bachelor's degree, supplicated successfully for his MD. Irrespective of the expense incurred in travelling to Oxford from Somerset and back again, the enterprise cost him £89 15s 2d, including tips, 'entertainments', the loan of a scarlet gown and £56 12s 2d paid to the university for fees.

The cheaper fares available on the Leyden physic line were the more significant because the outlay necessary at the English universities, already high in the 1680s and 1690s, went on rising. By how much it is difficult to say; but there are some indications that the change may have been substantial. Even in 1697 Thomas Brown, physician-turned-playwright, put the cost of a regular physician's education, from matriculation to final degree, at £1,000. This was approximately what James Jurin was said to have saved nearly twenty years later from a short but successful career in schoolmastering and lecturing in order to finance the training at Cambridge which was to pave the way for a distinguished London medical practice; and if he had not already had an excellent general education and the beginnings of a medical training at Leyden in 1709 he would clearly have needed to accumulate more. Perilous though it is to hang too much on the words of pamphleteers or on other literary evidence, it is notable that in the course of an acrimonious demarcation dispute at Henley-on-Thames in the 1740s between Drs Russell and Addington, Addington roundly asserted that whereas his rival's medical education, at Paris and Rheims, could not conceivably have cost him more than £500, his own Oxford training in the time-honoured mould had involved an outlay of £1,500. Although it was never widely used, there was one way round the problem for parents who were not able to provide even a short Continental training and were not anxious to let a boy serve his time in an apothecary's shop or with a surgeon. There were physicians to be found in the early eighteenth century willing to take promising young men as pupils and assistants for a period of years and prepare them either for the Royal College's extra-licentiates' examination or for an application to the Church authorities. The apprenticeship might well be informal; and this seems to have been the case with Messenger Monsey, who after being schooled by his father was sent first to Cambridge to take a BA and then to Norwich to study physic under Sir Benjamin Wrench. Alternatively, it could be formal. In September 1711 George Vaux, MD, of Reigate, a Leyden-trained physician, took on one Richard Smith as his apprentice for seven years; while John Aery, the son of a yeoman farmer at St Bee's, Cumberland, was indentured the following May for six years to 'John Heslopp of Whitehaven, Doctor of Physic' for a premium that in the circumstances was astonishingly low, a mere £30.

When Dr Thomas Brown put his figure of £1,000 on the training of a 'university doctor' in 1697 it was with the relative cheapness of entry into the two major apprentice-based branches of medicine that he inevitably contrasted it. He treated the premiums payable to good London surgeons at that time, taking £120 as a not unlikely figure, as small beer but reserved his most derogatory comparisons for the physicians' other rivals, pointing to the sums as low as £50 required by apothecaries of their apprentices even in the capital. Thirteen years before, in the preface to his treatise on *The Royal College of Physicians* Charles Goodall had written of the apothecaries: 'We have to deal with a sort of men not of academical but mechanic education . . . either actually engaged in the late Rebellion [*sic!*] or bred up in some mean and contemptible trade.' Of course, no one doubted that the social origins of the great majority of apothecaries throughout the seventeenth century had been, and remained, far lowlier than those of the average physician. Dr Hamilton had expressed the opinion that even in the eighteenth century the bulk of apothecaries were drawn from the ranks of small tradesmen and shopkeepers, of farmers who had a respectable freehold acreage, and of craftsmen. Undoubtedly there is a good deal of truth in all this. Yet too much can be made of the social gulf between the background of Augustan physicians and apothecaries. It was a gap rather than a gulf, and it was not unbridgeable.

One of the aspects on which the College's protagonists monotonously harped, the indifferent education of the apothecaries, can very easily be got out of proportion. Before their seven years of practical training (five or six in a small minority of cases) almost all apothecaries' apprentices had had a grammar-school education, taken at least far enough to enable them to acquire a modest proficiency in Latin – for that was the language of the physicians' prescriptions which they had to interpret. In addition, most apothecaries with serious ambitions to practise general medicine and all who looked to be licensed for this end would have been expected to be familiar with at least some of the basic medical classics in the original (there were few English translations available before the eighteenth century, although by the 1720s the number was on the increase). William Broghurst, one of the select group of London apothecaries who as early as the Restoration, in his own words, 'stood upon their own legs and lived by their [general] practice', was doubtless very much the exception among his kind in being 'skilful in his profession and in the Greek and Latin tongues, delighting in the study of antiquity'. And yet when the Warwickshire doctor, Henry Stubbes, gave the apothecaries careful advice on their reading in his *Lex Talionis* of 1670, exhorting them to keep up with the physicians in theoretical knowledge, he recommended the works of La Framboisière – seven volumes, in French – and of Willis for diagnosis, and among others, Primrose's *Enchiridion Medicum* for therapeutics. He can hardly have believed that even at that time he was wasting his sweetness entirely on the desert air. By 1730, however, such a high-powered bibliographical commentary could have been addressed to a more receptive audience than that of 1670 and a better-qualified one. The author of *Tentamen Medicinale* (1704), a temperate apologia for the new branch of an old profession, made much of the point that the apothecary 'now has the theory in one hand and practice in the other. He may read the best authors at home, the same perhaps the doctors themselves do.' By George II's reign it was possible to find apothecaries, even in small market towns, who, like Abraham Sutcliffe at Settle in north Yorkshire, could read Latin and French with ease and possessed libraries which were good enough to launch their apprentices on a career in either physic or surgery.

This rise in academic standards reflected the new capacity of the apothecaries, with their breakthrough to professional status, to attract recruits from a far wider social background than had generally been the case fifty years earlier. Even in the second half of the seventeenth century by no means every apothecary was of modest or obscure origins. Francis Bernard (1627–98), whose younger brother became one of the wealthiest surgeons in post-Revolution England, was the son of a doctor of divinity, the rector of Croydon, while the parents of James Sherard (1666–1738) were well-to-do enough to give another of their sons a protracted Oxford education which eventually brought him an Ll. D., a Cambridge fellowship and ultimately the post of British consul at Smyrna. But by the years 1700–30, as it became clear that the apothecaries were moving steadily up the status ladder and that many could expect much higher rewards than fifty years earlier, the career became increasingly attractive to younger sons of gentle birth and good education. The claim by the London Society of Apothecaries in 1724 that their membership 'chiefly consists of those that have been the sons of the reverend the clergy, and of gentlemen' was, of course, an exaggerated one; but it had its point, and forty years before it would not have been made at all.

The Stamp Office registers of apprenticeships to London master-apothecaries between 1711 and 1730 do indeed reveal a very strong link between parsonages in many parts of England and the blue aprons of the capital; in fact, in the later years of Anne the clergy supplied apothecaries country-wide with more apprentices than did any other occupational group. Non-armigerous country gentlemen, such as Gervase Barker of Haydon, Lincolnshire, John Beech of Holly Grove, Staffordshire, and William Williams of Isleworth now readily placed their boys with good City apothecaries; and the pseudo-gentry of the larger towns and cities, while normally preferring to take advantage of local facilities for training young men in pharmacy and medicine, quite often looked to London as well. The profession also began to pull in many more sons of prosperous urban tradesmen and master manufacturers, those of Dissenting background being well represented. And very occasionally an overseas merchant of some standing is to be found among the sources of recruitment. Indentures sealed in June 1716, for instance, took a son of the Virginia merchant Thomas Booth into the shop of Job Matthew, a London apothecary and liveryman of the Society of Apothecaries, for a premium of £80. There was certainly an element among those young men from backgrounds in domestic trade, manufacture and commerce who brought with them into their new profession of medicine an existing familiarity with the lifestyles and expectations associated with gentlemen. There was not much of the 'rude mechanic' about Dudley Ryder's cousin Watkins, like himself a Dissenter and a wealthy tradesman's son, who was able to afford 'a great deal of money' to fit up his London shop in 1715; while another apothecary acquaintance of the young Ryder who figures much in his diary, Mr Porter, was greatly admired by him as 'a man of very good sense and thought', who looked on 'physic . . . [as] a very pleasant and delightful study', was musically gifted, and cultured enough in other respects to be able to hold his own with confidence in debates on Berkeley's notion of abstract ideas.

One of the considerations which made the apothecaries' vocation more attractive than orthodox 'physic' to needy gentry or respectable business families with sons to establish was the fact that by 1700 it was able to offer a combination of clearly rising status and expectation with low cost of training. There is evidence that in the early decades of the eighteenth century apprenticeship premiums did begin to move upwards in response to a changing market; but it seems to have taken a long time for this trend to have any appreciable effect outside London. Even in Surrey it has been shown that between 1711 and 1733 some 52 per cent of the premiums paid to master-apothecaries were still less than £50. In the capital there was a more marked rise in premiums in the course of these two decades. But the inflation was in no way dramatic before 1730, if we except the demands of a few particularly successful and prosperous masters. In the years 1711–12 the norm of £50 disparagingly referred to by Dr Thomas Brown in William III's reign was still being exceeded relatively rarely. By 1715–16 rather more sums of £70 or even £80 were being written into indentures. By 1730–1 top-notch apothecaries such as William Gataker and George Bewe were asking as much as £105 with some apprentices, and in March 1730 William Dellingham made a remarkable agreement with William Lloyd, a wealthy citizen of Chichester, in which the price of training the latter's son Francis in London for eight years was fixed at £157. The fact that Lloyd could have placed him in many a good London attorney's office for less, vividly illustrates how high the apothecaries' star had risen in the previous fifty years. But setting aside the odd exceptional case, the average London premium in the early years of George II's reign remained below £70 – less than £9 a year – and some parents still got away with as little as £40. With the provincial basement £10 lower than London's and not short of occupants even in 1730, and with the average country premium not yet more than £50, it is not difficult to discern one broad, inviting door which kept this part of the medical profession of late Augustan England genuinely 'open'.

By this time most surgeons – in sharper contrast than ever with the old-style barber-surgeons – had begun to rate their services as instructors distinctly higher and, in London, sometimes far higher than those of the average apothecary. Little has been published which throws light on the expense involved in training for a career in surgery before 1700. But what printed evidence there is, and what can be deduced retrospectively from the voluminous material bearing on the cost of apprenticeships to surgeons from the later years of Anne onwards, does suggest that while Brown was right in assuming in 1697 that surgeons' premiums were generally stiffer than those asked by apothecaries, he was well wide of the mark in suggesting that even in London they were on average more than twice as high.

A revealing source for the state of the market in the late-seventeenth-century provinces is James Yonge's journal. Yonge took a series of apprentices between 1673 and 1684, the years when he was establishing an outstanding reputation in the West Country. He usually asked no more than £50 for seven years and once as little as £40, although with the stipulation in all these cases that the parents or relatives of the young man should provide his clothes. On the one occasion he did go much higher he agreed to clothe the apprentice himself. By 1712 the surgeon to Plymouth dockyard, Wiliam Bacon – a worthy man, no doubt, but not a second Yonge – was able to command £64 10s 0d with the son of Christopher Warwick of St Austell; and this is not the only indication that already rates had begun to rise. In the last three years of Anne it is not unusual to come across provincial surgeons' premiums as high as £60 and occasionally £75 or £80; though it is also clear that the range was very wide and that surgeons who asked no more than £25 to £35 for the usual seven-year period, like Robert Heslopp of Newcastle upon Tyne, were still not uncommon. Freakish though it was, a pointer to the way the wind was already blowing is that it cost a Staffordshire yeoman £60 in April 1712 for only one-and-a-half-year's instruction from a master-surgeon of Ashby de la Zouche. By the years 1729 and 1730 £60 had become a relatively low sum for a normal seven-year indenture to a provincial surgeon, and by the very best of them,

men of the calibre of Jonathan Lippeatt of Newbury, £100 or even
£105 could now be hopefully anticipated from a well-off parent.

In London the inflationary process had begun earlier, with the most
accomplished practitioners naturally leading the way. In 1692 James
Yonge himself, then a very prosperous man, actually abandoned his
plans to place his son John with 'Mr Horsnel, an eminent surgeon in
Hatton Garden', after discovering 'that the price would be too high'.
Even so, in the first year after the Stamp Office began to compile
records of apprenticeships in 1711 only a tiny minority of the members
of the London Barber Surgeons' Company accepting pupils – a handful
of surgeons in very good practice like George Dottin, John Dobyns or
Peter Lamarque – received as much as £100 or more. Dobyns's charge
of £139 15s in October 1711 for taking on Nathaniel Noble, a Wiltshire
gentleman's son, was unusually stiff at the time. It was not to appear so
for long. William Cheselden, a decade before he began to approach the
peak of his astonishing reputation, felt no inhibitions about asking
and receiving £200 when he accepted his own 18-year-old brother as a
pupil in September 1714. By the years 1715–30 the very high fees some
surgeons could command for operations and the hospital facilities and
other tuition they could provide or arrange for their pupils were, in
general, forcing premiums up, and sums of £150 or £200 became less
startling than before. Although no one else approached Cheselden's
asking price of £350, achieved in 1730, a London druggist named
Joseph Webb had paid Robert Gay of Hatton Garden, a recognised
grand master of the scalpel, £250 for initiating his son in the mysteries
of his profession in the summer of 1716; three separate surgeons in one
year, 1719, priced their services at £200; and when Thomas Reynolds
of Wellingborough went up to London in July 1730 to complete his
surgical training with George Coldham of Covent Garden he was
charged £52 10s, all in, for twelve months' instruction. Richard Kay's
single year at Guy's and St Thomas's in 1743, to perfect the skills and
knowledge he had long been acquiring in his native Lancashire, cost his
father intially 24 guineas, but since on top of that board and lodging
had to be paid for and a private course in midwifery subscribed to, the
experience can hardly have cost less than £50.

As with the apothecaries, however, such figures as these have to be
kept in strict proportion. Only a very tiny minority of London's
trainee surgeons could afford to seek out the star performers. Neither
was it necessary to do so. In the 1720s a perfectly sound surgical
grounding could still be had in the capital for around £100 from good
surgeons such as William Pierce, James Wilkie and James Pringle of
Westminster, and there were still many run-of-the-mill practitioners
prepared to take apprentices for considerably less than that. Among
the bargains to be picked up in late Augustan London which illustrate
how much more accessible the surgeon's branch of the profession still
was compared with the physician's, perhaps the most remarkable came
the way of Abraham Chovet. Chovet was to become one of the finest
surgical demonstrators of the 1730s, and yet he was able to serve his
time from 1720–7 under Peter Lamarque, a distinguished Foreign

Brother of the Barber Surgeons' Company and himself one of the most gifted teachers of his day, for only £105.

Of course, when the apprentice had completed his normal seven years of training he still had to set up and fit out his surgery and equip himself with instruments and at least the bare minimum of a medical library. In the provinces the surgery was commonly referred to throughout the period as 'the shop'. James Yonge records how 'I had fitted up my shop' on his return from his last voyage to Newfoundland, in March 1671. The inventory of William White, a Sussex surgeon who practised at Midhurst in Charles I's reign, suggests he had his 'shop' in a wing of his house with a bedchamber over the top; and as late as 1730 new houses for surgeons, as at Blandford, were being built over or immediately beside their shops. In 1743 Richard Kay's day as a senior apprentice of 24 still normally began when he 'waited on Father in the shop' in the family residence (which was the size of a small manor house) just to the north of Bury. 'Fitting up' could be done at a pinch for £20 or might cost up to five or six times as much, according to means. Yonge was fortunate in being able to anticipate the £150 he had been promised with his bride. Surgical instruments became more sophisticated and more expensive between 1660 and 1750, and so did drugs. William White's entire collection of 'instruments, mortars, stills and drugs' was valued at only £8 10s 4d in 1632, and seventeen 'books on physic and surgery' at £10. A century later William Cheselden used fourteen separate instruments in the performance of his famous lateral lithotomy operation alone, some of them clearly made to his own specifications – an awesome array, captured for posterity in a drawing by G. Van der Gucht in July 1731. And without attempting to compete with the crack London specialists, the progressive provincial all-rounder felt the need to move with the times. Before Richard Kay left London in 1744, after the last year of his training, he bought a whole case of 'new chirurgic instruments' under the careful guidance of Mr Stead, Apothecary to Guy's Hospital, to replace the old ones he had been using for the past seven years.

If Yonge's experience is a reliable guide, even in the second half of Charles II's reign an appreciable number of recruits into surgery (leaving aside migrants from the armed forces) were coming from the respectable urban middle class and yeomanry, and some at least from the lower-gentry and pseudo-gentry. One of Yonge's apprentices was the nephew of John Edgecombe, apparently one of the nearby Mount Edgecombe family; another was a yeoman's son from Boscastle in Cornwall, vouched for by Dr Sprague; yet another was 'the son of Mr Christopher Wyat of Exeter, recommended by my friend Dr Waterhouse'; a fourth, the son of Mr Winston of Brixham; and a fifth, a parson's son from the neighbourhood of Tavistock. However, this neither was nor remained the whole picture. The young surgeons who began practising in the early decades of the eighteenth century came from exceedingly diverse backgrounds. Symbolic of surgery's rise in public esteem was the fact that one of Cheselden's apprentices in the 1720s, John Belchier, had been educated at Eton. The families of 'gentlemen' now provided three recruits out of every ten: and the sort of small, non-armigerous, parish-gentry background from which Cheselden himself emerged, one step away from the upper yeomanry, remained especially strongly represented. This apart, budding surgeons were more likely to come from parsonages or farms than from any other homes. But the provision trades were another steady source of supply to the profession, as were small manufacturers, craftsmen and master-mariners. A Maidstone paper-maker, a Buckinghamshire 'laceman', a London tinplate worker (no small craftsman, this, for he put up £107 to indenture his son to a leading city surgeon), a Norwich cloth merchant, a Hayes gardener and a Bristol cook were among the many scores of parents who started sons on the road to a career in medicine via 'chirurgery' between the summer of 1711 and the middle of 1712.

Connections between the Church and the surgeons' profession were probably at their strongest between 1700 and 1725. Joshua Symonds, a successful anatomy lecturer under George I and one of the Surgeons to St Thomas's Hospital in the following reign, was a clergyman's son from Clapham. His father must have been a man of means, for Symonds served his time from 1709–16 under Cheselden's teacher, James Ferne, who took on a further pupil towards the end of that period for a premium of £215; and subsequently he fitted with ease into that social milieu which men such as Charles Bernard had enabled the new generation of London surgeons to inhabit. Symonds mingled with leading physicians on terms of amity and equality, for he was a cultivated man, an enthusiastic classicist as well as a good surgeon. (Appropriately, among the provisions of his will was the bequest of his Foesius's translation of Hippocrates to 'my friend, Dr Jonathan Gouldsmith'.) By and large, however, clerical recruits were more likely to be found searching the bargain basement for low premiums than going, like Symonds, to the best London masters. Few clerics were ready to pay even as much as the £60 which Richard Pickering, vicar of Featherstone, found in 1730 to place his son with a surgeon in Pontefract, and not infrequently they had to settle for second best. William King, a clergyman from Eastham in Worcestershire, paid £25 in December 1711 to apprentice his son for seven years to Thomas Page of Bristol, barber-surgeon, and it has been noted earlier how a barber-surgeon in Manchester catered even more cheaply for a boy from the parsonage at Lyme (above, p. 110). (There were a great many barber-surgeons after 1700, in London as well as in the provinces, who still took on apprentices for five, six or seven years at a minimal charge – for anything from £12 down to £5, in fact. It can be safely assumed that they dispensed little in the way of a genuine medical training, however, and indeed in the provinces some of them advertised the fact by describing themselves as 'barber surgeons and periwig makers'.)

William Kay of Doncaster wrote in 1652 that he had 'served his father, and . . . been bred in the art of surgery under his father'. James Yonge of Plymouth, like Richard Kay of Baldingstone two generations on, was the son of a surgeon. William Barman, a surgeon in practice at Wilmington, Kent, in the reigns of William III and Anne, died before his son, Thomas, had reached the age when he could be bound apprentice; but not before he had made provision in his will for the boy to be trained under Peter Lamarque in London. As with the physicians – as, indeed, with most professions by this time – family tradition was becoming an increasingly important factor in recruitment. In London there was no more remarkable example of this than the careers of the Hawkinses. Caesar Hawkins, who was in established practice in Bloomsbury before 1735, having previously served for seven years as an assistant to John Ranby, was the son of a country surgeon and had begun his apprenticeship in the provinces. Apart from his father, his brother Pennill, his nephew George, his son Charles and his grandson Caesar all became not only surgeons but distinguished ones. He himself became Surgeon to the Prince of Wales in 1737, when he was only 26.

The dynastic chains which drew not merely surgeons but the whole body of medical practitioners closer together by the early eighteenth century were studded with links that were socially as well as professionally significant. Here and there a bright apprentice would marry his master's daughter, as did Ambrose Dickens, a future Serjeant Surgeon, after he had served his time under the famous London surgeon, Charles Bernard. Bernard himself, as we know, had an elder brother who was one of the most prosperous apothecaries in London before his death in the late 1690s. Some Augustan apothecaries became well-to-do enough to train their sons as physicians; and among the beneficiaries was at least one, Thomas Dale, who had an apothecary uncle of great repute, Samuel Dale of Braintree, as well as a father in the same line. On the other hand, John Hawes, who had an apothecary's shop and flourishing practice at Rickinghall in Suffolk, was one of several of his kind in Augustan England who chose rather to give his son a surgeon's education, in his case at Bury St Edmunds. It is particularly striking how many surgeons in England between the 1680s and the 1740s had brothers, cousins or uncles in other branches of medicine as well as in their own. The Bernard brothers, surgeon and apothecary respectively, had a number of counterparts. Nathaniel Smith, a surgeon at St Barts, whom Abel Boyer described on his death in 1723 as 'a celebrated anatomist', had a brother, Lawrence, who was a physician. John and James Douglas, both of whom practised, pioneered, lectured and wrote prolifically in London between c. 1700 and 1740, were frequently confused at the time (and still are) because each had a consuming interest in anatomy; but whereas John, the inventor of the supra-pubic stone operation, was a surgeon first and last, his brother James (of 'Douglas's pouch' fame) was a qualified physician with a doctorate from Rheims. Having a relative already in the profession frequently provided the spur to a young man's interest in medicine and to his commitment to it as a career. When Cheselden was a lad he was most probably influenced by a kinsman, Dr George Cheselden, practising twelve miles away in the town of Leicester. Robert Kay, who practised surgery and general medicine in the Bury area from Anne's reign until 1750, was, so far as we know, the first of the Kays of Baldingstone to take up this profession. But one of his nephews, Samuel Kay, became a notable Lancashire physician, graduating MD in 1729 and practising in Manchester for more than fifty years thereafter; and as the diary of Robert's son, Richard, shows, his Manchester cousin exercised a deep and lasting influence on his career, not least in footing part of the bill for the expensive year in London which completed his training as a surgeon.

The cost of the long training for all the three main branches of the medical profession did, as we have seen, increase during the Augustan period. But down to 1730 it never reached the point of inhibiting recruitment into the two junior branches from a very wide range of social classes and occupational groups; neither had it managed to restrict entry to the senior branch to those socially exclusive channels to which the bar had now become increasingly tied. It is also clear by the years 1710–30, both from Stamp Office records and from much biographical work on the graduates of Leyden and on the Fellows and Licentiates of the Royal College, that many families of good standing below the level of the most substantial landed squirearchy now regarded the surgeon's and apothecary's vocations as desirable careers for their sons. At the same time, both landed and bourgeois families were quick to respond to the obvious appeal of Leyden and the other major Continental medical schools in their palmy years from 1700–40. They were no less ready from the 1720s, especially if they were Dissenters, to hitch their sons' wagons to the rising northern star in Edinburgh. That some of these young men felt a sense of vocation is not in doubt. But a prime attraction of the profession of medicine lay in the growing professional rewards which the successful practitioner at all levels came to anticipate over the course of the seventy years after 1660. Contemporary records of all kinds, from wills to the evidence of brick and stone, are profuse with examples of the wealth and the style of living which practitioners of medicine might enjoy in late Stuart and early Hanoverian England.

In general it would be true to say that most of the great fortunes made in medicine between 1680 and 1730 were accumulated by formally qualified London physicians. However, their monopoly was certainly less total in the last two decades of our period than in the first two; and even by 1700 there were a few exceptionally successful apothecaries and surgeons in practice in the capital whose wealth and repute made nonsense of differences of formal status. One for whom this was certainly true was James Chase, an unusual phenomenon among the apothecaries of London in the 1680s by reason of his Oxford degree. Admittedly Chase had come into the world with a silver spoon in his mouth. The family had prospered by medicine during the seventeenth century and had acquired an estate at Hughenden in Buckinghamshire. For much of William III's reign James Chase supplemented his large private practice with a salary of £500 a year as Apothecary to the Court and he kept this post throughout Anne's reign, though it seems that by this time he was in the happy position of being able to forsake the London shop on which the Chase fortune had been founded. As well as inheriting Hughenden he had bought an estate at Marlow in Bucks, and represented Great Marlow borough in the Commons for twenty years. He acquired lands in Bedfordshire; he invested towards the end of his life in South Sea stock; and he accumulated an excellent medical library which he left to a kinsman, Dr Stephen Chase. Equally eminent in his own field and just as irreproachable socially was Charles Bernard (1650–1710), whose skill as a surgeon earned him much acclaim and eventually some notoriety, when his professional conscience triumphed over his staunch High Churchmanship and allowed him to save the leg of the latitudinarian divine, Ben Hoadly. Bernard practised as a Freeman of the Barber Surgeons' Company for thirty-three years until his death (appropriately, for such an aristocrat among professionals, while on a visit to Longleat) in 1710. For twenty-five years he was Surgeon to St Bartholomew's and for the last eight of them Serjeant Surgeon to Queen Anne. The Bishop of Carlisle was vastly impressed by a visit he paid in February 1707 to Charles Bernard's house, and full of admiration for his host 'whose library and frank entertainment very fine'. Much of Bernard's wealth had been devoted to building up one of the finest private collections of books in London and at the auction of his library after his death, at which Swift bought several items, one small book was sold for the almost unheard-of price of £28.

Shortly before the Revolution Edward Chamberlayne, an astringent commentator on the contemporary professions, remarked that some eminent London physicians had already 'received in fees yearly two or three thousand pounds, and purchased great estates'. Most physicians who became thoroughly established in Augustan London did well for themselves; in a period of fifty years spanning the seventeenth and eighteenth centuries less than a dozen cases of doctors in poverty were brought to the notice of the Royal College. But if it was true in the 1680s that exceptional prosperity was already within the grasp of those whom a trusting public confirmed at the head of the profession, this was even more true three or four decades later. By then the élite was larger and a few of its individual successes of startling proportions.

With wicked pen Dr Samuel Garth described his colleagues, the ultra-prosperous fashionable physicians of Augustan London, thus:

> Triumphant plenty, with a cheerful grace
> Basks in their eyes, and sparkles in their face.
> How sleek their looks, how goodly is their mien,
> When big they strut behind a double chin.
> Each faculty in blandishments they lull,
> Aspiring to the venerably dull.

Yet Garth's memorable stereotype ought not to persuade us that the profession's highest peaks could be scaled only by a single unedifying route and that its conservatism left no room for individualists to prosper. Nothing more effectively belies this assumption than the career of Samuel Garth himself. A translator of Ovid as well as the author of *The Dispensary*, he sometimes appeared to take far more delight in hobnobbing with the Whig aristocracy and their literary acolytes in the Kit Cat Club than in following his chosen vocation. A favourite anecdote of Queen Anne's day related how he lingered so long over his bottle one evening at a meeting of the club that even Dick Steele felt constrained to put him in mind of his duty to his patients. Garth's reply was at least refreshingly free from cant: 'It was no matter whether he saw them that night or next morning, for nine had such bad constitutions that no physician could save them, and the other six had such good ones that all the physicians in the world could not kill them.' But though he loved to play the iconoclast, Garth kept on good terms with Mammon. He lived in the grand manner at his town house in Covent Garden and by George I's reign had collected a knighthood, an appointment as one of the royal physicians and eventually the post of Physician-General to the Army.

Success as a physician could be made up of combinations of many different ingredients, of which official patronage might be one. It was certainly a great spur to the career of the young Scotsman William Cockburn that he contrived to scoop the profitable appointment of Physician to the Navy in 1694 at the very early age of 25. More important in the long run, however, was that six years later he invented a specific for dysentery. By the time he died in 1739 he had made a very substantial fortune, partly from his London patients but even more, perhaps, from his patent drug. Cockburn benefited, of course, from the sheer length of his career. But longevity was no more essential to membership of the medical aristocracy than was official favour. Garth did not take his MD until he was 30 and when he died in 1719 he was only in his fifties. John Freind had no more than sixteen years in established London practice, having been abroad, privately or with the army, for much of the time between 1705 and 1712; yet even without the benefit of the Whig patients who boycotted him for his Jacobite sympathies, he enjoyed the income of a grandee. Freind purchased a country mansion at Hitcham in Buckinghamshire, and it was said – no doubt apocryphally, but not without point – that 5,000 guineas-worth of fees had accumulated for him while he was in the Tower as a political suspect in 1723.

Large-scale operations in the land market, as opposed to minor dabblings, appear to have been less popular with the medical élite than with lawyers, army or navy officers and some civil servants. Physicians such as Freind, Radcliffe (a singular case, as we shall see) or Edward Hulse, junior (who was able to retire after less than thirty years in practice with a manor at Dartford and a very large estate in Hampshire) were very much exceptions to the rule. On the other hand, house property in the capital or in its satellite settlements certainly interested Hans Sloane as a major investment, and it may have appealed in the same way to others of the fraternity. Moreover, Dr P. G. M. Dickson had found at least two London physicians, Nehemiah Grew of Racquet Court and Robert Pitt of Princes Street, who were prominent early investors in the short-term National Debt and original stockholders of the Bank of England; and Grew acquired £5,000 more of Bank stock in the subscription of 1709. Sir David Hamilton, who bought an estate in Scotland out of the profits of the first phase of his medical career, sold it after his appointment as one of the Queen's Physicians in 1704, purchased over £10,000 of Bank stock between 1710 and 1719, and was closely interested in the affairs of the South Sea Company. He probably lost heavily in the collapse of 1720, though whether to the tune of £80,000, as one contemporary source would have it, cannot be definitely substantiated. Other London doctors, too, figure in stock and loan subscription lists in the two decades after 1694; but most of them, including even such notable figures as Sloane and Arbuthnot, appear to have involved themselves on a relatively modest scale. One exception, almost inevitably, was the great Radcliffe who put £35,000 into a new Annuity Loan and into Bank stock in the years 1707-9. Another was Dr Caleb Cotesworth, who had £25,010 invested in East India stock in 1723-4. Yet, in general, physicians were not as active as either lawyers or government officials in the fields of investment opened up by post-Revolution finance; and it is striking how very few even of the wealthiest London physicians felt the urge to set themselves up as country gentlemen, despite the fact that the opportunities to acquire small estates in the Home Counties that could be comfortably combined with continuing practice were plentiful enough. Most successful doctors were content with a single fashionable town house. James Jurin and James Douglas can be picked out as fairly typical of a marked general trend. Jurin (see above, p. 209), who became Physician to Guy's Hospital in its early years from 1725-32, made a fortune conservatively described as 'ample' out of medicine. But it was his old school, Christ's Hospital, which profited as much as anyone from his success and the house in Lincoln's Inn Fields which he bought in the 1720s remained his home to the end. As for Douglas, while he admittedly lived in high style in Red Lion Square, he spent a good deal of his large income, as Charles Bernard did, on his library which included several hundred volumes of or about the works of Horace.

Fortunes of the scale of Cockburn's and Garth's, Freind's or Hamilton's or Cotesworth's were not freakish among eminent London physicians of late Augustan England. Some achieved their 'triumphant plenty' wholly creditably; others, like Richard Morton, owed too much of it to what was disparagingly referred to at the time as 'chamber-pot practice'. But none could approach the exceptional wealth accumulated by the three giants who dominated the profession between 1685 and the middle of the eighteenth century, Radcliffe, Sloane and Mead. John Radcliffe had practised for almost a decade in Oxford before he came to London in 1684. With astonishing speed he thereafter captured the bulk of the great practice formerly enjoyed by the most noted physician of Charles II's reign, Richard ('Cock') Lower of Covent Garden; and he then proceeded to add to it spectacularly. In many ways a rough diamond, who made something of a fetish of his disdain for orthodox book-learning, he built up over thirty years incomparably the biggest medical fortune England had yet seen. His famous gold-headed cane, which passed to Mead and is now one of the coveted possessions of the Royal College of Physicians, came to symbolise a new pinnacle of professional splendour which at the Restoration would have seemed quite unattainable. At his death in 1714, aged 62, Radcliffe owned houses in Bloomsbury Square, Hammersmith and Carshalton, held large estates in Yorkshire and at Wolverton in Buckinghamshire, and other land in Northamptonshire and Surrey. His landed properties were managed by agents and out of them were funded, among other things, two travelling medical fellowships of £600 a year at University College, Oxford, and eventually the building of the Radcliffe Infirmary and Observatory in that city. Although his fortune had long been legendary, contemporaries were still staggered by the terms of his will, which included £45,000 in capital gifts to his university, most of it to be devoted to the building of the library known as the Radcliffe Camera, and £3,130 a year in other bequests, a fifth of it going to St Bartholomew's Hospital. Yet, as his account books confirm, he had lived handsomely. One of his rivals in the years 1695–1710, Sir Edward Hannes, made some attempt to keep up with Radcliffe in worldly parade – down to his coach-and-six and his coachmen decked out in glittering livery – but, benefactor though he was by his own lights, he could not come near the great man's lavish standard of munificence. Few early-eighteenth-century Englishmen, of any vocation, could.

The case of Hans Sloane, the first medical baronet (1716) and President of the Royal College for a record period (1719–35), was a rather different one from Radcliffe's in that he had some private means, especially after his marriage; so he was not entirely dependent on the income from his fees, from his 'corner' in quinine and his patent milk chocolate. He was also a shrewd businessman who by the end of Anne's reign already owned a sizeable part of Chelsea. Yet property speculations apart, much of Sloane's income was spent on his great natural history and manuscript collection which he left to the nation in return for £20,000 and which formed the original core of the holdings of the British Museum. Not merely a baronet but the father-in-law of a peer, his lofty standing in society was unshakeable for the last thirty to forty years of a long and unequivocally distinguished life. It was, however, Richard Mead rather than Hans Sloane who inherited the mantle of Dr Radcliffe, as well as his cane – even to the point of buying Radcliffe's house in Bloomsbury Square in 1714. But Mead's interests were far wider and his culture deeper. He bought no great agglomeration of landed acres; in fact, although in due course he acquired a country house near Windsor, his private life was squarely centred on the metropolis. He, like Sloane, was an avid collector. His house in Great Ormond Street, to which he eventually moved from Bloomsbury Square, housed his vast library of over 10,000 books, his manuscripts, paintings, coins and statuary, a treasure trove which after his death was sold for over £16,000, the books alone fetching £5,518. What Mead did share with Radcliffe was an insatiable appetite for medical practice. Having first begun to practise without a licence in Stepney in 1696, he pursued his career far into George II's reign. At the height of his vigour and professional prowess Mead's income from fees, on the evidence of

Mr Hocker, his librarian, was for some fifteen years between £5,000 and £6,000, and in one year surpassed £7,000. It is doubtful whether Radcliffe ever achieved more than £6,000 a year: and Mead's income would have been higher still but for his well-known generosity in waiving fees in innumerable cases of hardship, and his firm principle – understandable, perhaps, in a minister's son – of always treating the clergy free of charge. It is hard to credit that his standard charge was only 1 guinea for a consultation at home and 2 guineas for a visit; but so it is said.

Whether the rewards of provincial practice in Augustan England kept pace, at a scaled-down level, with those of London practice is hard to say, since the evidence tends to be selective. Clearly in the main urban centres of England the leading physicians (or, as was quite often the case, the sole physician) were for the most part prominent and prosperous members of the local community. Diarists and travellers from the 1690s to the 1720s rarely mention a 'university doctor' without making it plain that he was well-to-do and often well connected. Such was certainly the case with Dr Marsh at Dunstable, whose house was visited twice by Celia Fiennes, and with Dr Gerard at Durham, who entertained Squire Blundell of Crosby in style for a week in 1706. Dr Thorpe at Rochester struck Lord Harley on a visit to the city in 1724 as a cultivated man, deeply versed in local antiquities in whose study he clearly had some leisure to indulge himself. The Dr Beeston mentioned by Defoe in his description of Ipswich in 1723 as the possessor of a 'physic garden adjoining to his house in the town' and of 'a collection of rare and exotic plants, such as are scarce to be equalled in England', was a greatly respected figure in East Suffolk. Two hall-marks of the success and status of these urban provincials were the houses they lived in and the wives they married. Dr Francis Worthington had a house large enough to enable him to board members of the Lancashire gentry, along with their maids and menservants, when they went to Wigan to take the cure by drinking 'the Hilton Spaw waters'. Dr William Johnson had only been in practice for seventeen years in Warwick when in 1692 he began building Landor House, a town mansion fit for a baronet, and Claver Morris had been practising for an even shorter time at Wells when he was able to put the cathedral clergy in the shade with his fine new residence. Dr John Castle's 'Great House' in Burford, Oxfordshire, and the grandiloquent town mansion in Ponte-fract, later dubbed 'Dr Burgess's Folly', were among other monuments to the social consequence of provincial physicians which all went up within a few years of each other in the last decade of the seventeenth century. Their ability to make socially advantageous or profitable marriages is also striking. Gerard allied himself with one of the Catholic gentry families which were still entrenched in County Durham at the beginning of the eighteenth century. Marsh of Dunstable captured a daughter of Sir Charles Wolseley of Wolseley for his bride. Dr Dickens, who practised in Liverpool under Anne and George I and was a trustee of the Blue Coat Hospital in the town, married the daughter of a wealthy local merchant, Richard Houghton.

Of course, there had been provincial doctors in the first half of the seventeenth century who had grown rich, lived handsomely or married advantageously. But they are much less easy to locate. The will of John Symcotts of Huntingdon is an interesting yardstick against which to measure the apparent change in the prospects of the profession between 1650 and 1700. Symcotts died in 1662 after over forty years of practice, in the course of which he appears to have built up and maintained for some time a near-monopoly among some of the best families in Huntingdonshire – Cromwells, Montagus, St Johns, Lukes, Cottons and Howards. He left a house in Huntingdon, where he also owned an inn, but otherwise little to suggest more than modest affluence: various plots of land, one small estate of 63½ acres, legacies up to a maximum of £34 a year and £201 in cash. A comparable practice sixty years later, town-based but with a good county clientele, would, in possibly nine cases out of ten, have been much more rewarding; though whether 'country physicians', properly speaking, were emphatically better off by the early eighteenth century than they had been in the mid-seventeenth is less clear. It may well be necessary to make a distinction between the two types of provincial practice. Messenger Monsey tried for fifteen years from the early 1720s to break into the charmed circle of Bury St Edmunds. But until a fortuitous encounter with Lord Godolphin translated him to London and to professional success he had to seek his bread mainly in Bury's rural hinterland. It was a depressing experience. A later biographical sketch depicted him 'in a rusty wig, dirty boots and leather breeches', condemned to 'the common fate of country practice – constant fatigue, long journeys and short fees'.

We do know that medical fees, like legal fees, were in a state of flux by the years 1680–1700, and not only in London. Edward Chamberlayne declared in 1682 that although the traditional doctor's fee was 20s per consultation for an MD and 10s for 'one that had not taken that degree', there was 'at present . . . no certain rule'. The 10s fee was probably the norm in the provinces around 1670, and if a Scots visitor to England at the time of the Union of 1707 had got his information right, this charge was still quite common, even for a visit (for surgeons as well as for physicians). But the fluctuations by now were very considerable. While Drs Dunning and Towgood in Dorset were charging the old standard 10s for each visit to the Nonconformist preacher, John Pinney, in his final illness in 1705 (the Pinney account books do not tell us whether either of these gentlemen held degrees, or whether it would have made any difference if they had), Richard Mead's London patients were paying four times as much for a visit and yet were thought to be very moderately charged. When a Lancashire squire's daughter fell sick with a lingering and puzzling complaint in the winter of 1723–4, her father boarded her for seven weeks at Wigan and Liverpool to allow her to be regularly treated by two physicians, Worthington and Broomfield: the latter's fees came jointly to £19 2s 6d, though how they were concocted is not known. There were even physicians in the provinces by George II's reign, and well respected ones too, who appear to have had no set scale of fees at all. Few can have been more altruistic than William Chambers of Hull, of whom a junior colleague, Dr John Alderson, later wrote that he 'frequently returned one half of the money which his patients thought he deserved, but which he thought them imprudent in giving'. Sadly, but not surprisingly, Chambers died poor.

The best documented (in print, at least) of the provincial physicians of Augustan England is also the most revealing on the question of fees. Claver Morris of Wells was by 1707, and probably from the early years of his practice, operating the carefully judged 'sliding scale' which became a widely accepted convention in Hanoverian and Victorian times. In Wells itself his fees for seeing patients, at his house or theirs, ranged from 2s 6d for the poor and 5s for the smaller tradesmen to half a guinea for the substantial townsmen and 1 guinea for the gentry and clergy. On the other hand, his fees for country visits were generously low, rarely more than 1 guinea unless the distance was unusually long and never more than the 12 guineas he charged on two isolated occasions for visits to Sandwell in Gloucestershire and to Exeter. Morris already had a very extensive clientele by the beginning of Anne's reign, being the only physician in the little city of Wells and treating almost all the country gentlemen and peers within a thirty-mile radius, and not a few (such as Frank Gwyn of Ford Abbey and Thomas Strangeways of Melbury) outside the county. He was clearly 'in very good practice' by the standards of the provincial physicians of his day; and we know a great deal about his income and life-style. From his medical fees, for example, he made from £100 to £150 a year between 1707 and 1710 and from 1710 until 1723 his income was consistently between £200 and £300. Unfortunately for purposes of comparison within the profession at large Morris was not a typical case. He lived like an affluent country gentleman; but many of his luxuries – his handsome house in Wells, built for £807 from 1699–1702, his carriage, his splendid cellar of often-smuggled wines, the boarding schools for his children, his wide social and sporting interests – could be afforded more because he had married well at the age of 26 and twice more, advantageously, by 1703, than because of his professional success. He accumulated landed property, including two estates bought during the Spanish Succession War for a total of £3,500, and by the end of his life two-thirds of his income of £600 a year was coming from rents, with some help from his investments in stock and the income from local loans and mortgages. So that although Morris worked quite hard, sometimes spending forty hours a week in the saddle, he also enjoyed life and did not have any pressing need, certainly in his last twenty years, to inflate his fees unduly or to scramble for custom in competition with the local apothecaries, to whom he cheerfully surrendered many patients.

It would seem that a very strong and determined provincial physician, with a similar monopoly of town and hinterland to that of Morris, might just succeed in making £500 a year out of his profession in the late Augustan period. But that would probably be a fairly exceptional achievement; and there are clear indications that, in most cases, competition, or the lack of it, was a very important factor in determining a doctor's chances of high rewards. Despite the shortage of physicians there was a limit to what the better-class market in almost any provincial centre could bear. Even in the wealthy port of Bristol, which for many years boasted two such medical notables as William Logan and Thomas Dover among its graduate doctors, the latter is reputed to have made as much money out of his famous powders (a compound of opium and ipecacuanha) as out of his attendance on patients; and although it is rather hard to accept, Bristol tradition later had it that it was not until the 1730s that the first physician (Dr Middleton) set up his carriage in the city. Norwich was the second city in England in Anne's reign, half as populous again as Bristol, and had the highest number of MDs in the provinces; but not all of them prospered, and judging from the fact that he was forced to apprentice one of his sons to a local worsted weaver, Dr Francis Colombine was well down the pecking order. There were two physicians in Reading in the 1740s; but one of them vehemently protested when a new arrival settled at Henley, eight miles away, and suggested he move to High Wycombe instead. John Arbuthnot fled from Dorchester as a young doctor, because he could not make a living there (though the indecently healthy air, he claimed, contributed to his plight!); whereas William Battie, later Physician to St Luke's Hospital, spent the early years of his career most successfully at Uxbridge where he was presented, it is said, with 'a fair opening' and took it. Plainly, in towns of around 3,000 inhabitants or less – in other words in the vast majority of Augustan towns – peaceful co-existence between physicians was rarely possible, though sole possession could be very profitable.

Although the worlds of London medicine and provincial medicine were in some respects so different, we must not imagine that commerce between the two was minimal. A few London physicians did from time to time opt for a quieter professional life away from the teeming, notoriously unhealthy metropolis. But it was more common for men who had accumulated enough capital from the building of a profitable provincial practice to move successfully to London, as Battie did from Uxbridge. Edward Baynard, for example, was over 40 when he migrated from Preston in the early 1680s, but by 1687 he had been elected a Fellow of the Royal College. Thomas Dover had thirty years of profitable practice in Bristol behind him (punctuated by three extraordinary years spent privateering in the Caribbean) before he came to London around 1721. By contrast, Richard Blackburne, a Leyden graduate of the later years of Charles II, practised at Tunbridge Wells during the summer season and in London for the rest of the year; and it is very probable that there were a number of other physicians in the Home Counties who found profit in keeping a foot in two camps in this way, particularly with an eye to the spa traffic at Tunbridge and Epsom.

Whatever fresh evidence may come to light about medicine in Augustan England, it is unlikely to reveal any provincial physician who earned as much by the beginning of the eighteenth century as the cream of the London apothecaries. The latter's soaring prospects, underlined by the fact that after the Great Fire the Apothecaries' Hall was sumptuously rebuilt six years before the Physicians' College, were grudgingly acknowledged even by the city's physicians and their polemicists. One pamphleteer writing in the middle of Anne's reign plausibly suggested that there were then eight or ten apothecaries in London whose incomes ranged from £1,500 to £2,000 per annum. By business and practice combined, an apothecaries' élite unquestionably emerged with wealth enough to be able to rank socially with the very top crust of the medical profession. James Chase has been mentioned already. It was well known that Radcliffe's apothecary, Dandridge, had made a fortune from his great patron's prescriptions: some contemporaries put it as high as £50,000. James Sherard, made a freeman of the Society of Apothecaries in 1690 after his apprenticeship under one of the great botanical specialists of his day, John Watts, did likewise. He owned a country house at Eltham and left an estate valued in 1738 at £150,000. Joseph Nicolson, Master of the Society in 1721, did not aspire to these heights, but he lived prosperously, occasionally bailed out indigent relations, and in company with his brother, the Bishop of Carlisle, entertained Cumbrian gentry and some of the leading *virtuosi* of his day at his house in Salisbury Court.

In London, as well as in the provinces, apothecaries were of growing importance in municipal affairs – eight of them were common councillors by 1695 – and there were other apothecaries, besides Chase, influential enough to gain a parliamentary seat. James St Amand, for many years an alderman of London, was elected to James II's Tory Parliament of 1685. George Bruere, admittedly a man with some family connections (his father being a government official in the Excise Office), set up shop in Covent Garden during King William's reign; yet before 1710 he was already rich enough to buy an estate at Great Marlow in Bucks, and fortified by a relationship with Sir James Etheridge he was able to represent that borough in the Commons from December 1710 to 1722. The rapidity of the fortunate London apothecary's prospects of wealth, as a result of combining trade with general practice, was one point stressed by a witness in 1748: 'Few chemists and druggists . . . build themselves fine houses, purchase country seats, and have large sums out at interest, or ride about in their chariots; & yet the honest apothecary can do all this in five or six years' time.' If this was a hostile witness, a perfectly neutral one, writing a year earlier, was quite clear that there was now no other vocation in London where there was a surer prospect of high success for so small an outlay. We must bear in mind the lucrative appointments to be had in the capital city which were not available elsewhere, jobs that could be easily combined with private practice; not just appointments to the Royal Household, but to the Admiralty, the War Office, the Chelsea and Greenwich Hospitals and, of course, the public hospitals, old and new. And as medical practice itself became more commonplace and above board after 1704, and the apothecary-doctors took more and more patients from among the well-to-do, so not a little of the unprecedented business and professional wealth generated in London between 1680 and 1730 found its way into their capacious pockets.

Here and there, even in early-seventeenth-century England, there were provincial apothecaries whose affluence surprised and irritated their contemporaries. By 1644, for example, Thomas Mynshall, a Cheshire man who had made the shrewd decision to set up business in Manchester, had made enough money to purchase Chorlton Hall. But by the late seventeenth century it was the expectations not simply of a handful but of a significant minority of the profession which were attracting notice. The ambitious apothecary might find his nirvana in any area where there was a thick concentration of affluent families, whether of commercial men or urban and landed gentry. By 1700 cathedral cities, assize towns, the larger ports and growing manufacturing centres, and not least the select new company of spa towns and other health and leisure resorts, all offered him ample scope.

No port expanded faster than Liverpool between Charles II's reign and 1720, and with it grew in prosperity not just its merchants, shipowners and traders but its leading apothecary, John Pemberton. A pugnacious Nonconformist, he was already well-established in shop and practice at the Restoration (he was forced off the borough council for religious Dissent in 1662); he erected a house in the most fashionable new street built in Liverpool between 1660 and 1680, Moor Street, and died in 1705 a very wealthy man, having set up his son as a successful merchant, married his daughters to advantage and left much property both in and out of the town to his heirs. By the 1720s the ailments of Mancunians had proved as profitable to Edward Holbrooke as those of Liverpudlians had been to Pemberton. Of the two apothecaries we know of in and around Wells in the second and third decades of the eighteenth century, Messrs Cupper and Hillard, the former lived in the city in comfortable style, mixing on apparently good terms with the urban gentry and on terms of friendship, as well as profitable professional association, with Dr Claver Morris. When Morris was seriously ill in 1709 Mr Cupper was one of the 'night watchers' for whom the doctor, in gratitude, gave a dinner after his recovery. There were greater possibilities, however, in wealthier cathedral cities than Wells, in 'gentry towns' like Warwick, Derby and Nottingham, in Bath or Tunbridge Wells, or in such popular regional resorts as Beverley, Preston and Bury St Edmunds. The Canterbury apothecary, Anthony Houghton, appears to have achieved by the early years of George I's reign a prosperity and reputation that were exceptional by any provincial standards. William Francys, apothecary of Derby and thrice mayor of the town 1697–1700, had an opulent house in the Corn Market with painted ceilings modelled on those of Chatsworth, and hobnobbed with the Cokes of Melbourne and other major county families. John Bradshaw, the leading apothecary-doctor in Warwick at the turn of the century and mayor of the town in 1717–18, waxed fat on the patronage of the local gentry who consulted him as one of their two general medical advisers, as well as on the profits of his drug sales. The value of his house and goods was put at over £350, a very high figure, at the time of the devastating Warwick fire of 1694; and in the subsequent rebuilding his richly ornamented, three-storied new dwelling became the showpiece of the town centre, 'the Crossing'.

It was just before this, in 1693, that Thomas Macro had built the 'Cupola House' in Bury St Edmunds which so impressed Celia Fiennes when she came there five years later: 'The market cross has a dial and lanthorn on the top, and there being another house pretty close by it, high built with such a tower and lanthorn also . . . made it appear nobly at a distance. This high house is an apothecary's, at least 60 steps up from the ground, and gives a pleasing prospect of the whole town.' Macro differed from his chief local competitor, Samuel Batteley, in being very much of the town; whereas Batteley, a later alderman and, briefly, MP for the borough (1712–13), inherited his father's apothecary's shop in Bury in 1681 but lived on a country estate at nearby Horringer. Like Pemberton, Francys and Bradshaw, Macro was active in local politics and government and was elected mayor of Bury on no fewer than five occasions. Indeed, he was a ripe example of social mobility in the provinces through the Augustan medical profession; for he had started in business as a grocer, yet was able to give his son, Cox, a gentleman's education at home and on the Continent and rejoiced to see him make his mark as a scholar, while he himself, before he died in 1737 at the age of 88, was the possessor of a handsome landed property close to his home town. Thomas Macro had been 'esteemed a very rich man' in his mid-forties when he built his town house 'in the new mode'; for, as Fiennes saw for herself, it had '4 rooms of a floor, pretty sizeable and high, well furnished, a drawing room and chamber full of china and a damask bed, embroidered, 2 other rooms, camlet and mohair beds, a pretty deal of plate in his wife's chamber, parlours below and [the key to all this sophistication] a large shop'. An apothecary mayor of down-at-heel Leicester lived in a house with only three taxable hearths in 1670. Macro, on the other hand, would not have found fault with Defoe's opinion, thirty years after Fiennes's visit, that 'the beauty of [Bury] consists in the number of gentry who dwell in and near it, the polite conversation among them, the affluence and plenty they live in, the sweet air they breathe in . . .' They, in turn, breathed sweetly on their leading apothecary.

Nicholas Batteley, Samuel's father, had sent his two eldest sons into the Church. Cox Macro was encouraged to crown his liberal education by entering on 'the physic line' at Leyden: but although he gained his MD he seems never to have practised seriously. Henry Francys, on the other hand, took a degree at Cambridge but was happy enough in 1724 to take over his father's gentleman's practice and business in Derby. We learn a good deal about the place of the apothecaries in early-eighteenth-century society by noting how they provided for their sons. Apprenticeship records, a most revealing guide in this respect, lay bare significantly few examples – remarkably few in the twenty years from 1710 to 1730 – of sons whose careers involved some measure of social relegation. Most of the movement is emphatically in the other direction. As already seen (see above, pp. 217–18), an appreciable number continued the family tradition of medicine: a handful, like Thomas Dale, as physicians, but many more as surgeons, especially in London. The premiums required by good London surgeons, apart perhaps from the hospital surgeons, were well within the capacity of flourishing city apothecaries such as George Blackaller; and those whose resources were less ample could usually find a competent surgeon in the out-parishes, like William Hepburne of Chelsea, ready to train their sons for £50 or £60. Of course, many fathers were content to see their sons follow them as apothecaries; but affluent provincials were often anxious to see them well established in London rather than in their own locality. A son of Edward Halfhyde, a Cambridge apothecary, had the clear promise of climbing higher up the professional and social ladder than his father when the latter sought out Thomas Barrow in 1716 and persuaded him to take the boy into his shop; for Barrow belonged to the upper aristocracy of the London Society, and put a higher price on his services as instructor than the great James St Amand. Good openings in wholesale trade or commerce, such as came the way of the Pemberton boys in Liverpool, were also sought after. By the early 1700s London premiums in this field could rarely be contemplated by any but the well-to-do, but this was no deterrent to some leading City apothecaries: Richard Malcher, for instance, found £300 in the summer of 1715 to apprentice his son, Cecil, to a drysalter. Usually the foundations of a good career in the law would be laid for about a third of this investment in the capital or for £20 or £30 less elsewhere; and during the first half of the eighteenth century a steady traffic developed between apothecaries' households and attorneys' offices, particularly in London. Among the former were a few high spenders: Charles Jenner, for one, paid £200 in 1719 to seal his son Thomas's articles to Richard Harcourt of the Inner Temple.

Among country surgeons there were more casualties than among provincial apothecaries, for reasons that are obvious. There was, in fact, greater diversity of reward in the practice of surgery than in any other branch of Augustan medicine. Even London surgeons here and there hit hard times and could afford nothing better than respectable manual trades for their sons. And it may be that for every country surgeon of comfortable means by the opening years of the eighteenth century, like William Barman of Wilmington, there was another more akin to George Wakeman, a struggling practitioner at Cople, who in February 1712 could afford to lay out only £5 to train his son Richard as a glazier in Bedford. The Sandwich surgeon William Spratt may have been a little better off; yet he had left only enough money at the time of his death to bind his boy for £20 to a tallow chandler in Deal. While Wakeman laboured for meagre returns in the backwoods of Suffolk, however, in that county's largest town, Ipswich, it was not (as at Bury) an apothecary but a surgeon, 'one Mr. White', who rivalled Beeston, the leading physician, in professional eminence and local status. Defoe was usually too interested in the condition of merchants, manufacturers and tradesmen to find much time in his *Tour* for doctors; but he found space for White, a 'gentleman' as noted for his culture as his manual dexterity, and one whose collection of coins, medals and antiquities had become one of the tourist attractions of the shire by the closing years of George I. White's case, like that of William Becket, an eminent contemporary practising in Abingdon who was an author and a Fellow of the Royal Society, illustrates how far the status gap between the Oxbridge-trained physician and the highly esteemed local surgeon had shrunk in the provinces by 1730; and with it, the economic gap too (in the larger towns at least). Another White of this period, the distinguished Manchester physician Thomas White (1696–1776) did not hesitate to train his son Charles, born in 1728, as a surgeon, in Lancashire, London and Edinburgh. There were palpable opportunities for surgeons to prosper in rapidly growing towns such as Manchester, Liverpool or Plymouth. James Yonge's first apprentice, Sampson Symonds, 'set up in Plymouth and fell into good business' immediately he had finished serving his time in 1682, although by that time his master was already making many hundreds a year out of his own practice in the town and dockyard.

The best documented example of a provincial surgeon in this period is, of course, James Yonge himself. It would be wrong to take his success story as being in any way typical; for clearly he was an exceptionally gifted as well as a fiercely energetic man. But it shows what might, in certain circumstances, be achieved. He himself had glimpsed these opportunities as early as 1662 when the master to whom he had been bound apprentice almost five years earlier, a ship's surgeon such as he himself became, surrendered his indentures 'intending to strike off from the sea and settle at Liverpool, Lancashire (where he now lives in great splendour and credit)'. With the aid of a prudent marriage, which brought him good custom from his wife's relatives at the outset and compensated for the 'little coolness' caused by her propensity for Nonconformist conventicles, and profiting further from his appointment as surgeon to the naval hospital at Plymouth, Yonge had built up by 1679 a practice that was to prove as valuable as any physician in the south-west could boast. He got 20s a day, on average, for the thirty-six to thirty-eight men in the hospital, did a roaring trade treating the pox – 'by that one disease I got this year [1679] above £120' – and had extended his country practice by 1682 as far as Tavistock, Liskeard and Fowey. Eventually all the great gentry and aristocracy of the neighbourhood came into his practice – including Sir William Morice, Sir Bouchier Wray, the Earl and Countess of Bath and the Earl of Radnor; and Yonge could charge 25 to 30 guineas for 'tapping' a rich patient, £20 for four days' attention to a gentleman severely wounded in a duel, and in 1698 between £30 and £70 each for curing nine cases of piles and 100 guineas for curing 'Mr G. C. of a great carnosity which had baffled the skill of great men in London and abroad'. By now there was certainly every incentive to use all his forty years of accumulated experience to keep his patients alive. 'January 30th [1702]', he wrote in his journal, 'died Mr. W. Addie, another good friend and profitable patient; he had an ulcer in the bladder, 4 years, in which time I had of him near £200.' His comfort was that in 1703 and again in 1704 he still had 444 patients on his books, 'a pretty good estate', as he modestly put it, and 'more business than I was desirous of'. Little wonder Yonge could command a fee of £50 for embalming the body of Sir Cloudesly Shovell after the admiral's flagship was wrecked off the Scillies in 1707.

Of the growing number of aspiring young surgeons during the first half of the eighteenth century who began their training in the provinces and came to London to complete it, there were always those who, unlike Richard Kay or Charles White, did not go back. The lure of the capital was not simply financial. For with William Cheselden beginning his celebrated run of anatomy lectures in 1711 (140 a year for twenty years) and with the hospitals crossing the threshold into what was to be the first golden age for the surgeon, London was now an exciting place to be for any ambitious young man in this profession. There was also no denying the financial inducement to settle in the capital: somewhere around the turn of the century the fees that star London surgeons could command for single operations or for a course of surgical treatment had quite suddenly 'taken off' into an altitude where the most sought-after provincial could not compete, and where even the leading physicians were left some distance behind. In 1714, less than four years after starting practice as a fully qualified surgeon, Cheselden was already able to invest £1,000 in South Sea stock. Whereas James Yonge, even in the second half of his long career, counted his highest fees in scores of pounds, the giants of the late Augustan Barber Surgeons' Company counted them in hundreds. The record was probably the £500 an operation charged to private (not hospital) patients by Cheselden himself at his zenith for cutting for the stone, a surgical miracle by any eighteenth-century standards. With the improved technique he first used in March 1727, he quickly reduced the time of performance (as an astounded French observer of one operation carefully noted) to fifty-four seconds, and by 1731, according to Dr James Douglas, 'performs . . . with so much dexterity and quickness that he seldom exceeds half a minute' in straightforward cases.

Just as run-of-the-mill surgeons in Augustan London owed much of their livelihood to their treatment of syphilis with mercury (see above, p. 198), so, too, the great incomes of their wealthier brethren often rested on more than the profits of the operating table. Charles Peters of St Martin's Lane, who rose from being an army surgeon in the Dutch Wars to becoming Surgeon to the Household in the 1690s, is said to have 'acquired an ample fortune' mainly from the sale of a nostrum which, he declared, *prevented* venereal disease! And in 1705 he was still advertising, in addition, the daily preparation of 'his cordial tincture and pills, which have cured thousands of the colic, stone, gravel, scurvy and dropsy, etc.'. Neither did the great London surgeon princes scorn to pick up their half guineas or guineas by 'cupping' their well-to-do patients, many of whom were bled as a matter of routine every spring and autumn, let alone during every indisposition. Caesar Hawkins, quite apart from his justly earned reputation for skill with his knife, was thought to earn £1,000 a year as a phlebotomist. And though many top surgeons in late Augustan London – men of the calibre of Ferne, Gay, Douglas, Bamber and Cheselden – appear to have been little involved in such lucrative sidelines, they clearly did make handsome profits out of their pupils with the level of premiums starting to soar at much the same time as operating fees. Even the fees charged for private lectures and demonstrations were not to be sneezed at. One of the most popular and effective demonstrators of the 1730s, Frank Nicholls, delivering two courses a year, expected 4 guineas from each subscriber for the first course and 3 guineas for the second. Nicholls gave good value – each of his courses contained thirty-nine lectures and a demonstration of cutting for the stone – and William Hunter was later to pay tribute to the profound influence they had on him; but as a practitioner he was not in the highest flight. That men of the reputation of Cheselden and John Douglas could, at their prime, command more than 4 guineas a course for lecturing is highly likely.

Cheselden, a principal surgeon at St Thomas's from 1719 to 1738 and Surgeon to Queen Caroline from 1727, had begun to learn his craft in Leicester, apprenticed (tradition has it) to a local surgeon called Wilkes. But he was in London by the time he was 15, and there had the good fortune to be taken under the wing of one of the most justly celebrated surgeons of post-Revolution London, William Cowper. Cowper was a Fellow of the Royal Society and he wrote the best work on anatomy yet to be published in English. He also built up so valuable a surgical practice in the eighteen short years of his active work (1691–1709) that the dozens of able young men who were training or beginning to establish themselves in the first decade of the eighteenth century were allowed a glimpse of the untarnished prestige as well as the great financial returns which the surgeon's art could now achieve. With lucrative hospital appointments and government posts to be contended for, and with pupils from the 'better sort' of families being increasingly drawn to the metropolis or streaming into the profession from London's own bourgeoisie, successful London surgeons who could stand the pace could grow very rich within anything from ten to twenty years. Their exceptional prospects are reflected in the fact that before the dissolution of the Barber Surgeons' Company in 1745 the fees for the admission of a surgeon to the full livery had risen to £131 16s 0d, not counting the £4 3s 6d which each new entrant was expected to contribute to the Poor's Box. An additional bonus for a lucky few was the chance of sharing in the Court and government financial patronage which, irrespective of official appointments, began to come the way of doctors in London. As Edward Hughes discovered over a quarter of a century ago, it became not uncommon in the 1720s to make payments to members of the medical profession out of secret service monies or royal bounty. Thus between 1721 and 1725 the surgeon Charles Maitland received a 'gift' (so recorded) of £1,000 for inoculating Prince Frederick against the smallpox. Dr Gideon Harvey, a Leyden graduate of the 1690s and the son of the Gideon who had been one of the more controversial figures in London 'physic' between

1660 and 1700, had a handout of £300 for 'visiting the State prisoners in the Tower' (not ungenerous considering he held the salaried post of Physician at the Tower at this very period). At much the same time, Thomas Rentone received a staggering £5,000 of public money 'for making known his art, skill and mystery in cutting ruptures', and Dr James Douglas (the physician brother of John), who discovered the 'Douglas pouch' in the peritoneum, was granted £500 'for his performance and publishing his Anatomical Observations'.

That London surgeon-princes shared in such munificent official largess is one measure of the fascination which the technical and even the academic achievements of a once-maligned occupation had come to hold for early-Hanoverian society. It was not coincidental that after ten years of dispensing strictly professional instruction as a lecturer, Cheselden felt the time was ripe by the years 1721–3 for a public relations venture (a profitable one, naturally), in which he and Francis Hawksbee combined to give three courses of subscription lectures in anatomy. They were, as an advertisement in the *Daily Courant* put it, 'chiefly intended for gentlemen; such things only will be omitted as are neither instructive nor entertaining, and care will be taken to have nothing offensive'. No less symbolic of the fact that surgery had arrived socially was a grandiose gesture by Edward Greene, senior surgeon of St Bartholomew's and Master of the London Barber Surgeons in 1711. When Greene sat for his portrait he had both the social panache and the money to commission the leading French court painter of his day, Rigaud, to put him on canvas – an artist for whom Louis XIV himself had sat not many years before.

Few great surgeons of the early eighteenth century appear to have felt it necessary to buy social acceptance by acquiring estates: their interest in the land market was even less evident than that of the physicians. But more and more they are to be found owning or renting large town houses in fashionable areas, houses that, in many cases, had to be large enough to contain lecture and demonstration rooms and even small operating theatres. One can gauge John Douglas's rise in the world from the fact that his first course on anatomy and surgical operations was given at his house in Fetter Lane, whereas by the time he died in 1743 he had been resident for a number of years in Downing Street. Peter McCulloch, one of London's best known anatomists and lecturers of the 1720s and 1730s, lived in Golden Square; John Ranby, FRS, in Bloomsbury – first in King Street, then in Southampton Street; Peter Coltheart in Bedford Court and Chandos Street.

The third of the 'great professions' of Augustan England was thus transformed socially as well as structurally in the last quarter of the seventeenth century and the first quarter of the eighteenth. And it was already clear by the 1730s – and clearer still by the time Hans Sloane, Richard Mead and William Cheselden died, within a year of one another, in the early 1750s – that the social dimensions of this great change involved more than the material prosperity of medical men, and more than the trappings of status. They entailed a notable increase in the capacity of a restructured profession to sustain social mobility to a degree unequalled by any other. Above all, they involved a fundamental change in the public reputation and the corporate self-respect of the greater part of those who could now, loosely but justly, be desscribed as 'doctors'.

To this last change the contribution of the physicians was certainly not negligible. There were still 'sleek' men among them, 'strutting behind a double chin', replete with portentous and largely useless booklearning, as a reminder of the obloquy they had not long ago aroused. But by 1740 much of this unfortunate image had been dispelled: partly by new developments – the Dispensary experiment, the involvement of many physicians in the hospital movement after 1720, the influx of Leyden and Edinburgh graduates; but mostly by individual example. The existence of so many admirable, hardworking and often well-loved physicians among the doctors of early Georgian England could not but redound to the credit of the medical profession at large. In the provinces bright beacons burned in the shape of men like John Huxham of Plymouth, Christopher Packe of Canterbury and William Chambers, whose philanthropy and care for the poor in Hull became a by-word. In London, too, there were physicians who earned respect by their research and writing and who, like Edward Strother, were patently more interested in advancing medical knowledge than in lining their pockets with fees.

On the other hand, if only because so few Englishmen even in George II's reign ever came into direct contact with a physician, the major credit for the new standing of the medical profession in society should probably fall elsewhere: to the pharmaceutical knowledge, the accessibility and the emancipation from the shop of the apothecaries; to the increasingly impressive all-round competence of the surgeon-apothecaries; above all, to the skills of the surgeons. Campbell, writing in 1747, found scarcely any vocation he could enthuse over as warmly as the surgeon's. It was a noble calling; it invoked some of the highest qualities of the human character; and it was, quite simply, indispensable. There were 'none of the liberal arts more likely to procure a livelihood'. 'An ingenious surgeon', Campbell rhapsodically concluded, 'let him be cast on any corner of the earth, with but his case of instruments in his pocket, he may live where most other professions would starve.' The surgeons of late Augustan England were, at their best, the most persuasive of all ambassadors for medicine as a profession.

PART THREE

The New Professions: the Service of the State

8

The State and the Professions: the New Men of Government

Professional men provide society with certain specialised services. The fledgling groups we looked at earlier, together with those who practised 'liberal arts and sciences', existed or came into being to serve the needs of individuals and private or corporate groups. Essentially this was true of 'the great professions' too. There were, of course, many vital points at which their interests and responsibilities interlocked with more public concerns. The Church of England was a state church, and its clergy were only too aware of their special relationship with the Stuart monarchy, while after 1714 they accepted (though more grudgingly) their responsibilities within a Whig Erastian polity. The 'twelve men in scarlet' presided over the king's courts of law, and it was primarily before these courts that the barristers pleaded and accredited attorneys appeared. As for medicine, there were in time of war several hundred 'doctors' in the army and navy. All other calls acknowledged, however, the clergyman's first duties were to his God and to the individual human souls in his care: very few divines were publicly employed and virtually none were paid from public funds. The proportion of lawyers in the Crown's employ was larger, but it was still small in relation to the great bulk of counsellors, attorneys and solicitors whose incomes derived overwhelmingly from private fees given in return for private services. Whether they were rendered to individual persons or to corporate bodies such as municipalities or trading companies, the services were essentially non-public. The position of the medical profession was even clearer in such respects.

By 1730, however, there flourished in England a substantial body of professionals who were directly employed by the state either in civil office or in the armed forces and whose vocational justification lay entirely in serving the state's needs, as opposed to private needs. It had been clear for many years – certainly since the end of Queen Anne's reign – that this body, which in numbers was possibly as large as the lawyers and the doctors put together, had come to stay: it was now an integral part of the middle storeys of the English social structure. For all that, the three groups which comprised it were astonishingly youthful when compared with the clergy, the lawyers and the medical profession. Only one had tap-roots which ran back into the Middle Ages; and even here there were only tenuous connections between the small band of career officials, many of them clerics, who serviced the household administration of the medieval monarch and the 'civil officers' (or, as we should say, civil servants) of the early eighteenth century. There had been no standing army in England before the 1640s: and during the ninety years that preceded the outbreak of the Civil Wars there was only one interlude of any length, between 1585 and 1603, when 'the profession of arms' was not of necessity a mercenary vocation. It is even arguable whether, despite the naval achievements of Henry VIII and Elizabeth I, there was a *peacetime* Royal Navy of any size, offering semi-permanent employment, before the 1630s; and even Charles I's 'ship-money navy' consisted of fewer than twenty warships supplemented by some armed merchantmen. Just how much the service of the state, in professional terms, owed to the particular needs of Augustan England, a glance back at the beginning of our period will reveal.

In 1680, twenty years after the civil service of the English republic had been cut down in its youth, very little worthy of the name, considered as a lifelong career possibility for the sons of the gentry or of professional men and businessmen, had taken its place. The personnel of government, outside the Royal Household and the new Customs service (inaugurated with the change from farming to direct collection in 1671) were few. Such departments of State as there were could guarantee little in the way of permanency to their members. The Exchequer was a notable exception and the competition for places there was fierce. But in the still tiny Treasury office, in the equally small offices of the Secretaries of State, to a lesser extent even in the Navy Office, clerks and secretaries still moved in and out with unsettling frequency. Here and there, through luck or exceptional talent (usually he needed both), a Bridgeman or a Pepys took root. But these were rare cases. There were a few men, too, who specialised in diplomatic skills; yet the *corps diplomatique*, if such it can be called, was minuscule and crippled by lack of adequate funds.

As far as the military service of the Crown was concerned the situation was even worse. Early in 1679 the commissioned ranks of Charles II's army barely constituted a profession at all, judged by the standards of the New Model from 1645 to 1660 or by those of the armies of William III and Marlborough after the Revolution of 1688. With the twenty-three new regiments raised during the war scare of 1678 all under sentence of disbandment, the number of regimental commissions available on the regular establishment shrank to under 300, not strikingly higher than the 210 that existed before the outbreak of the second Dutch War in 1665. Most of these were held by courtiers and gentlemen dilettantes, who had seen no action and desired none. The true professionals of this period, who had officered most of the regiments sent to Flanders in 1678, prepared to do again what they had done for much of the reign, that is, seek service abroad, especially in the Anglo-Dutch brigade. The navy was larger than the army and was certainly taken more seriously, but it was in poor shape in 1680 after some years of mismanagement; and although 'the sea service' was now regarded as a lifetime's vocation, its status was not high and it was by no means clear in 1680 that it was a profession suitable for fulfilling the proper aspirations of the sons of gentlemen. For much of Charles II's reign the genuine professionals among the officers of the Royal Navy were the 'tarpaulins'; and they emphatically were not gentlemen, by birth or even by transmutation.

Three developments transformed the service of the Crown and of the state during the next twenty to thirty years. The first was the strengthening of central authority in the years from 1681 to 1688, the period of the so-called Stuart reaction which followed the failure of the Exclusion campaign. There was a notable expansion, and some reform, of civil government, both processes being governed above all by the needs of the king's revenue, and owing much to the promptings of the Treasury. They were accompanied by the revitalisation of the Royal Navy in Pepys's last great phase at the Admiralty. And there was also built up in these half dozen years before the Glorious Revolution a standing army which, though neither so large nor so formidable as the republican army of 1649–60, was appreciably bigger than the Crown had previously mustered; and while its expansion is normally associated with the authoritarian and pro-Catholic policies of James II, it is noteworthy that as early as 1684 the number of regimental and garrison officers serving his brother Charles had risen to 613.

The second development in point of time, and one which had far more spectacular effects on career opportunity in all three branches of the state's service, was the twenty years of warfare which ensued during the quarter-century between 1689 and 1713. In spite of the justifiable apprehension felt at the increase of James II's army in the late 1680s, the strength of the regiments that could be put in the field in the autumn of 1688 was no more than 23,000. Yet by 1695–7 there were more than twice this number of native troops fighting overseas, irrespective of home garrisons and reserves, while over the years 1706–11 the total strength of the army in all theatres, excluding officers, was maintained at an average level of 120,000 (though see below, p. 264). Nothing to compare with such a force had been mustered by any previous English generation. And so it was with the navy, too. King James's 100 ships of the line of December 1688 were even at that time the largest battle fleet in Europe, in terms of numbers if not weight of ships. By the summer of 1714, however, that fleet had swollen to 131 battleships; and these were supported by 65 fifth- and sixth-rates (the rough equivalent of the later frigates and sloops), 57 more than at the time of the Revolution, while yet another 42-gunner was on the stocks at Sheerness. What is more, the 131 ships of the line now included 20 of the new first- and second-rates, of 100 or 96 guns, with their massive complements each as big as an infantry battalion. The repercussions of the Nine Years' War and the Spanish Succession War on the professions were not confined to the fighting services. To organise, equip and direct such armed forces, and to raise and administer the revenue for a military and naval budget that was eventually five times as large as James II's, called not only for a much larger and more complex executive than that of 1688 but for a new attitude towards the officials who composed it. In the more peaceful years from 1713 to 1730 the armed forces were kept at a much lower active strength. Even in intervals of emergency such as 1715–16, 1718–19 and 1726–8, their numbers and cost were well down on the record levels of 1702–12. But the transformation which had taken place in the structure of the professions since 1689 could not be, and was not, reversed. Within this structure the naval, military and civil service of the Crown had by the end of Queen Anne's reign come to assume a role without precedent, even in the 1650s. Three fully fledged new professions had arrived; and they had been, however reluctantly in some quarters, accepted.

The third factor which transfigured the shape and social importance of these new professions between 1680 and 1714 affected primarily the bureaucracy. Over this period there took place a fundamental change in attitudes towards public service in England. In part, this change was brought about by deliberate government policy in fostering continuity of service, policy in which three leading ministers of the late Stuart monarchy played a key role; in part, it was wrought by back-bench parliamentary pressure on the governments of William III and Anne to curtail the political activities of public employees, pressure before which, paradoxically, those ministries bent with considerable reluctance. These pressures appeared to be pushing for a long time in different, if not irreconcilable, directions. But, in the event, this proved not to be the case. Both proved in the long run powerfully instrumental in creating a large career bureaucracy, a body that was largely non-political and in essentials professional, out of what had been for most of Charles II's reign little more than a small group of individuals, practised survivalists in a world in which staying in an executive office for five years on end had been a substantial achievement in itself.

The New Men of Government

The drive for greater administrative efficiency in the 1680s, especially in revenue raising and collection, had its mainspring in a rejuvenated Treasury. Behind most of the creative and reforming initiatives of the years 1680–7 the hand of Lord Rochester, First Commissioner of the Treasury and finally Lord High Treasurer, can be seen at work. The establishment in 1683 of the Excise department, by far the largest and most consciously professionalised government department yet seen in England, was his outstanding concrete legacy. But it was also Rochester – a far more courageous innovator than his father, the Earl of Clarendon – who deserves much of the credit for the less tangible steps taken in these years to create an embryonic bureaucracy, in which continuity of efficient service and the development of a civil service tradition were positively encouraged at all levels among men whose loyalty to the Stuart regime was considered reliable. When the wars arrived to put the fragile foundations of the 1680s under appalling

strain, the need for a large corps of officials who would regard dedicated service to the state as a permanent commitment, whatever
ministry was in power at the centre, became urgent. But it was only
after a period of great upheaval in the early and mid-1690s, in which
the Excise, especially, became the field for a violent tug-of-war between
Whigs and Tories to control its abundant patronage, that the determination of a tiny handful of post-Revolution 'managers' overcame
the chaotic influence on government of the party spoils system.

Two of these statesmen, Godolphin and Harley, had twelve successive years between them at the head of the Treasury (1702–14); and
these were the years when a major, though not wholly unqualified,
victory was achieved for the principle that the non-political government official should be inviolate from political interference and ejec-
tion. Although they never used the term explicitly, it is perfectly
clear that what Anne's two leading ministers were fighting for was
the concept of the civil service as a profession. Robert Harley's role in
the moulding of this new profession was especially critical, for during
his first year in office in 1710–11, with Toryism rampant and vengeful,
he was under insistent pressure to purge the officials whom his predecessor, the fallen Godolphin, had either appointed or preserved. One
of the many courageous decisions he took at this time was to keep
George Townshend on the Excise Board where he had served since
1699, after being first appointed by the Whig Junto. Furthermore,
when he needed a man of ability and experience to get the new Leather
Office off the ground in 1711, it was to Townshend that Harley turned,
even allowing him to keep his place at the Excise at the same time.
To most Tory backbenchers such moves as this seemed indefensible;
but to a raw colleague on the Commission for the Leather Duty, young
Justinian Isham, himself the son of a Tory knight of the shire, it
made very good sense to have a man as 'very well versed in business'
as Mr Townshend to guide his steps. Townshend saw the Leather
Office through into George I's reign and ended his career as the senior
Commissioner of Excise in 1726, having served there for over a quarter
of a century.

It in no way depreciates the achievement of Harley, or of Godolphin
before him, in professionalising the civil service to point to one
extraneous factor of real importance which, we can now see, greatly
eased their task in the long run. This was the successful outcome of
'Country' campaigns in Parliament between 1694 and 1706 which
resulted in the exclusion of large categories of placemen from the
House of Commons. Ironically, the ministries of the day resisted, or
at least resented most of these moves: for the motives of the 'Country'
leaders were seen, quite correctly, to be more political than administrative. And yet without them it would have been infinitely more difficult
for dozens of executives in such departments as the Customs, the
Excise, the Stamp and Salt Offices, or the Navy Office to carve out
professional careers in post-Revolution England that could last for
anything up to twenty-five years.

That there were so many more posts available to such executives, and to many others of comparable rank, by 1714 than there had been thirty years earlier was the result not merely of wartime expansion but also of the total commitment of the leading politicians (and also the monarchs) of Augustan England to committee-government. In a country where the emphasis had traditionally been on the individual responsibility of ministers to the king the committee-conscious interlude of the Civil Wars and the Interregnum marked a decisive change of direction. As new departments were created after 1680, and in particular after 1689 when they came along thick and fast, they were almost all put under the control of boards (in contemporary parlance 'put in commission') from the beginning. The three English revenue boards of 1693 had become eight by 1711 – nine if the Commissioners for Taxes, strictly under Treasury aegis, were included. The Treasury itself was in commission from 1687 to 1702 and again, continuously, after 1714, and the Admiralty for the whole period, except from 1702–9; while the Navy Board swelled at one time to as many as sixteen members. Of course, there was more behind this trend than mere devotion to a principle. No government, even in wartime, was entirely innocent of patronage considerations; and no government was unaware that many bodies presented a more difficult target to the often-withering fire of parliamentary criticism than one. But whatever the motives, there were by the early months of 1714, 113 commissioners at the head of eighteen different offices; most of these commissioners, outside the Admiralty, the Board of Trade and the Board of Ordnance, were essentially non-politicians; and each board had its own secretariat and, in the case of the revenue boards, at the very least its own comptroller, receiver-general and cashier, and frequently its own legal adviser.

Apart from the tradition of security which Godolphin and Harley worked so hard to foster, the commissioners and executives of the revenue departments, and the chief clerks likewise, were also protected from the ravages of the party spoils system by the high degree of professional skill which many of their operations demanded. A few high-powered bureaucrats, such as George Townshend or Thomas Everard, inventor of the 'sliding rule' for excisemen, might move from department to department in the revenue, exercising their reforming zeal or their personal brand of hyper-professionalism. The most notable case in point was John Danvers, whose reputation as a scourge of the inefficient was first earned as a Customs Searcher and then as an Excise Commissioner before finally he was appointed by Godolphin to oversee the launching of the new Salt Office in 1702 and presided over it as chairman of the commissioners until he died in 1716. However, there were many more officials of the first rank who from the 1690s or early 1700s onwards could expect to live out their working lives in a single finance department, acquiring an unshakeable grasp of the minutiae of its practice, earning a more modest reward than the highflyers, but enjoying the benefit of security for themselves and conferring the benefits of continuity on their own special corner of the field. Among the more important professionals in this category were the permanent secretaries of the revenue boards, a new post-Revolution race of specialists of whom William Bridges was a not-untypical example. Appointed the first Secretary to the new Stamp Office in 1694, he was still in the same post thirty years later: and in the course of that time his salary advanced from £100 a year to £300, which was as much as many commissioners earned outside the very biggest departments. At the more modest levels three Salt Office employees, Matthew Greenwood, William Johnson and William Sumpter, illustrate the kind of departmental profile which is repeated again and again across the field of the Augustan central revenue administration from William III's reign through to George II's. They were still serving in the mid-1730s as Correspondent and Clerk of the Securities, Departmental Solicitor and Chief Accountant respectively, having all been appointed initially when the Salt Office was set up in 1702.

The cementing of a permanent, professional tradition of state service made possible the forging of many long, uninterrupted official careers outside the revenue departments, too. The Treasury, the Navy Office, the Admiralty, the Post Office, the offices of the two or three Secretaries of State, the clerical and technical establishment of the Ordnance Office and the secretariat of the new Board of Trade office (1696) all began to offer increasingly secure prospects after the Revolution and, in the case of the Treasury and the Post Office, for some years before it. Some careers were cut short in the early years of the Whig supremacy after 1714, but they were a small minority. A most revealing case cropped up in the Ordnance Office in 1709 when Alexander Eustace, one of the Storekeeper's clerks, appealed vigorously to the Board of Ordnance against his dismissal by an incoming officer who wished to accommodate one of his own clients. The Eustace affair illustrates just how far the process of consolidation had already gone at the ordinary clerical level and how far 'the good of the service in general' (in the words of the Secretary to the Treasury) had begun to take precedence in so many departments over personal as well as political considerations. Eustace had served in the Ordnance Office, seemingly without blemish, since December 1693 and had been promoted from third to second clerk in 1705. The board, having ascertained after careful inquiry that there had only been two instances in the department since 1683 of clerks being dismissed at the whim of an incoming principal officer, instructed the new Storekeeper, Robert Lowther, to reinstate Eustace – who then continued his career peacefully into George I's reign. Howard Tomlinson has discovered that in this office alone two of the seventeen clerks who were in employment at the end of 1714, Nicholas Whittaker and John Allen senior, served all told for between thirty and forty years and at least half a dozen others for more than twenty years.

Clerkships in the Treasury carried status and rewards above those in more run-of-the-mill departments. The business of the office was considered uniquely responsible as well as highly specialised. Even the more senior under clerks received salaries of £100 a year with an entitlement to fees, in addition, and all under clerks were paid as much by 1733. The four Chief Clerks were prosperous men and the Secretaries of the Treasury wealthy ones. That men should wish to find a permanent berth in the office was not surprising, therefore, and their opportunity came with a deliberate change of policy towards Treasury clerkships during the Rochester regime and in Henry Guy's first period as Secretary (1679–89). Most of the clerks appointed in those years negotiated the watershed of the Revolution, as did their most able predecessor from the 1670s, William Lowndes. Christopher Tilson graduated to the post of Chief Clerk of the Revenue, which he held from 1695 to 1714, completing thirty years in the department. Contemporaries of Tilson such as Samuel Langford, Robert Squibb and William Shaw would most probably have survived at least as long as he did had they not died prematurely in the 1690s. The next generation proved more durable, and between 1690 and 1730 many notable Treasury marathons began. With chief clerkships few in number it was quite common for a man to remain an under clerk throughout his working life at the Treasury, moving slowly up the seniority ladder over the years: Christopher Lowe did this for nearly thirty-three years, for instance (1721–54) and Edward Webster for as many as sixty-four years (1691–1755), though he was a pluralist for all but twenty-five of them with his main duties elsewhere. Death or resignation might interrupt an under clerk's career; by the eighteenth century dismissal scarcely ever did so. Only one is recorded between 1714 and 1758. Experienced chief clerks were very occasionally drafted into the Treasury from elsewhere (Henry Kelsall, appointed in 1714, survived for over forty-one years and died in harness), but it was more usual for the Treasury to make internal promotions. When men such as Mark Frecker and Thomas Bowen were promoted in 1723 and 1738 respectively, their qualities had already been tried and tested for over twenty years. No ministry would have contemplated removing them thereafter. After William Lowndes (see below, pp. 250, 260) only one Treasury clerk before George III's reign, John Taylor, had the distinction of working his way through the whole departmental system from junior clerkship to a Secretaryship of the Treasury. He did so between 1690 and 1715, and ironically this feat made him politically vulnerable – in view of Lowndes's long entrenchment in the First Secretaryship – in a way the clerks had ceased to be.

Appropriately, the foundations of the new bureaucracy of Augustan England were nowhere more securely laid than in the two departments where the legacy of Samuel Pepys was of vital importance. In the Admiralty and the Navy Office from about 1680 onwards two generations of public servants – well over 500 of them all told, not counting the staff of the dockyards – were taken in and trained. With a wider range of jobs to be filled than in any other sector of government service, many of them calling for specialist skills or knowledge and some carrying considerable responsibility, the able and dedicated man had unusually good opportunities for internal advancement, sometimes involving transfer between the two departments. Apart from Pepys and William Hewer, both of whom had served the navy since the

Restoration, Sir Anthony Deane was the only notable figure to fall at the hurdle of 1688–9, which also left the clerical staffs almost completely unscathed. The casualties at the rather stiffer fence of 1714–15, when the victorious Whigs were showing somewhat less sympathy than the previous regimes of Godolphin and Harley to the principle of absolute bureaucratic security, were very slightly more numerous, and a tiny handful of clerks suffered in the process: John Newson and Philip Barnett paid off after seven and ten years, respectively, in the Admiralty Office, and Henry Beach, Chief Clerk of Victualling Accounts, more startlingly discharged after twenty-four years of service to the Navy Board. Yet although the axe fell on one or two more distinguished heads as well – notably that of Benjamin Timewell, Controller of Victualling Accounts, whose association with the Navy Office went back more than forty years – the overriding pattern was one of survival, either until death or until retirement, for almost everyone except temporary clerks.

In the process scores of lifelong careers were forged, including a few that were, by any standards, distinguished. None was more remarkable than Josiah Burchett's almost continuous sixty-two years in the Admiralty, forty-eight of them in the key position in the department which Pepys had held until 1689, that of Secretary to the Board. Burchett had begun as a precocious 14-year-old, a junior clerk to Pepys himself, in 1680, and it was fitting that the last four years of his life, following a voluntary retirement when 'worn out with age', should be solaced by what must have been the most richly earned pension of a pension-happy century, the £800 a year paid to him from 1742–6. On the other hand, the man whom Richard Ollard has described as the 'true administrative heir' of Pepys, Charles Sergison, never held any position in the Admiralty. He began his working life as a dockyard clerk in 1671, got his first appointment, a temporary clerkship in the Navy Office in Crutched Friars in 1675, and served as Clerk of the Acts (Pepys's first major office) from February 1690 until an enforced retirement, aged 65, in May 1719. On several occasions since the 1690s Sergison had pleaded to be relieved from the treadmill of an exceptionally demanding post, and it seems that in the end he was taken at his word – and felt somewhat aggrieved in consequence! His first appeal to be allowed to resign, embedded in a letter to William III, could hardly have been more self-defeating; for it was so impregnated with the stern sense of departmental pride and professional achievement that were hallmarks of the great figures in the first generation of Augustan civil servants that it advertised the very qualities which, in wartime at least, made Sergison irreplaceable. He and his colleagues at the Navy Board had

> struggled with many difficulties, such as remote and deficient funds, stubborn and refractory officers, insulting superiors ... But nevertheless, by our adherence to the ancient rules and methods of the Navy [Office], [the] regularity of our payments and constant diligence and attendance, we have overcome them all.

Among those colleagues of the 1690s were Sir Richard Haddock and
Dennis Lyddell. Haddock was a former admiral who transferred to the
shore service of the government as an extra Navy Commissioner in
1673 and was preserved into a doddering old age in the senior post
of Controller, from which, after a tenancy of over thirty years, death
finally wrested him in 1715. Two years later Lyddell, too, died in office.
A more dynamic figure than Haddock, his career from 1676 to 1717
ran in a closely parallel course to that of his great friend Charles
Sergison, culminating in sixteen and a half years as Controller of
Treasurer's Accounts.

   The professionalism which the administration of a large and, until
1715, ever-growing navy demanded imbued a whole squad of Admiralty
and Navy officials, less prominent than the Burchetts, Sergisons and
Lyddells but noted as a body for their loyalty and commitment. Many
of them seem humdrum-enough figures. Michael Howen and Henry
Johnson, for instance, both gave forty-seven years of continuous
service before they died in the 1720s; neither rose above chief clerk's
status (Howen for thirty-five years at the Ticket Office and Johnson
for thirty-one in Bills and Accounts), and each confined himself in
nearly half a century to just two of the Navy Office's eight main
subdepartments. Yet their responsibilities were enough to make them
very necessary cogs in a machine which by the time of the Spanish
Succession War was running with a smoothness unforeseeable in the
1660s; in fact, Howen's salary – by then £200 – was as much as some
departmental secretaries were paid. Edward Burt, another unsung but
invaluable servant of the Augustan navy, progressed more enterpris-
ingly. Having served his apprenticeship in the Navy Office from 1683
to 1694, he moved to the Admiralty as Joint Chief Clerk in 1694,
became Secretary to the new Office for Registering Seamen from 1696
to 1705, but returned to his old post, solo, at the Admiralty in November 1705 and was earning £400 a year there by the time he died in
1722. Among those who rose ultimately well above the clerkships they
occupied during the Nine Years' and Spanish Succession Wars were
Thomas Pearse, who began in 1693 as a lowly clerk in Seamen's Wages
and ended (1726–43) as Clerk of the Acts and John Fawler, who after
sharing the Chief Clerkship of the Admiralty with Burt, and later
holding it alone from 1696 to 1705, first became Deputy Secretary
under Burchett and finally served for thirty years on the Navy Board,
mostly as Commissioner of Victualling Accounts. The opportunities
for advancement, from bottom to top, in the Navy Office were there
for every ambitious professional government servant to see. Between
1660 and 1673 no fewer than seventeen men who had begun their civil
service careers as clerks in the office ended them as Navy Commissioners, though frequently their experience was broadened along the
way by periods spent in the dockyards, the Admiralty or the Victualling
Office. At the same time both the Admiralty and Navy Office were
fiercely resistant to the penetration of their avenues of promotion
from outside their own condominium. For a century after the 1688
Revolution it became almost unknown for chief clerks in the Navy

Office to be appointed from anywhere else than the lower reaches of the same department.

The growth of specialisation and departmentalism were both inevitable developments in a bureaucracy which emerged so swiftly after 1680, expanded so rapidly, and in the war years of 1689–1713 had to adapt itself to a governmental machinery of increasing complexity. Nevertheless an older and more versatile tradition, that of the gifted all-rounder, still survived here and there in the established profession of the early Hanoverian period. It was a tradition exemplified well before the Revolution by Sir George Downing – diplomat, Treasury Secretary and Customs Commissioner: a tradition more appropriate to the relatively unsophisticated executive in which other pioneers of a non-political civil service, like William Bridgeman and William Blathwayt, were reared. The 'very ingenious' Bridgeman (as John Evelyn described him in 1680), who had spent over a quarter of a century from 1667 in the department of the Secretaries of State, was transferred to the Admiralty in 1694 to deal with a crisis and within a few years made a considerable impact there, while still holding down a Clerkship of the Privy Council and the chairmanship of Greenwich Hospital. His record paled, however, when set beside Blathwayt's astonishing range of activities, spanning over a period of thirty-nine years the diplomatic service, the Plantations Office, the War Office, the Privy Council and the new Board of Trade, and including, in addition, the acting Secretaryship of State during most of King William's visits abroad. From May 1696 to April 1704 this super-drudge, with his inhuman energy and single-minded acquisitiveness, took on four different offices simultaneously, not one of them a sinecure, and managed to discharge them without giving his critics any serious ammunition to use against him.

The pre-Revolution tradition of the civil service utility-man, carried over to the early years of the eighteenth century by Blathwayt (who did not quit his last office until 1710), could still claim a few representatives in the 1720s and 1730s. One was Sir Philip Ryley, whose early appointment as Serjeant at Arms in the Treasury from 1684 to 1689 proved to be a springboard for a post-Revolution career which lasted a further forty-four years and involved him in five departments or individual offices. Another was James Vernon, junior – fifty-three years a public servant – who, having made his début as a clerk to one of the Secretaries of State in 1697, moved with scarcely a stutter in the middle of Anne's reign from the embassy at Copenhagen, via a brief sojourn in the Royal Household, to the Board of Excise, where he soon earned the confidence of his fellow commissioners sufficiently to be unleashed on a general survey of the northern counties in 1712. By the 1720s he was a major pillar of the revenue, and except for a two-year intermission when he fell foul of Walpole remained so for more than forty-five years.

In the meantime, another tradition was being established in the new bureaucracy – a family tradition of public service. It was evident to some extent in the case of the Vernons, for James Vernon the elder was an Under-Secretary and finally a Secretary of State in William III's reign and remained a placeman under both Tories and Whigs in that of Queen Anne, and there was another Vernon ready to succeed James junior in the Excise Office not long after his death in 1756 (his younger brother, Edward, had meanwhile chosen the navy as his vocation and had become one of George II's most controversial admirals). The public's gradual recognition of the civil service as a profession, promising permanence as well as profit, and the growing tendency of young men to follow fathers or other close relatives into it and then to pass the baton on, can be clearly seen in the rise of notable Treasury families like the Lowndeses and the Tilsons (no fewer than nine Lowndeses served in this department between 1680 and 1767); in the presence of five Popples on the establishment of the Board of Trade between 1696 and 1745; and in the prominence of three generations of Frowdes in the administration of the Post Office between the Restoration and the reign of George II. The same tradition of public service grew up in several other bureaucratic families, such as the Delafayes in the Secretaries of State's department, and in many minor dynasties that were relatively obscure – the Johnsons in the Navy Office, for example – or wholly provincial. It would be a mistake to look for the dead hand of nepotism in all or even the great majority of these cases. They rather reflect the fact that, in conditions far more promising and more secure for the careerist than had been known before 1680, fathers prepared their sons, and sons in turn brought up their sons, 'to business'.

Beyond this, however, relatively little worthwhile generalisation is possible in the present state of research about the background of the Augustan civil servants. Information of this nature, even on those in the upper ranks of the bureaucracy, is hard to come by: there are, for example, no admissions registers and very few apprenticeship records to serve as a basis for further inquiry, as there are in the case of the Church or of the legal and medical professions. As for the origins of many thousands further down the column, including those provincially based officials who made up a large majority of the whole, fleeting, isolated glimpses are the most we can hope for, without the most laborious and protracted biographical investigation. There is some evidence, however, patchy though it is, to suggest that a fair proportion of the more successful of the new men of English government came of minor or necessitous gentry stock; and this would be in harmony with what is clearly a major motif in the pattern of recruitment to other large Augustan professions. The archetypal government official of the whole period from the 1680s to the 1720s, the great 'Ways and Means' Lowndes, who was a clerk and later Chief Clerk in the Treasury from 1675–95 and Secretary to the Treasury from then until his death in 1724, was a classic product of that job-hungry class, the non-armigerous parish gentry of small estates. But even local offices of £50 a year or thereabouts in the revenue, given prospects of promotion, were far from being beneath the notice of the lesser gentry or of their younger sons. When a Dutchman was committed for trial at Lancaster assizes on a charge of murder in 1695, Thomas Kenyon expressed shock at the incident but no surprise at the discovery that the victim was an offshoot of an old Lancashire county family, 'a gentleman, Mr Walmisley, born at Bury and then a[n Excise] gauger at Preston'.

As other professions expanded it was natural that there should be a certain cross-flow between them and the civil service. The 'Robert Maidstone of St. Andrew's, Holborn' who got his son into the Pipe Office in 1721 was described as 'gentleman', but may well have been a professional man, most likely an attorney. The law, indeed, was a natural provider. One of the recruits to the Exchequer in 1715 was the son of a very wealthy Chancery lawyer and court official, John Hammond; while among the more prominent established bureaucrats of this time, Philip Ryley had had a lawyer father and so perhaps had John Fawler – certainly he was trained as a civil lawyer before entering the Admiralty. Another civil lawyer by training, William Aglionby, was the son of a Cumbrian clergyman: 'having but small encouragement' in his original profession (according to another government functionary, John Macky), he became first a Post Office official and then, from shortly after the Revolution until 1705, a diplomat employed in Savoy, France and Switzerland. On the other hand, Sir John Werden, a pillar of the Customs for a generation, had a military pedigree. In addition to the contribution of other professions the business world supplied valuable recruits. The Cardonnel dynasty, which had branches in the War Office and the Customs and its main trunk in the Salt Office, and the Popples both came from trading families; Sir Lambert Blackwell, a prominent diplomat under William III and Anne, was 'bred a merchant' in the Italian trade; while John Scrope, Walpole's choice as successor to William Lowndes at the Treasury, was the son of a Bristol merchant and the grandson, on his mother's side, of another. One thing beyond doubt is that a number of extremely successful Augustan civil servants emerged from total or near obscurity. This was certainly true of William Blathwayt; of Thomas Everard, who worked his way up from ground level in the Excise with the aid of his 'sliding rule' and his treatise *Stereometry made Easie*, and was always regarded as something of an upstart; of Josiah Burchett, the tradesman's son from Sandwich who described himself in 1687, when temporarily out of employment, as 'a poor young man who is entirely at a loss to keep himself'; and of the incomparable Charles Sergison of the Navy Office, who had emerged from the anonymity of the dockyards and whose epitaph in Cuckfield church studiously omits all reference to his family and education. But how representative were such cases? What common denominators, if any, can be found among them and their like? Clearly the civil service was not a career closed to talents: but how 'open' was it, relatively speaking, when compared with other professions in the late seventeenth and early eighteenth centuries? At present the answers to such questions can only be speculative.

Two things we do know, however. One is that in the overwhelming majority of cases influence, sponsorship or patronage of some kind was necessary to secure an aspirant his first foothold in this new profession. There were no automatic passports to employment that could be earned either by academic study or (a few instances excepted) by serving out indentures. Neither, except in a tiny proportion of cases, could entry be bought, as commissions in the army were bought. A crucial change took place in this respect between 1680 and 1720. Some very important working offices could still be purchased before the Revolution – Blathwayt, after all, bought the Secretaryship at War in 1683 – but by 1700, outside the Royal Household, a purchasable office was almost invariably a sinecure or a quasi-sinecure. Purchase had very little bearing by the early eighteenth century on the efficiency either of the profession or of government itself. But influence was a very different matter. Even in the most open and, in some respects, democratic of all departments, the Excise (as in the later Salt and Leather Offices whose procedures were modelled on those of the Excise), every candidate for probation had to be vouched for by two citizens of some status, who were expected to act as guarantors of his good behaviour in office, to the tune of sureties of £200 each. Likewise, although entrance examinations were instituted in the Customs early in William III's reign, and passing these written and oral tests became a normal condition of acceptance for training for all duty-collecting posts, these examinations were only open to those whose candidacies had already been approved by the commissioners on the basis of recommendations received; and there seems little doubt that they were sometimes waived as a result of a word in the right ear from an influential quarter.

Yet this is just one side of the coin; and the reverse side shows us how important it is not to be misled by the obverse. However powerful the influence they could muster, most non-political entrants into the public service after the early 1690s (and many before that time) had to start on the bottom rung of the ladder. This normally meant beginning with a plain clerkship – quite often a temporary clerkship – in one of the central departments of state, or in a humble desk job in the dockyards or, after serving probation, as a rank-and-file 'revenue-man' (Excise gauger, salt officer, landwaiter, etc.) in the provinces. And the average civil servant's career ran, up to a certain point, in a fairly predictable groove: he could expect to serve a long and not very lucrative apprenticeship in the lower, if not the lowest, reaches of his office or branch of the service before, by his own efforts, in the main, he earned promotion. As such conventions consolidated, resentment against queue-jumping became marked, and not least in the revenue departments. The prevailing attitude is summed up by an incident in 1714–15. At the end of Anne's reign the department of Excise had sacked a certain Mr Ferryman, who had joined the service as a supernumerary in Hampshire in 1684 and risen to be a collector of the duties in Wales, 'for intermeddling in an election contrary to law and repeated orders': this being a rule which Harley, as Earl of Oxford and Lord Treasurer, had insisted on enforcing. The new and entirely

Whiggish Treasury Board which succeeded his regime at the beginning of George I's reign tried to replace Ferryman with a candidate who bore all the marks of being a political nominee. The Commissioners of Excise promptly objected, and in the strongest terms, their long memorial ending with the words, 'that the placing of persons who were never concerned in the revenue, at the first step into the office of Collector will not only be a discouragement to those in that service [the Excise], but to all other officers who have served long and faithfully in the revenue'. After some huffing and puffing the Treasury, under the veteran Charles Montagu, Lord Halifax, eventually concurred.

The mature Augustan civil service had this in common, therefore, with most of the other thrusting professional groups of the period, that it usually expected a lengthy apprenticeship of its new recruits. Of course, the 'apprenticeship' of new entrants into the government service was not exactly comparable with that required of attorneys, surgeons or apothecaries. For one thing, it was paid. It was also, on the whole, informal; although the practice in the Excise of appointing young men initially as 'expectants' or 'supernumeraries', and the private coaching they received from the established gaugers with the Excise Board's approval, came very close to formality in practice, as did the system of 'preferable men' which came to be adopted by the Customs Commissioners for filling positions in their London and larger outport establishments. Indeed, the formal indenturing of trainees was still practised in parts of the dockyard service, in certain branches of the Exchequer and in some of its ancillary departments, for example, the Pipe Office. All in all, therefore, the new bureaucracy as it had developed by 1700 was almost as much an apprentice-based profession in practice as was the Royal Navy, with its 'servant' or 'volunteer' streams of entry (see below, pp. 275–6, 277).

The exceptions to the rule that every entrant worked his passage had been sufficiently numerous before 1685 to excite relatively little comment (the speed with which Thomas Aram, thanks to Sir Robert Howard's powerful patronage, achieved a chief clerkship in the Treasury and the Solicitorship of the Excise in 1671–2 is a good example); but by the turn of the century they had, by and large, been brought within a fairly narrow and generally recognised compass. The very nature of committee-government gave the ministries of William III, Queen Anne and George I the chance to mix inexperienced with seasoned men on departmental boards; and this was one way (another being in the filling of specialist posts, such as cashier and office solicitor) in which men could still move directly from outside the service into administrative or executive jobs of a nonpolitical character. Young Vernon could be slotted into the Excise Commission in 1710, or Justinian Isham, eldest son of a prominent MP, on to the Board of the Leather Office in 1711, without moving up the normal pecking order, because there were enough experienced heads round each table to ensure that their early steps would be carefully guided. But it would be misleading to attach overmuch weight to the experience of these fortunates. It is significant, for example, that the only direct route on to the Navy Board after 1688 – the only route, that is, which could by-pass either the clerical causeway within the London headquarters itself or the road that led to the new Navy Office building in Crutched Friars via the dockyards – was that available to men who had already had considerable sea service behind them. Such commissioners almost invariably came to their shore appointments, like Sir Richard Haddock and George St Loe, as 'flags' or senior captains. And while there is no doubt that the role of patronage in influencing both initial appointments and promotions in the embryonic bureaucracy of Charles II's reign was a stronger one than it subsequently became, it is striking, none the less, how many even of the first generation of distinguished Augustan civil servants, who had begun their careers well before 1689, had themselves started at the bottom, as Sergison, Blathwayt, Bridgeman and Lowndes did.

How large had this new civil service become by the end of the period? And what rewards did it offer to its members? Gregory King's table of ranks and incomes (see above, p. 19) throws no helpful light on these questions: on the contrary, it befogs and distorts both issues. His estimates – of 5,000 'persons in greater offices and places', earning an average of £240 per annum, and of 5,000 lesser office-holders with mean incomes of £120 per annum – were, in any case, meant to relate only to the year 1688: so they can tell us nothing of the unprecedented wartime expansion of the bureaucracy, much of which (though not all) survived the postwar retrenchments of 1712–17. But far more important is the fact that King's figures, if they are taken seriously at all, must be applied to all 'placemen' in late-seventeenth-century England and not simply to that one category which can reasonably be labelled 'civil servants'.

In common with the compilers of the many contemporary lists of office-holders published periodically by Edward and John Chamberlayne, by Guy Miège, Abel Boyer and David Jones, as well as by a variety of anonymous writers coursing 'Country' political hares, Gregory King naturally included the occupants of what we should call 'ministerial' posts. These were those offices which, by conventions which evolved gradually after 1680 and had mostly been settled by 1714, were regarded as fair game for those whose chief concern was politics, not the service of the king's government whatever its complexion. There were not many such positions in relation to the whole spectrum of places: less than 300 all told during Queen Anne's reign. But among them, naturally enough, was a high proportion of the most lucrative jobs in the Crown's gift; and an average income figure for 'persons in greater offices and places' which includes the earnings of these politicians has no direct relevance to the salaries of 'higher' civil servants. To take one of the smaller departments as a case in point: the work of the Board of Trade in the 1720s was carried on by eight political appointees, earning £1,000 a year but subject to a fairly rapid turnover, and by nine civil servants. Two of the latter, the Secretary and Deputy Secretary, were of executive status, being paid

£500 and £200 a year respectively, while seven were clerks with salaries ranging from £80 down to £40 a year. Besides those competing for political spoils King's supposed 10,000 civil office-holders also embraced those who served the courts of common law and equity, whether in a major or minor capacity, or who were attached to one of the provincial Crown courts: legal officials, in fact, rather than government officials. Finally, and most significant numerically, there were those who had jobs in some branch or other of the Royal Household. Modern scholarship has confirmed that there was a considerable shrinkage in this sector during the seventeenth and early eighteenth centuries, from around 1,450 posts in the 1630s down to roughly 950 by George I's reign. Part of this slimming process took place after the Revolution and a reasonable guess for James II's Household might not be far short of 1,100. Of course, the Household was not hermetically sealed off from other groups of office-holders: most of its plums – the offices of Lord Chamberlain, Vice-Chamberlain, Lord Steward, Master of the Horse, Treasurer of the Chamber, and so forth – were greedily gobbled up by active politicians; and a number of its lesser sinecures were used to supplement the salaries of favoured civil servants. An early Hanoverian Receiver-General of Excise, for instance, was gratified with the post of Yeoman of the Jewel Office, while the Cashier of the Salt Office doubled up as Clerk of the Robes. Nevertheless, the vast majority of Household officials were personal servants of the Crown as opposed to public servants of the state, and the general level of their incomes was higher than the ordinary run of officials in government departments could expect.

Leaving aside its political placemen and its legal and Household functionaries, England had still accumulated a corps of public servants by the mid-1720s that numbered over 12,000 permanent employees and many more auxiliaries of one kind or another. The 'army of civil officers' referred to so apprehensively by Archibald Hutcheson, a prominent member of the House of Commons, during a debate in 1716 represented an already very substantial increase even since 1688 (let alone since 1680). And the fiscal measures of the early Walpole era, with their emphasis on greater efficiency in the Customs and on increasing the yield of internal duties, served further to consolidate the ranking of the new civil service as being, by now, one of the largest of contemporary professions. This lends credence to the calculations of Joseph Massie, who attempted in 1759 to update Gregory King's social table and estimated the number of 'civil officers' by then at 16,000, as compared with King's 10,000. As an unusually well-informed as well as prolific pamphleteer in the government's pay, Massie is unlikely to have been far astray with this particular figure; and since the size of the Royal Household and the legal bureaucracy changed very little between 1688 and 1760, and the same was true of the number of political placemen, Massie's total reflects first and foremost the swelling of the civil service, not only by two major wars between 1689 and 1713 but as a result of further long periods of warfare between 1739 and the date of his exercise.

Around 1725 there were probably close on 2,700 posts open to career officials in the London offices of the government, including diplomats serving overseas under the direction of the Secretaries of State (though not colonial administrators). A small proportion of these offices, it is true, were shared among pluralists; on the other hand, I have not counted as 'civil servants' for present purposes men in peripheral establishments such as the Heralds' Office, Greenwich Hospital or the Office of Works. At the same time, the provincial civil service in the closing years of George I contained well over 5,000 established revenue officers. These were employed by the Customs, the Salt and Stamp Offices, and by the now mammoth department of Excise which by 1725 claimed almost a third of all government officials, including some 3,250 of those stationed in the provinces. The other major provincial components of the state's civil employees were the two groups – between 4,000 and 5,000 men in all – employed under the authority of the Navy Commissioners and the Postmasters-General. The 'officers' and clerks of the six royal dockyards, local postmasters, and the agents, captains and crews of the packet boat service accounted for some 1,200 of these, and the dockyard workers for the rest. It was the latter who supplied the only major variable in the total number of the state's servants by the later 1720s, when the executive had at last settled down to a period of relative stasis. From the early 1690s onwards, even in the most peaceful conditions, the dockyards never employed less than the 3,300 men who were in pay there in 1725; so that such a number can fairly be regarded as permanent employees. But the complement could rise very sharply at the breath of an emergency, as it did in 1727 when it shot up to 4,800. As well as dockyard auxiliaries, there were many other part-time or non-established public employees in Augustan England whom I have not considered as properly a part of the new civil service – temporary clerks, sub-postmasters, supernumeraries in the Excise and the Salt Office, 'extraordinary men' and 'preferable men' in the Customs service. Their numbers ran into thousands: there were, for example, reputedly around a thousand part-time customs officers in the port of London alone by the early eighteenth century.

The Augustan state was not an ungenerous paymaster, nor an inflexible one. What is more, many thousands of its professional servants between 1680 and 1730 were able to depend on the fact that if they proved competent, conscientious and, of course, durable, their prospects of promotion at some stage were bright. Nevertheless, only a very small proportion of them, well under 10 per cent at any one period, could ever hope to achieve the relative comfort of a three-figure salary, or better. The overwhelming bulk of the government's office staff and 95 per cent of its local revenue men earned between £40 and £80 a year. Among those civil service posts whose remuneration was wholly or primarily by salary, and where that salary has been ascertained,* I have found at the end of George I's reign just 506

*This has not proved possible in a small minority of cases: namely, with the diplomats; with the clerks in the War Office or with the local Collectors responsible for some of the supplementary excises dating from Anne's reign.

which carried emoluments of £100 a year or more. In 301 cases the salary was between £100 and £190 (mostly at the bottom end), and in a further 121 cases it was between £200 and £450 a year. The select group of career bureaucrats to whom the Treasury paid £500 a year or more totalled only eighty-four, twenty-nine of whom received four-figure salaries: the two highest of all, it should be said, being up to a point artificial, in that the Comptroller and Receiver-General of Excise had to pay deputies and clerks out of their £2,020 and £2,740 per annum respectively.

However, the favoured circle was wider than these figures by themselves would suggest; for some of the most prosperous civil servants were in offices where the rewards lay entirely in fees and commission, while others – by no means an insignificant number – were allowed to take fees to boost their salaried income. Of approximately 230 posts in the Upper and Lower Exchequer in 1716, all but a tiny fraction were feed and they included many succulent offerings. Clerkships in the Privy Seal Office and the Signet Office were in the same category, though in general less sought after. The four English Under-Secretaries of State were paid solely by fees; and it is highly probable that the two principal Under-Secretaries could safely rely on more than £500 a year. The principal Secretary to the Treasury and the Chief Clerks of the Treasury carved up the fees of that department to their mutual benefit; and to the former, by the 1720s, the job must have been worth over £2,000 a year, despite having to share the profits with a Joint-Secretary, a political nominee, first appointed in 1712.

Among officials who were able most profitably to supplement their salaries from fees and poundage were a number of the Ordnance officers, the patent officers of the Customs, both in London and the outports, and virtually all the executives of the Post Office together with the six Clerks of the Road. Mr Ellis's study of the eighteenth-century Post Office has shown just how nominal some paper salaries could be as a result of such bonuses. The Secretary to the Post Office was paid annually £200 from the Treasury; but by the 1760s he was making in the region of £1,000, year in, year out, from his office. The place of Solicitor to the Post Office, officially valued at £200 per annum, was reckoned to be worth nearly three times as much, and its holder could take on private business as well. The Comptrollers of the Inland and Foreign Offices in the same department, with salaries of £200 and £150 a year after 1688, were actually earning £980 and £1,260 a year, respectively, by 1788. Even if their fees were only half as high in 1730 as they were to become by the 1780s, they still ranked with the bureaucratic élite of late Augustan England.

Important as fees still were (and continued to be until the practice came under systematic attack in the 1780s) in determining the rewards of office in old-established departments, those who profited from them represented, well before 1730, very much the exceptions to the general rule of a *salaried* profession. In every one of the new departments erected between 1671 and 1711, as well as in the earlier Navy Office, three practices were adopted from the start. All employees from top to bottom were appointed 'during pleasure' (the traditional patent offices in the Customs being the only important exception); all were paid realistic salaries; and all were forbidden to take either fees or any other payments on the side. So by 1714 the vast majority of England's civil servants were, officially at least, in this position. Their salaries were kept under review. Between the 1680s and the 1720s, but more especially after the Revolution, pay rises were a fairly frequent occurrence. Whenever the Treasury was convinced that a case had been made out (for example, on the grounds of increased work load, or on the basis of comparability) it was prepared to countenance a revision of salaries. Thus the Commissioners of the Stamp Office got a rise of £100 a year after the imposition of new stamp duties by Parliament in 1712, and many of their executives and subordinate officials were rewarded in proportion; while £40 had been added in 1704–5 to the salaries of the first seven clerks of the Ordnance Office in acknowledgment of a substantial increase in their business and to bring them into line with clerks in other war departments.

However, it was not only the salaries it offered which helped to attract, and hold, men to the civil service at a time when other professions beckoned enticingly. Many senior government officials, dockyard officers and even head clerks had rent-free lodgings or houses provided. The importance attached to this can be gauged from the fact that the Clerk of the Ordnance received a £100 supplement to his salary in lieu of the house that most of his colleagues on the Ordnance Board enjoyed, while the Clerk of the Deliveries in the same department had £40 compensation for the same reason. Another more widespread and persuasive perquisite was the remission of land tax payments for virtually all government employees with salaries of £80 or less, and for many earning up to £100: this came about as a result of a series of concessions by the Treasury between the later 1690s and the middle years of Anne. In addition, a serious attempt was made by most large departments, with Treasury blessing, to guarantee some recognition for long and faithful service, not only by offering fair prospects of promotion but by insulating retiring officials against penury in old age. A pioneering contributory pension scheme for the Excise was inaugurated as early as February 1687, and by 1713 roughly half of the established posts in the entire civil service were superannuable. At the same time, in many departments which lacked organised pension schemes, such as the Ordnance, informal arrangements were often made to take care of deserving cases.

Few officials who reached the higher plateaux of the profession, however, and who stayed there for any length of time had need of protection against the buffets of fate as they drew close to retirement. One of the tiny handful of Augustan civil servants whose careers have been studied in any detail is Charles Delafaye, who gave nearly forty years of service to the state, beginning as an unpaid temporary clerk in 1697 and culminating in seventeen years as an Under-Secretary of State. His burial memorial was explicitly worded to 'remind his neighbours that piety, honesty and industry will secure a fair character, a comfortable subsistence here, and everlasting felicity hereafter'. Whether the splendid confidence about his after-life was justified we cannot know. But, beyond doubt, Delafaye's subsistence throughout the second half of his career could have been described as 'comfortable' without fear of distortion. J. C. Sainty tells us that before he resigned his place in the Duke of Newcastle's office in 1734 after a bout of ill-health he had acquired the lease of a property in Whichbury, and to that he retired. An Under-Secretaryship could be worth anything from £400 to £500 a year; and Delafaye's savings during his active years, plus the profits from various sinecures he secured in the 1720s – one of which, the Clerkship of the Signet, was a useful pension in its own right – ensured that his unexpectedly long retirement, down to the age of 85, would be handsomely provided for. They also enabled him to build up a large collection of books, mathematical instruments and antiques. For a man whose Huguenot immigrant father had had a salary of no more than £52 a year as French translator of the *Gazette* the new bureaucracy had proved a wise choice of profession.

The indications are that only a tiny minority of Delafaye's predecessors and colleagues in the permanent bureaucracy between the 1680s and the 1730s were able – or chose – to buy estates of any size or to build fine houses; the number who did both was minimal. It was 1733 before James Vernon junior purchased an estate (and that a small one, for which he paid £15,000), although it is true that he had five years earlier inherited land in Lincolnshire worth £200 a year. For most, of course, social aspirations had to be trimmed to the demands of their work and this usually meant living either in London itself or no further away than the residential towns or villages on its outskirts. Greenwich and Blackheath became popular settlements for civil servants, especially Ordnance and Navy Office officials, as well as for retired army and navy officers. Adam de Cardonnel bought a house at Chiswick and Josiah Burchett inherited one at Hampstead, where Richard Houlditch of the Stamp Office and Sir Philip Ryley also lived. Even such relatively mild suburban splendours were not normally within the means of a London government clerk, although the prosperity to which chief clerks in some departments might eventually aspire, if they were lucky, and which the Treasury and the Exchequer allowed to all their clerks, given time, is clear enough from occasional evidence which comes to light. Peter Leheup, who was an Under Clerk in the Treasury for thirty-one years from 1721, was in a position to lend £4,500 to the government when England became involved in the Austrian Succession War. One of his predecessors in the office, Thomas Bendish (Under Clerk from 1694 until his death in June 1710), had a house in Hatton Garden, a fashionable street: it gave him and his family an armchair view – too close for comfort – of the ugly Sacheverell riots of March 1710. And the competition for places in the Exchequer can be understood when we read that John Grainger, a First Clerk and Deputy Teller there under Anne and George I, subscribed £5,000 to a land tax loan in 1720 and owned £10,000 of Bank of England stock in 1724.

The involvement of civil servants in the City or in 'the Funds' in the early decades of London's financial revolution ranged from small investments by clerks, such as Thomas Jett and Edmund Ball of the Exchequer, to the heavy buying of Bank stock by John Taylour, First Secondary in the Lord Treasurer's Remembrancer's Office (he owned £20,000 worth by 1724). Three other government officials with heavy commitments in the City were the diplomat Sir Lambert Blackwell, Francis Hawes of the Navy Treasurer's Office and later of the Customs, and Richard Houlditch, all three of whom became directors of the South Sea Company before the Bubble of 1720. Other investments, as well as stock, shares and government bonds, attracted the new men of government. Several of them were, like Delafaye, avid collectors; this was true of Blathwayt, Francis Hawes and, not least, of Burchett, who had accumulated a houseful of Old Masters by the time he retired. Sir Philip Ryley operated in the property market on a very broad front. His will shows that when he died he owned, in addition to a country estate on which he had his principal seat and his suburban house at Hampstead, the tithes and advowsons of Little Hockham; a house in Thetford 'and the shopyard against it'; other lands in Norfolk and Suffolk; the Bear Inn at Hampstead; and other miscellaneous parcels of real estate, as well as having the lease of a town residence in very select company in Dover Street.

The small group of higher civil servants who used professional success to buy their way into the landed squirearchy, as Sergison and Lyddell of the Navy Office did in the early 1690s, were often among those who had travelled farthest socially; although this was not so of Sir Basil Dixwell, long-serving Auditor of the Excise, who had a seat near Canterbury with gardens that John Macky thought 'worth seeing'; nor was it the case with Lambert Blackwell – of Irish gentry extraction and the son of a governor of Pennsylvania – who built up estates worth £4,000 a year in Norfolk between 1700 and 1720 (many of them acquired, it is true, after he had left the diplomatic service in 1705). Neither was it the case with Temple Stanyon, the younger son of a Middlesex gentleman and younger brother of another well-known diplomat, who became a long-serving Under-Secretary of State and acquired a fine country seat in Oxfordshire. Charles Sergison and Dennis Lyddell bought ready-made manor houses at Cuckfield and Wakehurst, and so did Francis Hawes at Purley, near Reading, and Philip Ryley (son of a failed barrister) at Great Hockham in Norfolk. But just a handful had both the means and the ambition to build for themselves on a substantial scale. William Lowndes, having bought his Buckinghamshire manor of Winslow in 1697, soon after his promotion to the Secretaryship of the Treasury, commissioned Sir Christopher Wren to design him a house of elegant simplicity and London and Wise to landscape its grounds. The 'delicious seat' and gardens at Totteridge into which John Charlton ploughed the profits of thirteen years in the Ordnance Office, sixteen in the Royal Household and a brief spell in the Excise, was thought by Defoe to outshine that of his noble neighbour, the Earl of Anglesey. But it was left to just one civil servant, William Blathwayt, the grand factotum of the bureaucracy, to erect a mansion that would bear comparison with anything planted in the English landscape by a professional man in his lifetime. The baroque grandeur of Dyrham Park in Gloucestershire was, and has remained, the supreme monument to the arrival of the civil service on the social stage.

Blathwayt himself, however, was unique in more than one sense among professional servants of the central government in this period. No other official remotely approached the total of £4,415 which his biographer has estimated he drew annually between 1694 and 1700 from his remarkable agglomeration of offices. At the very opposite end of the scale it might seem natural to assume that the social impact of provincial officialdom, despite its ever-extending arm between 1680 and 1725, was negligible. Yet it was not. A weighty consideration was the extent to which the lower cost of living outside London enhanced the relative value of salaries paid to provincially based civil servants. In the second decade of the eighteenth century, for instance, the 188 Supervisors of the liquor excise, who received £90 a year with £10 riding allowance, were nearly all better off in real terms than the Secretary of the Leather Office and the Comptroller of the Leather Duties in London, both in 1717 earning salaries of £115 a year. Neither had they any reason to envy the third clerk in the Admiralty Office, despite his £120 a year. In the larger outports, the Collectors of Customs were men of considerable substance, at least as comfortably circumstanced as the Excise Supervisors and sometimes more so. The Collector of Customs at Newcastle upon Tyne, though he ranked only third to his counterparts at Bristol and Liverpool, was still counted a wealthy man in his own society, even if he had to pay the wages of a clerk out of the £190 he earned in 1723 (£20 was the going rate for a local clerk). The Collectors of Milford Haven and Bideford were sitting pretty on £100 a year each; while Thomas Kennedy at Topsham – the port of Exeter – with his £90 and Hugh Mason, esquire, at Hull (£110 for himself and a clerk) could keep up a gentleman's lifestyle in Devon and Yorkshire in the 1720s with little difficulty. Many a Devonshire squire, as Professor Hoskins has shown, had a lower income than Kennedy, and their expenses, in nine cases out of ten, would be higher. In fact the Augustan civil servant had this in common with his fellow professionals in the law, medicine, the Church and the liberal arts: his social profile could not be captured solely in the metropolis and, through rare estate purchases, in the county society of the south. Before 1730 the new man of government had become, if as yet only in a modest way, a social personage in the provincial town as well.

9

The Armed Services of the Crown

I The Army Officers

There is ample evidence that in the course of the 1690s and of the first decade of the eighteenth century the existing social hierarchy grew acutely aware of the rapid advance of a new class of public servants. One of the clearest indications we have of this are the attempts that were made through the House of Commons to ensure that the activities of this class remained professional and not political. Despite various setbacks, the successful exclusion from the House from 1694 onwards of Stamp officers, officials of the Customs and of the Excise and Salt Offices, and finally in 1706 of the Navy Commissioners in the Outports and the chief executives of four other small departments represented a notable victory for this principle. These measures made a major contribution, as we saw, to the future professionalisation of the civil service; and so, too, did an equally important clause in the Regency Act of 1706 which excluded from the Lower House the holders of all freshly created offices, a provision which brought in its first harvest in 1711 when some 500 officials of the Leather Office were barred from a political career.

After the qualified victory of the Country members in the struggle with the ministry over the Regency Bill, Sir John Cropley, MP for Shaftesbury, had boasted: 'I defy any sessions to pass without bills and divisions against the army and household'. In February 1708 another Country Whig, James Lowther of Whitehaven, was confident that those army officers who were by then crowding the benches of the Commons during the non-campaigning months of every winter would 'certainly be routed sooner or later'. Cropley and Lowther were to be proved wrong. For after the successes of the years 1694–1706 all efforts to force through further place legislation in the second half of Anne's reign were frustrated; and because of this all attempts to extend the parliamentary exclusion of 'officers' from the civil to the armed services of the Crown came to nothing.

Although an abortive measure of 1705 had the design of bringing naval as well as army officers into its net, it was the dramatic climb of the latter to social as well as political prominence since the Revolution which aroused most controversy. To thousands of country gentlemen this seemed by the middle of the second of the wars against Louis XIV a particularly dangerous threat both to the foundations of the old social structure and to the constitution – more dangerous in many eyes than the rise of the bureaucrats. 'Though the civil officers should not be increased,' complained Edward Wortley Montagu in the Commons in January 1710, 'the continuance of the war must make the military officers more numerous and more powerful . . . Promotions may be made every day in the old regiments, and new ones raised, and a very great share of these preferments falls to this House.' The rapid accumulation of wealth by careerist colonels and generals of the army was as politically undesirable as it was socially unacceptable:

> Those who have no other fortune, depending on the war, than the command of a regiment, have nothing else to do but to make a proper disposition in the clothing of it; by which means such an interest may be made in most of the corporations as no gentleman in the country is able to resist . . . The heavier the [war] debt is upon the nation, the more of those who receive the public money will sit here, and impose the taxes out of which they are paid.

It is sometimes thought that such sentiments were the preserve of the backwoods Tories. Yet Cropley, Lowther and Wortley Montagu were all staunch Whigs. The ground swell against the 'military men' was as much a social as a political phenomenon. It is true, however, that the longer the Spanish Succession War lasted, the more the commanding influence of the Marlborough circle over promotions seemed to most civilian observers to be favouring officers of committed Whig views; and this explains why it was the Tory squire, in particular, striving as often as not to maintain his own income and status, who tended to link army officers with 'monied men' as the most baleful social legacy of the long struggle against France. It was on such Tory prejudices that Swift unerringly played in his early numbers of the *Examiner* in the winter of 1710–11.

> It is odd, that among a free trading people, as we call ourselves, there should so many be found to close in with those counsels, who have been ever averse from all overtures towards a peace. But yet there is no great mystery in the matter. Let any man observe the equipages in this town; he shall find the greater number of those who make a figure to be a species of men quite different from any that were ever known before the Revolution; consisting either of Generals and Colonels, or of such whose whole fortunes lie in funds and stocks: so that power, which according to the old maxim was used to follow land, is now gone over to money; and the country gentleman is in the condition of a young heir, out of whose estate a scrivener receives half the rents for interest, and hath a mortgage on the whole, and is therefore

always ready to feed his vices and extravagancies while there is any thing left. So that if the war continue some years longer, a landed man will be little better than a farmer at a rack rent, to the army and to the publick funds.

Just as 'a new interest' had been created in the City by 1709, and, as St John put it, 'a sort of property which was not known twenty years ago' had threatened to undermine the old divine right of landed property in society and politics, so likewise since the 1680s a new profession had carved out a large place for itself that was almost as disturbing to traditional values.

Partly it was the exceedingly rapid growth in the sheer size of this profession that lay behind much of the alarm. By the peak years of the army's strength in the Spanish Succession War, when the number of native British troops reached roughly 70,000, there were well over six times as many active commissioned officers as there had been at the end of Charles II's reign. There were more than 3,000 in the foot regiments and foot guards alone, and some 3,600 in the foot and horse together; and this took no account of the officers of the Horse Guards and Horse Grenadiers, units which were not regimentally organised. The officers of the independent companies (each company had three or four), plus officers of marines, the artillery men and the engineers accounted for several hundred more. As the end of the war approached hopes were widely entertained of a dramatic relief from the encroaching tide of military men. 'I hope every gentleman here is satisfied', Wortley Montagu had told the Commons in 1710, 'that, in time of peace, we shall want no greater number of men for guards and garrisons than before the war.' But two circumstances combined to demonstrate in the years down to 1730 how over-sanguine hopes of this kind had been. One factor was the series of emergencies and alerts which caused Parliament to vote an army estimate for 1716 of 36,000 men, led Walpole to insist in 1722 on a 50 per cent increase in the home establishment to 18,000, and caused a further substantial rise to 26,000 in 1727–30. Even in the three years 1719–21, when the estimates were down almost to post-Ryswick levels, many extra regiments (as at all times in the early Hanoverian period) were, as Fortescue put it, 'hidden away' in Ireland. The second factor was much more basic: the final acceptance of a fully fledged, organised, half-pay system for the holders of the king's commission. An early prototype of this system had operated for the few true 'regulars' even in the post-Restoration army, and such retentions became common practice during the French wars after 1689. But the system was only institutionalised for the peacetime army in consequence of a vital Commons' resolution of 1713 and the queen's response to it, to the effect that

Whereas upon the disbanding of our forces, we have thought fit that half pay shall be allowed to the commission officers who shall by that means be discharged our service until they shall again be provided for therein; which it is our royal intention they shall be in the first vacancies that may happen amongst our forces that shall be kept on foot, in preference to all other persons.

It was because of the half-pay system that the periodic contractions of the army from 1712 onwards (by 1714 it was already down from over 100,000 to under 30,000) were not accompanied by a proportional contraction of the profession. Hundreds of officers, of course, were never employed again, even in periods of partial remobilisation such as 1715–16 and 1727–9; and there were others, as we shall see, who were not even retained, because their allegiance seemed suspect to the new Whig masters after 1714. But the majority of the army officers who were still on active service when fighting ceased in the Spanish Succession War in 1712 were kept on the new king's payroll. And for the fortunate among them those precious interludes of activity in George I's reign and in the early years of his successor provided the opportunity to scramble from the slippery lower rungs of the army ladder to the firmer upper rungs of the older and permanently established regiments.

To illustrate this process we may take at random one of a profusion of case histories that can be pieced together from Dalton's invaluable lists: that of a man with few strings to pull, for whom the wars of 1689–1713 brought no startling promotion and who had patiently to wait a very long time for all his opportunities. William Brereton was commissioned as a young ensign in the Horse Grenadiers in 1695. Perhaps because others blocked his path he moved first to the dragoons and then to the infantry. In August 1710 he at last reached the rank of captain, in Bradshaigh's regiment of foot, but since this was disbanded in 1713 he found himself on half-pay for more than two years. The impending Jacobite rebellion gave him his next chance and from July 1715 he spent three years as a captain in James Tyrrell's freshly raised regiment of dragoons. But it was not until 1722, after four more years on half-pay, that Brereton at last found a permanent niche, in the 2nd troop of Horse Grenadiers where he at length got a captaincy in 1734. He was still in harness, then a major, when the Horse Grenadiers went to Flanders during the Austrian Succession War and was wounded at Fontenoy, fifty years after he had been first commissioned. But he recovered, and on 9 April 1746 a lifetime of professional service was rewarded with promotion to the rank of lieutenant-colonel.

Under the early Hanoverians, therefore, the half-pay system, for all its undoubted faults, represented a lifeline for the individual officer. But far more than that, it maintained cohesion in a profession whose future was now effectually assured. It also benefited the army by ensuring that a very large pool of war-seasoned experience could be drawn on right through George I's reign. In fact an Army List published privately in 1740 shows that a surprisingly high number of officers who had begun their careers during the wars against Louis XIV were still in military employment in the twilight of the Walpole era. It was not, however, until the mid-1740s that the strength of the active 'officer corps' again approached the levels of 1711–12. Even by 1759, the *annus mirabilis* of the Seven Years' War, it has been calculated that there were not far in excess of 4,000 commissioned officers serving, although, again, this number did not include officers in the artillery and the engineers. And when in 1759 Joseph Massie tried to estimate the size of the profession in normal times the total he arrived at was no more than 2,000 active serving officers. With such perspectives we can well understand how startling the mushroom growth of this new profession must have seemed to the post-Revolution generation – from 300 to roughly 4,000 in the space of thirty years after 1679 – and why it disturbed yet more deeply the many still alive then who had been reared on that deep antipathy to standing armies, bred in the bone of later Stuart England by the experience of the New Model.

Yet it was not just the size of the profession but its wealth, or at least the wealth of its upper ranks, to which Englishmen had become so sensitive by the closing years of Queen Anne. Of obvious relevance to the rewards which a military career could offer by this time were two distinctive circumstances of the years from 1689 to 1712 which were closely related. One was that by pre-Revolution standards, and similarly by the later standards of 1713–39, prospects of promotion in the army of William III and Queen Anne were exceptionally good: and they beckoned not merely the aristocratic sprig and every other well-connected youth who had a pair of colours bought him during the French wars but, in some degree, many other newly commissioned ensigns and cornets or established lieutenants and captains. There were certainly no fortunes to be made low down in the hierarchy of regimental officers; and it was with this majority in mind that Massie was to put the average income in the profession in the mid-eighteenth century at £100 a year. A captain in a cavalry regiment might, if he were paid all he was owed (an unlikely contingency at most times in our period), receive about £400 for a full year's service; but over half of that was by way of allowances for forage and servants. A lieutenant of foot was lucky to get £85 in a year, and even a captain in a foot regiment, though credited with a nominal £180, was expected to devote a quarter of his pay to the maintenance of three servants. It was consequently of prime importance to every subaltern, lieutenant and captain, as it was higher up the scale, too, that for some twenty years new units continually proliferated in the army, and that potential rivals were regularly removed by death and disablement in action and by the diseases that were the scourge of most campaigning theatres. For an ambitious officer finding himself in a position comparable with that of Robert Carr in 1706, 'who is the youngest captain in Sir Charles Hotham's regiment and sees little chance of promotion, not being a neighbour or relation of Sir Charles, as are most of the other captains', there were new regiments regularly being formed to which he had a chance to transfer. Carr himself used the offices of his brother William, the Newcastle merchant and MP, in his bid to procure such a move.

The other singular element in the post-Revolution situation was the unprecedented number of general officers which the wars threw up, plus the fact that most of them were able to draw their rank allowances for periods that were equally without precedent. By the beginning of

1710 the British army found itself with no fewer than sixty-eight generals, and their allowances (paid only while the officers were on service) ranged from 10s a day for brigadiers and £2 a day for major-generals up to £10 a day for commanders-in-chief. Even when not on service, generals still drew their double pay as colonels of regiments and commanders of companies (which virtually all of them were) together with the various allowances and perquisites – forage money, clothing money, servants' allowances – which the conventions of the service allowed all colonels to accumulate. There were at least a hundred full colonels by 1710, and their standard 'pay of rank' in foot and marine regiments, the barest bones of their emoluments, was still 12s a day, as it had been in the peacetime army, on top of which they drew a further 8s a day for their companies and 4s for servants. A company of guards was an even more valuable perquisite for a general, – as it was for a more junior officer. When James Stanhope, then only 22 years of age, secured such a company in 1695, his father rated its value to him as '£600 to £700 a year, and honour equal to the degree of a colonel'.

There were some remarkable mass promotions of general officers in both the French wars, but especially in 1706 and 1710. On 9 May 1710 Luttrell noted: 'Her Majesty has made a promotion of general officers, viz. 13 lieutenant generals, 22 majors general, and 24 brigadiers.' It was Marlborough's last fling; and largely as a result of it the number of general officers three years after the end of the Spanish Succession War stood at eighty-four, of whom forty-one were brigadiers-general. Many had risen to general's rank with enviable rapidity. Lord Shannon set probably the hottest pace of all. Having entered the Horse Guards as a cornet in February 1694 he was promoted a major by 1696 after two campaigns in Flanders, and by 1709 he was a lieutenant-general. Philip Honywood joined an ordinary foot regiment in the same year as Shannon, was colonel of the 68th Foot by 1709 and a brigadier-general by 1710. Shannon, who eventually became a field-marshal under George II, admittedly had a flying start. As a Boyle, grandson of an Irish peer and successor to a viscountcy himself in 1702, he owed his opening in the Horse Guards to family influence; but it is fair to add that over the next fifteen years he fought with great distinction in both the Low Countries and the Peninsula. By contrast, Honywood had no exceptional family pull; his elder brother was an ordinary country gentlemen with an estate in Kent and another in Essex. The main stroke of fortune in his career (and, as we shall see, it was to prove double-edged) was to become a Marlborough protégé. But, in or out of fortune, he remained a committed professional and he was to command a division at Dettingen in 1743.

Although facility of promotion, rapidity of turnover and the infla-tion of the generals' list all played their part, the unique opportunities the army could offer during the French wars to Swift's 'species of men quite different from any that were known before the Revolution' were also shaped by the operation of the purchase system. Throughout the wars, except in the artillery and the engineers, this system remained substantially intact. William III, like George I after him, was hostile to the buying and selling of commissions, and the practice was, in theory, forbidden by royal warrant from 1693–5 and from 1705–11, and by statute from 1695–1700. But the natural desire of existing holders of commissions to protect their property rights in investments already made proved far stronger than the fear of perjury, and both William's and Anne's governments had to content themselves with eliminating some of the worst abuses. In Anne's reign it probably cost the average father between £150 and £200 to procure for his son an ensign's commission in a regiment of the line, and in a crack regiment the outlay could be more than double that amount. Yet lack of substantial private means was certainly not the barrier to professional advance which it subsequently became under George II. For one thing, the need for young ensigns and lieutenants to stock hastily raised new regiments was on numerous occasions too desperate for colonels to insist on an unreasonably high initial sum; and, for another, promotions on the battlefield into dead men's shoes enabled many officers on campaign to evade paying the price of at least some of their subsequent changes of rank. And although in the years that followed the Peace of Utrecht George I failed to realise his unconcealed wish to abolish the 'merchandise' in commissions, he and his ministers did succeed in authorising an official tariff of prices not to be exceeded, the cheapest of which was £170 for an ensigncy in a foot regiment on foreign or colonial service. They also managed to protect the right of men on the half-pay list to succeed to vacancies in the teeth of competition from the fatter purses of others; while queue-jumping was also checked, and professional standards were further safeguarded, by a regulation of 1720 that promotion to captain's rank must be preceded by at least ten years' service as a subaltern.

Even a cursory glance down the generals' and colonels' lists of 1708–23 reveals, as one would expect in the circumstances, that a good aristocratic or wealthy gentry pedigree remained no small advantage to the career officer under the last Stuart and the first Hanoverian. Yet they are far from being exclusive catalogues of Campbells, Hamiltons, Stanhopes, Lumleys, Cholmondeleys, Seymours, Butlers, Windsors, Suttons, and the like. Indeed, if the lists bear one mark more prominently than any other it is not the domination of the profession by the great landed families so much as the dominant influence of the Duke of Marlborough over higher promotions in the years between 1702 and 1710. The case of one beneficiary, Honywood, has been noticed already. Those who knew him as a dyed-in-the-wool Whig, and later rejoiced that he was one of the three Whig generals forced to sell their regiments for drinking damnation to Harley's ministry in the winter of 1710, found it not entirely coincidental that he was given his most significant hand up the ladder in 1709–10 when Whig influence with the Captain-General was at its height. If his social advantages were not conspicuous, the other two Marlboroughites involved in what St John called the 'licentious insolence' of December 1710 started with even fewer. And, like their colleague, both had profited to the full from war's open-handed bounty to durable and talented professional soldiers: George Maccartney to reach the rank of brigadier by 1705 and major-general five years later, and Thomas Meredith to rise to a captaincy by 1691, to major-general's rank by 1707 and to a lieutenant-generalship by January 1709. Their friend William Cadogan's ascent was even giddier. An 18-year-old cornet at the Boyne in 1690, he was a major before the age of 29 and thereafter, as Marlborough's quartermaster, rose meteorically. He was still only 36 when he was made a lieutenant-general on New Year's Day 1709. How powerful the Churchill network was can also be seen from the experience of Metcalf Graham, who needed only nine years from his first commission in Cadogan's regiment of horse in 1702 to become a colonel of horse and adjutant-general to the forces in Flanders. As one of Marlborough's favourite aides-de-camp he was picked to carry the news of Malplaquet to England in 1709 and, at the duke's request, received £500 out of the Treasury for his pains.

The number of obscure family names in the 1710 and 1716 lists of general officers published in John Chamberlayne's *Magnae Britanniae Notitia* is particularly striking. Except during the Interregnum there were few, in any, periods before the final illegalisation of purchase in 1871 when the self-made man flourished in the army to the extent that he did for the quarter-century after the 1688 Revolution. Maccartney, Cadogan and Thomas Whetham, another beneficiary of the Marlborough regime who took fifteen years to reach the rank of major by 1700 but after Anne's accession never looked back, were just three successful careerists who came of plain bourgeois stock, mercantile or legal. Defoe was later to reflect with special pride in *The Complete English Tradesman* how 'in the late wars . . . was our army full of excellent soldiers who went from the shop, and behind the counter, into the camp, and who distinguished themselves by their merits and gallant behaviour! as colonel Pierce, [Generals] Wood, Richards, and several others that may be named'. He could easily have cited others: General Sabine, for example, whose family had been in trade in Canterbury and Phineas Bowles, younger son of a London glass manufacturer, who got a lieutenant-colonelcy with great rapidity at the end of the war and was to end his career as a lieutenant-general in the 1740s. Among the generals of the Spanish Succession War there were many more who rose from social anonymity largely on the strength of their conduct in the Flanders campaigns of William III and Marlborough: Cornelius Wood, for instance, a country clergyman's son from Staffordshire; Sir Charles O'Hara, later General Lord Tyrawley, who was given his first chance in the army in Charles II's reign through having been a private tutor in the household of the Earl of Ossory; or Charles Wills, the general who checked the Jacobites' southward march at Preston in 1715, who was one of the six sons of a debt-harassed Cornish yeoman.

What was perhaps more important still, in terms both of social mobility and of the gradual, grudging acceptance of a permanent military profession by the tax-paying squirearchy, the Augustan army became a much-favoured resort for the younger sons of impoverished gentry. Its commissioned ranks absorbed numerous hopefuls whose families could not pay to educate them expensively but could scrape together purchase money at the bargain rates of the 1690s and the early 1700s. Some, like the celebrated George Wade, fought their way to the top by both character and ability. Others did so by sheer dogged determination. Joseph Wightman, the major-general who played a prominent part in mopping up the Highlands at the end of the 'Fifteen, was a third son from a very minor landed family in Kent, and no military genius: just, in Marlborough's view, 'a very careful and diligent officer'. Yet he got to major-general's rank in almost exactly eighteen years, after starting at the bottom in December 1690. Many others, less happy in their accidents or timing, just missed the flood-tide before the Peace of Utrecht arrived and drastically slowed down the pace of promotion. Such was the lot of Archibald Hamilton, eighth son of a Donegal squire, who battled his way slowly up from a cornetcy in 1688 to a lieutenant-colonelcy in September 1711, having had the bad luck in the meantime to be captured at Almanza. Unfortunately his unit was disbanded in 1712, so that although he got back on to the regular establishment in 1715 it was 1732 before he got a regiment of his own and 1739 before he became a brigadier. And we cannot doubt that there must have been many, too, from shadowy backgrounds, embedded deep in the substrata of the profession, who lacked the ability or the drive or the money or the connections to rise at all. John McQueen was commissioned an ensign in the Royal Scots in May 1694. He saw action enough in both wars in the Low Countries and was wounded at the Schellenberg. But he had to wait until 1704 to get lieutenant's rank and until 1717 before he was made a captain. He had risen no higher when, still in the same regiment, he left the service in the late 1730s.

Social groups apart, two sources, in particular, supplied a notably high proportion of the successful professional soldiers of the French wars and after. First, Ireland proved a fertile seed-bed, and has remained so to this day. Of those mentioned already who attained general-officer rank in Anne's reign or later, Shannon, Maccartney, Meredith, Wade, Cadogan, Bowles and Hamilton were all of Irish birth. But so, too, were William Steuart (a full general by 1711–14), Charles Cholmondeley, John Pepper, Robert Echlin, Thomas Pearce, Richard Ingoldsby and Lord Barrimore. The list is not exhaustive. Secondly, by the middle and later stages of the wars family traditions of military service, already of importance even in Charles II's few standing regiments, were becoming a source of great value in supplying the large mid-Augustan army with new officers. With the Cornwalls, the Bowleses, the Handasydes, Godfreys and Braddocks, as with Carpenters, Cadogans, Killigrews, Dormers, Hothams and Molesworths, sons followed fathers, or younger brothers followed elder, often in a lifelong career. Patient research would undoubtedly uncover numerous other examples, especially in the unpublicised lower and middle reaches of the profession. It is quite possible that between 1690 and 1740 they ran into hundreds.

Was the wealth and importance of the new generation of army

grandees as great or their lifestyle as pretentious as the groans of the landed gentry appear to affirm? One useful indicator is the number of officers who found their way into Parliament. Certainly the civilians did not exaggerate the extent to which 'military men' invaded the House of Commons, especially from the later years of William III onwards. In the last brief Parliament of William, technically a peacetime Parliament, thirty-nine army officers sat. After the Spanish Succession War, despite the existence on the statute book of the Landed Qualifications Act (1711) which had been partly aimed against them, they appeared in no less strength than they had mustered in the notorious Whig Parliament of 1708–10. 'Between the army and the City', wrote John Ward despondently in 1715, 'there's very little room left for the country gentleman.' To that Parliament, which lasted until 1722, fifty-eight officers were elected and in that of 1722–7 there were only five fewer. They constituted about 10 per cent of the entire House. By this time, if not invariably in Anne's reign, most of them were duly qualified by land purchase with at least the £300 a year in real estate stipulated by law. Indeed, the great estates and houses of the generals, so often observed by travellers of the later Augustan years, seemed to hard-pressed country gentry not so much new embellishments to be admired as unambiguous tokens of the unseemly prosperity which long years of hostilities had brought to the profession of arms. 'Behind the park [at Greenwich] is a large plain called Black Heath, where are several gentleman's seats, very fine', wrote Macky at the beginning of George I's reign: 'Mr Sims, a famous gamester, hath a very noble one, and well kept. Lieutenant-General Withers, General Palm[e]s, Brigadier Richards, and several others whom we have known abroad, have each their pleasant retreats here.' There were flourishing plantations to the west of London, too: Maccartney and Major-General 'Jack' Hill, the brother of Queen Anne's favourite, Abigail Masham, had properties and houses side by side in Egham, though politics must have made them uncongenial neighbours; while habitués of Richmond were familiar with a splendid house on the Green, with its own private ballroom attached, built by Colonel William Duncombe of the Guards.

But the broad acres, and quite frequently the splendid new mansions, of the military men were also well in evidence by the first two decades of the eighteenth century far beyond the peripheries of the Home Counties. Richard Sutton, Colonel of the 19th Foot until he was forced to sell out on suspicion of Jacobitism in 1715, returned to his native Nottinghamshire in Anne's reign to buy the Scofton estate near Worksop and soon afterwards the manor of Kelham, which gave him virtual control of a parliamentary seat at Newark. It is not recorded what his new neighbours felt about the close proximity of a man whose 'atheistical, debauched' reputation earned him, while governor of Hull, the nickname 'governor of Hell'. In Wiltshire, close to the little borough of Ludgershall which he represented, Lieutenant-General John Richmond Webb, the battle-scarred hero of Wynendael, erected Biddendon House in 1711. He did so on land which he had bought there as long ago as 1692, after seven years in the army and three as a captain and lieutenant-colonel of the Grenadier Guards, though presumably with some of his new wife's money to help him. The generals certainly had no lack of company from colonels, lieutenant-colonels and occasionally even majors in jostling in the queue for property, and at times building country houses or standing for Parliament. Colonel Thomas Stringer, an infantry officer whose main claim to fame was as a duellist, bought an estate at Sharlston in Yorkshire; though the fact that he sat for Clitheroe at various times between 1698 and 1706 was due less to his own interest than to that of his father, an extremely wealthy lawyer said to have made £30,000 as a practiser and cursitor in the Court of Chancery. By 1718 James Tyrrell, colonel of a regiment of dragoons but not yet a general, had completed Shotover Park in Oxfordshire which his father, historian and Whig squire, had started to build just after the Spanish Succession War. Similarly, Henry Hawley, who was later to come into prominence as a general who fought at Dettingen and Fontenoy in the 1740s, built West Green House in Hampshire at much the same period as Tyrrell and while still a lieutenant-colonel in the 4th Hussars.

These were quite small pickings, however, compared with the great landed properties, and sometimes honours, which accrued to those who had already achieved professional distinction by the end of the war and whose careers continued to gather momentum thereafter. William Cadogan made a vast fortune, bought the Caversham estate near Reading in Berkshire, became a baron in 1716 and two years later an earl. General Carpenter, too, got a peerage, though in his case an Irish one, and having early acquired property in Ireland with the proceeds of his wife's portion in 1703, eventually settled at Longwood House in Hampshire. Maccartney, it is true, died in a state of near-bankruptcy in 1730, despite having been cleared of the Duke of Hamilton's murder, restored to lieutenant-general's rank in 1716, given the colonelcy of the Royal Scots Fusiliers and eventually the general command of the forces in Ireland. Also, when Major-General Joseph Wightman died suddenly of a stroke at Bath in 1722 his daughter was forced to petition George I for relief on the ground that 'her mother and she were left in a sad and deplorable condition, lacking even the barest necessities of life'. But these were exceptional cases. Maccartney had been a dissolute prodigal all his life, and while 'poor Jo. Wightman' was a brave and apparently capable officer he had been prey to a series of misfortunes. Most of their contemporaries on the generals' list trod the primrose path. Joseph Sabine, for instance, bought the Tewin estate in Hertfordshire in 1715 and is said to have spent £40,000 rebuilding the house and furnishing it in princely style. Orkney acquired the showy palace in Berkshire built in Charles II's reign for Buckingham of the Cabal; and Major-General Whetham, on land in Middlesex close to Postmaster-General Frankland's house at Sutton Court 'hath built a most magnificent seat of free-stone', it was said in 1714, 'and is laying out also spacious gardens'. Wade, by contrast, preferred the town life of Bath where he bought a fine house in Abbey Courtyard and, as befitted his position as Member of Parliament for the borough from 1722 to 1748, became a lavish benefactor both of the corporation and the inhabitants.

It was provincial towns with good amenities, well patronised by the leisured gentry and professional men but not too costly to live in, that became magnets after 1713 for that essentially new phenomenon, the half-pay officer. John Macky in the two volumes of his *Journey*, published in 1714 and 1722, paints some deft pictures of these gentlemen – presumably captains and majors, for the most part, with some of the better-off lieutenants and here and there a leavening of lieutenant-colonels – enjoying good company cheaply and hanging out for rich wives: at worst, targets for mild satire, but certainly not objects for that vituperative alarm which the 'military men' had aroused in 'Country' circles in the last war. At Stamford, which 'abounds with good company', Macky 'saw at the coffee-house several officers in half-pay, who retired hither for cheapness and sport'. He also found such weekly assemblies as those at Salisbury and Winchester

> very convenient for young people; for formerly the country ladies were stewed up in their fathers old mansion houses, and seldom saw company, but at an Assize, a horse-race or a fair. But by the means of these assemblies, matches are struck up, and the officers of the army have had pretty good success, where ladies are at their own disposal; as I know several instances about Worcester, Shrewsbury, Chester, Derby and York.

One military conquest – though by a serving officer, not a half-pay man – was related to Timothy Thomas when he arrived in Doncaster with Lord Oxford's retinue in 1725. He found cavalry quartered in the town and troopers' horses grazing by the river; 'but their commanding officer, Colonel Foley, was then absent, having the day before married a wife, Mrs Sunderland, a young lady of about £2,000 fortune in that neighbourhood'.

Macky observed one significant sign of the times when he visited York, a place where 'plenty and cheapness . . . brings abundance of strangers . . . for the conveniency of the boarding'. The Earl of Carlisle's efforts after 1716 to remove the Whig and Tory labels from the city's two assemblies were being much assisted by 'the officers of the army making no distinction' between them. That army officers should have been ready to bury the old political hatchets after George I was safely established, and the Jacobite threat had receded, was not altogether surprising. For always excepting the accidents of war itself, politics was for much of the Augustan period the one major threat to an able officer's professional advance. Naturally, many of James II's officers left or were forced out in 1688–9. What is less well known is that, while George I quickly repaired the dismemberment of Whig-infested regiments by Bolingbroke and Ormonde in 1714, a large number of officers – not simply generals such as Webb, Echlin, Steuart, Sutton and Hamilton but lieutenant-colonels, majors and captains –

were, in Craggs's words, 'displaced, either with leave to sell or otherwise' on political grounds between late 1714 and 1717. Even an imprudent vote in Parliament could on occasion prove expensive. Walpole's revenge on the army Excise rebels is a celebrated case; but as early as the middle of Anne's reign Colonel Lord Windsor had lost his regiment for voting against the Godolphin ministry, and it was no coincidence that one of Ormonde's sacrificial offerings to political expediency in March 1714, William Egerton, who lost his company of Guards, had a staunch Whig voting record as MP for Brackley.

In general, however, by the 1720s and the 1730s the profession, while not apolitical, was less politicised and assuredly much less agitated by politics than had been the case in the three previous decades. And under a Whig oligarchy and a more stable political order than England had known for generations those army officers who chose to enter politics normally remembered which side their bread was buttered on: and never more clearly (as Edward Wortley Montagu had forecast in 1710) than when voting against Place Bills! Nothing would make the regular army of Hanoverian England a popular institution in peacetime. The system of quartering and methods of recruitment were, by themselves, enough to account for that. And 'Country' distaste for the officers still made itself felt from time to time. But most of the political opposition, at least, was becoming ritualistic. As a profession the army was no longer seriously disturbed by the ingrained fears and deep and genuine animosities of the past.

II   The Navy as a Profession

Because the great expansion of the royal navy between 1680 and 1715 was viewed in a totally different light from the swelling of the army, the development of the naval service as a profession in the Augustan period was not conditioned by the atmosphere of parliamentary suspicion or hostility which accompanied the rise of the military men. While not entirely insulated from political influences and pressures – and latterly, especially, from the operation of the Whig patronage system – it was subject to them only to a relatively minor degree before the 1730s. Addison's quintessential country gentleman of *The Freeholder*, a Little Englander to his fingertips, who in 1715 admitted 'frankly, that he had always been against all treaties and alliances with foreigners', rested his case almost entirely on the strength of the navy: ' "our wooden walls," says he, "are our security, and we may bid defiance to the whole world . . ." ' This is not to say that the professionalisation of the navy between Charles II's and George I's reigns was a matter of solving purely professional problems. There was, on the contrary, a complex social equation that had to be resolved in the course of this decisive half-century: but the elements involved in it were fundamentally different from those which made the relations of the army officers with the society of their day a tense and uneasy one for two decades or more.

To Samuel Pepys, who was Secretary of the Admiralty from 1673 to 1679 (and later from 1684–9), the root problem which the navy still had to come to terms with at the start of our period was that as a career, certainly as a career for officers, it was socially as well as professionally undesirable. 'Have any of our Heralds allowed in express words the seaman for a gentleman?', he wrote in his *Naval Minutes*, pithily realistic as ever. The lowly place of naval officers in the Lancaster Herald's 'Scheme' for 1688, and the fact that Gregory King credited them with an average income smaller than that of 'freeholders of the better sort' gave point to Pepys's question. Mr Secretary's dream throughout the 1670s and 1680s was of a profession that could offer to those who chose it permanency, profit and honour in equal measure, 'as that not only the younger brothers of England might be encouraged to seek their fortune in that way, . . . but that even the elder might esteem it, for the dignity of it'. There were deterrents enough against going into the navy, after all, which in the foreseeable future were beyond the control of any administration, however well-intentioned. Nothing could banish the privations and hazards which, even for those who held the king's commission, attended active service at sea: they might be reduced during the long intervals of peace which punctuated the period from 1660 to 1688, but they were not removed. In this respect, the small and largely ornamental pre-Revolution army offered to men bred as gentlemen a feather-bedded alternative with which the navy could scarcely compete.

All the more reason, then, as Pepys (and also, to their credit, the royal brothers) fully grasped, for demolishing the other obstacles that still blocked the way to the creation of a class of regular naval officers, combining professional skill as seamen with good social standing. The long-standing tradition that officers, like ratings, were paid only when actively employed (which for many meant rarely, if at all, in peacetime and discontinuously even in time of war) had been eroded at the higher levels between 1668 and 1675; it had yet to be comprehensively eradicated. The pay itself had to be substantially improved. There must be adequate inducements at each stage to persuade the right men to seek lieutenants' commissions, to work hard to achieve post rank and earn promotion as captains from the lowest to the highest rates of ship, and ultimately to aspire to a flag. The captain of a man-of-war, to put it no lower, ought to be acceptable beyond question as a gentleman by his lifestyle and status, whatever his social origins. Not least important, the system of gentlemen-'volunteers' on midshipmen's pay, which Charles II had encouraged after 1661 (and which wa˜ ᴺᵒᵗ abandoned until 1730) had somehow to be married harmoniously w . . traditional methods of recruitment to the service and promotion within it: for only thus could the social gap between officers of this type and those who had been raised from the lower deck or drafted in from the merchant service be diminished, and only thus could the gulf in professional competence between 'gentlemen' and 'tarpaulins', still distressingly wide in 1680, be closed entirely. All these problems demanded solution. For as things stood, Pepys gloomily noted,

where a . . . seaman gets an estate, he either out of pride or some
other less satisfactory reason seldom brings up a son to his own
trade, but advances him in the Law, the Court, the University,
or disposes of him some otherwise than to the sea; whereas you
shall have lawyers and gownmen of all sorts, soldiers and courtiers,
continue their trades from father to son for many generations . . .

The years between 1677 and 1720 were ones of momentous change
in the whole nature of the profession; and it was fitting that Pepys
himself lived long enough, even in retirement, to know in his heart that
the change was irreversible. It was almost inevitable in view of its
pedigree and its recent history that the navy should develop along
different fines from the army: certainly it was in every way desirable
that it should do so. Most obviously there remained, even in George I's
reign, a pronounced 'social mix' in the commissioned ranks of the
Royal Navy; it was by no means absent from the army, as we have
seen, but in the navy it was a prominent feature. The naval officer was
a far less stereotyped social being than the cavalry or even the infantry
officer. Keen as it was to attract young men of good family into the
service as officer material, the Admiralty by the end of the Nine Years'
War had been taught by bitter experience the utter folly, in a profession where experience and seamanship counted for so much, of
countenancing a system of admission, training and promotion which
offered 'a very great discouragement to such persons as have . . . served
many years as mates and midshipmen [that is, as petty officers], and in
every respect qualified themselves to perform the duty of lieutenant'.
In consequence, during the war years of 1702–12 the 695 men newly
commissioned as lieutenants included no fewer than 303 who had
previously seen service in the merchant fleet, many of them 'old tars'
who had transferred to the navy in the first place as petty officers. But
the great difference between their situation and prospects and those of
their predecessors under Charles II was that by the early eighteenth
century the men of humble or modest origins who rose professionally
through 'the sea service' now aspired to, rather than despised – or
affected to despise – gentlemanly manners and styles of life. On the
other hand, the scores of officers in the fleet who were of aristocratic
or gentle birth in the 1720s were no longer found wanting on the score
of seamanship, as was so often the case with their counterparts of the
1660s and 1670s. Technical revolution and social evolution had proceeded side by side.

The professional officer corps whose construction had begun in the
second half of Charles II's reign and whose shape and character had
been very largely determined by 1720, acquired in the intervening years
three features of decisive importance. Its most basic acquisition was a
high measure of technical competence. At individual level this was not
only assessed before commissioning but also, in this most competitive
of professions, remained subject to regular scrutiny. Secondly, its
members were able to rely increasingly on their proficiency being rewarded, whether or not they were on active service: in other words,

they served a navy which was prepared to retain them either in regular employment or on the reserve as long as they were fit for it, and afterwards give them some support in their retirement. Thirdly, so far as the highest ranks in the service were concerned, a system of promotion had developed which was governed, by and large, (and certainly to a much greater degree than was the case with the army) by the principle of seniority.

The key to the imposition of basic standards of seamanship on the new breed of directly recruited gentlemen-officers – whether they were volunteers per order (alias 'King's Letter Boys') or whether they had entered the navy in their early or middle teens as captains' 'servants' (in effect, apprentices) – was the examination for the lieutenant's commission. This was first introduced on Pepys's initiative in 1677 and was permanently entrenched by the Order in Council of 19 February 1678. The examination was no formality. It was conducted at the Navy Office by a board of three, including one admiral and one senior captain, and even the immediate results of its institution were immensely gratifying to the Admiralty Secretary: 'I thank God,' he wrote, early in 1678, 'we have not half the throng of those of the bastard breed pressing for employments which we heretofore used to be troubled with, they being conscious of their inability to pass their examination, and know it to be to no purpose now to solicit . . . till they have done it.' The prior qualifications expected of candidates for the examination were subject to a good deal of alteration in the light of experience over the next fifty years. The original three-year minimum period of qualifying service at sea before examination had become firmly consolidated at six years by January 1730. In the meantime recruitment to the lieutenants' list for most of the Spanish Succession War, when the profession was fuller than at any time before the 1740s, and also during George I's reign had been governed by an Admiralty order of May 1703 to the effect that

to prevent the inconveniences that happen by persons coming too young to that station, no one shall be qualified for the future to be a lieutenant in the fleet till he is arrived at the age of twenty years, and has passed his examination . . . and has served four years, and two of them at least as midshipmen in some of her Majesty's ships; and that no one shall be capable of receiving the Lord High Admiral's letter (or Commissioners of the Admiralty's) to be borne as volunteer in any of her Majesty's ships but between the ages of thirteen and sixteen.

Although the age limit for receiving a commission was sometimes evaded (by the 1720s there was said to be a brisk trade in forged certificates of baptism), it is clear that the quarterdecks in Queen Anne's navy were well stocked with experience. Even in 1702, before the new order came into force, the average age of the candidates who presented themselves for examination was almost 27. It was very much lower by

1730: but passing the examination did not get a man his commission. Only appointment to a ship could do that and in the peacetime navy, when a candidate lacked connections, this might take several years, sometimes as many as four or five. Subsequently, the far higher pay and infinitely larger prospects of supplementary income enjoyed by captains made rapid promotion to post rank the ambition of every lieutenant worth his salt, and provided the best of all guarantees that he would continue to apply himself conscientiously to his vocation. Over the heads of the idle or incompetent there hung the Officers' Instructions of Charles II's reign, carefully spelling out the duties of each rank and specifying penalties for negligence or flouting of regulations. For the backsliders and for those deficient in judgement or nerve there was the ultimate sanction of the court-martial, which could break a man's career overnight and at worst, as with Kirby and Wade in 1703, lead to execution for cowardice.

The second basic change of policy towards the navy during the period 1680–1730 which reflected an essentially new attitude towards 'sea-officers' as a profession involved their pay and permanence. Until 1694 the rates at which commissioned officers were paid while on active service, despite some revision in 1686, still reflected the old assumption that they would be drawn largely from the same seafaring community as the petty officers and senior ratings who served under them. Thus the bosun, gunner, purser and ship's carpenter of a first-rate man-of-war (100 guns), at £4 per month, were only minimally less well paid than the lieutenants on the same ship (£4 4s). The same ratings on the second-rate earned as much (£3 10s per month) as the lieutenants on third-, fourth- and fifth-rates. Even if his ship was not laid up at all, there was no way in which the captain, even of the largest fighting vessel in the navy, could earn, in any one year, from salary alone, more than £252 in the 1680s and early 1690s. The comparable ceiling for the captain of a fourth-rate was £120, and for the captain of a sloop or large yacht, £84.

It is true that there had long existed various recognised ways whereby officers could legitimately augment their earnings. They were permitted to take servants on board – the number regulated according to rank – and to draw the pay of these servants, or probationers, making them allowances entirely at their own discretion. Both in peace and war many captains took 'freight money' from the captains or owners of merchantmen for carrying bullion safely back from overseas stations. Most valuable of all sidelines was the prize money that came the way of the fortunate in wartime, of which everyone got his cut in some proportion – from the admiral of the squadron, who took an eighth, even though his flagship was hundreds of miles away from the scene of the capture, down to the humblest member of the crew. It was the captain who stood to gain by far the most from prize money (one quarter of the whole value, and even more if he was on an independent mission and not under a flag); but lieutenants in such circumstances could also do very well for themselves. Even in the early years of the war of 1689–97 there were some colossal hauls, none bigger than the entire convoy of seventy-one Danish ships bound for France, brought in in 1693 by a Channel squadron commanded by Admiral Sir Ralph Delavall. Although privateer crews engrossed a substantial share of the total prize booty of £443,402 in the Nine Years' War, it is clear that a few naval officers made fortunes out of their share of the proceeds (Sir George Rooke, for one) while many more were enabled to live in plenty for years on theirs. It was largely because the smaller ships in the fleet, cruisers and sloops, were considered far more likely to make captures in wartime than ships of the line that such striking discrepancies in officers' pay existed up to 1694, according to the rate of ship on which they served.

Prize money and freight money, nevertheless, were fortuitous and indiscriminate rewards. They could not disguise the fact that naval officers before and for some years after the Revolution were deplorably paid: their remuneration compared miserably, for example, both with that of officers in Colbert's French royal navy and with that of officers in most English ocean-going merchant ships. Still less did they alter the fact that up to 1694, in spite of the special provision of half-pay made in the years 1668–74 for flag officers and captains of first- and second-rates, the great bulk of sea-officers had no guarantee of regular employment in the navy. In peacetime as like as not they were unemployed and they were usually paid off for part of every year even in wartime. This was a far more formidable barrier to the creation of a permanent professional service even than inadequate rates of pay.

Two great steps forward were taken in the new establishment of 1694. On the one hand, levels of pay throughout the commissioned ranks of the service were more than doubled; and even if servant allowances were cut in partial compensation the change was none the less a momentous one. A full admiral on active service could now earn up to £1,460 a year, a vice-admiral £1,095, the captain of a first-rate nearly £550, a cruiser captain (fifth-rate) £182 10s and a senior lieutenant about £120 a year. It is true that in 1700 the rates were revised again, downwards; with fairly light reductions for lieutenants and admirals, and much more substantial ones for captains. Yet, at the same time, the servant allowance for captains was made more generous than ever (the captain of a first- and second-rate could take on up to thirty-one and twenty-seven respectively and even the captain of a fifth-rate was allowed eight), so the officers lost little, if anything, materially by the change. A proposal by the Admiralty in 1730 to return to the 1694 system of pay met with no response from Walpole and his colleagues.

Meanwhile, however, the navy had taken in 1694 an even more significant change of course. The half-pay system was crucially extended at this time to take in all captains of ships together with the first lieutenants and masters of the first three rates. By 1700, although the number of recipients was modified to the first 50 names on the captains' list and the first 100 on the lieutenants' list, the object of the new system was now being explicitly laid down by the Admiralty: 'to have always a competent number of experienced sea-officers supported on shore who [would] be within reach to answer any sudden or emergent occasion'. With half-pay officers forbidden to go abroad (and therefore to accept posts on merchantmen), prohibited from holding any other public office and required to keep the Admiralty apprised of their whereabouts, the foundations of a permanent officer corps involving the maintenance of a regular reserve had been securely laid. It now needed only the new establishment of November 1713 after the Peace of Utrecht, providing 'that an allowance of half pay be also established on all captains and lieutenants (according to the bigger rates wherein they have served) *who now do, or shall hereafter, stand fair to be employed when there shall be occasion . . . at sea or on shore*' (my italics) to make the new system almost universal among those officers who had not already voluntarily retired or transferred to merchantmen. Pensions had been regularly allowed since 1674 to officers (as to petty officers and ratings) wounded in the king's service. Provision for superannuated officers was a logical extension of this. Yet it was not until 1748 that a formal superannuation scheme was adopted; and although retirement pensions had been fairly regularly paid since 1690 the fact that this had been done at the Crown's discretion had meant, in the case of lieutenants, no certain provision even for long-serving men.

The third cornerstone of that officer hierarchy which by 1720 had realised Pepys's dream of a thoroughly professionalised naval service was an accepted pattern of promotion. In the patronage-ridden world of early Hanoverian England it was unavoidable that sooner or later connection would become the most decisive single factor – certainly among men of average, or better than average, competence – influencing promotion from lieutenancies to the captains' list and advancement up the various rungs of the captains' ladder. Having said this, it becomes necessary to qualify the statement in at least four important ways. For one thing the conditions governing promotion in the twenty-three war-dominated years between 1689 and 1712 were very different from those which slowly supervened in the predominantly peaceful quarter of a century from 1714 to 1739. It was, for example, very unlikely indeed in wartime that a genuinely able officer, even though entirely without influence, would get permanently stuck (as could happen in peacetime) as the commander of a sloop or a storeship. Secondly, the right of commanders in overseas stations to promote to vacancies as they occurred regularly made nonsense of the schemes of private patrons, and even of the Admiralty itself. So far as official Admiralty policy was concerned, ability was regularly acknowledged throughout the entire Augustan period to be the ideal criterion for appointments: even under the first two Georges it was quite frequently able to assert itself, overcoming political influence or private patronage, interrupting the upward plod of mere seniority; and it was at all times rare for outstanding merit in an officer to go unrewarded. The final qualification to the power of connection, however, equally affected the prospects of the exceptionally able. Promotion to flag rank, the height of every naval officer's ambition and normally a passport to a fortune, after being somewhat eccentrically bestowed in the first half of our period became almost exclusively a matter of seniority by the second half. Whatever defects the system had by then, it was at least not at the mercy of 'influence'; and the advent of predominantly peaceful foreign relations in the quarter century after the Utrecht settlement spelled a long and frustrating wait even for officers with no lack of patronage strings to pull. Lord Vere Beauclerk's aristocratic friends may have procured him the captaincy of a frigate in the 1720s at the age of 22; but they were powerless to get him a flag until he was very nearly 50. The publication of the first Navy List in 1718, in which all officers were ranged in strict seniority order within their ranks, had been the clearest possible indication of the Admiralty's new thinking; it was in sharp contrast to the situation in the first two years of Anne's reign when Prince George's Admiralty Council was still 'of opinion that the Crown never tied itself to seniority in choosing their [flag] officers'.

We can see the effects of this change very clearly if we compare the fortunes of two able officers, wholly without important connections, who were commissioned about the time of the 1688 Revolution with those of three younger men, with no lack of social or political advantages, whose careers began later in William III's reign. John Baker was commissioned lieutenant in November 1688 at the age of 28, almost certainly after many years' experience in merchant ships. He was a commander by 1691, a full captain by 1692 and after just over nineteen years of brave and worthy (though unspectacular) service he was appointed rear-admiral of the White Squadron in January 1708. Sir Charles Wager, perhaps the most universally popular and respected of all Augustan admirals, hoisted his flag in the same year as Baker, following a brief but remarkably successful turn of duty as a commodore on the West Indies station. He was then 42, and it was sixteen years since he had first been posted captain – originally, to nothing more elevated than a fireship. By contrast, it took Philip Cavendish, a bastard son of the first Duke of Devonshire, thirty-four years of commissioned service and twenty-seven years at post rank (from 1701) to achieve the status of rear-admiral. And among others who missed the early post-Revolution tide were Edward Vernon, a Secretary of State's son, who entered the navy in 1700 and became a captain in 1706, but had to wait for his flag (admittedly through a career punctuated by political activity) until 1739, and Tancred Robinson, an officer with excellent Whig connections and fewer distractions than Vernon, who had to serve twenty-eight years as captain before being promoted rear-admiral of the White in 1736.

By this time it was certainly possible to contrast the fairly stern application of the seniority rule at the top with the wider opportunities for queue-jumping lower down. Nevertheless, Professor Daniel Baugh has observed that even when Newcastle's patronage machine was functioning at peak efficiency, in the 1740s and 1750s, 'ordinarily, political connection could not advance an egregiously incompetent officer very far'; and between 1700 and 1730 its power was distinctly less, even in peacetime. The Hence the astonishment and solemn disapproval with which John Charnock, the late-eighteenth-century naval biographer, noted the exceptional favour doled out in the first decade of the century to James Berkeley, Viscount Dursley, the son of the second Earl of Berkeley. Joining the navy as a volunteer in the mid-1690s, while his elder brother Charles was still alive, Dursley was made a frigate captain in April 1701, only two months after his 21st birthday. He commanded an 80-gun ship of the line at Malaga in 1704, was promoted (now a peer in his own right) rear-admiral of the Red Squadron in January 1708 when he was still a stripling of 27, and was made a vice-admiral at 30. 'We have in no instance', Charnock censoriously remarked, 'found the established rules of the service so repeatedly broken through as to make room for his particular promotion.' It was impossible to deny that Dursley was a good seaman and a gallant, energetic and, in terms of action and prizes, lucky young officer. But the deep unease which his vaulting career aroused underlies emphatically the widely recognised professional standards governing promotion which the navy had set itself by the late 1690s.

If we define the Augustan naval profession strictly, including in it only duly-commissioned officers on sea pay or on half pay, and by the same token excluding probationers and all warrant officers (even the highly valued ships' masters), its proportions were relatively modest. Even towards the end of the Spanish Succession War, when numbers were at their highest point, it is likely that they fell short of a thousand. In the light of the navy's massive expansion since the 1670s such a total may well seem surprising: for even the peacetime navy of 1723 still had a paper strength of 180 rated ships and 45 others. Two factors explain the apparent discrepancy. One is that although scores of battleships were either built or rebuilt between 1689 and 1713, among them large numbers of the highest rates of eighty guns or over with great complements rising from 520 to 850 men, much of the wartime effort of the shipyards went into the production of the fifth- and sixth-rates that were particularly needed for commerce protection and destruction. Such ships normally carried only one lieutenant each, although the biggest fifth-rates, in common with all ships of forty guns or more, did have their establishments increased by an extra one in 1719. In addition, however, even the biggest ships of the line had commissioned establishments that seem to us tiny in relation to the number of men and, more particularly, to the number of warrant officers they carried. For example the *Royal Anne*, the second biggest ship in the fleet by 1713, carried 780 men and 24 midshipmen, but – in common with other first- and second-rates of the day – no more than 5 lieutenants. Eighty-gun ships such as the *Devonshire*, built in 1710, or 70-gunners such as the *Grafton* (1709) were permitted an establishment of only three lieutenants, though they carried 520 and 440 men respectively. So the entire line-of-battle fleet of 131 ships in 1714 required only about 500 captains and lieutenants to officer it.

Even so, the call for new recruits was then, and at all times, strong.

That it was so is a sobering commentary on the amount of wastage in the profession, through death, disablement and voluntary or involuntary retirement. The West Indies station was particularly deadly. Quite apart from those dispatched by enemy action, it is said that more than fifty captains died of disease while on service in the Caribbean in the first half of the eighteenth century; and to make matters worse, the Admiralty decided in reviewing the case of George Smyth, the captain of the *Warwick* who died at Barbados in 1704, that widows of victims of a 'pestilential distemper' did not qualify for a pension in the same way as widows of those struck down by cannon ball or musket shot. Periods of war naturally raised the demand for new officers to an intense level. At the height of the Spanish Succession conflict, in the space of four years (1706–9) 332 men successfully presented themselves for the lieutenants' examination in London and home ports alone; while altogether, between 1702 and 1712 there may well have been around a thousand fresh recruits coming through with commissions from the ranks of volunteers and petty officers, including many who qualified overseas. This was more than three times as many as in the previous war.

After the Spanish Succession War there were many retirements. Scores of officers who knew that their chances of being retained on half-pay were slim or non-existent, and dozens of others who were too ambitious – or could not afford – to mark time for years on a low retaining salary, transferred to the merchant service while the going was good. In the short-term trade boom which followed the Peace of Utrecht this made good sense (a similar emigration after the Peace of Ryswick in 1697 had accounted by 1700 for almost a fifth of the 523 lieutenants as well as six of the captains who had served during the Augsburg War, and at the same time there were smaller defections to the customs and packet boat services and to foreign navies). When the peacetime establishment of the navy was finally settled in 1715, therefore, fewer than 650 officers were retained. Of these a mere 168, including 70 captains, continued to draw full pay, with only a third of the king's ships in service. The lists were further eroded over the next few years, especially the captains' list which shrank from 258 to 197 between 1715 and 1720. As for lieutenants, although 196 new ones were commissioned between 1715 and 1732, on the eve of the next great phase of warfare in 1739 the number in pay was still only fractionally more than had been established in 1715.

In spite of the high casualty rate which its entrants had to reckon with, it is clear that the navy was seen by many of those who sought commissions after 1680, and the majority of those who sought them after 1688, as potentially a lifetime's occupation. And for those who survived, and at the same time resisted the peacetime tug of the merchant service, this is substantially what the profession became in Augustan England. Of the captains on the Navy List in March 1720, 6 had been posted thirty years or more earlier, 36 had commissions of Williamite vintage, while 122 had received their first commands during Anne's reign. The 341 lieutenants in pay in 1726 included some officers commissioned as early as 1693. If salaries alone had been their reward few of these men, and for that matter not many admirals either, would have had the slightest chance of making those fortunes they had dreamed of when they first became volunteers or transferred to the navy from merchant ships as petty officers. By 1730 the basic salary scale which had seemed tolerable in wartime to lieutenants and junior captains had become a standing source of grievance, partly because payments were so irregular, but mainly because peacetime prospects of promotion were so drastically reduced. The Admiralty did try in this year to persuade the Treasury to agree to higher salaries; but the attempt was frustrated and it was to be 1754 before it was made again. It was the sidelines rather than the pay which brought the luckier sea-officer his golden returns, and with one exception these were mostly the bonuses of war. There was prize money, above all, to be hoped for; but also convoy money (until it was made illegal in 1694); freight money (see above, p. 278); 'head money' (paid by the Admiralty from 1708–12 for prisoners taken on enemy men-of-war); and, not least, servants' allowances. Such windfalls could comfortably line the pockets even of mere lieutenants: the sole lieutenant of a 32-gun 'cruiser' might get anything up to an eighth of the value of a captured prize. To captains, as we have already seen, they could spell wealth of no mean order; and to admirals, with their assured share of every prize taken under their flags, and perks allowed on anything from fifteen to fifty 'servants', they could almost guarantee it. The snag was that there was no necessary correlation between the highest rewards and the most deserving officers. Of Captain Richard Leake, a wastrel and a great disappointment to his distinguished father, it was said by his cousin that 'being made a captain in the navy very young, in a few years he got more by prizes than his father did in his whole life'.

The successful naval officer, like the successful army officer, was usually marked out by his estates. There were exceptions; and Sir John Leake, whose ill-luck in the matter of prizes throughout two wars was compounded by enforced early retirement in 1714, was one of them. At the time he was appointed Rear-Admiral of Britain he appears to have been still living in Stepney; and though he did buy a country house at Bedington, Surrey, some time before Queen Anne's death, a retirement pension of £500 a year at the end of his service on the Admiralty Board (1709–14) allowed him little scope for late excursions into the land market, and according to his nephew 'a little box' at Greenwich was the only purchase of his closing years. In general, however, few professional men of the Augustan age appreciated *terra firma* more warmly than the seadog on the make. Sir David Mitchell, who had been ship's boy and mate in the merchant marine in the 1660s and early 1670s, eventually bought land and a country seat at Popes in Hertfordshire and married the co-heiress of a Shropshire squire. Cloudesley Shovell, who in 1690 became a rear-admiral after being a cabin-boy at 14, had already made a handsome profit out of his com-mands in the Mediterranean prior to the Revolution and was a big landowner in Kent long before he was drowned off the Scillies in

1707. Matthew Aylmer, unlike many of his fellow-admirals, inherited an estate from his family, comfortably-off Irish gentry; but he could hardly have supported the Irish peerage he was granted in 1718 without the lands in Kent which were the fruits of a successful active career at sea from 1678–98 and of his later appointment (1701) as Admiral of the Fleet.

Kent was the favourite resort of wealthy, distinguished sea-officers. Sir John Norris, who rose from junior lieutenant's to full admiral's rank between 1689 and 1709, bought up the Guldeford family's estates there and in Sussex and seated himself in 1718 at Hemsted. Nicholas Haddock, posted captain at the tender age of 21, purchased Wrotham Place in 1723 when he was still only 37; while one of the heroes of Malaga, John Baker, had likewise acquired the manor of East Langdon, near his birthplace of Deal, when he was still captain of the *Monmouth*, of seventy guns. On the other hand, another of Queen Anne's ablest admirals, Sir John Jennings, put down his roots in Hertfordshire when he was in his 40s, and Commodore Wager's handsome share of the £50,000 of Spanish booty taken in a captured galleon off Carthagena in 1708 was invested in the soil of his native Cornwall.

More than twenty years later Sir Charles Wager was to accept the post of First Lord of the Admiralty; but only with some reservations, having managed to persuade both himself and Walpole that although his estate was not of patrician proportions, he was 'not altogether an upstart'. Sir Charles, the son of a naval officer from Deal though brought up in the West Country, was but one of many passengers on the remarkably crowded social escalator which naval service offered during and soon after the French wars of 1689–1713. Among his fellow-travellers was Francis Hosier, whose father was a Gravesend dockyard official. He became a lieutenant at 19, a captain at 23 (in 1696) and after enriching himself with prize money in two golden years of the Spanish Succession War and surviving a period of suspension for alleged Jacobite sympathies (1715–17) hoisted his flag at the age of 46. Others got on to the staircase much lower than Wager and Hosier. The cases of Shovell and Mitchell, referred to already, are well known. Among those in the fast-dying tradition of the 'old tars' there was no rougher diamond than John Benbow, the son of a Shrewsbury tanner; yet he died, at 49, a vice-admiral and commander-in-chief of the West Indies fleet. Admiral Hopson, knighted and pensioned off with £500 a year in 1702, may not have started his working life as a tailor's apprentice, as was once thought, but he certainly rose from the lower deck (as did Sir George Walton after him) and took ten years to claw his way to lieutenant's rank on the eve of the Second Dutch War.

The list of those who were able through the quarterdeck and the captain's cabin to improve their social prospects out of all recognition is long and impressive, especially before 1715 when the profession was most genuinely open to talents. Baker was the stepson of a carpenter. Norris is known to have been born and brought up in Ireland but we know nothing whatever about his family, and his difficulty in making headway during the first nine years in the service (1680–9) suggests he had few, if any, social connections of value at that stage. Thomas Swanton and Sir George Saunders, both of whom captained line-of-battle ships during the French wars and graduated to comfortable shore berths in the Navy or Victualling Offices under George I, were Londoners whose parentage has defied discovery. On the other hand, Sir John Jennings certainly came from a landed family of sorts; but as the fifteenth child of a financially embarrassed Shropshire gentleman he might, with good reason, have jibbed at his background being described as favoured. Even Sir George Byng, the victor of Cap Passaro, who was rich enough to send his heir on the Grand Tour from 1713 to 1715 and who ended his days (1721–33) as Viscount Torrington, was by no means as fortunate in his early years as his landed gentry origins in Kent might suggest. Although he was the eldest son, there were virtually no family estates left for him to succeed to when his impoverished father died in 1683; and the decision which transformed his life – sending him into the navy as a 'king's letter boy' at the age of 15 – had already been taken five years before.

Nevertheless, the years of Byng's active career as a commissioned officer in the royal navy, from 1684 to 1720, unquestionably saw the accomplishment of that social transmutation in the profession for which Pepys had hoped and worked. The fact that so many relative parvenus during these three and a half decades achieved a social recognition through their sea service which the old tarpaulin officers could never have aspired to was not a matter of increased financial rewards alone. It owed just as much to the way in which the whole standing of the naval profession was raised, almost year by year, in the eyes of polite society; for it proved as successful in offering an acceptable vocation for the sons of noblemen and gentlemen as in utilising the talents of the sons of nobodies. Among those who commanded ships, squadrons and, in some cases, fleets during the four reigns which followed Charles II's death the aristocracy was represented, for example, by a Greville, a Russell, an Osborne, a Berkeley, a Fitzroy, a Beauclerk, a Forbes, a Stewart, a Maynard, a Cavendish (albeit of the bar sinister) and a Clinton. In the same period old-established county families like the Drakes, Trevanions and Trefusises in the West Country, the Ogles, Fairfaxes, Blacketts and Delavals in the north, or the Daverses and the Walpoles in East Anglia sent their sons to sea as readily as others bought commissions for theirs in the army. As time went by the navy shared increasingly in a process we have already observed elsewhere, the cross-fertilisation between professions. Among the lieutenants commissioned between 1727 and 1734, for instance, was the eldest son of a barrister and the younger son of a successful Whig divine. Yet over time, as one would expect, self-replenishment from within naval families themselves proved more important by far than recruitment from any other profession. Delaval, Haddock, Hardy, Hubbard, Leake, Norris and Byng were only some of the names which recurred in successive generations in the late Stuart and early Georgian navy. Josiah Burchett, the heir of Pepys, had no reason to complain, as his illustrious predecessor had complained, that 'where a . . . seaman gets an estate, he . . . seldom brings up a son to his own trade.' The navy illustrates, as well as any other sector examined in this book, the rise of the professional dynasty in Augustan England.

Appendix

Table 1   *Recorded Bar Calls, Middle Temple and Inner Temple*
1580–1639,   1670–1729

	Middle Temple	Inner Temple
1580–9	85	62
1590–9	94	92
1600–9	108	89
1610–19	155	78
1620–9	111	88
1630–9	120	142
TOTAL, 60 years, 1580–1639:	673	551

Source: W. R. Prest, *The Inns of Court under Elizabeth and the Early Stuarts 1590–1640* (1972), table 8.

	Middle Temple	Inner Temple
1670–9	173	173
1680–9	233	184
1690–9	201	138
1700–9	168	147
1710–19	149	119
1720–9	193	142
TOTAL, 60 years, 1670–1729:	1,117	903

Sources: H. A. C. Sturgess (ed.), *Register of Admissions to the Honourable Society of the Middle Temple*, Vol. 1 (1949); F. A. Inderwick (ed.), *Calendar of Inner Temple Records*, Vol. 3 (1901).

Table 2   *Recorded Bar Calls: Lincoln's Inn and Gray's Inn*
1570–1639,   1660–1729

	Lincoln's Inn	Gray's Inn
1570–9	63	21[a]
1580–9	105	73
1590–9	101	93
1600–9	97	89
1610–19	123	107
1620–9	147	55
1630–9	148	101
TOTAL, 70 years, 1570–1639:	784	539[a]

Source: Prest, op. cit., table 8, p. 52.
Figures incomplete for 1570s.

TABLE 2—*continued*

	Lincoln's Inn	*Gray's Inn*
1660–9	103	275
1670–9	99	202
1680–9	74	144[a]
1690–9	45	88[b]
1700–9	60	75
1710–19	65	69
1720–9	64	64
TOTAL, 70 years, 1660–1729:	510	917

Sources: For 1660–79, W. P. Baildon *et al.* (eds), *The Records of the Honourable Society of Lincoln's Inn: The Black Books* (4 vols, 1897–1902), Vol. 2 (1899); for 1680–1729, Paul Lucas, 'A collective biography of students and barristers of Lincoln's Inn, 1680–1804', *Journal of Modern History*, vol. 46 (1974), table A7, p. 251, and R. J. Fletcher (ed.), *The Pension Book of Gray's Inn 1569–1800*, Vol. 1 (1901), Vol. 2 (1910).

[a] Including 2 called 'by grace' at Jeffreys's request and 8 RCs 'recommended' by James II 1686–7.

[b] For the ravaging of Gray's Inn by fire see above, p. 144.

Table 3   *Total Recorded Bar Calls, 1580–1639 and 1660–1729*

[1570–9]	–?–[a]	1660–9	714
1580–9	325	1670–9	647
1590–9	380	1680–9	635
1600–9	383	1690–9	472
1610–19	463	1700–9	450
1620–9	401	1710–19	402
1630–9	511	1720–9	563
TOTAL CALLS, 1580–1639: 2,463		TOTAL CALLS, 1660–1729: 3,783	

Sources: as for Tables 1 and 2; except for the grand total for the years 1660–9 which I owe to the kindness of Mr R. W. Pearce and which incorporate *inter alia* his work on the MS Bar Book of the Inner Temple.

[a] Calls in the 1570s were certainly much lower than in the 1580s but incomplete records rule out firm enumeration. The total for the 70 years, 1570–1639, cannot have exceeded 2,700, over a thousand less, that is, than for the 70 years, 1660–1729.

Bibliographical Notes

Abbreviations

A number of titles recur under several subject headings in the notes that follow. They are abbreviated thus:

Angliae Notitia   Edward Chamberlayne, *Angliae Notitia, or the Present State of England* (various edns 1669–1704).
Campbell, *London Tradesman* R. Campbell, Esq., *The London Tradesman: being a Compendious View of all the Trades, Professions, Arts, both Liberal and Mechanic, now practised in the Cities of London and Westminster* (1747).
Defoe, *Tour*   Daniel Defoe, *A Tour through the Whole Island of Great Britain* (first published 1724–7: Everyman edn, 2 vols, reproduced from 1927 edn, intro. by G. D. H. Cole).
DNB   *Dictionary of National Biography.*
Fiennes, *Journeys*   C. Morris (ed.), *The Journeys of Celia Fiennes* (rev. edn, 1949).
GEC Complete Peerage   V. Gibbs (*et al.*), (eds), *The Complete Peerage by G. E. C[ockayne]* (14 vols, 1910–59).
HMC   Reports of the Historical Manuscripts Commission.
Macky, *Journey*   John Macky, *A Journey through England* (2 vols, 1714, 1722).
Magnæ Britanniæ Notitia John Chamberlayne, *Magnae Britanniae Notitia, or the Present State of Great Britain* (various edns, 1708–32, and after).
Sedgwick   Romney Sedgwick, *The History of Parliament: The House of Commons 1715–1754* (2 vols, 1970).

Place of publication

Unless otherwise stated the place of publication is London.

Note

There are no separate bibliographical notes to Chapter 1. The views referred to on pp. 11 and 15–16 are developed in Peter Borsay, 'The English urban renaissance: the development of provincial urban culture *c*. 1680– *c*. 1760', *Social History*, vol. 5 (1977); Lawrence Stone, 'Social mobility in England, 1500–1700', *Past and Present*, no. 33 (1966); Richard Grassby, 'Social mobility and business enterprise in seventeenth-century England', in D. Pennington and K. Thomas (eds), *Puritans and Revolutionaries* (Oxford, 1978).

Chapter 2 (pp. 19–42)

My interpretation (pp. 19–21) of the 'social table' in Gregory King's 'Natural and Political Observations upon the State and Condition of England' (in G. E. Barnett [ed.], *Two Tracts by Gregory King* [Baltimore,

Md, 1936]) is based on the arguments put forward in my 'Gregory King and the social structure of pre-industrial England', *Transactions of the Royal Historical Society* 5th ser., vol. 27 (1977). See the appendix to that paper for both versions, that of 1696 and that of 1698–9, of King's full 'Scheme'.

For the training of surveyors the best printed sources are probably E. G. R. Taylor's two standard works on mathematical practitioners (see p. 295 below). I have also utilised the apprenticeship records in the Stamp Office registers (see below, p. 301). E. Hughes, 'The eighteenth century estate agent', in H. A. Cronne, T. W. Moody and D. B. Quinn (eds), *Essays in British and Irish History in Honour of James Eadie Todd* (1949) is still the best compact treatment of its subject. J. D. Hunt and P. Willis, *The Genius of the Place: The English Landscape Garden 1620–1820* (1975) and C. Hussey, *English Gardens and Landscapes 1700–1750* (1967) are valuable on the emergence of the professional garden-planner and landscapist. A 2nd edn of Batty Langley's *New Principles of Gardening: or, the Laying out and Planting Parterres, Groves, Wildernesses, Labyrinths, Avenues, Parks etc.* (1728), quoted above, p. 23, appeared in 1739. Langley's *A Sure Method of improving Estates by Plantations* (1728), a companion work, also illuminates the range of competence of this new breed of professionals. The quotation from Switzer's *Ithnographia Rustica* (1718), p. 23 above, is taken from Hunt and Willis, op. cit., p. 23. Accounts of gardens in the Home Counties, *c.* 1714–25, in Macky, *Journey,* vol. 1, and Defoe, *Tour,* vol. 1, are made use of in this section, as the *DNB* articles on Langley and Switzer.

The paragraphs on architects are heavily indebted to: H. M. Colvin, *A Biographical Dictionary of English Architects 1660–1840* (1954), and not least to Dr Colvin's introductory essay on 'The architectural profession' (ibid., pp. 10–25); J. Lees-Milne, *English Country Houses: Baroque 1685–1715* (1970); and Sir J. Summerson, *Architecture in Britain 1530–1830* (4th edn, 1963). The only contemporary source directly consulted for this section was the chapter on architects in Campbell, *London Tradesman,* pp. 155–8. John James's letter to Bishop Robinson (see above, p. 27) is quoted in Colvin, op. cit., p. 314, from Bodleian Lib. MS Rawlinson B. 376; the quotation from Loveday on Beverley, 1732, is taken from Colvin, op. cit., pp. 612–13, and that from Roger North's *Of Building* (Brit. Lib. Add. MSS 32540), from ibid., introduction.

Another chapter of Campbell's invaluable handbook of professions and trades of 1747 provides a lively, if partial, contemporary view of musicians, and J. Wilson (ed.), *Roger North on Music* (1959), transcribing North's *Memoirs of Musick* (1728), the far more wide-ranging view of a cultivated layman whose musical experience went back to Charles II's reign (see above, p. 29). A voluminous basic work of reference is *The New Grove Dictionary of Music and Musicians* (ed. Stanley Sadie, 20 vols, 1980). Other secondary works relied on for this section of Chapter 2 are: E. Walker, *A History of Music in England* (3rd edn, rev. by J. A. Westrup, Oxford, 1952); E. D. Mackerness, *A Social History of Music* (1964); J. Harley, *Music in Purcell's London* (1968); the intriguing work by W. W. Wroth, *The London Pleasure Gardens of the Eighteenth Century* (1896, repr. 1979); and a well-researched local study, T. Fawcett, *Music in Eighteenth-Century Norfolk and Norwich* (Norwich, 1979). There are important references to musical entrepreneurs and the provision of concerts in J. H. Plumb, *The Commercialization of Leisure in Eighteenth-Century England* (Reading, 1974) and in M. Foss, *The Age of Patronage: The Arts in Society 1660–1750* (1971).

Foss, op. cit., and Plumb, op. cit., should also be consulted for journalism and, in the case of Foss, for the rewards that might come the way of the fortunate few in the world of letters. My brief picture of Thomas Brown (above, p. 31–2) draws heavily on Foss's more extended treatment of him. I have used the standard lives of Addison and Steele by P. Smithers, *The Life of Joseph Addison* (Oxford, 1954) and C. Winton, *Captain Steele* (Baltimore, Md, 1964) and *Sir Richard Steele MP* (Baltimore, Md, 1970). A number of worthy books discuss the politics of Augustan literature but have disappointingly little to say about the economics. A notable exception is Kathleen M. Lynch, *Jacob Tonson: Kit-Cat Publisher* (Knoxville, Tenn.: University of Tennessee Press, 1971) – see above, p. 32. For another famous publisher, Henry Clements, see my *Trial of Doctor Sacheverell* (1973). On journalists, in general, Pat Rogers, *Grub Street: Studies in a Subculture* (1972) explores some unusual backwaters. W. B. Ewald, jnr, *The Newsmen of Queen Anne* (Oxford, 1956) is more orthodox: Dunton's remarks on de Fonvive, quoted above, p. 33–4) are from ibid., p. 232. Fonvive is one of the journalists treated in a lively chapter on 'Grub Street' in Michael Foot, *The Pen and the Sword* (1957). More authoritative and embodying much modern research as well as its author's own is J. A. Downie's, *Robert Harley and the Press: Propaganda and Public Opinion in the Age of Swift and Defoe* (Cambridge, 1979), especially the introduction for its information on printings, circulation and financial returns; and some very helpful Augustan data on the same subjects can be extracted from Pat Rogers's essay 'The writer and society' in P. Rogers (ed.), *The Eighteenth Century* ('The Context of English Literature', 1978). H. L. Snyder has discussed *The Circulation of Newspapers in the Reign of Queen Anne* (Bibliographical Society, 1968). See also the introduction to I. Maxted, *The London Book Trade 1775–1800* (1977) for some interesting early eighteenth-century statistics and the argument that 1714 marked the eighteenth-century peak of the London book market. For Lewis Theobald, William Arnall and John Gay, see *DNB*. G. C. Gibbs has written on Abel Boyer's 'Early life, 1667–1689', *Proceedings of the Huguenot Society*, vol. 22 (1978).

Robert Harley was the most press-conscious politician of his day, prior to Walpole, and both his published and unpublished papers (HMC *Portland MSS* and Brit. Lib. Loan 29) have supplied material for Chapter 2. See, in particular, HMC *Portland MSS*, Vol. 8, p. 201 (letter of Pittis on risks of persecution) and pp. 187–8 (letter of Fonvive, 1705, including reference to his income from *The Postman* – above, p. 33); Loan 29/38/6: MS memo. 17 December 1715 for observations on Fonvive's wealth.

Professors, readers and lecturers at Oxford and Cambridge are enumerated from the lists in *Magnae Britanniae Notitia* (1727) to which I have added two new Regius Professors of Modern History. Information on Gresham College is taken from Stow's *Survey of London*, Vol. 1 (1754 edn), incorporating John Strype's revisions of 1720. *The Remarks and Collections of Thomas Hearne* (Oxford Historical Society, 11 vols, 1885–1921) – the diary, 1703–35, of one of the university's most celebrated antiquaries – is full of spicy but frequently loaded passages on Oxford academic life. (The strictures quoted above, p. 37, are from Vol. 1, pp. 99–100, 292). See the earlier A. Clark (ed.), *The Life and Times of Anthony à Wood 1632–1695, Described by Himself* (5 vols, Oxford, 1891–1900) and J. R. McGrath (ed.), *The Flemings in Oxford . . . 1650–1700* (Oxford Historical Society, 3 vols, 1904–24). Fiennes, *Journeys*, includes a refreshing account of a visit to Oxford *c.* 1694 and records a visit to Cambridge in 1697 above, pp. 38, 40 on New College and St Catharine's). The letter from William Stukeley, quoted p. 41, is from the Osborn Collection at Yale and is printed in the *Yale University Library Gazette* (January 1978). It is reproduced here with the kind permission of the Curator of the Collection.

I base my version of the career pattern of the early-eighteenth-century don largely on the account of Arthur Engel, 'Emerging concepts of the academic profession at Oxford, 1800–1854', in L. Stone (ed.), *The University in Society: I. Oxford and Cambridge from the 14th to the 19th Centuries* (Princeton, NJ, 1974). Professor Stone's own contribution to this volume supplies undergraduate admission figures for the Augustan period super-seding those given in idem, 'The educational revolution in England, 1560–1640', *Past and Present*, vol. 28 (1964). W. R. Ward, *Georgian Oxford* (Oxford, 1958) is principally concerned with university politics, but see pp. 72–3 for the extraordinary Thomas Hoy (cf. *DNB*) and pp. 84–7 on the Whig attempts to 'regulate' the universities under George I. N. Sykes, *William Wake, Archbishop of Canterbury 1657–1737* (Cambridge, 1957), Vol. 2, likewise discusses these attempts (1716, 1719) and G. V. Bennett, *The Tory Crisis in Church and State 1688–1730* (Oxford, 1975), the earlier designs of 1709. Dr Bennett memorably illuminates some corners of the Oxford scene during Francis Atterbury's heyday as student and Fellow, and later Dean of Christ Church. D. Douglas, *English Scholars 1660–1730* (rev. edn, 1951) is not primarily concerned with the universities but a number of his individual portraits are pertinent, for example, that of Edward Thwaites (above, p. 42) and Thomas Gale (p. 39).

V. H. H. Green, *The Young Mr. Wesley* (1961) includes much on Wesley as a Fellow of Lincoln College in the 1720s and 1730s. Chapters 11–13 of the same author's *The Commonwealth of Lincoln College 1427–1977* (Oxford, 1979) deal authoritatively with one of the smaller academic com-munities from 1660 to 1750. The final quotation in Chapter 2 is from Sir G. N. Clark, *The Later Stuarts 1660–1714* (2nd edn, Oxford, 1955), p. 415.

Chapter 3 (pp. 43–80)

L. Stone, 'The educational revolution in England, 1560–1640', in *Past and Present*, Vol. 28 (1964) did much to foster the notion that a period of unprecedented expansion and wide opportunity in education before 1640 stands in sharp contrast to the regression which set in after 1660 and which foreshadowed the dismal decline of the eighteenth century. (He was, how-ever, concerned as much with universities as with schools.) D. Cressy, 'Levels of illiteracy in England, 1530–1730', *Historical Journal*, vol. 20 (1977), pp. 10, 12, 22–3 and W. A. L. Vincent, *The Grammar Schools: Their Continuing Tradition 1660–1714* (1969) have given more recent support to this theory; as have other contributions to the literacy debate', for example, L. Stone, 'Literacy and education in England, 1640–1900', *Past and Present*, vol. 42 (1969) and D. Cressy, 'Literacy in pre-industrial England', *Societas*, vol. 4 (1974). The high priest of the 'decay' school, however, was A. F. Leach, in his numerous sections on county schools in the *Victoria County History of England* and in his article on 'Schools' in the *Encyclopaedia Britannica*.

There is an emphatic rejection of the 'decay' theory as regards later Stuart Leicestershire by Joan Simon, 'Post-Restoration developments: schools in the county 1660–1700', in B. Simon (ed.), *Education in Leicester-shire 1540–1640* (Leicester, 1968). This essay is one reason why Leicester-shire figures quite prominently in Chapter 3. A larger-scale county study, the best of its kind for the period, is D. Robson, *Some Aspects of Education in Cheshire in the Eighteenth Century* (Chetham Society, 1966). It should be required reading for all who utter the fashionable platitudes about English schools and schoolmasters in the years 1660–1730, and most of my Cheshire references are drawn from it (for example, to the grammar schools at Macclesfield and Chester; the severity of the churchwardens at Frodsham; longevity at Congleton, salaries at Witton and cheap labour at Lymm grammar schools; Barthomley and Rostherne parish schools; Christleton and Nantwich charity schools). New foundations in Nottinghamshire in the late seventeenth and early eighteenth centuries (e.g. Tuxford) are discussed by J. D. Chambers, *Nottinghamshire in the Eighteenth Century* (1932), especially pp. 305–7.

The wider-based conclusions of R. S. Tompson, *Classics or Charity? The Dilemma of the 18th Century Grammar School* (Manchester, 1971), derived from a close study of fifteen English counties, suggest that even the Hanoverian grammar schools might have to be retrieved from the historian's trash can. Tompson's work has proved valuable for statistics as well as illustrations (e.g. p. 55 above). Even more damaging to the 'decay' theory in the period 1660–1730, and a rich vein of information on the development of the schoolteaching profession, is M. Seaborne, *The English School: its Architecture and Organization 1370–1870* (1971). It is illuminating both on the 'modern' type of endowed grammar school and on those older 'public' schools (e.g. Eton and Winchester) which developed after the Restoration into major boarding establishments or institutions with a large fee-paying clientele. I have used it for, *inter alia*, Pierrepont's, Lucton; Moore's, Appleby Magna; Risley, Witney, Leeds and Southampton grammar schools; Kirkleatham School; Osgathorpe; and Sedbergh.

A standard work of an earlier vintage is N. A. Carlisle, *A Concise Description of the Endowed Grammar Schools in England and Wales* (2 vols, 1818). A few outstanding grammar-school teachers, e.g. Holyoake of Rugby, are the subject of articles in *DNB*. Vincent, op. cit., is an admirable work of reference for many more: see also his analysis of a sample of 559 masters 1660–1770, ibid., p. 120. On grammar-school masters in individual counties the essays of A. F. Leach in *The Victoria County History*, suspect though they are in their general bias, are prolific in detail. I have used, in particular, his articles on Buckinghamshire (especially for Aylesbury and Eton) in *VCH Bucks*, Vol. 2; on Yorkshire (especially for Wakefield), *VCH Yorks*, Vol 1; on Lincolnshire (Corby Glen), *VCH Lincs*, Vol. 2; on Berkshire (Reading, Wallingford, Newbury), *VCH Berks*, Vol. 2; on Durham (Darlington, Durham Grammar School and Cathedral School), *VCH Durham*, Vol. 1; and on Warwickshire (Nuneaton), *VCH Warwicks*, Vol. 2. A much more recent and model local study, allowing insights into the profession and the structure of educational provision, is John Lawson, *The Endowed Grammar Schools of East Yorkshire* (East Yorks Local History Society, 1962): NB especially for Beverley, Malton and Hull. Some references in Chapter 3 to Cumberland and Westmorland grammar schools are taken from C. M. L. Bouch and G. P. Jones, *A Short Economic and Social History of the Lake Counties* (Manchester, 1961), though that to Lowther College is from J. V. Beckett, 'Lowther College 1697–1740: "For None but Gentleman's Sons" ', *Transactions of the Cumberland and Westmorland Antiquarian and Archaeological Society*, vol. 79 (1979). C. Gill, *History of Birmingham . . . to 1865* (Oxford, 1952) is informative on the endowments, estates and masters of King Edward's School. G. Lipscomb, *History and Antiquities of the County of Buckingham*, Vol. 2

(1847), p. 63 has an excellent account of the new model grammar school at Aylesbury (above, p. 60–1).

School histories comprise a vast species (more than 300 are listed in P. J. Wallis, 'Histories of old schools: a preliminary list for England and Wales', *British Journal of Educational Studies* (vol. 14, 1965). They vary bewilderingly in quality; but the best ones together contain a mass of information on the Augustan teaching profession which has never been synthesised. A sample of those drawn on in Chapter 3 includes I. E. Gray and W. E. Potter, *Ipswich School 1400–1950* (Ipswich, 1950); F. Henthorn, *History of Brigg Grammar School* (1959) (quotations on pp. 49, 60); C. E. Woodruff and H. J. Cape, *Schola Regia Cantuariensis* (1908) (pp. 72–3, 74); A. A. Mumford, *Manchester Grammar School 1515–1915* (1919); A. L. Murray, *The Royal Grammar School, Lancaster* (Cambridge, 1952); H. C. Maxwell Lyte, *Eton College* (1877) (see above, pp. 57, 67–8); R. Austin Leigh, *Eton College Lists 1678–1790* (Eton, 1907) for table of numbers at Eton, Winchester, Harrow and Rugby; A. F. Cook, *About Winchester College* (1917); A. F. Leach, *History of Winchester College* (1899); E. H. Pearce, *Annals of Christ's Hospital* (1901); M. F. J. McDonnell, *History of St Paul's School* (1909); J. Sargeaunt, *Annals of Westminster School* (1898) and E. P. Hart (ed.), *Merchant Taylors' School Register, 1561–1934* (2 vols, 1936). J. Rogers, *The Old Public Schools of England* (1938) quotes Rev. Gideon Murray (1759) on Beverley Grammar School as 'the Westminster of the North' and deals with the boarding enterprises of Richard Pocock at Southampton, of Sedbergh *c.* 1714, etc.

One of the main themes of Chapter 3 is the rapid progress of 'modern' schools and subjects and the consequent demand for teachers of those subjects. A pioneering work in this field is Foster Watson, *The Beginning of the Teaching of Modern Subjects in England* (1909). For teachers of mathematics and mathematics-based subjects, e.g. navigation and surveying, the biographical researches of E. G. R. Taylor are invaluable. See idem, *The Mathematical Practitioners of Tudor and Stuart England* (Cambridge, 1954) and *The Mathematical Practitioners of Hanoverian England* (Cambridge, 1966). They are the sources for reference to, *inter alia*, Anthony Thacker, John Holmes, John Dougharty, John Grundy, John Colson, John Buchanan, John Jeffreys, Thomas and William Watts, and George Donn. For the mathematics master at Parkyn's School, Bunny (p. 50) see Tompson, op. cit. What Taylor does for one group of the new specialist instructors, A. Heal, *The English Writing Masters and their Copy Books* (Cambridge, 1931), does for another: see the references in Chapter 3 to John Bland; William Addy and John Sturt; William Benson of Newcastle; also to Christ's Hospital Writing School. A much earlier work containing brief professional pen portraits is W. Massey, *The Origin and Progress of Letters*, pt 2 (1763): it has been drawn on for references to Edward Powell at Wandsworth and John Ayres of Fetter Lane. Both Tompson, op. cit., and Seaborne, op. cit., supply valuable information on mathematics, modern language and calligraphic teaching in the endowed school sector.

Statistically unreliable but informative on private schools and schoolmasters is N. Hans, *New Trends in Education in the Eighteenth Century* (1951). See references (pp. 51, 57 above) to Watt's Academy and (pp. 51, 69 above) to Clare's Academy. Newspaper advertisements for private schools are discussed in J. H. Plumb, 'The new world of children in eighteenth-century England', *Past and Present*, vol. 67 (1975). Hans, op. cit., pp. 54–62, also serves as a supplement and corrective to the more traditional secondary sources on Dissenting academies and schools: e.g. on Doddridge's Academy, and the boarding schools of Singleton and Gilling. See also, H. McLachlan, *English Education under the Test Acts* (Manchester, 1931); Irene Parker, *Dissenting Academies in England and Wales* (Cambridge, 1914); H. P. Roberts, 'Nonconformist academies in Wales, 1662–1862', *Transactions of the Honourable Society of Cymmrodorion* (1928–9).

On elementary and charity schools, V. E. Neuburg, *Popular Education in Eighteenth Century England* (1971) promises more than it delivers but serves as a timely reminder that there are other indicators of literacy levels than those used by Stone and Cressy. It also allows useful glimpses of individual teachers; see references in Chapter 3 to Thomas Dyche, Ford and Shanks at Soho, and Henry Dixon. M. G. Jones, *The Charity School Movement of the 18th Century* (Cambridge, 1938) should be the starting-point for any assessment of elementary education in Augustan England. The book contains a section on the recruitment and conditions of work of charity-school teachers. Some of Jones's statistics have to be used with care, as indicated by Joan Simon, 'Was there a charity school movement? The Leicestershire evidence', in Simon (ed.), *Education in Leicestershire*; but her conclusions are far from being invalidated. Some of A. F. Leach's articles in *The Victoria County History* are illuminating on blue-coat and other charity schools, e.g. *VCH Berks*, Vol. 2, for Reading and Winkfield. On the very large number of endowed, as opposed to subscription charity schools founded in the early eighteenth century, an essential complement to Jones's work is David Owen, *English Philanthropy 1660–1960* (Cambridge, Mass. and London, 1965), although his educational conclusions are not confined to the elementary sector. Summarised in Owen, op. cit., pp. 250–1, are the findings of the Taunton Commission (*Schools Inquiry Commission Report, 1867–8*) referred to above, p. 44. For other references to these findings, see Vincent, op. cit., ch. 1.

Contemporary Sources
Augustan travellers occasionally took note of both schools and school-masters and sometimes of the latter's incomes and conditions. The references in Chapter 3 to Doncaster Free School and its masters and to Williamson's School, Rochester, Morpeth Grammar School and Queen Mary Free School, Ripon, are taken from Timothy Thomas's account of journeys in 1723 and 1725, HMC *Portland MSS*, Vol. 6. Those to Shrewsbury School in the 1690s and 1720s come from Fiennes, *Journeys* and Defoe, *Tour*, Vol. 2. Fiennes also comments on the reputation of Beverley and on the teaching staff at Eton; Defoe on the endowments and library of St Bee's School, Whitehaven and the master's provision at Blundell's, Tiverton. C. S. Whiting (ed.), *The Autobiographies and Letters of Thomas Comber* (Surtees Society, Vol. 157, 1947) includes the letter from John Burton to Comber, 1699, on Durham School (quoted above, p. 63). Peter Collier's ambitions at Clitheroe (p. 73) can be traced in HMC *Kenyon MSS*, p. 272, and *Magnae Britanniae Notitia* (1716 and 1723 edns) supplies information on the staffing of Christ's Hospital and Westminster Schools.

One of the classic near-contemporary county histories, P. Morant's *History and Antiquities of the County of Essex* (Chelmsford, 1768) has an important section on schools (Vol. 1, pp. 171–9). I have used it for Colchester Charity School. A similar work, Francis Blomefield, *An Essay towards a . . . History . . . of Norfolk* (5 vols, Fersfield, 1739–75, Vol. 2, is the source for Norwich Grammar School. The views of Gilbert Burnet,

Bishop of Salisbury, on education (1708) are quoted from *A History of My Own Times* (Oxford, 1833), Vol. 6, pp. 212–13. Bishop William Nicolson's diaries (MSS at Tullie House, Carlisle) and his visitation records of 1703, printed in *Miscellany Accounts of the Diocese of Carlisle* (see below, p. 301) have been used for schools in his diocese. Bishop Francis Gastrell's comparable *Notitia Cestriensis* (see below, p. 301) is equally valuable on Lancashire and Cheshire schoolmasters, c. 1715. The Schism Bill debates (1714) in the House of Lords, which yield information on dissenting schools, academies and teachers, are partly printed in W. Cobbett, *Parliamentary History of England*, Vol. 6 (1810), 1352.

Several contemporary treatises, pamphlets, sermons and periodicals were consulted. Those quoted from are [Francis Brokesby], *Of Education with respect to Grammar Schools and Universities... To which is annexed A Letter of Advice to a Young Gentleman*, by F. B., B. D. (1701); John Houghton's *A Collection for the Improvement of Industry and Trade* (1692–1703), a periodical which regularly advertised private schools, especially writing schools; and James Talbott, *The Christian School-Master: or the Duty of those who are employed in the Public Instruction of Children, especially in Charity Schools* (1707). Extracts from Charles Hoole, *A New Discovery of the Old Art of Teaching School* (1660) and M. Nedham, *A Discourse concerning Schools and Schoolmasters* (1663) are taken from David Cressy, *Education in Tudor and Stuart England* (1975), a helpful brief anthology of contemporary writings. (For Nedham, see also Vincent, *Grammar Schools*, p. 167.)

The MS surveys of schools by Christopher Wase in the Bodleian Library, Oxford (MS C.C.C. Oxon 390/1–3, 391/1; see *Bodleian Library Record*, vol. 4, 1952) is a well-known source for the 1670s. It has been well exploited by Vincent, op. cit., and from it are derived various figures on grammar-school salaries and the reference (above, p. 69) to private schoolmasters at Eltham. The quotation (above, p. 76) from John Urmston, *A New Help to Accidence* (1710) is taken from Neuburg, *Popular Education*, p. 18, and that from Mandeville (p. 79) from Jones, *Charity School Movement*, p. 102. References to, and quotations from, SPCK reports on charity schools, ibid., *passim*. Sir Christopher Wren's letter to Sir John Moore, 1693, is quoted by Seaborne, op. cit., p. 75, from *Wren Society Publications*, vol. 11 (1934).

Chapter 4 (pp. 83–114)

A pioneering study of the clergy as a vocational and social group in the late sixteenth and early seventeenth centuries, Rosemary O'Day's, *The English Clergy: The Emergence and Consolidation of a Profession* (Leicester, 1979) appeared as the final draft of Chapter 4 was being written. For the transformation to a graduate profession, referred to above, p. 83, see ibid., pp. 3, 55, 141–2, and for O'Day's comment on the early social implications, quoted above, p. 87, ibid, p. 138. Now badly needed is a comparable study of the profession in the years from 1660 to 1720 or 1730. John H. Pruett, in his article 'Career patterns among the clergy of Lincoln Cathedral, 1660–1750, *Church History*, vol. 44 (1975), has indicated the kind of questions that should be asked, and can be answered in the case of particular groups. Unfortunately, A. Russell, *The Clerical Profession* (1980) takes the early nineteenth century as its effective starting-point: what it has to say on the seventeenth- and eighteenth-century background is sadly dismissive and of little weight.

Fortunately church history for the period in question has been in many respects well served, in particular as regards biography. Figures for diocesan ordinations given in note on p. 85 above were partly derived from two biographies, G. V. Bennett, *White Kennett, Bishop of Peterborough* (1957) and W. M. Marshall, *George Hooper, Bishop of Bath and Wells* (1976), but partly from N. Sykes, 'Episcopal administration in England in the eighteenth century', *English Historical Review*, vol. 47 (1932). Without Sykes's heroic work from the 1920s through to the 1950s it would still be desperately difficult to put together from secondary sources an acceptable picture of the clerical profession in our period. His *Church and State in England in the 18th Century* (Cambridge, 1934) was, and remains, a masterly work, and the chapters on 'The ladder of preferment' and 'The clerical subalterns' are invaluable on the structure of the profession, on personnel and promotion (ibid., pp. 110–11 for the source of Stillingfleet's views on the overcrowding of the late-seventeenth-century profession, mentioned above, p. 95). Sykes's first book, *Edmund Gibson, Bishop of London* (Oxford, 1926) is also one of his best and yielded plentifully for Chapter 4 on Lincoln diocese, as well as on London, Middlesex and Essex clergy, 1715–48. His *William Wake* (2 vols, Cambridge, 1957) is less helpful as a synthesis but very useful for its voluminous extracts from Wake's correspondence in Christ Church Library (see below, p. 301). Wake's own career from the 1680s took in a rich West End rectory and Lincoln diocese as well as Canterbury. More than thirty years' accumulated wisdom is distilled in Sykes's *From Sheldon to Secker . . . 1660–1768* (Cambridge, 1959).

The acute problems facing the post-Revolution Anglican clergy, not least the financial and economic pressures of war and agrarian depression, are lucidly discussed in G. V. Bennett, *The Tory Crisis in Church and State 1688–1730: The Career of Francis Atterbury, Bishop of Rochester* (Oxford, 1975). See also, 'The Church', ch. 2 of G. Holmes, *The Trial of Doctor Sacheverell* (1973). The contrast with the softer climate of the mid-late eighteenth century, despite the continuing hardships of perpetually disadvantaged groups, e.g. assistant curates, is pointed by E. J. Evans, *The Contentious Tithe* (1976); see especially ch. 1 (p. 9 for the assistant curates of Worcester diocese). G. F. A. Best, *Temporal Pillars* (Cambridge, 1964) is the standard work on Queen Anne's Bounty; and although most of the illustrations and statistics used in my section on the Bounty are derived or calculated from the contemporary work of Ecton (see below, p. 299), Best's book along with A. Savidge, *The Foundations and Early Years of Queen Anne's Bounty* (1955), provided much of the necessary framework.

At a more elevated clerical level, the work of Henry Compton, the aristocratic Bishop of London 1675–1713, is assessed by E. Carpenter, *The Protestant Bishop* (1956); that of Lloyd at St Asaph and Worcester, by A. T. Hart, *William Lloyd 1627–1717* (1952); that of William Nicolson as Archdeacon and Bishop of Carlisle in F. G. James, *North Country Bishop* (New Haven, Conn., 1957); and that of Burnet in T. E. S. Clarke and H. C. Foxcroft, *A Life of Gilbert Burnet, Bishop of Salisbury* (Cambridge, 1907). Particularly helpful, not least for its generous quotations from the archbishop's papers (see below, p. 301), is A. T. Hart, *The Life and Times of John Sharp, Archbishop of York* (1949). *DNB* articles on Sir George Fleming, Dean of Carlisle, Isaac Maddox and John Robinson also provided material for Chapter 4. But so far as the rank and file of the Anglican clergy are concerned, except very rarely at county or diocesan level (e.g.

H. I. Longden, *Northamptonshire and Rutland Clergy from 1500*, 15 vols, Northampton, 1938–43), there is no biographical source book to compare with the estimable A. G. Matthews, *Calamy Revised: being a revision of Edmund Calamy's Account of the Ministers Ejected and Silenced 1660–2* (Oxford, 1934). I have made extensive use of this in my brief treatment of Dissenting clergy.

For my discussion of the social background of the higher clergy I was very fortunate in being able to refer to an unpublished paper by Prof. D. L. Hirschberg, 'Social mobility in early modern England: the Anglican episcopate 1660–1760' (1977). The figures cited above, pp. 90–1 are taken from this paper (table 2); also one version of the social origins of Bishop John Robinson. Prof. Hirschberg has also contributed an article on the government's influence on ecclesiastical patronage, 1660–1760, to the *Journal of British Studies*, vol. 20 (1980), which from a close analysis of the contemporary researches of Browne Willis (see below, p. 299–300) throws new statistical light on the control of advowsons generally within the Augustan Church of England. See above, p. 101. John Findon has produced a valuable social analysis of 488 Anglican clergy of the years 1689–90 in his unpublished Oxford D. Phil. thesis (1978), 'The Nonjurors and the Church of England 1689–1716', pp. 52–3; with his kind permission I have referred to it above, pp. 87–8. J. H. Pruett, in his Princeton University PhD dissertation, 'The Clergy of Leicestershire, 1660–1714', investigates the social and academic background of the incumbents of that county; and he has helpfully summarised some of his conclusions in his article on Lincoln Cathedral clergy, cited above p. 297. There is no general study of the university education and vocational training of the Anglican clergy in the period 1680–1730; but for the training of Dissenting ministers see H. MacLachlan, *English Education under the Test Acts* (Manchester, 1934). For a guide to the 'Evans census' (see below, p. 300) John Creasey's *Index to the John Evans List of Dissenting Congregations and Ministers 1715–29* (1964) is a necessary companion, and for references to a further Non-conformist survey of the same vintage, by Daniel Neal, see E. D. Bebb, *Nonconformity and Social and Economic Life 1660–1800* (1935), app. 2. M. R. Watts, *The Dissenters*, Vol. 1 (Oxford, 1978) is an admirable survey.

Contemporary Sources
The best contemporary history of the whole period is Burnet's *History of My Own Times* (6 vols, Oxford, 1823, 1833). Burnet was a leading Anglican divine, Bishop of Salisbury 1689–1715, and his comments, particularly in Vols 4–6, on the Church and the clergy are astringent as well as informed. Vol. 5 contains his account of the inception and inauguration of Queen Anne's Bounty (see above, p. 86) and his comment on Dawes (above, p. 89), while the 'Conclusion' of the *History*, Vol. 6, written in 1708, contains a fine section on the clerical profession of his day – including the deficiencies of its vocational training – written by one who was himself a dedicated professional.

The prefatory list of benefactions in John Ecton, *Liber Valorum* (1728 edn) was the main source of information on private augmentations of clerical incomes linked with the Bounty, 1711–27 (above, p. 86). It was used in conjunction with Ecton's *A State of ... the Bounty of Queen Anne* (2nd edn. 1720). My estimate of the extent of the Lord Chancellor's patronage over livings and chapelries (above, p. 101) is based on the comprehensive catalogue of advowsons in Browne Willis, *A Survey of the Cathedrals* (3 vols, 1742), collated with [J. Ecton], *Thesaurus Rerum*

Ecclesiasticarum (3rd edn, by Browne Willis, 1763). Guy Miège's account of the Church of England, quoted p. 92 above, is taken from *The New State of England* (1699 edn.), Vol. 2, p. 158; and John Chamberlayne's, including his 'not 15,000' estimate of clerical numbers, from the 1723 edn of *Magnae Britanniae Notitia*. A typically uncompromising chapter on the clergy appears in Campbell, *London Tradesman*, and is quoted above, p. 111. A near comprehensive census of the bulk of the Nonconformist ministry in 1715–16, subsequently updated, was made by John Evans, minister of Hand Alley Presbyterian meeting, and is preserved in Dr Williams's Library, MS 34.4. Gregory King's estimate of the number of canons and prebendaries among the dignified clergy, of 'double-beneficed clergymen of £120 per annum' and of 500 Dissenting pastors and 9,500 Anglican ministers *in toto* are taken from his so-called 'Burns Journal', reproduced in *The Earliest Classics: John Graunt and Gregory King* (intro. by P. Laslett, 1973) and Harley's comments from the copy of the *Natural and Political Observations* in Nat. Lib. Australia, Kashnor MSS. Relative, if not exact, income figures and accurate numbers for the higher clergy can be extrapolated from the authoritative *List of Archbishops, Bishops, Deans and Prebendaries . . . [1762]*, in Sir J. Fortescue (ed.), *Correspondence of King George III*, Vol. 1 (1927), pp. 33–44.

The correspondence, diaries and autobiographies of Augustan divines have been drawn on for illustrative detail and here and there suggested independent lines of thought. Part of the correspondence and the journal of White Kennett as a London rector, Archdeacon of Huntingdon and Bishop of Peterborough is in Brit. Lib. Lansdowne MSS 1013, 1014, 1024. Kennett's reference to Samuel Bradford's promotion to Carlisle, quoted above, p. 88, is from ibid., 1013, f. 228. J. Nichols (ed.), *The Epistolary Correspondence . . . of . . . Francis Atterbury* (4 vols, 1783–7) is more valuable for secular and ecclesiastical politics than for professional matters. The MSS collections in the Bodleian Library seethe with ecclesiastical correspondence dating from the fifty to sixty years after the Restoration, notably in the Rawlinson, Tanner and Ballard MSS. In Chapter 4 I have drawn directly only on the letters to Arthur Charlett in MS Ballard 3, 5–7, 9, 15. The struggles of a man seeking to make his way in the Church without influence are illuminated in R. Trappes-Lomax (ed.), *The Diary and Letter Book of Thomas Brockbank 1671–1709* (Chetham Society, 1930). It is his expenses at Oxford in the 1680s and 1690s (ibid., p. vii) which are used as one yardstick in discussing the cost of training for the profession, above p. 108. Two infinitely more fortunate clerics are revealed in E. M. Thompson (ed.), *Letters of Humphrey Prideaux, sometime Dean of Norwich, to John Ellis . . . 1674–1722* (Camden Society, 1875) and in C. E. Whiting (ed.), *The Autobiographies and Letters of Thomas Comber, sometime Precentor of York and Dean of Durham*, Vol. 2 (Surtees Society, Vol. 157, 1947). For the references, above pp. 89–90, to the accumulated preferments of John Montagu see ibid., p. 194. Letters in J. R. Magrath (ed.), *The Flemings in Oxford*, (Oxford, 1904–24), Vol. 3 contain information on the singularly undistinguished university career of a later Dean of Carlisle (see above, p. 90), and 'The Diary of John Thomlinson' [curate of Rothbury, rector of Glenfield] is in *Six North Country Diaries* (Surtees Society, Vol. 118, 1910).

A neglected source for the Anglican clergy in the 1720s are the acute observations of Timothy Thomas, the chaplain who accompanied the 2nd Earl of Oxford on a long journey in 1725: HMC *Portland MSS*, Vol. 6. I have made specific use of his comments on Croft (Yorks), Doncaster, Leeds, Northallerton, Thirsk, Durham, Newcastle upon Tyne, Jarrow and

Northumberland north of Alnwick. The travel journal of Sir John Perceval, 1701 (Brit. Lib. Add. MSS 47057) is the source of the references to the bishopric and deanery of Durham, above pp. 93, 94. Other travellers interested in the clergy and clerical buildings and lifestyles are Thomas Baskerville in the 1670s and 1680s (HMC *Portland MSS*, Vol. 2); Macky, *Journey,* Vols 1 and 2 (see abvoe, p. 94 for Lichfield); Defoe, *Tour,* Vols 1 and 2 and Fiennes, *Journeys* (most examples quoted being from 1697).

A remarkably full picture of the early-eighteenth-century clergy in one region of the country, the north-west, from Cheshire to the Scottish border, can be pieced together from (1) William Nicolson, *Miscellany Accounts of the Diocese of Carlisle . . . delivered to me at my primary Visitation* [1703], ed. R. S. Ferguson (Carlisle and London, 1877) and (2) Francis Gastrell [Bishop of Chester], *Notitia Cestriensis*, ed. F. R. Raines (Chetham Society, 2 vols in 4, 1845–50). The latter is based largely on information gleaned by Gastrell in his primary visitation of 1715, though a lot of the material is updated to the 1720s. These sources, especially the *Notitia*, have been used or quoted extensively in Chapter 4. See also, R. E. G. Cole (ed.), *Speculum dioeceseos Lincolniensis, sub episcopis Gul: Wake et Edm: Gibson . . . 1705–1723* (Lincolnshire Record Society, pt 1, Lincoln, 1913). Nicolson's diaries, both those local sections printed *passim* in the *Transactions of the Cumberland and Westmorland Antiquarian and Archaeological Society* and the voluminous London diaries (MSS in Tullie House, Carlisle, being prepared for publication by Mr Clyve Jones and the present author) are replete with references to the clergy. I have used them sparingly here, but see above, p. 100 on Wigan.

Edmund Calamy, *An Historical Account of My Own Life* [*and Times*], *1671–1731* (ed. J. T. Rutt, 2 vols, 1829) is mostly concerned with high matters of state and church, but chs 4 and 5 in Vol. I (1692–1702) offer some fine insights into the Nonconformist ministry. For the end of the period, see [B. Gough], *An Enquiry into the Causes of the Decay of the Dissenting Interest* (1730) and Philip Doddridge, *Free Thoughts of the Most Probable Means of Reviving the Dissenting Interest* (1730).

I have made some use in Chapter 4 of clerical obituaries in the *Gentleman's Magazine* for 1732 and 1733. For admissions to the inns of court from clerical families (above, p. 109) see below, p. 302, especially the references to Sturgess and Lucas. Apprenticeships of clergymen's sons have been studied in the Stamp Office registers, PRO IR 1/1–12 and 1/42–9 though the summary for the years 1710–20 is derived from P. Bezodis, unpublished fellowship thesis, Trinity College, Cambridge, cited in R. Robson, *The Attorney in 18th Century England* (Cambridge, 1959), p. 55n. and app. The quotation from the Tenison papers (Beaw on Adderbury, 1699) is taken from Sykes, *Church and State*, p. 16. Two quotations from Wake's correspondence in Christ Church Library – Robert Wake on Buxted, 1720 and the extract from Wake's Lincoln Register (above, pp. 100, 107) – are from *Church and State*, p. 213 and Sykes, *Wake*, p. 185. The quotations from Lord Thanet on Westmorland livings, Nicolson on Carlisle diocese livings in his gift, John Boulter on Harwood, and Timothy Ellisonne on Haworth and his plans for his son are all from the Lloyd–Baker–Sharp MSS, printed in Hart, *Life of Sharp*, pp. 158, 160, 152–4, 162, 20.

Chapter 5 (pp. 115–65)

Contemporary Sources
The basic sources for the barristers of 1680–1730 are the records of the inns
of court. Despite their variable accuracy the printed editions of these records
remain indispensable to the researcher; and much use was made in Chapter 5
of H. A. C. Sturgess (ed.), *Register of Admissions to the Honourable Society
of the Middle Temple*, Vol. 1 (1949) – this also registers bar calls; F. A.
Inderwick (ed.), *Calendar of Inner Temple Records*, Vol. 3 (1901); R. J.
Fletcher (ed.), *The Pension Book of Gray's Inn*, Vol. 2 (1910); and J. D.
Walker (ed.), *The Records of the Honourable Society of Lincoln's Inn: The
Black Books*, Vol. 3: 1680–1775 (1899). (For admissions to the bar at
Lincoln's Inn, however, I have relied heavily on the analysis of the original
Black Books in Paul Lucas, 'A collective biography of students and barristers
of Lincoln's Inn, 1680–1804', *Journal of Modern History*, vol. 46, [1974],
table A7, p. 251.) A. R. Ingpen (ed.), *Master Worsley's Book on the History
and Constitution of the Honourable Society of the Middle Temple* (1910) is
valuable for the comments of a Treasurer of the inn, *temp.* George II, on
the social calibre of its entrants and the expenses of reading for the bar.

Magnae Britanniae Notitia (1708–32) contains a good brief sketch of the
judiciary and the business of the courts. The quotation on p. 121 above is
from the 1727 edn. John Chamberlayne, its author, omits the pungent
comments of his father Edward in the earlier *Angliae Notitia* on the fees,
incomes and land purchases of members of the legal profession (see above,
pp. 123–4, 126, 131). William, Lord Cowper's memorandum to George I
(1714) on the legal profession, printed in John, Lord Campbell, *The Lives
of the Lord Chancellors* (1846), Vol. 4, pp. 349–50, shrewdly assesses leading
figures of the bench and bar, including Sir T. Powys, Sir E. Northey, Sir P.
King, Sir J. Pratt, Nicholas Lechmere and Littleton Powys. Campbell's
London Tradesman has a searching chapter on barristers, including the cost
of their training, as well as other chapters on attorneys and solicitors, notaries
and scriveners. For appointments to the Great Seal, especially the shambles
after Somers's dismissal in 1700, see Burnet, *History of My Own Times*,
Vols 4 and 5. The seedy practices involving Masterships in Chancery (see
above, p. 122) were revealed at the trial of Lord Chancellor Macclesfield:
see T. B. Howell (ed.), *State Trials*, Vol. 16 (1812), especially for the
references to Medlicott, Kinaston and Elde. The political factors dictating
the choice and tenure of Welsh judges, and their appointment by letters
patent rather than commission is illustrated, for example, in the appointments and dismissals of 9 June 1711, *Calendars of Treasury Books*, Vol. 25,
pt 2, (1961). *The Art of Thriving, or the Plaine Path-way to Preferment*
(1635), republished in the 1690s and printed in *Somers Tracts*, Vol. 7, pp. 197–
200, is a useful source on local courts and court-keeping (above pp. 140–1).

The works of Roger North are rich beyond comparison in biographical
and professional information on the law in the 1670s and 1680s (L.
Schwoerer discusses the dates of his writings in *Huntington Library
Quarterly*, vol. 22 (1958–9) and concludes that all were written after 1709
except for parts of the autobiography.) The *Life of Lord Guilford* and
Roger's own invaluable *Autobiography* (his legal career ended in 1689) were
brought together in A. Jessopp (ed.), *The Lives of the Norths* (1890, repr.
with new intro. by E. Mackerness, 1972), Vols 1 and 3. An earlier edn of
the life of Lord Keeper Guilford (1826) was also used in Chapter 5. Most
quotations from these two works of North are clearly signposted in the text

of this chapter; but see p. 127 on the 'small profits' of the serjeants-at-law. In addition, I have utilised and quoted from Roger North's *Discourse on the Study of the Laws* (1824).

P. C. Yorke, *The Life and Correspondence of Philip Yorke, Earl of Hardwicke* (3 vols, Cambridge, 1913), Vol. 1 is the source of most of the references to Yorke's legal training in Anne's reign, including the practice of coaching by prominent attorneys, to his early career at the bar and to his caution in the land market; also to his father, Philip senior, the redoubtable Dover solicitor. Ibid., Vol. 3, p. 416 gives Hardwicke's view of the 'independence' and advantages of the legal profession, quoted above p. 116. The Hardwicke Papers in the British Library contain important legal correspondence from *c.* 1710 onwards. Add. MSS 35585 contains the letter from John Comyns to Hardwicke, endorsed 3 January 1735[-6] giving details of his career, the value of his practice and his lack of landed qualification (see above, pp. 127-8, 134-5). See also Add. MSS 35584, f. 132 for Comyns. Among other collections in the British Library, the Caryll Papers (Add. MSS 28277) throw light on Nathan Wright's landed ambitions in 1708, and the Corporation of Sandwich MSS (Add. 33512) on the Recordership of the barrister-MP, James Thurbane. Among the HMC reports, the following have been drawn on for quotations or other illustrative material on Augustan lawyers: *Kenyon MSS* (for George Kenyon; attorney clerks of the peace in Lancashire; King's Bench attorneys coming up from London for the Lancashire treason trials, 1694; the Lancashire barristers, Edward Herle and John Walmsley; and Alexander Leigh of Hindly and Wigan); *Portland MSS*, Vol. 4 (for Robert Raikes of Northallerton; Sir Simon Harcourt and the Great Seal in 1710; Sir Thos. Powys's letter to Harley on the Attorney-Generalship, 1710, above, p. 125); *Portland MSS,* Vol. 5 (for William Jessop and court-keeping on the Holles estate); *Portland MSS*, Vol. 6 (Lord Oxford's Journeys, for lawyers in Bury St Edmunds, 1732).

The anon. *Memoirs of Lord Somers* (1716) throw some light on the early legal career of the later Lord Chancellor. Sir Henry Chauncy, Treasurer of the Middle Temple and Welsh judge in the late 1680s (for his strictures on the profession, see p. 143) figures along with other members of his legal family in H. Chauncy, *The Historical Antiquities of Hertfordshire* (2 vols, 1700). 'The diary of Thomas Gyll', in *Six North Country Diaries* (Surtees Society, Vol. 118, 1910), throws light on a successful Durham barrister and official of the Palatine Court. Other individual lawyers, e.g. Samuel Gatwode, are the subject of obituaries in the *Gentleman's Magazine* for the 1730s, while Joseph Addison's essay on the professions in which he satirises the overcrowding of the Augustan bar (see above, p. 136) appears in the *Spectator*, no. 21 (Saturday, 24 March 1711).

The relevance to Chapter 5 of [Henry Philipps], *The Grandeur of the Law: or, An exact collection of the nobility and gentry of this kingdom whose honors and estates have by some of their ancestors been acquired or considerably augmented by the practice of the law* (1684) is self-explanatory. For the section on those counsellors' fees, including circuit earnings, which were the source of many of these 'estates' (above, pp. 129-132) a major source was MSS Turner 136 (Harvard Law School Library): the fee-book of Sir Edward Turner [or Turnour], for whom see *DNB*. The information on the fees of Pratt and King in the Annandale case I owe to Mr Clyve Jones. It is based on a bill of costs, 'Mr. Mason's Acct.', 12 November 1708-29 January 1709, in the Hope-Johnston Papers, Scottish Record Office (the permission of Major P. A. W. Hope-Johnston is gratefully acknowledged).

Finally, a number of primary sources were used for the civil lawyers and for court officials. Brit. Lib. Add. MSS 24,105 contains Sir Charles Hedges's account of fees and charges 1691–1702. The wills of a number of leading civilians, now in the Public Record Office, proved revealing: those of Sir Richard Raines, Henry Newton, John Bettesworth, Humphrey Henchman and Sir John Cooke. The bureaucracy of the Westminster courts is surveyed quite adequately in successive editions of *Magnae Britanniae Notitia*. More detailed information on the establishments and remuneration of officials of these courts can be gleaned from (1) *Lists of Officers and their Deputies belonging to the Several Courts in Westminster Hall and elsewhere, with the Lists, Accounts and Tables of the Fees claimed by them: presented by order to the House of Commons, March 1730* (1731); and (2) the report of the Commons' committee on fees [Wyndham Committee], printed as *A Report from the Committee to whom the Several Lists of the Officers and their Deputies belonging to the Several Courts [etc.] . . . were referred* (1732).

The early years of George II were indeed a time when much of the legal profession was subjected to close parliamentary scrutiny, and nowhere was this more sharply directed than at the 'lesser degrees' of the law. The *Journals of the House of Commons*, vol. 21, pp. 266–8, print the report of the Commons' inquiry into the numbers and practices of attorneys, solicitors and entering clerks, undertaken by a Select Committee under Sir William Strickland in 1729 (see above, pp. 150, 152, 153, 156–7). The repercussions of this inquiry later produced the two most comprehensive contemporary sources available at this period for studying any branch of the law: *Lists of Attornies and Solicitors admitted in pursuance of the late Act for the better regulation of Attornies and Solicitors: presented to the House of Commons* (1729[–30]); and the supplementary *Additional Lists of Attornies admitted in pursuance of the late Act* (1731). These have been extensively used in Chapter 5; as have the indispensable Stamp Office volumes in the Public Record Office at Kew (see p. 301 above) – the registers of apprenticeships kept by the office. Nineteen volumes cover the years 1711–31, twelve being officially 'London' registers (PRO IR 1/1–12), though in fact they contain abundant provincial material as well, and seven 'Country' registers (IR 1/42–9).

E. Freshfield (ed.), *Records of the Society of Gentlemen Practisers in the Courts of Law and Equity Called the Law Society* (1897), begin in 1739, shortly after the formation of the first professional organisation by attorneys and solicitors in the Home Counties. Of the various lawyers' manuals referred to above, p. 158, the most illuminating on the early part of our period is *The Compleat Solicitor, Entring-Clerk and Attorney: Fully Instructed in the Practice, Methods and Clerkship of all his Majesties' Courts of Equity and Common-Law* (1683). Use is also made (see above, p. 154) of the earlier (1668) edn of this work. T. M., *The Sollicitor* (1662 edn) is another early Restoration treatise quoted to throw light on solicitors' insidious extension of their activities into the common law courts. John Aubrey's comments on the great expansion in the number of attorneys during the seventeenth century, with particular reference to Gloucestershire and Worcestershire (above, p. 151) occur in his *The Natural History of Wiltshire* (ed. J. Britton, 1847), pt 2, ch. 16. There is more on the same general theme in some of the later entries of E. S. de Beer (ed.), *The Diary of John Evelyn* (Oxford Standard Authors edn, Oxford, 1959).

J. W. F. Hill, *Letters and Papers of the Banks Family of Revesby Abbey* (Lincolnshire Record Society, Vol. 45, 1952) chronicles the rise and prosperity of one of those families whose great wealth and county status was founded on a provincial law practice (see especially, pp. v–xxv). Other references to land purchases, housebuilding and sundry local activities of attorneys have been taken from: Gastrell, *Notitia Cestriensis* (above, p. 301), Vol. 2, pt 1, for John Starky and Heywood Hall, W. Nicolson's MS diaries for Lancelot Simpson; M. Blundell (ed.), *Blundell's Diary and Letter Book 1702–28* (Liverpool, 1952), for William Plumbe of Liverpool; Chauncy, op. cit., for Stephen Eure and Joshua Lomax; A. Browning (ed.), *Memoirs of Sir John Reresby* (Glasgow, 1936), for Robert Benson senr, of York and Wrenthorpe. The reference to Thomas Brereton's lowly social origins is taken from HMC *Egmont Diary*, Vol. 1, and that to tax evasion by Cornish attorneys from *Calendar of Treasury Books*, Vol. 14, p. 135: Treasury Lords to Sir Walter Moyle, 28 September 1698. Among the travellers who take note of prosperous provincial attorneys are Timothy Thomas, on Sheffield and its neighbourhood, and Thomas Wright (HMC *Portland MSS*, Vol. 6, Fiennes, *Journeys,* on the 'high-built' house at Preston, and Defoe, *Tour,* Vols 1 and 2, on Launceston and Preston.

Secondary Sources
W. Holdsworth, *A History of English Law*, Vol. 6 (2nd edn, 1937), ch. 8: 'The professional development of the law' (in the later seventeenth century) remains a valuable introduction to the institutional aspects of the legal profession at all levels. Although the editorial introductions to the records of the inns (see above, p. 302) do something to repair the gap, especially Fletcher's on Gray's Inn, there is an obvious need for a chronological sequel to W. R. Prest, *The Inns of Court under Elizabeth and the Early Stuarts 1590–1640* (1972). My task would have been far more difficult but for the admirable foundations laid by Dr Prest, and several of his conclusions furnished criteria against which to measure the development of the bar and the barrister's training in the second half of the seventeenth century and beyond. The same applies in some degree to W. J. Jones, *Politics and the Bench: The Judges and the Origins of the English Civil War* (1971). Edward Hughes, *North-Country Life in the Eighteenth Century: The North East 1700–1750* (Oxford, 1952) deals with methods and cost of training for the bar under George I, particularly with the coaching activities of Charles Saunderson (above, p. 146).

On Welsh judges the standard work is W. R. Williams, *The History of the Great Sessions in Wales 1542–1830* (Brecknock, 1899). On office-holding by barrister-MPs after 1714, see Sedgwick, *passim*; and for 1689–1702, H. Horwitz, *Parliament, Policy and Politics in the Reign of William III* (Manchester, 1977), pp. 359–66. W. L. Sachse, *Lord Somers: A Political Portrait* (Manchester, 1975) is helpful on Somers as a young barrister, law officer in the early 1690s and head of Chancery, and includes his law-reform measure of 1705. M. Landon, *The Triumph of the Lawyers 1679–1689* (Montgomery, Ala: University of Alabama, 1970) is disappointing on the profession as opposed to its political involvement, but has some information on incomes, especially from the fee-book of Sir Francis Winnington (above, pp. 125, 126). Information on the fee earnings of Sir John Cheshyre in the reign of George I (pp. 127–8) is tucked away in *Notes and Queries,* 2nd ser., vol. 7 (1859), pp. 492–3.

Various articles and essays enlarged my knowledge of the development of the profession at the level of the bench and the bar. E. Hughes, 'The professions in the eighteenth century', *Durham University Journal*, vol. 44 (1952), was a starting-point. Lucas, 'A collective biography', (cited above, p. 302) contributes information on the social background of the students and barristers of Lincoln's Inn and idem, 'Blackstone and the reform of the legal profession', *English Historical Review,* vol. 77 (1962), attempts less successfully a more general analysis of the 'professionalisation' of the inns post-1660 and of the social quality of their students; the article quotes tellingly from Blackstone's inaugural lecture of 1758 (see above, p. 143). P. Styles, 'The heralds' visitation of Warwickshire, 1682–3', *Birmingham Archaeological Society Transactions,* vol. 71 (1953), refers to provincially based barristers in one Midland county. W. R. Prest, 'Counsellors' fees and earnings in the age of Sir Edward Coke', in J. H. Baker (ed.), *Legal Records and the Historian* (1978) supplies the yardsticks against which to measure later rises in income levels. J. H. Baker, 'Counsellors and barristers: an historical study', *Cambridge Law Journal,* vol. 27 (1969), is a valuable article. To it I owe the information about barristers' abandoning the preparation of their own briefs; also the changes in conventions regarding counselling fees in the sixteenth and seventeenth centuries (above, pp. 119, 130–1) including the quotation from a pamphlet of 1707, *Proposals for remedying the great Charge and Delay of Suits at Law and in Equity;* and the Common Pleas case of *Messor v. Molyneux* in 1741 (above, p. 155).

The main biographical compilations utilised for material on barristers and judges are: *GEC Complete Peerage* for Cowper, Harcourt, Trevor and Macclesfield; Burke's *Peerage and Baronetage* on Lilford for Littleton Powys; *DNB* on John Maynard, Erasmus Earle, Nathan Wright (see also, J. H. Plumb, *The Growth of Political Stability in England 1675–1725,* [1967], Thos. Vernon, Roger North, Joseph Jekyll, George Treby, Gilbert White (for John White of Selborne), Matthew Lamb (for Peniston Lamb); Sedgwick, for James Medlicott, Thos. Kinaston, Francis Elde, Richard Wynn, John Pratt, John Comyns, Lawrence Carter and Thos. Vernon (in cluding Sir R. Temple's estimate of his income at the Chancery bar.) The value of Edward Foss, *The Judges of England* (9 vols, 1848–64), Vol. 7: 1660–1714; Vol. 8: 1714–1820, is by no means purely biographical. Vol. 8, for instance, discusses New Year's gifts (see above, p. 124), the trade in Chancery Masterships, and judges' salaries. G. C. A. Clay's Cambridge PhD thesis 'Two Families and their Estates: the Grimstons and the Cowpers from *c.* 1660 to *c.* 1815' (1966) deals with the financial and landed invest- ments of Lord Chancellor Cowper (see also my acknowledgements, above, p. xiii). P. G. M. Dickson, *The Financial Revolution in England . . . 1688– 1756* (1967) is the source of most of the other references to investment by lawyers in Bank and company stock and government funds. Much of the house-building by barristers and judges discussed in Chapter 5 can be traced in N. Pevsner and E. Hubbard, *The Buildings of England: Cheshire* (1971), for John Ward; J. Lees-Milne, *English Country Houses: Baroque 1685–1715* (1970), for the Trebys of Plympton, Thos. Vernon of Hanbury, James Medli- cott (Ven), Sir Peter King (Ockham); Sir J. Summerson, *Architecture in Britain 1580–1830* (4th edn, 1963), for John Maynard.

Postscript. Wilfrid Prest (ed.), *Lawyers in Early Modern Europe and America* (1981) appeared after the typescript of the present work had been submitted to the publisher. It contains an important short study of 'The English bar, 1550–1700' by Dr Prest (pp. 65–85) and an essay by Daniel Duman on 'The English bar in the Georgian era' (pp. 86–107). Comparisons with Chapter 5, above, will reveal some differences of interpretation and emphasis; but the only amendment to my text which seemed both necessary and possible for me to make in consequence was to lay a greater stress on the distinction between the bar and the 'practising bar' (above, pp. 137–8).

A third essay in this collection relevant to the Augustan period is B. P. Levack, 'The English civilians, 1500–1750'.

Civil Lawyers, Attorneys and Solicitors. G. D. Squibb, *Doctors' Commons: A History of the College of Advocates and Doctors of Law* (1977), is a recent book on the civil lawyers with useful material on the period 1680–1730; but neither it nor Levack's brief essay on the 'civilians', 1500–1750, cited above, are effective substitutes for the type of detailed study provided by B. P. Levack, *The Civil Lawyers in England 1603–1641* (Oxford, 1973), for the earlier seventeenth century. A. H. Manchester, 'The reform of the ecclesiastical courts', *American Journal of Legal History,* vol. 10 (1966), reflects on some aspects of the decline of the 'civilians'. Although error-prone, [C. Coote], *Sketches of the Lives and Characters of Eminent English Civilians* (1804) remains fruitful if used judiciously.

Holdsworth, op. cit., apart, the two standard works in print on attorneys and solicitors covering all or part of our period are R. Robson, *The Attorney in Eighteenth-Century England* (Cambridge, 1959) and M. Birks, *Gentlemen of the Law* (1960). (My debts to them are mostly indicated in the text, but mention must be made here of the debt books, 1688–1725, of Joseph Hunt of Stratford on Avon, p. 158 above, one of several important provincial sources utilised by M. Birks.) For the estimate of lawyers' numbers in 1759 (p. 154) see P. Mathias, 'The social structure in the eighteenth century: a calculation by Joseph Massie', *Economic History Review,* 2nd ser., vol. 10 (1957). W. Blake Odgers, 'The legal quarter of London', in idem (ed.), *Six Lectures on the Inns of Court and of Chancery* (1912), pp. 46–56, is informative on the surviving inns of Chancery. H. H. L. Bellot, 'The exclusion of attorneys from the inns of court', *Law Quarterly Review,* vol. 26 (1910) has some relevance to the theme of Lucas, 'Blackstone and the reform of the legal profession' (cited above, p. 306).

Several attorneys who attained some prominence in politics are the subject of short biographies in Sedgwick: see especially articles on Thos. Brereton, John Brace, Philip Hawkins and Joshua Lomax. M. Cox, 'Sir Roger Brad-shaigh, 3rd baronet, and the electoral management of Wigan', *Bulletin of John Rylands Library,* vol. 37 (1954–5) contains excellent material on Bradshaigh's legal man of business, Alexander Leigh (above, pp. 158, 159–60); it also includes references to the latter's son Robert, Town Clark of Wigan, and to his nephew John Wiswall. One of the rare book-length studies of an individual attorney, by R. Stewart-Brown, focuses on another Lancastrian, *Isaac Greene: A Lancashire Lawyer of the 18th Century* (Liverpool, 1921), and incidentally throws light on some of his local contemporaries, e.g. the Starkies of Preston (above, p. 165). J. A. Bradney (ed.), *The Diary of Walter Powell* (Bristol, 1907), though concerned with an attorney of an earlier generation (1603–54), illuminates many of the avenues, e.g. assiduous court-keeping and legal advice to the gentry and nobility, which his successors were later to exploit to their profit. C. D. Webster, 'Halifax attorneys', *Transactions of the Halifax Antiquarian Society* (1968–9), pp. 80–7, 117–19 of which cover 1680–1730, embodies assiduous local research and contains interesting information on the acquisition of estates and country houses.

The description in Chapter 5 of Edward Hoblyn's house at Croan, Cornwall, and Attorney Norris's at Chippenham are derived from J. Lees-Milne, op. cit., pp. 26, 276. Other secondary authorities utilised were: J. Patten *English Towns 1500–1700* (Folkestone, 1978) for statistics on East Anglia; Hughes, *North Country Life: The North East,* for Northumberland and

Durham (e.g. litigation of William Cotesworth); J. W. F. Hill, *Georgian Lincoln* (Cambridge, 1956), for Thos. Becke; H. S. Toy, *The History of Helston* (Oxford, 1936), for the Tremenheeres and other Helston legal dynasties; J. Simmons, *Leicester Past and Present*, Vol. 1 (1974), for Leicester's Town Clerks and Deputy Recorders; E. Stephens, *The Clerks of the Counties* (1961); W. A. Speck, *Tory and Whig . . . 1701–1715* (1970), for the Norwich Poll Book of 1715 (above, pp. 154–5).

Chapters 6 and 7 (pp. 166–235)

Contemporary Sources
There was no 'medical register', even of an unofficial kind, before 1779–83 when three issues of the *Medical Register* were produced by Samuel Foart Simmons, MD. (The 1st edn listed well over 4,000 practitioners of all legitimate varieties in England and Wales but is obviously incomplete, naming, for example, only 125 in Wales. The 3rd edn, *The Medical Register for the Year 1783*, is fuller and contains valuable retrospective material, notably on London and provincial hospitals.) For London, however, lists of the Fellows, Licentiates and Candidates, but not extra-licentiates, of the Royal College of Physicians for 1694–1727 were printed in successive edns of *Angliae Notitia* and *Magnae Britanniae Notitia* (1723 and 1727 edns used for the staffs of the London hospitals). A modern attempt to compile from contemporary sources *A Directory of English Country Physicians 1603–1643*, by J. H. Raach (1962), is an important pioneering effort, though open to methodological criticism. J. H. Bloom and R. R. James, *Medical Practitioners in the Diocese of London . . . An Annotated List, 1529–1725* (Cambridge, 1935), which prints much contemporary material from the licensing books of the bishops of London, was an important source for Chapter 6, especially on Essex and Middlesex (e.g. above, pp. 175–6). Ultimately there is no alternative to a comprehensive combing of ecclesiastical records, including archidiaconal visitation records, for locating those local licensed practitioners, *medici* and surgeons, who did not have university MDs or the imprimatur of the Royal College.

The Stamp Office registers of 1711–31 (see above, p. 301) are crucial to understanding the social context of changes in the structure of early-eighteenth-century medicine. Although the hundreds of apprenticeships recorded are overwhelmingly to apothecaries, surgeons and barber-surgeons, the registers also yield some information on surgeon-apothecaries (e.g. Edward Jacob, p. 203 above), licensed physicians (e.g. John Lambert, p. 189) and even MDs (p. 210 above). Campbell, *London Tradesman*, has lively chapters on all three main branches of the profession in the 1740s (see especially his reference to naval surgeons, quoted above, p. 193, and to profits from treating venereal disease, above p. 198).

Valuable diaries, journals and autobiographies of Augustan medical men are in print. The subject of E. Hobhouse (ed.), *The Diary of a West Country Physician AD 1684–1726* (1934) is Claver Morris, MD, of Wells. Of an earlier vintage was John Symcotts, MD, of Huntingdon (see above, p. 224), whose diary figures in F. N. L. Poynter and W. J. Bishop (eds), *A Seventeenth Century Doctor and his Patients* (Bedfordshire Historical Society, 1951). W. Brockbank and F. Kenworthy (eds), *The Diary of Richard Kay, 1716–51 . . . a Lancashire Doctor* (Chetham Society, 1968) is the best and most complete edition of one of the most vivid of eighteenth-century medical documents. It is of great value not only for its picture of general practice (by surgeon-apothecaries) in the Bury area in the 1730s and 1740s but for local medicine in general, including the profession in Manchester, and still more for hospital training in London. The extract from Thomas Braddock's funeral sermon on the death of Kay, which concludes Chapter 6, is printed as an appendix to this edition. A. Kay (ed.), *A Lancashire Doctor's Diary 1737-50* (Southport, 1895) retains some independent value; and cf. 'The diary of Richard Kay of Baldingstone, Bury, surgeon', extracts in *Medical History*, vol. 3 (1959). F. N. L. Poynter (ed.), *The Journal of James Yonge [1647-1721], Plymouth Surgeon* (1965) is a vivid source for the long career of one of the giants of Augustan provincial medicine, who became in time a licensed physician as well as a surgeon. He is the candidate for an extra-licence referred to above, pp. 171-2. P. Roberts (ed.), *The Diary of Sir David Hamilton 1709-1714* (Oxford, 1975) has much more on politics than on the medical career of one of Queen Anne's 'man-midwives'; but the editorial introduction is helpful. The 'Autobiography of Alexander Monro, *primus*', founder of the Edinburgh medical school, ed. H. D. Erlam, is in *University of Edinburgh Journal* (1954); and the 'Day Book of the Court Apothecary in the time of William and Mary, 1691', attributed to James Chase (see above, pp. 218-19), is described by L. G. Matthews, *Medical History*, vol. 22 (1978) with a biographical sketch of Chase.

References in Chapter 7 to secret service payments to physicians and surgeons in the 1720s are from Brit. Lib. Add. MSS 40843, ff. 9-11. The MS diary of Bishop Nicolson (see p. 301 above) allows insights into the lifestyle of the bishop's brother, London apothecary Joseph Nicolson; also see ibid, for library of Charles Bernard. HMC *House of Lords MSS 1702-4* prints minutes of proceedings in the Rose case. For London medicine, S. Young, *The Annals of the Barber Surgeons* (1890), also proved of occasional value, e.g. on phlebotomy, the Hawkins dynasty and the examination of prospective naval surgeons. J. F. South, *Memorials of the Craft of Surgery in England* (ed. Sir D'Arcy Power, 1886) has some contemporary anecdotes of interest, e.g. on the soldiers' raid on Tyburn, 1706, and the Barber Surgeons' Company rebuke to Cheselden. More important are the records of the governors of St Thomas's Hospital printed by South (ibid., pp. 248-9), especially for surgeons' dressers or 'cubs' (see above, pp. 200-1). R. D. Merriman (ed.), *The Sergison Papers* (Navy Record Society, 1950) contains important documents on naval medicine (see above, pp. 193, 197). Extracts from the town wardens' accounts of Torrington, Devon, with references to the doctors who treated the town's poor 1692-1731, are printed in J. J. Alexander and W. R. Hooper, *History of Great Torrington* (Sutton, Surrey, 1948). Nicholas Blundell's *Diary and Letter Book* (see p. 305 above) displays a rich assortment of medical practitioners who attended the squire of Crosby and his family 1702-28.

The statement was made in the text that medicine was 'the most pamphlet-ridden of late-seventeenth and eighteenth-century professions'. Among the pamphlets and also the more substantial contemporary treatises consulted directly, the following yielded material for Chapters 6 and 7: [Henry Stubbe], *Lex Talionis: Sive Vindiciae Pharmacop[oe]rum* (1670) – see above, p. 188 for the revealing English subtitle; Gideon Harvey, *The Family-Physician and the House-Apothecary* (2nd edn rev. 1678 [1st edn, 1670]); Charles Goodall, *The Royal College of Physicians* (1684); *Reasons on behalf of the Apothecaries Bill humbly submitted to the consideration of this present Parliament. In answer to the City of London's Petition against the said Bill* (broadsheet, 1695) – quoted above, pp. 188–90, 190; *The Apothecaries' Reply to the City's printed Reasons against their Bill* (broadsheet,

1695), which enumerates the master-apothecaries in London and 'the out-parishes' in that year; *The State of Physick in London* (1698), which has an account of the setting up of the Dispensary for the Sick Poor (above, p. 187) and is the source of the statement that there were then 'about eight hundred' apothecaries in London and Westminster (p. 191) and of the quotation (p. 201) upholding the merits of native surgeons; Samuel Garth, *The Dispensary* (1699). Of the extensive literature dating from the period of the Rose case I have made use of: Fran[cis] Brown, *The Case of the College of Physicians of London, wherein they are Defendants* [*c*. 1702–4]; *The Present Ill State of the Practice of Physick* (1702); *Tentamen Medicinale: or an Enquiry into the difference between the Dispensarians and Apothecarys, wherein the latter are prov'd capable of a Skilful Composition of Medicines and a Rational Practice of Physick* (1704), 'by an Apothecary' – particularly informative on the apothecary's training; and Robert Pitt, *The Antidote: or the Preservative of Health and Life* (1704), the source of the quotation about apothecaries' malpractices, p. 186 above. The preface to *The Antidote* is 'An Account of the Dispensaries'.

For fees and apothecaries' incomes (above, p. 227) see *Fair Play for One's Life: Or, the Sovereign Preservative of the Royal Family, Nobility, etc., and of the Arts of Physick and Surgery and the Apothecaries Trade*, by a Gentleman of Quality of North Britain (*c*. 1707). *Reasons humbly offered against Part of the Bill for the better Viewing, Searching and Examining Drugs, Medicines, etc.* (1724) makes the claim for elevated social status on behalf of the London master-apothecaries quoted above, p. 211. *An Address to the College of Physicians and to the Universities of Oxford and Cambridge occasioned by the late Swarms of Scotch and Leyden Physicians* (1747) is self-explanatory, but also fulminates against the 'bishops' doctors' (above, pp. 174–5). Quotations from three other pamphlets are taken from secondary sources: *Reflections on a Libel* (1671), see above, p. 168, from C. Wall, H. C. Cameron and E. A. Underwood, *A History of the Worshipful Society of Apothecaries of London* (Oxford, 1963), Vol. 1, p. 120; T. Brown, MD, *Physic lies a Bleeding* (1697), with its allusions to the relative cost of training for the three branches of medicine, from B. Hamilton, 'The medical professions in the eighteenth century', *Economic History Review*, 2nd ser., vol. 4 (1951), p. 163; and *A Dialogue concerning the Practice of Physic* (1735), quoted above, p. 168, from ibid., p. 160.

The following is a selection from those primary sources which have yielded incidental information on the 'doctors' W. Matthews (ed.), *The Diary of Dudley Ryder, 1715–1716* (1939) is the source of the quotation about apothecary Watkins and Dr Hulse (above, pp. 190–1) as well as for the conversation between Ryder and Marshall (p. 166), and HMC *Kenyon MSS* for 'Dr' Bromfield, the Warrington apothecary, and Dr Buck. Sir Edward Moore, *Liverpool in King Charles the Second's Time* [1667–8], ed. W. F. Irvine (Liverpool, 1889) has two superb pages (119–20) on John Pemberton of Liverpool (above, p. 228). The medical treatment of a Dorset pastor is mentioned in G. Nuttall (ed.), *Letters of John Pinney 1679–1699* (1939), app. 5. Among Augustan travellers Celia Fiennes has more interest than most in medicine and more connections than most with medical men. The descriptions of the Newcastle Barber Surgeons' Hall, of 'Dr Burgess's Folly' in Pontefract and of Macro's house in Bury St Edmunds are from *Journeys*, pp. 211, 94, 151–2. Dr Thorpe of Rochester (above, p. 223) figures in Edward Harley's Kent visit of 1723, HMC *Portland MSS*, Vol. 6. Defoe, *Tour*, as well as a reference to the profession in Ipswich includes good accounts of the building of Guy's Hospital and of Radcliffe's bequests to Oxford.

Secondary Sources

Any study of the personnel of medicine in the late seventeenth and early eighteenth centuries must begin at secondary level (as mine did) with the work of Bernice Hamilton and R. S. Roberts. Dr Hamilton's 'The medical professions in the eighteenth century', loc. cit., is a distillation of many of the arguments and conclusions in her doctoral thesis. Equally valuable is Roberts's 'The personnel and practice of medicine in Tudor and Stuart England, part I. The provinces', *Medical History*, vol. 6 (1962); 'Part II. London', ibid., vol. 8 (1964). General enlightenment apart, I owe to the latter (pt I) the reference to graduates in Exeter diocese in 1665 and the quotation from William Kay, 1652 (above, pp. 173, 216). Dr Roberts (pt II) dissents from the standard view of the Rose case as a landmark in the evolution of a medical profession; but as Chapter 6 will suggest, I believe he gives too little weight to the genuine anxieties of London apothecaries about the dubiety of their legal position. For understanding the rise to professional status of the apothecary in general, his essay 'The early history of the import of drugs into Britain', in F. N. L. Poynter (ed.), *The Evolution of Pharmacy in Britain* (1965) is essential (see above, pp. 184–5).

Two of the three main regulating bodies in Augustan medicine have been the subject of first-class histories. Vol. 1 of Sir George Clark's *History of the Royal College of Physicians of London* (Oxford, 1964) ends in the late seventeenth century; Vol. 2 (Oxford, 1966) begins approximately with the Revolution. Among much else of relevance Clark prints (Vol. I, pp. 418–25) the text of James II's charter, referred to above, p. 170. Just as valuable as Clark and to some extent complementary (e.g. in accounts of the Rose case) is Wall, Cameron and Underwood, op. cit., Vol. I of which carries the story of the London apothecaries from 1617–1815. It contains many references to leading figures in the Society of Apothecaries, e.g. James Sherrard and James St Amand, and on p. 109 prints the statement from the Company of Barber Surgeons, 1664, quoted above, pp. 195–6. Wider in its range is Mrs J. G. L. Burnby, 'A Study of the English apothecary from 1660–1760, with Special Reference to the Provinces' (unpublished London PhD thesis, 1979). To this I am indebted for the point about the overseers of the poor (above, p. 169) and for the two references (pp. 228, 229) to the Francys family of Derby: ibid., pp. 117, 158. A. G. Debus (ed.), *Medicine in Seventeenth Century England* (Berkeley and Los Angeles, Calif., 1974) is a collection of essays which are mostly concerned with advances in medical knowledge and techniques but occasionally – as with L. M. Zimmerman on 'Surgery', A. W. Franklin on 'Clinical medicine' and S. H. Radbill on 'Pediatrics' – include matter of relevance to the development of the profession (e.g. Franklin and Radbill on Richard Wiseman and on the treatment of venereal disease; Zimmerman on James Yonge's refinement of the technique of amputation).

Chapters 6 and 7 draw extensively on secondary researches of a biographical nature. Sir Zachary Cope has written (1953) a short biography of *William Cheselden 1688–1752*, the prince of Augustan surgeons, and C. R. Hone a *Life of Dr. John Radcliffe 1652–1714* (1950) which is rather slight but deploys some very interesting contemporary material, especially from Radcliffe's account book. The first chapter of G. C. Peachey, *Memoirs of William and John Hunter* (Plymouth, 1924) throws a good deal of light on the world of the London surgeons and their training in the early eighteenth century, particularly valuable on private lecture courses and demonstrations (above, pp. 198–9). It assembles biographical information on such surgeons as John Douglas the lithotomist, Rolfe, Buissière and Joshua Symonds (q.v.). Basic biographical material on Augustan medical men is most readily available, however, in the field of physic. The first two volumes of the 1878 edn of W. Munk, *The Roll of the Royal College of Physicians of London*, Vol. 1 on the seventeenth century, Vol. 2 on the eighteenth, is the standard work of reference and includes sketches of provincial extra-licentiates. My allusions to the following all owe something to Munk: Robert Taylor, Thomas Dover, Sir Richard Manningham, John Birch, George Lock of Alnwick, Messenger Monsey, Phineas Fowke, Edward Hulse, Gideon Harvey jnr, James Jurin and William Chambers (quoting MS account of John Alderson – see above, p. 224–5). A modern work of patient research, E. A. Underwood, *Boerhaave's Men: At Leyden and After* (Edinburgh, 1977) contains, in addition to analysis, scores of helpful biographical cameos. See references in my text to Thomas Dale, Charles Morton, David Ross, Edward Hody, Richard Conyers, William Brownrigg, William Hillary, John Huxham, James Mackenzie *et al.* (The whole section on Leyden in Chapter 6 owes much to Underwood, and his compendia on provincial hospitals were used in conjunction with Simmons's contemporary comments.) More but briefer biographical notices are contained in R. W. Innes Smith, *English-Speaking Students of Medicine in the University of Leyden* (Edinburgh, 1932).

[W. MacMichael], *Leading British Physicians* (1830) includes an early brief study of John Fothergill and information on John Huxham. It is much less useful, however, than an intriguing compilation of similar vintage, William Wadd, *Nugae Chirurgicae: or a Biographical Miscellany illustrative of a Collection of Professional Portraits* (1824): see Chapter 7 above, for John Belchier, Richard Morton, Richard Mead (pp. 222–3), Messenger Monsey, Charles Peters, William Battie, William Becket and James Cooke of Warwick. Several physicians and the occasional apothecary sat in the House of Commons. Charles Oliphant, Charles Cotes and George Bruere, the apothecary, are among those noted in Sedgwick. The *DNB* is naturally more informative on physicians than on surgeons or apothecaries – its account of Mead is outstanding; it does, however, contain a very full biography of Cheselden and covers, among other surgeons, Charles Bernard, William Cowper and Charles White. W. MacMichael, *The Gold-Headed Cane* (1st edn., 1827; 5th edn., ed. G. C. Peachey, 1923) conveys in an eccentric form some sound medical history of the age of Radcliffe and Mead.

P. G. M. Dickson, *The Financial Revolution* (1967), is the source of most references in Chapter 7 to the 'paper' investments of physicians and surgeons; but Cope, op. cit., has relevant information on Cheselden and P. Roberts (ed.), op. cit., on Sir David Hamilton. A Raistrick, *Quakers in Science and Industry . . . during the 17th and 18th Centuries* (2nd edn, Newton Abbott, 1968) has a good biographical sketch of Dr Fothergill, prints (p. 278) the provision in the will of Henry Lampe of Ulverston quoted at the end of Chapter 6, and discusses the education and library of apothecary Sutcliffe of Settle. The references to the house of John Bradshaw, Warwick apothecary (above, pp. 228–9), to the career of Samuel Batteley of

Bury St Edmunds (p. 229) and to the portrait of surgeon Edward Greene (p. 234) were kindly supplied by Dr Peter Borsay, Dr David Hayton and Dr R. A. Beddard respectively.

In addition to those cited at the beginning of this note, several other articles or essays are fruitful. This is particularly true of J. F. Kett, 'Provincial medical practice in England, 1730–1815', *Journal of the History of Medicine*, vol. 19 (1964). Part of R. McConaghey, 'The history of rural medical practice', in F. N. L. Poynter (ed), *The Evolution of Medical Practice in Britain* (1961) is of relevance to the theme of 'the coming of "the doctor"' (e.g. pp. 127–8) and contains statistics of bishops' licences granted in the dioceses of Hereford and Exeter. Sydenham's *bon mots* are quoted in K. Dewhurst, 'Thomas Sydenham: reformer of clinical medicine', *Medical History*, vol. 6 (1962). The rise in the living standards of country surgeons 1630–1730 can be gauged against the background found in F. W. Steer, 'The possessions of a Sussex surgeon [Wm. White]', *Medical History*, vol. 2 (1958) (cf. W. R. Le Fanu, 'A North Riding doctor in 1609', ibid., vol. 5, 1961) W. H. Harsand, 'Medical Bristol in the 18th century', *Bristol Medico-Chirurgical Journal*, vol. 17 (1899), uses valuable contemporary material on the city, including the medical 'census' of 1754. The information on Preston in Chapter 6 is based on P. N. Borsay, 'The English urban renaissance, 1680–1760', *Social History*, vol. 5 (1977) and that on Kendal on Samuel Foart Simmons, cited p. 308 above, and J. D. Marshall, 'Kendal in the late 17th and 18th centuries', *Transactions of the Cumberland and Westmorland Antiquarian and Archaeological Society*, vol. 75 (1975).

T. McKeown and R. G. Brown, 'Medical evidence related to English population changes in the eighteenth century', *Population Studies*, vol. 9 (1955) has long been accepted as a conclusive indictment of the failure of the progress of medicine to have any appreciable effect in lowering death rates in eighteenth-century England. Useful though it is as a warning against undue euphoria, it is astonishing that so influential an article should have made so little use of *eighteenth-century* evidence in reaching its conclusions, and its strictures are naïvely unrelated to the expectations of the time. It is especially cavalier, and quite at odds with contemporary impressions, in dismissing the successes of eighteenth-century surgery as of little account and, in general, presents an over-gloomy picture.

Chapter 8 (pp. 239–61)

The first English civil service worthy of the name was a short-lived one. It has been comprehensively chronicled and analysed in G. E. Aylmer, *The State's Servants: The Civil Service of the English Republic 1649–1660* (1973), the sequel to the same author's *The King's Servants . . . 1625–1642* (1961). Nothing comparable in authority or scope has been devoted to its late-seventeenth and eighteenth-century successor. Dr Aylmer himself glanced ahead as early as 1965 with his 'Place bills and the separation of powers: some seventeenth-century origins of the "non-political" civil service', *Transactions of the Royal Historical Society*, 5th ser., vol. 15 (1965). His important lecture 'From office-holding to civil service: the genesis of the modern bureaucracy', ibid., 5th ser., vol. 30 (1980), which ranges from the Restoration to the late eighteenth century, appeared after the final draft of Chapter 8 had been completed. I have dealt myself at some length with the institutional framework of the changes discussed in that chapter in a book whose first draft I completed some three years ago on 'The Transformation of English Government 1667–1725': I am preparing this for publication.

It was to facilitate changes in the field of the revenue that much of the expansion and selective reform of government that took place in the 1670s and 1680s was undertaken C. D. Chandaman, *The English Public Revenue 1660–1688* (Oxford, 1975) is an indispensable guide to the former and a valuable introduction to the latter. On a much smaller scale but judicious and instructive is H. C. Tomlinson, 'Financial and administrative developments 1660–88', in J. R. Jones (ed.), *The Restored Monarchy 1660–1688* (1979). A far earlier work, which first aroused my curiosity about the Augustan civil service, is E. Hughes, *Studies in Administration and Finance 1558–1825* (Manchester, 1934). It is an unfashionable work and an eccentrically documented one. But Hughes had a feel for the world of eighteenth-century government and a real interest in the people behind the dry entries in such stern sources as the *Calendars of Treasury Papers*. He illuminates political attitudes to the revenue departments in general, and more particularly the personnel of the Salt Office and the Excise. A nineteenth-century compilation on the Excise department, using contemporary material, is John Owens, *Plain Papers relating to the Excise Branch of the Inland Revenue Department from 1621 to 1878* (Linlithgow, 1879). See the references to guarantors of applicants for jobs in the Excise and to Thomas Everard, above, pp. 251, 252.

J. C. Sainty discusses 'The tenure of offices in the Exchequer' in *English Historical Review*, vol. 80 (1965) and 'A reform in the tenure of offices during the reign of Charles II' in *Bulletin of the Institute of Historical Research,* vol. 41 (1968). On the decline of purchase (see above, p. 252) the English sections of K. Swart, *The Sale of Offices in the 17th Century* (The Hague, 1949) are not particularly helpful. The best approach here is via departmental studies (see below). For guidance on the minutiae of personnel and tenure in the Augustan bureaucracy there are now five volumes relating to our period in the series 'Office-Holders in Modern Britain' (1972–8). Vols 1–4, by J. C. Sainty, deal respectively with *Treasury Officials* (1972), *Officials of the Secretaries of State* (1973), *Officials of the Board of Trade* (1974) and *Admiralty Officials* (1975); and Vol. 7, by J. M. Collinge, with *Navy Board Officials* (1978). They are essential works of reference which by their very precision have also made interpretation far easier than it previously was. In the Navy Office there is some extra biographical information in G. Jackson and G. F. Duckett, *Naval Commissioners . . . 1660–1760* (Lewes, 1889).

Much of my material on the civil service was pieced together from work done on individual departments or sectors of government. For the diplomatic corps a useful reference tool is D. B. Horn (ed.), *British Diplomatic Representatives 1689–1789* (Camden Society, 3rd ser., vol. 46, 1932). A first-class modern study of one important department and its officials is H. C. Tomlinson, *Guns and Government: The Ordnance Office under the Later Stuarts* (1979). The quotation on p. 245 above is taken by Tomlinson from a letter of William Lowndes to Harry Mordaunt, 12 July 1705, printed in *Calendar Treasury Books, 1705–6.* K. Ellis, *The Post Office in the Eighteenth Century* (Oxford, 1958) has little on personalities, but is sound on institutional history, good on establishments, conditions of service, remuneration, etc. H. Joyce, *History of the Post Office* (1893) contains a brief sketch of the office and its organisation *c.* 1680 which should be compared with J. A. J. Housden, 'The posts in 1720', *St. Martin's Le Grand*, vol. 17 (1907). On the Customs, E. E. Hoon, *The Organization of the English Customs System 1696–1786* (1938; 2nd edn, intro. R. C. Jarvis, Newton Abbot, 1968) is, for the most part, excessively desiccated administrative history of the old style; it has a bad starting-point and acquires little substance before the 1720s. Yet there is little else in print to rely on. By contrast, S. B. Baxter, *The Development of the Treasury 1660–1702* (London and Cambridge, Mass., 1957) is informative on both Treasury and Exchequer officials. A major study of the Exchequer and its officers from 1660 to the 1780s is long overdue. References to, and statistics on, the Royal Household (above, p. 255) are taken from Aylmer, *King's Servants* and J. M. Beattie, *The English Court in the Reign of George I* (Cambridge, 1967), p. 18.

Apart from Sainty, *Admiralty Officials* and Collinge, *Navy Board Officials* (see above, p. 314), the best introduction to the personnel of these departments in the 1690s, and also to the royal dockyards' establishment, is to be had in J. Ehrman, *The Navy in the War of William III* (Cambridge, 1953). From this is derived the figure for James II's fleet in 1688 (above, p. 241). That for 1714 is taken from R. D. Merriman (ed.), *Queen Anne's Navy* (Navy Records Society, Vol. 103, 1961), pp. 364–5, 369–71. Valuable for the latter part of our period is D. A. Baugh, *British Naval Administration in the Age of Walpole* (Princeton, NJ, 1965): table 16 is my source for the dockyard establishments of 1725 and 1727.

The leading Admiralty civil servant of the post-Pepys era is examined in G. F. James, 'Josiah Burchett, Secretary to the Lords Commissioners of the Admiralty, 1695–1742', *Mariner's Mirror*, vol. 23 (1937) (above, pp. 247, 259, 260). M. A. Lower, 'Some notices of Charles Sergison, Esq., one of the Commissioners of the Royal Navy . . .', *Sussex Archaeological Society Collections*, vol. 25 (1873) also mentions Dennis Lyddell. For their Sussex estates and houses see also T. W. Horsfield, *History, Antiquities and Topography of the County of Sussex* (Lewes, 1835). Of the major figures in the permanent service of the Crown after 1680, Pepys apart (for whom see R. Ollard, *Pepys: A Biography*, 1974), only one has inspired a full-scale biography. However, G. A. Jacobsen's, *William Blathwayt* (New Haven, Conn., 1932) would be a masterly work in any company, and because of Blathwayt's extraordinary range of activities (see above, p. 249) it illuminates quite a large part of the government stage. On a much smaller scale but well researched is J. C. Sainty, 'A Huguenot civil servant: the career of Charles Delafaye, 1677–1762', *Proceedings of the Huguenot Society of London*, vol. 22 (1975–6), pp. 398–413. I have also utilised *DNB* biographies of Adam de Cardonnel, James Vernon senr, and both Abraham and Temple Stanyan, and three short pen pictures of the officials Lambert Blackwell, Francis Hawes and Richard Houlditch in J. Carswell, *The South Sea Bubble* (1960), app. The will of Sir Philip Ryley, (above p. 260) is printed in E. C. Waters, *Memoirs of the Extinct Family of Chester of Chichelly* (1878), Vol. 1, p. 179. On civil servant investors (above, p. 260) I have again relied on P. G. M. Dickson, *The Financial Revolution*.

Contemporary Sources

Contemporary lists and names of offices and office-holders, sometimes with the relevant salary appended, exist in some profusion. I have used, in particular, those in the appendices to the *Calendars of Treasury Books* (1686–1718), *passim* (see also *Calendar of Treasury Books*, Vol. 8, 1687, p.

1,173 for the Excise superannuation scheme); in the various editions of *Angliae Notitia* and *Magnae Britanniae Notitia*, especially those of 1694, 1708, 1710, 1716 and 1723; in G. Miège, *The New State of England* (1699 edn); in [Abel Roper], *A List of the Principal Officers, Civil and Military, in Great Britain in the year 1710* (1710); in the 70 pp.-appendix to *The Laws of Honour* (1714), listing office-holders *c.* November 1713; and in an establishment list of the Treasury in 1711 in Brit. Lib. Loan 29/45B/12.

There are excellent selections of contemporary documents printed in Merriman (ed.), op. cit., and D. A. Baugh (ed.), *Naval Administration 1715–1750* (Navy Records Society, vol. 120, 1977). Another useful collection for the civil service is that in H. Roseveare (ed.), *The Treasury 1660–1870* (1973). Charles Davenant's *Political and Commercial Works* (ed. Sir C. Whitworth, 5 vols, 1771, repr. 1967) contain important allusions, especially in Vol. 1, to the revenue and its administration *c.* 1683–*c.* 1700. He stresses the advance of professionalisation in the Excise in the 1680s and the set-backs in the early and mid-1690s (see above, p. 243). Davenant was an Excise Commissioner before the Revolution and four of his diaries are most revealing on the nascent organisation of that office and on its local officials. See Brit. Lib. Harleian MSS 5121, 5020, 5022–3; also Harleian MSS 4077 for 'An account of the management of the officers of the Excise in the West of England [1685]'. Brit. Lib. Add. MSS 18903, *passim*, yielded good material on the early-eighteenth-century Customs department.

Some use has been made of the letters or papers of other civil servants as well as those of Davenant. The autobiography of James Vernon, jnr, diplomat and Excise Commissioner (see above, p. 249) is in Brit. Lib. Add MSS 40794. Letters and memoranda of Charles Sergison, Clerk of the Acts in the Navy Office, are printed in R. D. Merriman (ed.), *The Sergison Papers* (Navy Records Society, 1949); his memorial of 24 May 1699 is quoted above, pp. 247–8. There are letters relating to the new Leather Office and its commissioners in the correspondence of Justinian Isham and his father in Northants Record Office, Isham MSS. I have referred (above, p. 243) to the letters of 11 and 16 June 1911. The letter book of William Bridgeman, 1694–7, in Brit. Lib. Lansdowne MSS 1152B reveals a top-class late-seventeenth-century civil servant at work. At a much humbler level there is an Excise Collector's official 'diary' for the Richmond, Yorks, Collection in 1710, in Lansdowne MSS 910.

The *Calendar of Treasury Papers, Vol. 1: 1556–1696* has material on examinations for entry to the Customs service (see above, p. 252). There are a number of contemporary biographical sketches by a former Post Office official in John Macky, *Memoirs of the Secret Services of John Macky, Esq.* (2nd edn, 1733), pp. 123–54, *passim* (see references in Chapter 8 to William Aglionby, Sir Lambert Blackwell, James Vernon, senr). The reference to Mr Walmisley, the Lancashire Excise gauger (above, p. 251) is from HMC *Kenyon MSS*, p. 381. Other HMC volumes to provide evidence for Chapter 8 on various officials are *Ormonde MSS*, Vol. 8 (on Everard), *Portland MSS*, Vols 4, 5, and especially 8 (official papers of Robert Harley). Years ago, when occupied with post-Revolution politics, I worked through immense quantities of the correspondence of both Harley (including his unprinted correspondence in Brit. Lib. Loan 29) and Lord Godolphin (especially in the Blenheim MSS). Inevitably that reading has left its mark on this chapter, especially on pp. 242–3.

Chapter 9 (pp. 262–287)

Until recently army officers as a group, professional and social, in the late seventeenth and early eighteenth centuries have been astonishingly neglected in interpretative printed work. John Childs, *The Army of Charles II* (1976), especially ch. 2 ('Officers and men') and ch. 12 ('Society, the army and parliament') has pointed the way. His work ensured that filling in the pre-1685 background was the easiest part of the present brief study. Its sequel on James II's army (Manchester, 1981) is more political in emphasis and, in any case, appeared too late for me to make use of it. Dr Childs promises a study of William III's reign, too; and that will be welcome, for as yet little is known about the army of the 1690s. R. E. Scouller, *The Armies of Queen Anne* (Oxford, 1966), though a work of large scale and sound learning, had different priorities and devotes no single chapter to the officer corps of 1702–14. Sections on 'Regimental organization and strengths', 'Numbers and ranks' and 'Pay' (in chs 3, 4), together with ch. 6, which contains a brief passage on half-pay (see above, pp. 264–5) all supply important material, however, as do the ten pages devoted to the engineers and the artillery. Yet it is still worth consulting older work, e.g. J. W. Fortescue, *A History of the British Army*, end of Vol. 1 (1899) and beginning of Vol. 2, for some necessary background. There are some useful pages on the strength and organisation of Marlborough's armies in I. F. Burton, *The Captain-General* (1968), ch. 2. I was able to make a few amendments to my references to purchase (above, pp. 267–8) in the light of A. Bruce, *The Purchase System in the British Army 1660–1871* (1980), pp. 14–31.

Naval officers as a group after 1688 have been much better served than their counterparts, especially in J. Ehrman, *The Navy in the War of William III* (Cambridge, 1953), ch. 4 and D. A. Baugh, *British Naval Administration in the Age of Walpole* (Princeton, NJ, 1965), of which ch. 3, 'Commissioned officers', is first-rate. Ehrman's table of naval pay (op. cit., p. 138), his treatment of prizes and information on ships' establishments all proved valuable, as did some of Baugh's retrospective material, including the pay tables for 1694 and 1700 (op. cit., p. 110), the table of new lieutenants commissioned 1702–12 (ibid., p. 98) and the table of promotions (ibid., pp. 132, 133). Much primary material is printed by Baugh, including the extract from Prince George's letter to Rooke, 1704, quoted above, p. 28. For other periods in the development of the navy's officer corps, see also the brief but authoritative introduction to Merriman, *Queen Anne's Navy*, pt 9; R. Ollard, *Pepys: A Biography* (1974) for the late 1670s and 1680s; and J. R. Tanner's introduction to *A Descriptive Catalogue of the Naval Manuscripts in the Pepysian Library* (Navy Records Society, 4 vols, 1903–23).

Biographical compilations and printed lists have supplied a good deal of the meat of Chapter 9. For the army: C. Dalton, *English Army Lists and Commission Registers 1661–1714* (6 vols 1892–1904) and idem, *George the First's Army* (2 vols, 1910–12); (and see also p. 318 below for the valuable 'Army List of 1740'). The 'Navy Lists' used were contemporary ones (see below, p. 318). J. Charnock, *Biographia Navalis* (1794–8) is a basic, though not always accurate, biographical source, utilised for, *inter alia*, John Baker, Charles Wager, George Walton, Edward Hopson, Thomas Swanton, Francis Hosier and George Byng. Dalton's *George the First's*

Army, Vol. I, begins with a series of excellent biographies of the generals of the early Hanoverian period. Outstanding is that of Sir Charles Wills (see above, p. 269). See also references in Chapter 9 to Viscount Shannon, George Wade, Joseph Wightman, Henry Hawley, Archibald Hamilton (ibid., Vol. I, p. 115n.) and John McQueen (ibid., Vol. I, p. 294). Sedgwick, Vols 1 and 2, contains many up-to-date biographical notes on officers. I have drawn, in particular, on those of William Cadogan, George Carpenter (for both, see also *GEC Complete Peerage*), Thomas Whetham, Joseph Sabine, Geo. Wade, Richard Sutton, J. R. Webb, among the generals; and Baker, Wager, Philip Cavendish, Edward Vernon, Sir John Jennings, Matthew Aylmer (see also *GEC Peers*) and Sir John Norris, among the 'sea-officers'. For Norris, see also D. D. Aldridge, 'Admiral Sir John Norris, 1670 (or 1671) – 1749: his birth and early service', *Mariner's Mirror*, vol. 51 (1965). For biographies of George Maccartney and Admiral John Benbow, see *DNB*.

Basil Williams, *Stanhope: A Study in Eighteenth Century War and Diplomacy* (Oxford, 1932) illuminates the career of one of Britain's bravest army officers, including his acquisition of a guards' company (above, p. 267.

Contemporary Sources
A List of the Colonels, Lieutenant Colonels, Majors, Captains, Lieutenants and Ensigns of His Majesty's Forces of the British Establishment (1740), usually referred to as 'The Army List of 1740' and the first printed list of its kind, gives dates both of current and first commissions and is exceptionally important for tracing career patterns in the profession, with the help of Dalton, *English Army* and *George the First's Army Lists*. There are lists of general officers (usually complete and accurate) and of leading regimental officers (incomplete) in successive editions of *Angliae Notitia* and *Magnae Britanniae Notitia*. Narcissus Luttrell notes many army promotions and naval appointments in his *Brief Historical Relation of State Affairs [1678–1714]* (6 vols, Oxford, 1857). The first Navy List to be published, ranging all officers in strict seniority order within ranks, appeared in 1718. Lists of captains appeared in subsequent editions of *Magnae Britanniae Notitia* (I have used the 1723 edn which printed the official Admiralty list of 1720), and a lieutenants' list in the edn of 1726. J. Campbell, *The Lives of the Admirals and other Eminent British Seamen* (4 vols, 1742–4) offers a profusion of biographical information which repays sifting.

Sir George Murray (ed.), *The Letters and Despatches of John Churchill, Duke of Marlborough* (5 vols, 1845) and H. L. Snyder (ed.), *The Marlborough–Godolphin Correspondence* (3 vols, Oxford, 1975) are excellent sources for military promotions. For the list of displaced Tory officers 1714–17 (above pp. 273–4) see Brit. Lib. Add. MSS 22264. J. R. Tanner (ed.), *Samuel Pepys's Naval Minutes* (Navy Records Society, 1926) is a pungent source for the navy before 1689: the three quotations on pp. 275–7 above are from pp. 62 and 405–6. Merriman (ed.), *Queen Anne's Navy*, prints a number of key documents for the years 1702–14: including the Admiralty's instructions to the Navy Board, 6 January 1702, the Admiralty Order of 1 May 1703 and the Order in Council of 30 November 1713 (half-pay) (quoted above, pp. 279–80). A more recent collection of source material on naval officers is D. A. Baugh (ed.), *Naval Administration 1715–50* (Navy Records Society, Vol. 120, 1977): at pp. 57–62 is the

Admiralty Memorial to the King in Council, 30 January 1730, which among many other things confirmed the six-year qualification period for the lieutenant's examination laid down by Admiralty order in 1729.

S. Martin [–Leake] wrote a good near-contemporary *Life of Sir John Leake* (ed. G. Callender for Navy Records Society, 1918–19), from which the quotation on captain Richard Leake and the information on the admiral's modest estate (above, p. 284) are taken. Sir Charles Wager gave his own account of his origins and connections in a letter to Walpole, 12 July 1731, printed W. Coxe, *Memoirs of the Life and Administration of Sir Robert Walpole* (1798), Vol. 3, pp. 116–17. HMC *Portland MSS*, Vol. 8 is useful for Harley's correspondence relating to army and navy officers (see p. 266 above for the case of Captain Robert Carr, 1706); Vols 6 and 8 contributed the references to Cols Foley and Egerton respectively.

The quotations from Cropley and Lowther, 1706, 1708, which appear at the beginning of Chapter 9 are from the Shaftesbury MSS (Public Record Office) and Lonsdale MSS (Cumbria Record Office): see G. Holmes, *British Politics in the Age of Anne* (1967), pp. 134, 128 n. 45. Swift's celebrated attack on the military men is in the *Examiner*, no. 13, 2 November 1710 and his description of the excesses of the three Whig generals (above, p. 268) in his *Journal to Stella*, 13 December. Defoe's allusion to bourgeois army officers (above, p. 269) is in *The Complete English Tradesman* (1745 edn, written 1726), Vol. 1, p. 247. Macky, *Journey*, contains descriptions of generals' country houses at Blackheath, Egham, Sutton, Richmond, etc. (p. 271) as well as the telling picture of 'half-pay men' quoted above, p. 273.

Index